WRITERS AT WORK

Third Series

Writers at Work

The *Paris Review* Interviews

THIRD SERIES

Edited by George Plimpton
Introduced by Alfred Kazin

NEW YORK: THE VIKING PRESS

Contents

Introduction

THE *Paris Review* interviews (of which this is the third selection in book form) have been unusually sensitive and adroit exercises in getting contemporary writers to reveal themselves. They have been the best recent examples of the biographical art of the profile. The classic interview, which Boswell and Eckermann practiced in order to write their respective books on Johnson and Goethe, is surely something else—a form of Wisdom Literature. It seeks a Lesson From The Master (traditionally no smaller man is worth interviewing), and in it the interviewer plays the role of disciple. His job is to put the Master's views on life into book form—the most notable recent example is the book that Lucien Price called *Dialogues of Alfred North Whitehead*. Because he is usually dealing with a great thinker's comprehensive and universal philosophy, the many branches of one great tree, he will notice inconsistencies, will draw the Master out on fascinatingly unexpected topics, will provoke the Master into unpremeditated eloquence. The classic interview with a Great Man probably had its origins in religious discipleship, and the purest example of it is still Plato's Dialogues. What the interviewer really asks is: How Are We To Live?

A profile, by contrast, is a sketch; what used to be called a "character"—a personality is quickly built up before our eyes. It is not an intellectual biography, such as a book on a single man seeks to become; it is a close-up, a startlingly informative glance— usually sympathetic, and even when it is not openly so, the cov-

erage becomes a form of sympathy. A profile, by common understanding, is due someone currently important. The interview is
our way of understanding his fame. It is not wisdom that we are
trying to understand; it is exceptionality—in the case of a writer,
his reputation as a writer, his hold on our imagination, means that
for us he is like no one else. The interview becomes a way of
getting the writer to document this exceptionality himself.

It is not required of the writer in these interviews that he be
great and wise. We all know, we readers of contemporary literature, that our novelists and poets do not live better than we do.
What is required is that the writer be gifted, which ever since the
Romantic period has meant vividness, a heightened degree of involvement with himself, a sense of his particular gift or daemon.
When we interview a gifted, vivid, intense, highly charged modern
writer, we are really saying: What does it feel like to be this gifted?
What's it like, day after day, living with a gift like yours? The
writer is always glad to tell us. Montaigne, who began the modern
habit of painstakingly examining his own thoughts, doubts,
quandaries for immediate literary purposes, could not have been
interviewed as Norman Mailer, Saul Bellow, James Jones, and
William Burroughs are here interviewed—he could not have
cooperated. Although Montaigne regarded his consciousness as a
problem, he thought that it was the human problem. Montaigne
would not have imagined that a stranger, chatting with him at
home, could isolate this consciousness by describing him in his
room, at his work table. But the biographical close-up now satisfies
us because we identify the power of art with the uniqueness of
personality. Ever since the Romantic period, when the writer
became the hero of his own books, a hero to his culture, a hero to
himself, the writer has also been taken, not least by himself, as a
man of unbounded exceptionality. Trying to cheer up Henry
Adams in their old age, Henry James stressed the duty of cultivating one's own consciousness: "It's, I suppose, because I am that
queer monster, the artist, an obstinate finality, an inexhaustible
sensibility." This "finality" is so well established that by now a

writer's most trifling personal habits are precious to *everybody*. When a modern writer is interviewed in his study and invited to talk about his manner of life, he understands, under the helpfully flattering questions put to him, that he is being recognized as his ideal—a wholly individual artist-man, a unique force, a truly free man. In such an interview, the writer visibly expands to the truth about himself. Now he rejoices his soul in the fullness of his own idiosyncrasy—his giftedness. His work can hardly be covered in a short interview; only his approach is, and this is delightfully inter-mingled with himself.

The fascination of these contemporary interviews, for me, is that each brings vividly before us, as a person seemingly different, gifted with a more instinctive sense of freedom, a writer who can never be sure that his emotions, his habits, his childhood, his loves and enmities, are not crucial to his work. The modern writer is likely to feel that his life and his work speak for each other; when an interviewer gently presses him to tell more, he will gladly try, for in the writer's own mind clarity about a seemingly personal matter seems to advance that moral clarity which is tantamount to literary power. Power, technical and intellectual power, the power to shape words that open up new realities in the mind, is what writers live for. And since, in modern times, writers feel that this power is in themselves alone, one can see why the gifted writer is enthralled by his own experiences, is gripped by himself in ways that are of *technical* interest to the rest of us. There is always something professional and impersonal in a writer's concern with his own experience. Even his eloquence about it shows gratitude for what he can make of himself.

The *Paris Review* interviews have made the best profiles of con-temporary writers because writers are so adept at portraying them-selves. Writers have been interviewing themselves, in notebooks, diaries, and in the presence of their friends, most of their lives, and are enchanted to carry on in interviews that add to their confidence by eliciting further self-knowledge. Moreover, writers are so aware of other writers, are so much concerned with skill—which is an instinct—that the shop talk in these interviews, too sparse and marginal to build a rounded philosophy of art in the style of Johnson or Goethe, is further characterization of the person being interviewed. Even the playwrights Harold Pinter, Edward Albee, and Arthur Miller, working with supposedly the most "objective" of literary forms, portray themselves here as dependent on their creative daemon, working catch-as-catch-can to be "true"—Pinter's key word—to their immediate creative mood.

So it is the modern writer's sense that he inhabits some mysterious power over his own life, that his gift and his life are really versions of each other, that his habits and beliefs occupy some mysterious center of creativity that is still not the same thing as "himself" but is his private god, his daemon, the mystery of his own creativity—this is the fascinating subject of these interviews. The interviewers are all really saying to these gifted writers: What's it like being *You*? And the writer, equally fascinated, is saying: I can describe it all willingly—you can see how willingly!—but I don't really know, for it is my Gift that is really Me, yet I can only describe this Gift allegorically, as if it were the same thing as a Person—for instance, Me!

However, in the interview with Allen Ginsberg, the writer says plainly that writing consists only in being oneself. Writing is a public art, but we live privately. The way to write—to write well, to reach new ground—is to break through this convention of privacy, and to talk to the reader as you talk to your friends. "We all talk among ourselves and we have common understandings, and we say anything we want to say, and we talk about our assholes, and we talk about our cocks . . . anybody tells one's friends about that. So then—what happens if you make a distinction between what you tell your friends and what you tell your Muse? The problem is to break down that distinction: when you approach the Muse to talk as frankly as you would talk with yourself or your friends. . . ." This (like the whole Ginsberg interview) offers up the pure Transcendentalist or religious notion that literature is identical with sincerity, that we are all equally vessels of God's truth, but that only the poet-as-prophet has the vision to yield up what is in him. It has been my observation that this is notoriously unsafe doctrine for poets. Yet in his interview Ginsberg comes through as a singularly appealing person, and I now understand why he has become a kind of guru or spiritual authority to so many young people all over the world. He is always himself, and as himself is always before us, in his poetry and as a personal resistant to the big state and its heartless wars. How wonderful it must be, the reader thinks, to be as unself-conscious and radiantly confident as that! But the reader of these interviews is also likely to feel *that* about so wily a personality as Jean Cocteau, who talks about himself by talking about his friends. Cocteau invoking the freedom and audacity of Picasso is as charming a "personality" as Allen Ginsberg straightforwardly describing physical intimacies with his friends. In both cases, as with so many openly homosexual writers, there is an explicit reliance on the "difference," the exceptionality, as a wholly personal fact which honesty raises to creativity. As it happens, Cocteau makes this point by talking about his friend Marcel Proust. That is the point of the marvelous Proustian anecdote: "I beg of you, Jean, since you live in the rue d'Anjou in the same building with Mme. de Chevigné, of whom I've made the Duchesse de Guermantes; I entreat you to get her to read my book. . . ."

No proper writer in an interview of this type can afford to lie, for a kind of aristocratic self-approval, a sense of his own right and authentic power, is the blood that keeps him warm. But no writer can resist the invitation to explain himself further and further, to locate the myth, the imaginative setting, that keeps him in business. James Jones, who is obsessed with the "current of violence just under the surface," finds his necessary ideal in all those oddities, like Prewitt in *From Here to Eternity*, who can resist the tragic emphasis that the human race puts on "bravery . . . a horrible thing . . . left over from the animal world and we can't get rid of it." Saul Bellow praises Dreiser for being "rich in a kind of feeling which has been ruled off the grounds by contemporary writers—

the kind of feeling that every human being intuitively recognizes as primary. Dreiser has more open access to primary feelings than any American writer of the twentieth century." This leads Bellow to what he calls his internal prompter— ". . . a kind of readiness to record impressions arising from a source of which we know little." This prompter is Bellow's example of what the writer must depend on in order to be himself, and explains why, as a writer, "I seem to have the blind self-acceptance of the eccentric who can't conceive that his eccentricities are not clearly understood."

Norman Mailer, of course, finds his working myth in the writer's willingness to go the limit. Too often, he says, writers who lack the courage to risk the unknown settle for "craft." What are they afraid of? Of discovering the ignoble in oneself. As for himself, he cites the man who said he wanted to perform the sexual act under every variety of condition, emotion, and mood available to him, and says he "was struck with this . . . because it seemed to me that was what I was trying to do with my writing. . . . By the time I'm done with writing I care about I usually have worked on it through the full gamut of my consciousness." This vision of the writer as an athlete of existentialism, a man who must above all be a hero to himself, stands in interesting contrast to Evelyn Waugh's ideal—the writer is someone simply obsessed with language. "I have no technical psychological interest. It is drama, speech, and events that interest me." Waugh, as is well known, found his necessary image of the writer in a kind of aristocratic dandyism that he wore as an actor might wear a costume or recite a set speech. How delightful it is to find Waugh asking the interviewer who had mentioned Edmund Wilson—up to *Brideshead Revisited* Wilson had been one of Waugh's greatest admirers—"Is he an American?" "Yes." "I don't think what they have to say is of much interest, do you? . . ."

William Burroughs, whose work habits sound as technically complicated as the adding machine his grandfather helped to develop, comes on here—at least in his opening remarks—as an engineer of the pen, a calmly interested specialist in new processes. But the obsession that makes his work interesting reveals itself in his claims that his "cutups," the material he clips from newspapers, magazines, advertisements, and then mixes with his elaborate personal notes, offers us simultaneous perception of many different orders of reality. When Burroughs makes philosophic and scientific claims for his disorderly collections of data, we happily recognize, under the externally calm surface of the interview, the kind of inner frenzy that is his genius—and to which, in all of us, his books make an appeal. We are grateful to him for filling out our intuitive picture of him. It turns out that Burroughs has the same idea of himself—of the source of his power—that we do. When Evelyn Waugh arrives for his interview only to get into bed wearing a pair of white pajamas and smoking a cigar, we recognize with rapture that the comic genius behind *Decline and Fall*—a genius for small, deadly particulars—never left him in life. He always impersonated the value of tradition, and who, in an age that has seen modernism do its worst, can call him altogether mistaken? "Experiment? God forbid! Look at . . . Joyce. He started off writing very well, then you can watch him going mad with vanity. He ends up a lunatic."

The writers in these interviews usually offer their temperamental urges as their creative life stories. Yet the most remarkable interviews are often those in which the stuff of a writer's life is described but remains too deep for an interview. For this reason, my favorite interviews in this book are those with Blaise Cendrars and Louis-Ferdinand Céline. Some of the Americans in this book are perhaps a little too eager to explain themselves. All that has ever really happened to them, one feels, is the experience of being writers. When they talk about themselves, these "selves" become sacred objects. As so often happens with Americans, the terror of failure hangs over them. They have had to train themselves somewhat harder than writers from older cultures do, for in America writers always start from themselves, and knowing the perils of this better than anyone, they have to prepare their position, to anticipate their difficulties. This puts a further strain on the willed intelligence by which they work.

By contrast, Blaise Cendrars seems carelessly bountiful of everything, and recounts his life, his friends, his many countries and adventures simply as anecdote and observation, for the pleasure of talking about them. His interview makes an extraordinary impression on us who are saturated in literature: this is not merely a writer seeking to be a writer, this is a man who has lived. Encountering Cendrars' headlong directness, one recognizes the extraordinary simplicity of heart and boldness of mind, the natural love of life, freedom, chance, and experiment, that went to make up the great modern revolution, early in this century, on which we still live. Everything that was fresh, hopeful, radical, daring in the arts before 1914—and gave the illusion in the twenties that it would go on forever—can still be heard in the voice and pace of Blaise Cendrars as he is interviewed. The man gives himself. Writers, as he says, like to exaggerate the difficulties of writing in order "to make themselves sound interesting." But writing is a privilege "compared with the lot of most people, who live like parts of a machine, who live only to keep the gears of society pointlessly turning." The greatest danger for a writer is to fall victim to his own legend.

Louis-Ferdinand Céline was an extraordinary and terrifying presence in the twentieth-century novel. He was never altogether sane after suffering head wounds in the First World War, and by the Second, like other wounded and desperate French writers who had come to despair of history, he allied himself with the most evil forces in Europe in order to protest the cruelty and injustice that had always been under his eye when he practiced medicine in the slums of Paris. Céline was an amazingly powerful writer who when interviewed did not make very much of being a writer. He thought it enough for a man to tell a story; he must tell it in order to be released from life's order; only then can he die in peace. It is doubtful that Céline died in peace. But he was so strong and original a writer—surely he is the only genius of the

French novel since Proust—that when he tells his "story" the impact of his life experience becomes one of those blows which we suffer with gratitude. He describes his childhood in Paris—the mother, a lacemaker, made the family live on noodles because more pungent foods left odors in the lace—he touches on the First World War, on his doctoring. It is extraordinary how much, in these few pages, he says about the human condition. Politically, Céline was a maniac. Yet his gift for describing things as they are was great, and the compassion he shows in his books is striking. Still, he said (in another interview) that his books were defective, for "great literature is never personal, like that." The "personal" is more and more the theme, the opportunity, the dilemma of contemporary literature. Rarely will one see the eloquence and the danger of the personal mode so clearly revealed as it is in these interviews.

ALFRED KAZIN

WRITERS AT WORK

Third Series

1. William Carlos Williams

William Carlos Williams was born in Rutherford, New Jersey, on September 17, 1883. After schooling in Geneva, Paris, and New York, he was graduated from the University of Pennsylvania Medical School in 1906. He then did graduate work in pediatrics at the University of Leipzig. In 1910 he returned to Rutherford, where he practiced medicine until his retirement in 1951.

His first collection, *Poems* (1909), and those immediately following were strongly influenced by Ezra Pound (whom he had known in Pennsylvania and later in Europe). It was several years later that Williams developed his own style.

Among his many published volumes are *Collected Poems 1921–1931* (1934), *An Early Martyr and Other Poems* (1935), *The Complete Collected Poems of William Carlos Williams 1906–1938* (1938), *Collected Later Poems* (1950), *Collected Earlier Poems* (1951), *The Desert Music* (1954), and *Pictures from Brueghel* (1962). Most important, perhaps, is his "personal epic" poem, *Paterson*, which appeared in five stages (1946–1958). He wrote four novels: *A Voyage to Pagany* (1928), *White Mule* (1937), *In the Money* (1940), and *The Build-Up* (1952); and numerous books of nonfiction, most notably *In the American Grain* (1925), *The Autobiography of William Carlos Williams* (1951), and *Selected Essays of William Carlos Williams* (1954). *Many Loves, and Other Plays: The Collected Plays of William Carlos Williams* and *The Farmers' Daughters*, short stories, appeared in 1961. *The Selected Letters of William Carlos Williams* was published in 1957. In 1950 he was elected to the National Institute of Arts and Letters, and the same year won the National Book Award for poetry. He and Archibald MacLeish shared the Bollingen Prize for Poetry in 1952. Williams died in Rutherford in March 1963.

As Weehawken ### to Hamilton

to Provence we'll say, he hated it

of which he knew nothing and cared less

and used it inhis scheems   - so

founding the coun~~d~~ing which was to

increase to be the wonder of the world
in its day

which was to exceed his london on which he patterned it

(A key figure in the development)

                        If any one is important more important
            - point of a dagger-
than the edge of a knife or a poem is: or an irrelevance #

in the life of a people: see Da Da or the murders of a

Staline

                or a Li Po

                            or an obscre Montezuma

or a forgotten Socrates or Aristotle before the destruction

of the library of Alexandria (as note derisively by Berad Shaw)

by fire in which the poes of Sappho were lost

            and brings us (Alex was born out of wedlock)

        illegitimately perversion ###### righed though that alone

does not a make a poet or a statesman

- Wahington was a six foot four man with a wekk voice and a slow
mind which made it inconvenient for him to move fast - and so he
stayed. He had a will bred in the slow woods so that when he
moved the world moved out of has way.

Fragment of the continuation of Paterson

R. Seidler

William Carlos Williams

RUTHERFORD, NEW JERSEY: Number Nine stands on a terrace at the foot of Ridge Road, just where it angles into Park Avenue and the stores along the main street. For fifty years the sign beside the walk read WILLIAM C. WILLIAMS, M. D. *Now it carries the name of his son, with an arrow pointing to the side entrance, and the new office wing. In his last years, Dr. Williams's health suffered from a series of strokes that made it difficult for him to speak, and impaired his physical vigor, so that there would often be a delay before he appeared, pushing out the aluminum storm door and retreating a step or two, extending welcome with a kind of hesitant warmth. On the occasion of the interview, he moved more deliberately than ever, but his greeting was still at pains to be personal. A leisurely progress brought us upstairs past a huge, two-story painting of Williamsburg Bridge filling the stair well, to the study, a room at the back of the house, overlooking the yard. An electric typewriter, which Dr. Williams could no longer use, was at the desk, and, though he could scarcely read, a copy of* The Desert Music and Other Poems, *opened to "The Descent," was propped up in the open drawer. In a corner of the room, over a metal filing cabinet, was an oil painting hung against a wallpaper of geometric simplicity. We sat a little away from the desk, toward the window, with the microphone lying on a stack of small magazines between us.*

At the time of these talks, in April 1962, William Carlos Williams was in his seventy-ninth year, author of forty published volumes from Poems, 1909, *a collection so rare that Mrs. Williams has had trouble holding on to a copy, down through various collected editions and the successive books of* Paterson *to* The Desert Music *and* Journey to Love. *Both of these last volumes were written in an unusual recovery of creative power after Dr. Williams's first serious illness in 1952. Now, with customary impatience, he was fretting to see his latest collection,* Pictures from Brueghel, *scheduled for publication in June. The doorbell never rang but he expected some word from New Directions, though it was still early in spring.*

Because it was so hard for Dr. Williams to talk, there was no question of discoursing on topics suggested in advance, and the conversation went on informally, for an hour or two at a time, over several days. The effort it took the poet to find and pronounce words can hardly be indicated here. Many of the sentences ended in no more than a wave of the hand when Mrs. Williams was not present to finish them. But whatever the topic, the poet's mind kept coming back to the technical matters that interested him in his later years. One of these was his concern with "idiom," the movements of speech that he felt to be especially American, as opposed to English. A rival interest was the "variable foot," a metrical device that was to resolve the conflict between form and freedom in verse. The question whether one had not to assume a fixed element in the foot as the basis for meter drew only a typical Williams negative, slightly profane, and no effort was made to pur-

sue this much further. As a result, the notion of some mysterious "measure" runs through the interview like an unlaid ghost, promising enough pattern for shapeliness, enough flexibility for all the subtleties of idiom. No wonder a copy of "The Descent" was in evidence as we began; for however much one may argue over the theory of this verse, it is hard to resist the performance.

On March 4, 1963, William Carlos Williams died in his sleep, at home, of a cerebral hemorrhage that was not unexpected. Two months later Pictures from Brueghel was awarded the Pulitzer Prize for poetry, and Mrs. Williams accepted, in his name, the Gold Medal for Poetry from the National Institute of Arts and Letters. Though he did not see this interview in print, he approved it in its final stages. Mrs. Williams reports him as having been much entertained by her part in the second half of it.

WILLIAMS: Well, what's to be done?

INTERVIEWER: I would like to ask you about this new measure that I see here—

WILLIAMS: If I could only talk.

INTERVIEWER: Perhaps we might begin with Rutherford, whether you thought it was a good environment for you.

WILLIAMS: A very—bad environment—for poets. We didn't take anything seriously—in Ruth—in Rutherford. We didn't take poetry very seriously. As far as recording my voice in Rutherford—I read before the ladies, mostly.

INTERVIEWER: You mean the Women's Club? How did they like it?

WILLIAMS: Very much: they applauded. I was quite a hero. [Picking up a volume] I remember "By the Road to the Contagious Hospital" was one of the ones I read. The hospital was up in Clifton. I was always intent on saying what I had to say in the accents that were native to me. But I didn't know what I was doing. I knew that the measure was intended to record—something. But I didn't know what the measure was. I stumbled all over the place in these earlier poems. For instance, in this one here ["*Queen-Ann's Lace*"]. I would divide those lines differently now. It's just like the later line, only not opened up in the same way.

INTERVIEWER: You were saying that Rutherford was a bad environment for poets.

WILLIAMS: Yes. But except for my casual conversations about the town, I didn't think anything of it at all. I had a great amount of patience with artisans.

INTERVIEWER: Did you mean it when you said medicine was an interference which you resented?

WILLIAMS: I didn't resent it at all. I just wanted to go straight ahead.

INTERVIEWER: And medicine was not on the way?

WILLIAMS: I don't know whether it would be. I used to give readings at the high school and Fairleigh Dickinson. I was sympathetic with these audiences. I was talking about the same people that I had to do with as patients, and trying to interest them. I was not pretending: I was speaking to them as if they were interested in the same sort of thing.

INTERVIEWER: But were they? Perhaps they felt the double nature of your role, as both poet and doctor, was something of a barrier.

WILLIAMS: No, no. The language itself was what intrigued me. I thought that we were on common territory there.

INTERVIEWER: Did you write the short stories on a different "level" than the poems—as a kind of interlude to them?

WILLIAMS: No, as an alternative. They were written in the form of a conversation which I was partaking in. We were in it together.

INTERVIEWER: Then the composition of them was just as casual and spontaneous as you have suggested. You would come home in the evening and write twelve pages or so without revising?

WILLIAMS: I think so. I was coming *home*. I was placing myself in continuation of a common conversation.

INTERVIEWER: You have insisted that there cannot be a seeking for words in literature. Were you speaking of prose as well as poetry?

WILLIAMS: I think so. Not to choose between words.

INTERVIEWER: Certainly the word does matter though.

WILLIAMS: It does matter, very definitely. Strange that I could say that.

INTERVIEWER: But when you had come home, and were continuing the experience of reality—

WILLIAMS: Reality. Reality. My vocabulary was chosen out of the intensity of my concern. When I was talking in front of a group, I wasn't interested in impressing them with my power of speech, but only with the seriousness of my intentions toward them. I had to make them come alive.

INTERVIEWER: You have said you felt trapped in Rutherford, that you couldn't get out, never had any contact with anyone here. Do you still feel that Rutherford hasn't provided enough of the contact you managed to find during the twenties, in New York, with the Others group? Was that a genuine contribution to your development?

WILLIAMS: That was not a literary thing exactly. But it was about writing—intensely so. We were speaking straight ahead about what concerned us, and if I could have overheard what I was saying then, that would have given me a hint of how to phrase myself, to say what I had to say. Not after the establishment, but speaking straight ahead. I would gladly have traded what I have tried to say, for what came off my tongue, naturally.

INTERVIEWER: Which was not the same?

WILLIAMS: Not free enough. What came off in this writing, finally—*this* writing [*pointing to* "The Descent"]—that was pretty much what I wanted to say, in the way I wanted to say it, then. I was searching in this congeries. I wanted to say something in a certain tone of my voice which would be exactly how I wanted to say it, to measure it in a certain way.

INTERVIEWER: Was this in line with what the others in the group were trying to do?

WILLIAMS: I don't think they knew what they were trying to do; but in effect it was. I couldn't speak like the academy. It had to be modified by the conversation about me. As Marianne Moore used to say, a language dogs and cats could understand. So I think she agrees with me fundamentally. Not the speech of English country people, which would have something artificial about it; not that, but language modified by *our* environment; the American environment.

INTERVIEWER: Your own background is pretty much a mixture of English and Spanish, isn't it? Do you think the Spanish has had any influence on your work?

WILLIAMS: There might have been a permanent impression on my mind. It was certainly different from the French. French is too formal; the Spanish language isn't. They were broad men, as in *El Cid*, very much broader than the French. My relation to language was a curious thing. My father was English, but Spanish was spoken in my home. I didn't speak it, but I was read to in Spanish. My mother's relatives used to come up and stay two or three months.

INTERVIEWER: You have said you equated Spanish with the "romantic." Is that a designation you would shrink from?

WILLIAMS: No, not shrink from.

INTERVIEWER: What I was getting at is that you have kept the name "Carlos."

WILLIAMS: I had no choice but to keep the "Carlos."

INTERVIEWER: I understand Solomon Hoheb, your mother's father, was Dutch.

WILLIAMS: Maybe. The Spanish came from the Sephardic Jews. Though the English was strong indeed, through my grandfather.

INTERVIEWER: You've been more conscious of the Spanish, then, than of the other.

WILLIAMS: Yes! I've insisted on breaking with my brother's memory of the Williamses as English. All one needs to do is look at my nose. Flossie says, "I love your nose." And the hell with my nose, after all. The thing that concerns me is the theory of what I was determined to do with measure, what you encounter on the page. It must be transcribed to the page from the lips of the poet, as it was with such a master as Sappho. "The Descent" was very important to me in that way.

INTERVIEWER: You mean that is where it finally happened?

WILLIAMS: Yes, there it happened; and before that it didn't. I remember writing this (*trying to read*):

> *The descent beckons*
> > *as the ascent beckoned.*
> > > *Memory is a kind . . .*

INTERVIEWER: . . . *of accomplishment.*

WILLIAMS: *A sort of renewal*
> > > *even*

an initiation, since the spaces it opens are new places.

You see how I run that line? I was very much excited when I wrote this. I had to do something. I was sitting there with the typewriter in front of me. I was attempting to imitate myself (I think I can't even see it at all) but it didn't come alive to me.

INTERVIEWER: It seems to me you were reading it just now.

WILLIAMS: More or less. But something went wrong with me. I can't make it out any more. I can't type.

INTERVIEWER: Would a tape recorder or a dictaphone be uncongenial?

WILLIAMS: No, anything that would serve me I'd gladly adopt.

INTERVIEWER: The appearance of this poem on the page suggests you were conscious of it as a thing—something for the eye.

WILLIAMS: Yes, very good. I was conscious of making it even. I wanted it to read regularly.

INTERVIEWER: Not just to please the eye?

WILLIAMS: The total effect is very important.

INTERVIEWER: But the care in placing the words—did you ever feel you would be as happy painting?

WILLIAMS: I'd like to have been a painter, and it would have given me at least as great a satisfaction as being a poet.

INTERVIEWER: But you say you are a "word man."

WILLIAMS: Yes, that took place early in my development. I was early inducted into my father's habit of reading—that made me a poet, not a painter. My mother was a painter. Her brother Carlos won the Grand Prix—the Gros Lot it was called—then he financed her to go to Paris, to study painting. Then the money ran out.

INTERVIEWER: And she met your father through Carlos, whom he knew in—

WILLIAMS:—Puerto Plata. My father was a businessman, interested in South America. But he always loved books. He used to read poetry to me. Shakespeare. He had a group who used to come to our house, a Shakespeare club. They did dramatic readings. So I was always interested in Shakespeare, and Grandmother was interested in the stage—my father's mother. Emily Dickinson, her name was. Isn't that amazing?

INTERVIEWER: Quite a coincidence: I notice a picture of her namesake over the desk.

WILLIAMS: Emily was my patron saint. She was also an American, seeking to divide the line in some respectable way. We were all of us Americans.

INTERVIEWER: Then you did read a good bit of her at some stage, with your father?

WILLIAMS: My father didn't know anything about Emily Dickinson. He was sold on Shakespeare. [*Doorbell rings. WCW makes his way downstairs to answer it.*]

INTERVIEWER [*As he returns*]: You say you were hoping it might be the new volume?

WILLIAMS: Yes. I am keenly disappointed. But that's always the way it is with me—my life's blood dripping away. Laughlin has been a wonderful friend, but it's always so goddam *slow*! I have still the illusion that I will be able to talk when I make these connections. It's possible, because I am an emotional creature, and if I could only talk, to you for instance. Here is a person well-intentioned toward me, meaning yourself, and I can't talk to him. It makes me furious.

INTERVIEWER: It's good of you to put up with this business at all. We were talking about painting and the theater and poetry. Was that a natural progression for you?

WILLIAMS: More or less; stemming from frustration. I was wondering—I was seeking to be articulate.

INTERVIEWER: At one point you wanted to be an actor.

WILLIAMS: I had no skill as an actor. But through Dad's reading, the plays of Shakespeare made an impression on me. He didn't *want* them to necessarily, just to read them—as words, that came off as speech.

INTERVIEWER: How did this interest in words make you interested in poetry as opposed, say, to writing novels?

WILLIAMS: That didn't have any connection.

INTERVIEWER: The words weren't sufficiently important in prose?

WILLIAMS: No. I never thought I was a very good prose writer anyway. But when I speak of Emily Dickinson—she was an independent spirit. She did her best to get away from too strict an interpretation. And she didn't want to be confined to rhyme or reason. (Even in Shakespeare, the speech of the players: it was annoying to him to have to rhyme, for Godsake.) And she followed the American idiom. She didn't know it, but she followed it nonetheless. I was a better poet.

INTERVIEWER: You are speaking about language now, not form.

WILLIAMS: Yes; her native speech. She was a wild girl. She chafed against restraint. But she speaks the spoken language, the idiom, which would be deformed by Oxford English.

INTERVIEWER: This new measure of yours, in the later poems, is meant then to accommodate the American speech rhythms.

WILLIAMS: Yes. It's a strange phenomenon, my writing. I think what I have been searching for—

INTERVIEWER: You were suggesting that Emily Dickinson had something to do with it; and her objection to rhyme. But that you were a better poet.

WILLIAMS: Oh, yes [*laughing*]. She was a real good guy. I thought I was a better poet because the American idiom was so close to me, and she didn't get what the poets were doing at that time—writing according to a new method, not the English method, which wouldn't have made much sense to an American. Whitman was on the right track, but when he switched to the English intonation, and followed the English method of recording the feet, he didn't realize it was a different method, which was not satisfactory to an American. Everything started with Shakespeare.

INTERVIEWER: Because it was meant to be spoken?

WILLIAMS: Yes. But when the Shakespearean line was recorded, it was meant to be a formal thing, divided in the English method according to what was written on the page. The Americans shouldn't tolerate that. An Englishman—an English rhetorician, an actor—will speak like Shakespeare, but it's only rhetorical. He can't be true to his own speech. He has to change it in order to conform.

INTERVIEWER: You think it is easier for the English to conform, in poetry, to their kind of speech pattern than it is for an American? You don't think for example that Frost is as true to the American idiom as you are trying to be?

WILLIAMS: No, I don't think so. Eliot, on the other hand, was trying to find a way to record the speech and he didn't find it. He wanted to be regular, to be true to the American idiom, but he didn't find a way to do it. One has to bow down finally, either to the English or to the American.

INTERVIEWER: Eliot went to England; you stayed here.

WILLIAMS: To my sorrow.

INTERVIEWER: To your sorrow? What do you mean by that?

WILLIAMS [*yielding, perhaps*]: It is always better to stick to something.

INTERVIEWER: It's rare to find someone who has. Eliot says he would not be the same if he had stayed. You have said there was a great virtue in the kind of isolation you experienced here.

WILLIAMS: A key question.

INTERVIEWER: And you have been called our most valuable homespun sensitivity.

WILLIAMS: "Homespun sensitivity." Very good.

INTERVIEWER: But you still feel it was a bad environment.

WILLIAMS: It was native, but I doubt that it was very satisfactory to me personally. Though it did provide the accent which satisfied me.

INTERVIEWER: Do you think you could have picked a better one? Do you think you would have been happier in Boston, or Hartford, or New York, or Paris?

WILLIAMS: I might have picked a better one, if I had wanted to —which I did. But if I lived there—if its language was familiar to me, if that was the kind of conversation which I heard, which I grew up with—I could tolerate the vulgarity because it forced me to speak in a particular manner. Not the English intonation.

INTERVIEWER: Do you still feel that the English influence on Eliot set us back twenty years?

WILLIAMS: Very definitely. He was a conformist. He wanted to go back to the iambic pentameter; and he did go back to it, very well; but he didn't acknowledge it.

INTERVIEWER: You say that you could never be a calm speaker, so that this unit you use, which isn't either a foot or a line necessarily, and which works by speech impulses, this is meant to reflect also your own nervous habit of speech—in which things come more or less in a rush.

WILLIAMS: Common sense would force me to work out some such method.

INTERVIEWER: You do pause, though, in the midst of these lines.

WILLIAMS: Very definitely.

INTERVIEWER: Then what is the integrity of the line?

WILLIAMS: If I was consistent in myself it would be very much more effective than it is now. I would have followed much closer to the indicated divisions of the line than I did. It's too haphazard.

INTERVIEWER: The poetry? You admit that in prose, but—

WILLIAMS:—in poetry also. I think I was too haphazard.

INTERVIEWER: In the later poems—like "The Orchestra" here— you think there is still some work to do?

WILLIAMS: It's not successful. It would be classical if it had the proper division of lines. "Reluctant mood," "stretches and yawns." What the devil is that? It isn't firmly enough stated. It's all very complicated—but I can't go on.

INTERVIEWER: You mean you can't find a theory to explain what you do naturally.

WILLIAMS: Yes. It's all in the ear. I wanted to be regular. To continue that—

INTERVIEWER [*picking up a copy of* Paterson V, *from which some clippings fall to the floor*]: These opening lines—they make an image on the page.

WILLIAMS: Yes, I was imitating the flight of the bird.

INTERVIEWER: Then it's directed—

WILLIAMS:—to the eyes. Read it.

INTERVIEWER: "In old age the mind casts off . . ."

WILLIAMS: *In old age*
                   the mind

                         casts off
                      rebelliously
                   an eagle
            from its crag

INTERVIEWER: Did you ever think of using any other city as subject for a poem?

WILLIAMS: I didn't dare any mention of it in *Paterson*, but I thought strongly of Manhattan when I was looking about for a city to celebrate. I thought it was not particularized enough for me, not American in the sense I wanted. It was near enough, God knows, and I was familiar enough with it for all my purposes— but so was Leipzig, where I lived for a year when I was young, or Paris. Or even Vienna or even Frascati. But Manhattan escaped me.

INTERVIEWER: Someone remarks in one of these clippings that there is no reason the poem should ever end. Part Four completes the cycle, Five renews it. Then what?

WILLIAMS [*laughing*]: Go on repeating it. At the end—the last part, the dance—

INTERVIEWER: "We can know nothing but the dance . . ."

WILLIAMS: *The dance.*

> *To dance to a measure*
> *contrapuntally,*
> *Satyrically, the tragic foot.*

That has to be interpreted; but how are you going to interpret it?

INTERVIEWER: I don't presume to interpret it; but perhaps the satyrs represent the element of freedom, of energy within the form.

WILLIAMS: Yes. The satyrs are understood as action, a dance. I always think of the Indians there.

INTERVIEWER: Is anything implied, in "contrapuntally," about the nature of the foot?

WILLIAMS: It means "musically"—it's a musical image. The Indians had a beat in their own music, which they beat with their feet. It isn't an image exactly, a poetic image. Or perhaps it is. The beat goes according to the image. It should all be so simple; but with my damaged brain—

INTERVIEWER: We probably shouldn't be trying to reduce a poetic statement to prose, when we have *The Desert Music* here: "Only the poem . . ."

WILLIAMS: "The counted poem, to an exact measure."

INTERVIEWER: You think it should be more exact then, than you have yet made it.

WILLIAMS: Yes, it should be more exact, in Milton's sense. Milton counted the syllables.

INTERVIEWER: "And I could not help thinking of the wonders of the brain that hears that music."

WILLIAMS: Yes.

INTERVIEWER: "And of our skill *sometimes* to record it." Do you still feel that such modesty is in order?

WILLIAMS: Modesty is in order, God knows—facing the universe of sound.

INTERVIEWER: At least you are not talking about painting now.

WILLIAMS: No. I'm more or less committed to poetry.

[*Talking with Mrs. Williams—the Flossie of* White Mule—*is like going on with a conversation with Dr. Williams: the same honesty, the same warmth, mixed perhaps with briskness and reserve. The living room of their house reflects the interests they have had in common—the paintings, the flowers, the poetry. For fifty years the daily mail brought letters, books, journals, to accumulate in corners and cupboards and on tables around the edges of the room: books from authors and publishers, books with dedications to WCW, or titles borrowed from his poems; and the whole lot of those almost anonymous little magazines that he encouraged with contributions: poems, articles, the inevitable "visit with WCW." On the first day of these particular interviews, a new hi-fi set still in its crate stood in the middle of the room, a gift from the second son, Paul. Now, while waiting for Dr. Williams to come in, Mrs. Williams put on a record, and we listened to the poet's voice for a while, recorded in this same room with occasional sounds of local traffic coming through. It was an aging voice, unmodulated and didactic, but curiously effective in reading the late poems. Mrs. Williams talked about the town of Rutherford, and the poet's brother Edgar, an architect with plans for improving life along the Passaic. She talked of the house when they first moved into it, and of her early impressions of Bill Williams as a young man, at a stage of their life when he was generally off in New York at the clinics, or at various literary gatherings.*]

INTERVIEWER: Did you have to be converted to poetry, in those early days?

MRS. WILLIAMS: No, I was sympathetic. Of course, Bill never

paid much attention to me. He used to come to see my sister, who was quite a bit older. She played the piano, and Bill played the violin—not very well. And Edgar sang. Bill didn't read his poetry to me then. He read some to my sister, but she didn't think much of it. Bill's early verse was pretty bad.

INTERVIEWER: I understand Dr. Williams wrote a sonnet a day for a year, when he was at Pennsylvania. Edgar says he called it brainwash, or something worse.

MRS. WILLIAMS: Meeting Ezra Pound seemed to make a difference. It was not really a literary relationship at first. They were too wholly different, but I think that was the turning point. From that time Bill began seriously to want to write poetry. But he realized he couldn't make a living at it.

INTERVIEWER: How did he happen to become a doctor?

MRS. WILLIAMS: His father wanted him to be a dentist. Bill was willing to try. But he hated it. Bill was just too nervous to stand in one spot. But he loved being a doctor, making house calls, and talking to people.

INTERVIEWER: He didn't care to be a surgeon?

MRS. WILLIAMS: He didn't have the long fingers he thought a surgeon should have. That's why he was never a good violinist. But he and Edgar both had ability with their hands. Edgar was a master at drawing, and Bill used to paint. And of course he loves to garden. Two years ago he turned over that whole garden for me when he could scarcely use his right arm. Things would really grow for him.

INTERVIEWER: Was there much literary life in Rutherford?

MRS. WILLIAMS: Not until much later. We had no literary contacts in Rutherford at all: except for Miss Owen, who taught the sixth grade. She knew what Bill was trying to do.

INTERVIEWER: I had the feeling Dr. Williams felt there was no real response to his poetry, even when he read to local groups.

MRS. WILLIAMS: They took what they could get, and ignored the rest—it just wasn't for them. I think to this day very few people in Rutherford know anything about Bill's writing.

INTERVIEWER: Is that a comment on the town or the writing?

MRS. WILLIAMS: I think both. It's a lower-middle-class type of mind, and Bill has never attracted a general audience. My mother used to try to get me to influence him.

INTERVIEWER: To write more conventionally?

MRS. WILLIAMS: Yes. Some of it I didn't like myself, but I never interfered. And I was never blamed for not liking it. [*Telephone rings.*] I'll get it, Bill. [*Answering*] Is it an emergency? No, there are no office hours on Friday. [*Returning from phone*] A patient for young Bill. He left the answering service off. That's what happens.

INTERVIEWER: I suppose you are used to that by now.

MRS. WILLIAMS [*groaning*]: Yes, by now, I'm afraid I am.

INTERVIEWER: Is Dr. Williams not writing now?

MRS. WILLIAMS: No, not for over a year; he can't. He just can't find the words.

INTERVIEWER: Was he writing very much when you were first engaged?

MRS. WILLIAMS: No; once in a while he would send me a poem. But he was busy building up his practice. After we were married he wrote more. I saw to it that he had time, and I made it pleasant for people who came here—because I liked them myself. They were much more interesting than most of the local people. Everyone you can think of used to be in and out. We were the only ones who had a permanent address in all that time. For fifty years, this was headquarters for them all. There was Marsden Hartley—that was his only pastel, over the divan there. He was broke and wanted to go to Germany, so he had an auction at Steiglitz's gallery. An American Place. Bill bought another one at the same time, an unfinished oil up in the study. Maxwell Bodenheim came and stayed a couple of weeks once. He almost drove us crazy. (He was supposed to have a broken arm but Bill was never convinced of it.) He was quite dirty and disagreeable. He couldn't eat carrots, though we had to have them, for the children's sake. And he stuttered terribly. One day we received a telegram from him saying: SEND $200 AT ONCE AM GOING TO MARRY A VERY BEAUTIFUL GIRL. MAXWELL. He was later found murdered in his apartment in New York, with his wife, if she was his wife; probably not the one in the telegram. Then there was Wallace Gould, whom you may not know, a friend of Hartley's from Maine. His mother was an American Indian. And Marianne Moore used to come out with her mother. Bill's writing developed tremendously in that period. There was a group up at Grantwood, near Fort Lee. Malcolm Cowley was in it; and Marcel Duchamp, Man Ray, Alfred Kreymbourg. Robert Brown had the one solid house; the others all lived around in their little shacks. Later on they used to meet in New York, at Lola Ridge's place. She had a big, barnlike studio. I suppose today you would call her a communist, though I never heard any talk of that kind. She was older than most of the young writers. Then there was John Reed, who wrote *Ten Days That Shook the World*; and Louise Bryant —they were all in that group. And there we were. There were arguments; they were all very serious about their writing. They used to get up and read—they would always read. It used to be deadly sometimes. But then I wasn't *too* interested in the group, and after all I had two small children. And then in the thirties, there were the Friends of William Carlos Williams—Ford Madox Ford's group. Toward the end we had a big party for them out here. But that was rather ridiculous. Bill says it was poor old Ford's last gasp for—you know, a group around him. He was dying on his feet. And he did die a couple of years later.

INTERVIEWER: How did you get along with Ezra Pound?

MRS. WILLIAMS: Pound was never around. Pound came over in . . . I think, 1938 to get an honorary degree at Hamilton. And he spent two days with us when he was released from Saint Elizabeth's in 1958, before he sailed for Italy. I wouldn't know what to say of this last impression. He was self-centered, as always. You couldn't talk to him; it was impossible. The only one he ever talked to nicely was Win Scott. It just happened that Win came out to see us, and they got along beautifully. Ezra always tried to tell Bill off, but they got along as friends over the years. Bill wasn't afraid of him; their letters used to be rather acrimonious, back and forth.

INTERVIEWER [*to WCW looking in*]: Apparently those letters don't represent your final attitude?

WILLIAMS: No; the only thing that I remember was the attitude of Flossie's father—

MRS. WILLIAMS: But that has nothing to do with Ezra's last visit here, dear.

WILLIAMS: Just a passing comment. [*Withdraws.*]

MRS. WILLIAMS: Bill and Ezra wrote quite a number of letters to each other when the war started; they were on such opposite sides. Ezra was definitely pro-Fascist, much as he may deny it, and Bill was just the opposite. Not pro-Semitic but not anti-Semitic either, by any means.

INTERVIEWER: After the war, wasn't there some local concern about Dr. Williams's so-called communism?

MRS. WILLIAMS: That was in 1952, when Bill was going down to take the chair of poetry. Senator McCarthy was in the news then, and they were frightened to death in Washington. There was a woman who was lobbying for a reform in poetry, who had no use for free verse. She had a little periodical, I've forgotten the name of it, and she wrote a letter saying what an outrage it was that a man like that—

INTERVIEWER: Of course, this was all in the aftermath of the Bollingen award to Pound.

MRS. WILLIAMS: Bill had nothing to do with that. But if he had been a member of the Fellows then, he would certainly have voted for him.

INTERVIEWER: Was Dr. Williams ever asked to testify against Pound?

MRS. WILLIAMS: They questioned him two or three times. They wanted him to listen to some records, and swear it was Pound. Bill couldn't do that, but he said he would tell them frankly what he knew. And that was all. Every time we went down to Washington, Bill went to see him.

INTERVIEWER: Going back to the First World War: perhaps this isn't something you want to go into, but there were some local reactions then, weren't there?

MRS. WILLIAMS: Against Germans. Yes; that would involve Bill because he was married to me. Bill's mother made my life one hell because I was partly German. Though she wasn't living with us then.

INTERVIEWER: So with one thing and another—Greenwich Village, communism, and the Germans—

MRS. WILLIAMS: Bill was always in a controversy. But I think he stood his ground very well through it all.

WILLIAMS [*coming in, and with his hands on Mrs. Williams' shoulders*]: Maybe you've had enough.

MRS. WILLIAMS: Oh, Bill, it's all right. Don't worry about me. Go out and take a walk.

INTERVIEWER [*to WCW*]: Do you have any recollection of writing a play for the P.T.A. years ago? It was on some local issue, like putting in a school nurse, on which you took a liberal view.

WILLIAMS: I can't think. I was certainly interested in plays. But the only person I ever worked with was Kitty Hoagland.

MRS. WILLIAMS: That was *Many Loves*, much later. Kitty didn't come until the thirties. But Bill wrote four or five small plays during those early years. One about the Dutch around this area; and a very nice little play called *The Apple Tree* that was going to be done at the Provincetown, but Alfred Kreymbourg lost it. And a Puritan play, *Betty Putnam*, that was acted over at the Tennis Club. Do you remember the old tennis courts over on Montross Avenue? There was a very active young group connected with it.

INTERVIEWER: But the town itself didn't quite get all this, I suppose. [*To WCW*] Your brother Edgar says it's a narrow town, and what you have done is in spite of it.

WILLIAMS: Yes. There were some aristocrats back there who would have nothing to do with budding genius.

INTERVIEWER: Not to mention political matters. Edgar says that in the political club which your father started, you were always the liberal.

WILLIAMS: Yes, to my sorrow.

INTERVIEWER: To your sorrow?

MRS. WILLIAMS: He doesn't mean it! I don't see why—

WILLIAMS: Do I mean it? For Godsake, my friends have all been pretty disillusioned friends.

INTERVIEWER: Marianne Moore, who knows you pretty well, says you were always a bit "reckless."

WILLIAMS: I guess she's right. I was a Unitarian. And Unitarians are liberals.

MRS. WILLIAMS: I think Bill has always been willing to be reckless. There was the social credit business for instance, that Bill got involved in in the thirties. They wanted to give a kind of dividend to the people to increase purchasing power. There were large meetings in New York and down at the University of Virginia. But that was about the end of it. In fact many of those involved withdrew from it when they saw how things were going, with the war coming on and all. Some of them were so nervous about that whole episode they wouldn't even speak to Bill. That's the difference. I don't say Bill was naïve; perhaps it was honesty. Bill isn't a radical or a communist or anything else. He's an honest man. And if he gets into it with both feet, it's just too bad. That's the way it's been.

INTERVIEWER [*to WCW*]: Right?

WILLIAMS: [*Agrees, laughing.*]

INTERVIEWER: If we could talk a few more minutes about personal matters—how did you enjoy Saint Thomas? I understand you have just come back from there.

WILLIAMS: I could stay there forever, with reservations, of course. Saint Thomas is the place where my father grew up. I remember a photograph of the blizzard area—oh, for Godsake, I mean the hurricane, in eighty-eight.

MRS. WILLIAMS: Bill, dear, I'm sorry, but it must have been in the seventies. It was when your father was a boy.

WILLIAMS [*with a sigh*]: Yes, yes, yes. [*Laughs.*] I remember a story of the hurricane. Thoroughly documented. How first the water went out of the harbor and left it dry, the ships lying on their beams' ends, and then another shudder and an earthquake worse than they ever had in the area. And I have a distinct memory of some photographs of my father, taken at perhaps twenty-one years of age. I was very much interested in making contact with his memory.

MRS. WILLIAMS: It was a good trip, but Bill gets restless. And it's to difficult at our age.

WILLIAMS: I think we'll not go again.

INTERVIEWER: To get back for a minute to the troubles of 1952 —do you think you were working too hard at that time?

WILLIAMS: I was interested in the process of composition—in the theory of it. And I *was* working pretty hard at it. But I couldn't make much of it.

MRS. WILLIAMS: Bill had a contract with Random House for three books. There was no hurry; but that's the only way Bill can work. And he doesn't want to look things over, which is his worst fault. *The Build-Up* was written then. I'm afraid Bill garbled that one. It was just impatience. And he didn't want me to read the things either. I wish I had, there were so many errors in the *Autobiography*. That was inexcusable. Then, one night in the winter of forty-eight, Bill felt a pain in his chest, shoveling out the car. He kept going until February. I used to drive around with him on house calls. But it was too much.

WILLIAMS: I had a heart attack. Perhaps it was a good thing. I thought I was God almighty, I guess; in general. But I got over that one.

MRS. WILLIAMS: There wasn't any kind of cerebral trouble until 1950 or so. Bill had given up medicine and we were going down to take the chair of poetry in Washington. But in 1952, when we were up visiting the Abbotts, in New York, Bill had a serious stroke.

WILLIAMS: I tried to play it down. I was conscious, and rational; and I could joke about it. But I was in a strange house, and I needed to get home. I couldn't write—

MRS. WILLIAMS: Then suddenly you could hardly understand him.

WILLIAMS: That was the end. I was through with life.

MRS. WILLIAMS: No, it wasn't the end. You had a lot of life left. You had a whole play running through your mind while you were lying there, *The Cure*. You thought it out and dictated the notes to me. You wrote it when we got home.

INTERVIEWER: That was something of a change in approach.

WILLIAMS: Yes, the novels I just did as I went along, at first; though I tried to think them out as well as I could.

MRS. WILLIAMS: Of course the *White Mule* was about a baby; Bill's favorite subject. But most of the later poems were written after the stroke. Bill used to say things like spelling didn't matter, and he would never correct at all. I think he did much better work after the stroke slowed him down.

WILLIAMS [*perhaps grudgingly*]: The evidence is there.

INTERVIEWER: It was when you were at the Abbotts' that someone read Theocritus to you.

WILLIAMS: Yes, Mrs. Gratwick; I asked her to. Theocritus was always strong in my mind. But I wasn't capable of hearing it in the Greek. I'm in an unfortunate position, because I don't have the original language. For example, I started to take Latin at Horace Mann, but the teacher was withdrawn, to my infinite regret. That was the end of that—all my life, that was the end. And I always regretted too that I didn't know Greek. I don't know, as far as the Theocritus was concerned, whether it came first, or the stroke.

MRS. WILLIAMS: You had talked of doing an adaptation.

INTERVIEWER: Why Theocritus?

WILLIAMS: The pastoral nature of it gave me a chance to spread myself. It was Greek, and it appealed to me; and it was a wonderful chance to record my feeling of respect for the Greek classics.

INTERVIEWER: There was a change in the verse in the fifties. Was this the first time you tried the new measure?

WILLIAMS: "The Descent" was the first. I regard that as an experiment in the variable foot.

INTERVIEWER: You said earlier that you were almost unconscious when you wrote it.

WILLIAMS: Yes, I was. I was very much excited. I wasn't conscious of doing anything unusual but I realized that something had occurred to me, which was a very satisfying conclusion to my poetic process. Something happened to my line that completed it, completed the rhythm, or at least it was satisfying to me. It was still an irregular composition; but not too much so; but I couldn't complete it. I had written that poem to retain the things which *would* have been the completion of the poem. But as for picking the thing up and going on with it, I had to acknowledge I was licked. I didn't dare fool with the poem so that it would have been more rigid; I wouldn't have wanted that.

INTERVIEWER: You felt there was nothing more you could do with it?

WILLIAMS: Nothing more. I felt all that I could do with it had been done, but it was not complete. I returned to it; but the irregularity of that poem could not be repeated by me. It was too . . . I've forgotten.

INTERVIEWER: You feel it wasn't a perfect poem?

WILLIAMS: It was too regular. There were variations of mood which would have led me to make a different poem out of it.

INTERVIEWER: And you don't think anything after "The Descent" goes beyond it?

WILLIAMS: No. I always wanted to do something more with it, but I didn't know how.

MRS. WILLIAMS: There was one written quite a long time before: that was the start of it. Then there was the "Daphne and Virginia"—Virginia, of course, was Paul's wife, and Daphne is Bill's. That poem always makes me sad. "The Orchestra" was written in 1954 or 1955, I think. Bill wrote quite a lot after he had the stroke.

It's really amazing what he has done; and he gave readings, too, in Saint Louis, Chicago, Savannah—

WILLIAMS: I couldn't break through.

MRS. WILLIAMS: Harvard, Brandeis, Brown. We took two trips to the coast after that—to U.C.L.A., the University of California, Washington—

WILLIAMS: I've been going down hill rapidly.

INTERVIEWER: And the *Pictures from Brueghel*?

WILLIAMS: Yes, those are late; very late. But they are too regular.

INTERVIEWER: Did you ever grow any fonder of the academic world after your trips around the campuses?

MRS. WILLIAMS: *They* liked *him*, at least. And the girls' colleges all loved him.

WILLIAMS: The high point was the appearance at Wellesley. It was a very successful impromptu appearance; a reading. I always remember the satisfaction I got pleasing the ladies—the kids.

INTERVIEWER: Beginning with the Women's Club in Rutherford.

WILLIAMS: Always. I was always for the ladies.

MRS. WILLIAMS: Bill has always been fond of women, and terribly disappointed not to have had a sister. And he never had a daughter. But women liked him; they sensed that he was sympathetic, and they could talk to him.

WILLIAMS: *Very* sympathetic.

INTERVIEWER: Just one or two more questions. Do you think your medical training—your discipline in science—has had any effect on your poetry?

WILLIAMS: The scientist is very important to the poet, because his language is important to him.

INTERVIEWER: To the scientist?

WILLIAMS: Well, and the poet. I don't pretend to go too far. But I have been taught to be accurate in my speech.

INTERVIEWER: But not scholastic. Someone has said you would not make so much of the great American language if you had been judicious about things.

WILLIAMS: It's a point well taken. The writing of English is a great pastime. The only catch to that is when a man adds the specification "English." That is purely accidental and means nothing. Any language could be inserted in its place. But the restrictions that are accepted in the classics of a language enclose it in a corset of mail which becomes its chief distinction.

MRS. WILLIAMS: Bill has always experimented. He was never satisfied to keep doing the same thing. And he has been severely criticized. But I think some of the younger poets are benefiting from it. Like Charles Tomlinson, and Robert Creeley—they've learned a lot from Bill. David Ignatow—any number of them. Allen Ginsberg was a good friend for many years.

WILLIAMS: I am a little concerned about the form. The art of the poem nowadays is something unstable; but at least the construction of the poem should make sense; you should know where you stand. Many questions haven't been answered as yet. Our poets may be wrong; but what can any of us do with his talent but try to develop his vision, so that through frequent failures we may learn better what we have missed in the past.

INTERVIEWER: What do you think you yourself have left of special value to the new poets?

WILLIAMS: The variable foot—the division of the line according to a new method that would be satisfactory to an American. It's all right if you are not intent on being national. But an American is forced to try to give the intonation. Either it *is* important or it is not important. It must have occurred to an American that the question of the line *was* important. The American idiom has much to offer us that the English language has never heard of. As for my own elliptic way of approach, it may be baffling, but it is not unfriendly, and not, I think, entirely empty.

MRS. WILLIAMS: All the young people come out to see Bill. Charles Olsen has been here a lot. Denise Levertov was out last week. Then there is Robert Wallace, Muriel Rukeyser, Charles Bell, Tram Combs. Charles Tomlinson stopped in on his way back to England.

WILLIAMS: Yes. He is writing in my vein. He's even conscious of copying me. I don't think he is too popular with his contemporaries. But it does look suspiciously like the beginning of something in England. I defer to you. But—do you have an example of his poems there?

INTERVIEWER: He seems to be carrying on the new measure. Do you have any comment?

WILLIAMS: The lines are not as I would have done, not loose enough. Not enough freedom. He didn't ignore the rules enough to make it really satisfactory.

INTERVIEWER: But you think he shows your influence in England, finally. That must be a satisfaction.

WILLIAMS: It is.

MRS. WILLIAMS: I think Bill will shortly be published in England.

INTERVIEWER: You would think they might have appreciated the American idiom.

WILLIAMS: Not *my* American idiom.

MRS. WILLIAMS [*looking about among the books*]: These are some translations of Bill's poems in Italian—the early poems; *Paterson; The Desert Music.*

WILLIAMS: Yes, I was very pleased by those.

MRS. WILLIAMS: Here are some selected poems in German: *Gedichte,* 1962.

WILLIAMS: I'm alive—

MRS. WILLIAMS: There is a selection coming out now in Czechoslovakia. And here is an anthology of "American lyrics" in Norwegian—

WILLIAMS: I'm still alive!

STANLEY KOEHLER

2. Blaise Cendrars

Blaise Cendrars (real name Frédéric Sauser) was born in Chaux-de-Fonds, Switzerland, on September 1, 1887. He spent his childhood in Alexandria, Naples, Brindisi, and Neuchâtel, accompanying his father, who pursued innumerable business schemes, none successfully.

At fifteen, Cendrars left home to work for a jewel merchant. Together they traveled through Russia, Persia, and China, and several years later he described the voyage in his long poem *Transsibérien* (1913). In Paris in 1910 he met and was profoundly influenced by Apollinaire, then a leader of the avant-garde world of arts and letters. Soon after, in America, Cendrars wrote his first long poem, *Les Pâques à New-York* (1912), which, with *Transsibérien* and his third and last long poem, *Le Panama ou Les Aventures de Mes Sept Oncles* (written in 1918, published in America in 1931, in a translation by John Dos Passos), was important in shaping the modern spirit of poetry.

Cendrars published two novels, *Moravagine* (1926) and *Les Confessions de Dan Yack* (1929), and a number of "novelized" biographies such as *L'Or* (1924), based on the life of John August Sutter (published in America in 1926 as *Sutter's Gold*), and *Rhum* (1930), a *"reportage romancé"* dealing with the life and trials of Jean Galmont, a misfired Cecil Rhodes of Guiana.

During the early months of World War II Cendrars was a war correspondent attached to the British armies; when France fell in 1940 he retired to Aix-en-Provence. He stopped writing until 1944, then began the series of reflective reminiscences, *L'Homme Foudroyé* (1945), *La Main Coupée* (1946), *Bourlinguer* (1948), *Le Lotissement du Ciel* (1949), and *Trop, C'est Trop* (1957), which constitutes his last and most important work. He was disabled with illness soon afterward and died on January 21, 1961, in Paris.

Blaise Cendrars (Photo: Robert Doisneau)

Blaise Cendrars

The following is selected from a series of radio interviews with Michel Manoll, broadcast from October to December 1950, and later published as Blaise Cendrars Vous Parle *by Éditions Denoël.*

INTERVIEWER: All writers complain of the constraint under which they work and of the difficulty of writing.

CENDRARS: To make themselves sound interesting, and they exaggerate. They should talk a little more about their privileges and how lucky they are to be able to earn some return from the practice of their art, a practice I personally detest, it's true, but which is all the same a noble privilege compared with the lot of most people, who live like parts of a machine, who live only to keep the gears of society pointlessly turning. I pity them with all my heart. Since my return to Paris I have been saddened as never before by the anonymous crowd I see from my windows engulfing itself in the Métro or pouring out of the Métro at fixed hours. Truly, that isn't a life. It isn't human. It must come to a stop. It's slavery . . . not only for the humble and poor, but the absurdity of life in general.

When a simple character like myself, who has faith in modern life, who admires all these pretty factories, all these ingenious machines, stops to think about where it's all leading, he can't help but condemn it because, really, it's not exactly encouraging.

INTERVIEWER: And your work habits? You've said somewhere that you get up at dawn and work for several hours.

CENDRARS: I never forget that work is a curse—which is why I've never made it a habit. Certainly, to be like everyone else, lately I've wanted to work regularly from a given hour to a given hour; I'm over fifty-five and I wanted to produce four books in a row. That finished, I had enough on my back. I have no method of work.

33

I've tried one, it worked, but that's no reason to fix on it for the rest of my life. One has other things to do in life aside from writing books.

A writer should never install himself before a panorama, however grandiose it may be. Like Saint Jerome, a writer should work in his cell. Turn the back. Writing is a view of the spirit. "The world is my representation." Humanity lives in its fiction. This is why a conqueror always wants to transform the face of the world into his image. Today, I even veil the mirrors.

The workroom of Rémy de Gourmont was on a court, 71 rue des Saints-Pères, in Paris. At 202 Boulevard Saint-Germain, Guillaume Apollinaire, who had a vast apartment with large rooms and with a belvedere and terrace on the roof, wrote by preference in his kitchen, at a little card table where he was very uncomfortable, having had to shrink this little table even smaller in order to succeed in sliding it under a bull's-eye window in the mansard, which was also on a court. Edouard Peisson, who has a nice little house in the hills near Aix-en-Provence, does not work in one of the front rooms where he could enjoy a beautiful view of the valley and the play of light in the distance, but has had a little library corner constructed in back, the window of which gives on an embankment bordered with lilacs. And myself, in the country, in my house at Tremblay-sur-Mauldre, I've never worked on the upper floor which looks out on the orchards but in the lower room which looks in one direction on an impasse behind a stable and in another on a wall which encloses my garden.

Among the very few writers I've had occasion to see much of, only one man of letters, celebrated for his frenetic cult of Napoleon, installed himself before a panorama to work—a historical one —the window of his study had a full view of the Arc de Triomphe. But this window was most often closed because the living spectacle of the glory of his great man, far from inspiring him, clipped his wings. He could be heard through the door coming and going in his study, beating his sides, roaring his phrases, trying out phrases and cadences, groaning, weeping, laboring himself sick like

Flaubert in his *"gueuloir."* His wife then said to the servants, "Pay no attention. It is Monsieur castigating his style."

INTERVIEWER: You have read much during your life?

CENDRARS: Read enormously. It's my passion. Everywhere, in all circumstances, and all sorts of books. Everything that falls under my hand I devour.

INTERVIEWER: Reading isn't for you, you've said, a means of traveling, in time or space, but a way of penetrating without great effort into the skin of a character.

CENDRARS: No, reading has been a drug for me—I drug myself on printer's ink!

INTERVIEWER: Will you cite some of the unusual reading you've done?

CENDRARS: Captain Lacroix is an old sailor and his books are a feast. I've never had the luck to meet him. I looked for him in Nantes, at Saint-Nazaire. I was told that he is in his eighties and that he doesn't want to give up. When he was no longer able to navigate, he became a marine insurer, and it appears that he doesn't hesitate to put on a deep-sea diving rig in order to see for himself the state of his hulls. At his age, admirable. I imagine that the winter nights seemed long to him by the fireplace, when the wind from the sea poured down on his village of the Loire-Inférieure and blew around in his chimney, and I suppose it was to kill time that this man, who has knocked about on all the Seven Seas and aboard all sorts of ships possible and imaginable, began to write books. These are thick books, strongly built, full of solid documentation, sometimes a little too heavy but nearly always fresh, thus never tedious, all the less so in that the old seaman even searches out reproductions of illustrated post cards and photos of joyous ports of call of his youth, and he recounts things as they happened, his experience and all that he has learned and all that he has seen from Cape Horn to the China Sea, from Tasmania to Ushant, speaking of everything, of lighthouses, currents, wind, reefs, tempests, crews, traffic, shipwrecks, fish and birds, celestial phenomena and maritime catastrophes, history, customs, nations, people of the sea, relating thousands of anecdotes intimate or dramatic, all his life of an honest seaman carried along by the very movement of the sea and dominated by his exclusive love of ships. Ah, it is certainly not the work of a *littérateur*. His pen is a marlinespike, and each page brings you something, and there are ten big volumes! It's as moving as it can be and as simple as good morning. In a word, miraculous. One touches the globe with a finger.

And there are the divinatory quatrains of Nostradamus, written in a magnificent language which is a joy to me, although they remain indecipherable. I have read them for forty years, I gargle with them, I regale myself with them, I enjoy them, but I don't understand them. I've never searched for the key, I've read nearly all the keys that have been published, they are meaningless and all false since every two or three years someone invents a new mechanism without being able to spring the lock. But, as a great French poet, Nostradamus is one of the greatest. Still another to stick in my *Anthologie de la poésie française* if I ever compile it. All his impromptu turns invented from a conventional language beat by far the looniness of Dada, and the automatic writing of the surrealists, and the decalcomania of Apollinaire's *Calligrammes*.

INTERVIEWER: What have you discovered since? What do you read at present?

CENDRARS: The latest book I've discovered is the great dictionary of the Customs Administration that we owe to an edict of Vincent Auriol, then Minister of Finance. It is entitled *Répertoire général du tarif* and appeared in 1937. Two volumes quarto. Weight fifty kilos. I take them every place with me because I'm going to need them some day soon when I begin to write *La Carissima*, the mystical life of Mary Magdalene, the only woman who made Christ weep.

INTERVIEWER: You need the customs tariffs in order to write that book?

CENDRARS: My dear sir, it's a matter of language. For several years, each time that I prepare to write a book, I first arrange the vocabulary I am going to employ. Thus, for *L'Homme Foudroyé*,

I had a list of three thousand words arranged in advance, and I used all of them. That saved me a lot of time and gave a certain lightness to my work. It was the first time I used that system. I don't know how I happened onto it. . . . It's a question of language. Language is a thing that seduced me. Language is a thing that perverted me. Language is a thing that formed me. Language is a thing that deformed me. That's why I am a poet, probably because I am very sensitive to the language—correct or incorrect, I wink at that. I ignore and despise grammar which is at the point of death, but I am a great reader of dictionaries and if my spelling is none too sure it's because I am too attentive to the pronunciation, this idiosyncrasy of the living language. In the beginning was not the word, but the phrase, a modulation. Listen to the songs of birds!

INTERVIEWER: Language, then, you would say, is not something dead, frozen, but something in motion, fugitive, attaching itself always to life and reality.

CENDRARS: That's why this great dictionary of the Administration of the Customs fascinates me. For example, take the word "ribbon." I discover with amazement all the significations that the word "ribbon" can represent and above all in its ultramodern industrial usages: there are twenty-one pages!

INTERVIEWER: Where did your interest in folk literature begin?

CENDRARS: During all my life I have been profoundly influenced by the works of Gérard de Nerval. I owe to Gérard de Nerval my love of songs and of popular poetry, and in all the countries of the world I've made an effort to hear and note and read some of the music, poetry, literature of the people, notably in Russia, in China, in Brazil. Much Alexandre Dumas is read, cloak-and-sword novels, love stories for typists—to a considerable degree all the stenographers of the world have the same mind. But there are also in every country some sorts of works which are *exclusively* reserved to the popular interest, such as *The Key of Dreams*, *The Language of the Flowers*, and a thousand others. If this sort of peddler's literature is perhaps a little out of date in Paris, in a country such as

Brazil (which is a new country, everything seems new to it), entire levels of the population, who have barely learned to read, are discovering these stories of sorcery, of werewolves, of the headless mule, of the White Lady, of phantoms, of black humor, of romance, fairy tales, novels of chivalry, nursery tales, and adventures of highwaymen, celebrated crimes of passion; a collection of marvels that is no more stale and trashy for that matter than are, in much more advanced countries, the detective novels of England, the gangster stories of the United States, the grand love films in all the cinemas of the earth, which themselves also constitute a part of the old foundations of folklore, of popular literature.

INTERVIEWER: But in Brazil, isn't this folklore entirely borrowed from the Negroes?

CENDRARS: Not at all. The literary folklore is of Portuguese origin. The peddler's literature was imported from Portugal; it is, by the way, much more at the base of the national Brazilian literature than are the works of the Brazilian academicians, who, for their part, were always more or less influenced, until most recent years, by academic French literature, as all the latest generation of young writers in Brazil is now influenced by the new North American novelists of between-the-wars, who were for the most part living in Paris and much in evidence here, at Saint-Germain-des-Prés and Montparnasse: Hemingway, John Dos Passos, Henry Miller.

INTERVIEWER: But the Negroes who had been transplanted, did they write?

CENDRARS: The transplanted Negroes—that is to say, the slaves —did not write. It was forbidden for them to write and it was altogether exceptional that certain ones were able to learn to read or write. More than this, it was forbidden to print books in Brazil, all came from Portugal. The first printing press was not installed at Rio de Janeiro until 1818, under the Empire. Thus, the *Complete Poems* of Grégorio de Matos [1633–96], who was called with good reason the François Villon of Brazil and whom his contemporaries named *boca da inferno*, so violent were his satires of colonial society, was not printed at Rio until 1882. Until that date they had been transmitted by oral tradition and manuscript copies which circulated in a certain class of society: the bohemians of Bahia.

INTERVIEWER: He was a Negro?

CENDRARS: No, at most a very dark mixed-blood, a *pardo*, as they say there. His parents had a sugar-cane plantation and owned a hundred and thirty black slaves. He had had the good fortune of being sent to study law at Coimbra, the famous university of Portugal. When he came back to Bahia, his doomed mouth and his infernal invectives earned him a session of exile in Angola, from where he returned, more enraged than ever, to settle at Pernambuco, under house arrest. Far from mending his ways, he led a life of drunkenness and debauchery with the Negro girls of the port. All his love songs, and there are some very beautiful ones, celebrate the black Venus. He died in poverty. Tradition has it that he was buried, like the poorest of the poor, with his guitar, his only property.

INTERVIEWER: When you ran away from home, at the age of fifteen, had you planned your escape? Did you have an objective, or a hope of return?

CENDRARS: Do I know? I went east because the first train through the station carried me east; if it had been a train going west I would have gotten to Lisbon and I would have done America instead of Asia.

INTERVIEWER: This was an extremely important date in your life because, after this time, your life has been divided into two paths: your adventures in the Orient and your adventures in the West. Since that time you've never had a roof.

CENDRARS: Those are the things one says when one wants to tell stories, to put a little order into one's existence. But my life has never been cut in two. That would be too convenient: anyone can cut his life in two, in four, in eight, in twelve, in sixteen.

INTERVIEWER: I want to ask you why you haven't continued the experiment which you began with *Pâques à New-York*, *Transsibérien*, and *Panama*. In these poems, particularly in 19 *Poèmes Élastiques* which innovated a new poetic technique, there's a movement of stanzas which you've since abandoned.

CENDRARS: In 1917 I had just written a poem which astounded me by its fullness, its modernity, by everything I'd put into it. It was so antipoetic! I was delighted. And at that moment I decided not to publish it, to let modern poetry get along without me, to see what would happen to it. I nailed this unpublished poem in a chest; I put the chest in an attic in the country, and I set myself a limit of ten years before I'd take it out to publish it. That's more than thirty years ago, and I believe the time has not yet come to publish it.

INTERVIEWER: This poem is "Au Cœur du Monde"?

CENDRARS: Yes, and although unpublished, it's famous. The other day an editor offered me a million [francs—two thousand dollars] for it, but I didn't bite.

I told you the other day that I don't write any more poems. I make poems which I recite to myself, which I taste, which I play with. I feel no need to communicate them to anyone, even to people I like a lot. I don't write them down. It's so good to daydream, to stammer around something which remains a secret for oneself. It's a sin of gluttony.

To write . . . it's an ungrateful profession; in all sincerity, one gets little satisfaction from it. It's quite exceptional to be able to say to oneself, That's not too bad, Blaise; it's even quite good. One gives oneself this satisfaction very, very, very rarely, because one thinks, above all, when one has published a book, about all that one has failed to do, all that one hasn't put in it, all that one wanted to put in, all that one would add to be complete, because it's so difficult to hem things in with writing and to say everything with words. When the book is finished, one remains fatally disappointed.

INTERVIEWER: Your own *Pâques à New-York*, the *Transsibérien*, *Panama*, the—

CENDRARS: Tell me, since when has anyone spoken of them?

INTERVIEWER:—the 19 *Poèmes Élastiques*. They are spoken of and cited precisely because these poems are at the base of modern poetry, are at the source of modern lyricism.

CENDRARS: No, no, not at all, I'm not at the base of anything at all. It is the modern world which is at the base, "enormous and delicate" like the Middle Ages. And the source, it's Villon. If the correspondence of Max Jacob were ever published, you would find sources and bases and points of departure and of arrival. *There* was one who understood how to shake the coconut tree and bring tumbling down pell-mell the false geniuses and the true ones, the pure and the impure! And he had as wicked a tongue as you'd want, and could stir up more trouble than the devil in holy water.

Poets don't seem to have fun any more. What troubles me more than anything else these days is to see the seriousness with which they approach everything.

INTERVIEWER: Were you gay because your life was brighter in the good old days?

CENDRARS: My dear sir, in the Belle Époque space writers were paid one sou a line in the papers and an Apollinaire had to wait months and years before he could sign his articles and count on steady employment with regular pay. That was why he published pornography: to earn his bread. You can't imagine how solidly closed all doors were to us. I have the impression that today you're much better received. I run into young writers everywhere, on the papers, the radio, in the picture studios. Before 1914 those who wanted a job stood in line at the door, or at an employment window that never opened. The others contented themselves with playing the buffoon, the wild bull, in the streets. To hell with a job and a decent living. We laughed. The Paris girls were pretty.

INTERVIEWER: This present generation hasn't been too bad at buffoonery.

CENDRARS: Everyone has a taste of it, it's the right of every young generation. Fortunately the wild bull still exists and hasn't been put in cans for exportation as corned beef. One counsel: when you see an open door, newspaper, radio studio, cinema, bank, anything —don't enter. By the time you're thirty you'll be nuts because you left your laugh at the door. That's my experience. Poetry is in the street. It goes arm in arm with laughter. They take each other along for a drink, at the source, in the neighborhood bistros, where the laugh of the people is so flavorsome and the language which flows from their lips so beautiful. "Il n'est bon bec que de Paris."

INTERVIEWER: In 1912, you were in New York.

CENDRARS: In 1912, at Easter, I was starving in New York, and had been for a number of months. From time to time I took a job, by force of necessity, but I didn't keep it a week and if I could manage to get my pay sooner than that I quit sooner, impatient to get on with my sessions of reading at the central public library. My poverty was extreme and every day I looked worse, unshaven, trousers in corkscrews, shoes worn out, hair long, coat stained and faded and without buttons, no hat or tie, having sold them one day for a penny in order to buy a plug of the world's worst chewing tobacco. Time passed. Came Easter. Easter Sunday the library was closed. In the evening I entered a Presbyterian church which was giving an oratorio, Haydn's *Creation*, so said a lighted sign hung to the spire. In the church there was a scattered audience and, on a stage, fashionable young girls who played ancient instruments and sang divinely well. But a wretched bishop interrupted the oratorio every five minutes to preach I-know-not-what pious sanctimony and make an appeal to the good hearts of the faithful and, when the oratorio continued, another croaker of a preacher as tiresome as the first entered the stall where I had taken a place, and tried to convert me by surreptitious exhortation, all the time thumping my money pocket in an effort to draw out a dollar or two for expenses, shaking his leather money plate under my nose. Poor me! I left before the end and walked home to West Sixty-seventh Street where I was living, absolutely disgusted and dead beat. It could have been two or three o'clock in the morning. I gnawed a hunk of dry bread and drank a big glass of water. I went to bed. I went immediately to sleep. I woke up with a start. I began to write, to write. I went back to sleep. I woke up the second time with a start. I wrote until dawn and I went back to bed and back to sleep for good. I woke up at five o'clock that evening. I reread the thing. I had written *Les Pâques à New-York*.

INTERVIEWER: The whole thing?

CENDRARS: As it was published. There were three erasures.

INTERVIEWER: This manuscript, where is it now?

CENDRARS: The original, I don't know, I had to sell it one rainy day. But the friend of poets, the publisher Pierre Seghers, who devoted a little volume in his series of *Poètes d'aujourd'hui* to me in 1948, spoke to me of a copy of the manuscript, a copy which belongs today to Paul Eluard, if I'm not mistaken. On landing in Paris, I remember having deposited this copy with Guillaume Apollinaire, who lived in Passy, rue Gros, across from the gasworks. Who sold it, or from whom could Paul Eluard have bought it, and when? I don't know, and I've never asked him, because I don't know Eluard. But Seghers, who had had this copy in his hands, asked me for precisions on the appearance of the manuscript and what I told him seemed to fit with what he had noticed, American paper, right-hand writing, et cetera.

INTERVIEWER: Your poem was published how many years after having been written?

CENDRARS: After writing it I had only one desire, to get out of New York, and I embarked within a week to return to Paris. I paid five dollars, some twenty-five francs. Imagine that at that time one could return from New York to Paris for twenty-five francs! It is true that it was a cattle boat. As soon as I arrived in Paris, I published my poem.

INTERVIEWER: Under what conditions? You had found a publisher?

CENDRARS: Not on your life! I found a printer, an anarchist who had a little clandestine press installed in a piano crate, at the Buttes-Chaumont, rue Botzaris, Villa des Boers. I worked with him to earn a little money against the cost of the edition. I profited from the occasion to undergo my apprenticeship in typography. I composed more than half of the text myself. The little book was published with an ugly picture of me. The thing cost me something like a hundred francs. There were one hundred twenty-five copies published. I offered them for sale at twenty sous. I never sold one.

INTERVIEWER: Not a single one?

CENDRARS: No.

INTERVIEWER: What became of all these copies?

CENDRARS: Where does old paper go? I don't have a copy of that edition myself.

INTERVIEWER: That made you known among the poets?

CENDRARS: I was already known enough among poets to have mocked them and to have disturbed their assemblies at the Closerie des Lilas, at the Café Fleurus, at the Procope; and so I didn't need to publish something in order to be known by the poets. But to have published *Les Pâques à New-York*, in October 1912, brought me the enmity of the bonzes and the pontiffs who, the following year, when I published *Le Transsibérien*, "the first simultaneous book," in June 1913, called me an epigonus and accused me of plagiarism. It was not good to be a young authentic among all those old glories on the tail of Symbolism, who all took themselves for sacred bards. Beards, yes, which I laughed in. At that time, Apollinaire was the only poet that I went to see. He was always kind to me and he got work for me so I could make a few sous. Don't listen to the evil gossips! They say today that he was influenced by me, and I say I couldn't care less. I sang of the Eiffel Tower. He sang of the Eiffel Tower. And plenty of others have sung of it since.

INTERVIEWER: All the same, it is an extremely mystifying thing, Apollinaire's change of poetic orientation after your meeting.

CENDRARS: It was Jules Romains who first remarked this change of front. Me, I pay no attention. It's not my affair. It's critics who say that. This is not my job. I'm not equipped for it. I wrote about the Eiffel Tower when I felt like it.

INTERVIEWER: This doesn't have to do with the Eiffel Tower. This has to do with—

CENDRARS:—with the influence I might have had on Guillaume Apollinaire. It was Robert Goffin who hung up this bell and there have been I don't know how many people come along to ring it, as if it's a crime to experience the influence of someone. I have, sometimes, the impression in regard to this alarm bell that I'm not dealing with critics, with students of poetry, with historians, but with amateur detectives who measure, mark, take fingerprints.

INTERVIEWER: Is there always this long delay—of ten years or so —between the lived adventure and the moment of writing it, as in *Panama*?

CENDRARS: A very long incubation. There's a whole unconscious labor of bringing to a point that must be carried out. Generally I start off with a title. I first find the title. I generally find pretty good titles—people envy me for them, and not only envy me but quite a few writers come to see me to ask for a title. When I have my title, I give myself to reflection. Things pile up. A crystallization both conscious and unconscious is produced around the title and I write nothing solid as long as I don't know everything about my characters, from the day of their birth to the day of their death, and can't make them evolve in all circumstances possible and imaginable according to their character and their situations fictional or real. This can last for years. I take notes. In this way I build up dossiers stuffed with notes and sketches. They are imaginary and not factual. Factual documentation bothers me.

INTERVIEWER: You've spoken to me of your next novel, a "real novel."

CENDRARS: Yes, a real novel or it won't appear.

INTERVIEWER: In any case, there'll be certain elements of your life in it?

CENDRARS: No, no, no, no, not at all, you won't find me in it, I shall write a novel-novel, and I won't appear in it, because they don't see but one character in all my books: Cendrars! *L'Or* is Cendrars; *Moravagine* is Cendrars; *Dan Yack* is Cendrars—I'm annoyed with this Cendrars! Anyway, one shouldn't believe that the novelist is incarnated in his characters—Flaubert isn't Madame

Bovary. It didn't do him any good to get sick when he described the poisoning of Emma—he still wasn't Madame Bovary, even though he believed he was, and said, "I am Madame Bovary!" That solid Norman an old aunt??? The greatest danger for a writer is to fall victim to his own legend, to fall into his own trap.

INTERVIEWER: You've announced thirty-three forthcoming books. Why thirty-three?

CENDRARS: The list of thirty-three books which I've been announcing for forty years is not exclusive, restrictive, or prohibitive; the number thirty-three is the key figure of activity, of life. So this is not at all a black list. If it has an index, it is not a putting on The Index. It doesn't include the titles of novels which I will never write—the other day I was surprised to discover that *La Main Coupée*, which I published in 1948, had been on this list since 1919. I had completely forgotten that! On the list are books which I will take up again and which will appear in the future. Also listed are the ten volumes of *Notre Pain Quotidien*, which are written but which I left in various strongboxes in South American banks and which, God willing, will be found by chance some day—the papers aren't signed, and are left under a false name. I've also listed a group of poems which I value more than my eyes but which I haven't decided to publish—not by timidity or pride, but for love. And then, there are the books that were written, ready for publication, but which I burned to the great detriment of my publishers: for example, *La Vie et la Mort du Soldat Inconnu* (five volumes). Finally, there are the bastards, the larvae, and the abortions which I will probably never write.

INTERVIEWER: John Dos Passos consecrated a chapter to you in *Orient Express* and he called you the Homer of the Transsibérien.

CENDRARS: When John was married, I was in the Périgord. I was in the process of hatching my book on Galmont. He came on his honeymoon directly from New York to Monpazier, of which Galmont was a native. Monpazier is a historic little city. It's a fortified village, built by the kings of England, that dates from 1426. It's very small, six hundred twenty-five inhabitants at most.

It's laid out like an American city. There are two principal arteries and all the cross streets cross these two principal arteries at right angles. One could number them as in America, I think there are twenty-one. I was staying in the best hotel in the vicinity, the Hôtel de Londres, where one eats like a god. It's kept by Madame Cassagnol—her husband is a double for Charlie Chaplin. Madame Cassagnol wears a mustache and the pants of the household. When John Dos Passos told me he was coming, I said to Madame Cassagnol: "I have some friends who are arriving directly from New York to stay here with you. Try to distinguish yourself." And I didn't give another thought to either the menu or the wine. For a week Madame Cassagnol fed us on that good Périgordine cuisine, setting up the menus herself, progressively, giving us a surprise each day: truffles, *pot-au-feu* with garlic to make you sop up your plate— with a little wine, country style; *buisson d'écrevisses, champignons à la crème*, boletus mushrooms *à la bordelaise*, fried fish, fish of the Dordogne and of the Garonne, *brochettes* of little birds, woodcock *à l'armagnac, game* feathered and furred, poachers' venison of which the main supplier was the curé of a neighboring village, roasts, *terrine de foie gras*, wild lettuce, peasant cheeses, figs in honey and crushed nuts, *pruneaux d'Agen, crêpes flambées*, as much strong red wine as you wanted, a bottle of Monbazillac for two, coffee, liqueurs, all for twelve francs fifty, plus fifty centimes extra for the surprise of the last day. The last day, the day of the departure of John and his wife, we ate a wild swan. I didn't even know there might still be wild swans in France, even in migration. What an astonishing country is the black Périgord!

I've seen John often, but always in Paris. It's curious, by the way, but never, never, never have I met one of my friends among American writers in the United States, as often as I've gone there. They are never home, as if by chance, and if I've insisted I've been told over the phone that the master for whom I was asking was on vacation, or on a tour, or in Europe. I've tried in vain to find one at his newspaper, his club, or at his publisher's. The response was the same everywhere: "He isn't here!" I used to hang up the phone with a bizarre feeling. I don't want to draw from it any conclusion disparaging to anyone, but I finished by admitting to myself that American writers are not free in their country and that those who come back from Europe don't have an easy conscience, reproaching themselves with little frolics painful to recall. They have a fear of public opinion and, contrary to the English, don't even have a bread-and-butter courtesy. It's a typically American complex.

INTERVIEWER: Among American writers, you know Henry Miller. Is he one of your great friends?

CENDRARS: Henry Miller, I've seen him in Paris and I've never seen him anywhere else but in Paris. He was a gay, joyous companion.

INTERVIEWER: You know still others?

CENDRARS: Yes, surely, crowds, crowds of poets, who have come, who have gone away; I've forgotten their names, so numerous were they in Paris on the eve of the last war.

INTERVIEWER: It is claimed that you have served them as a model and that you have strongly influenced certain American novelists.

CENDRARS: That's absolutely false. If I've been able to influence this one or that without my or his knowledge, I haven't served as a model. It's Victor Hugo, it's Maupassant who served as models for them when they came to establish themselves in Paris at the end of the other war. They came to France without an afterthought, be it as soldiers, ambulance drivers, diplomats; the war over, they sojourned for a time, short or long, in Paris, where certain ones stayed during the entire time between the two wars; they frequented Montparnasse, then Saint-Germain-des-Prés, and if they were influenced it was rather by the *ambiance*, the air of Paris and the way of living in France rather than by this or that French author. John Dos Passos declared to me one day: "You have in France a literary genre that we don't know at all in the United States, the *grand reportage à la Victor Hugo*."

INTERVIEWER: That's an astonishing statement.

CENDRARS: I was surprised by it because, like you, I believed reportage to be a strictly American genre. Well, it appears not. From the point of view of reportage, then, we have terribly influenced young American novelists, who didn't yet write for the great magazines and had a tendency to fortify themselves in their ivory tower in order to dedicate themselves to letters, to belles-lettres. Since then they've caught up with themselves; it's only necessary to read the latest war reporting or other reporting by a Seabrook, a Hemingway, a John Dos Passos himself, which bear our imprint and which are marvelous. They have renewed the genre. *Asylum* by Seabrook is a masterpiece of reportage, as Victor Hugo's *La Mort de Balzac* is another and the first model of the genre. Dos Passos was right.

INTERVIEWER: And Faulkner, you know him?

CENDRARS: No, I don't know Faulkner. I've never met him. Malraux asked me to do a preface for the translation of *Light in August*; I didn't want to do it, finding it too regional, too literary, and written as one doesn't write any more, too well.

INTERVIEWER: Was it in New York that you met Hemingway?

CENDRARS: No, at the Closerie des Lilas in Paris. I was drinking; he was drinking at a table next to mine. He was with an American sailor on leave. He was in uniform—probably that of a noncombatant ambulance aide, unless I'm mistaken. It was at the end of that other war, the "last of the last." We talked between tables; drunks like to talk. We talked. We drank. We drank again. I had an appointment in Montmartre, at the home of the widow of André Dupont, a poet killed at Verdun. I went there every Friday to eat bouillabaisse with Satie, Georges Auric, Paul Lombard, and sometimes Max Jacob. I brought my boozer American friends with me, I thought I'd give them something good *de chez nous* to eat. But the Americans aren't fond of good food; they have no good food at home, they don't know what it is. Hemingway and his sailor didn't care for my arguments—they preferred to drink until they weren't thirsty any more. So I planted them in a bar on the rue des Martyrs, and I ran to treat myself at my friend's widow's house.

INTERVIEWER: You knew Sinclair Lewis, too?

CENDRARS: Yes, that's another story. . . . It was in 1930, in Rome. He'd already been widely discussed in Italy, where he was trailing about with a squadron of jolly New York girls who were causing a scandal. One fine day he landed in Rome, where I was making a movie. He let me know that he urgently wanted to meet me. I asked him to come to the studio, but he answered that he had a cold, he didn't like movies, and anyway he didn't have the time because he was leaving the next morning for Stockholm to collect the Nobel Prize. I didn't have the time either, I was busy working, but there was a breakdown at the studio around ten o'clock so I went to his hotel, where I found half a dozen American girls completely drunk, making a gigantic cocktail in a soup tureen full of whipped cream, into which—while quarreling with each other about how much to put in—they were pouring two, three liters of vermouth. I didn't think I could join this scene of mad women right away—one of them held out some scissors to me and dared me to cut her hair—so I thought I'd take a little stroll. But I changed my mind and decided to search the apartment for the master of the séance, whom I hadn't seen yet. The door of the bathroom was half open, and boiling water was coming out. I went in. The bathtub was overflowing and the faucets were wide open. Two feet, dressed in polished dancing pumps, hung out of the tub, and at the bottom a man in a tuxedo was drowning. It was my Sinclair Lewis. I pulled him out of his unfortunate position, and that was how I saved his life so he could take the train the next morning for Stockholm and his prize.

The next day I put him on the train—he didn't even buy me a drink. It's true he had a hangover and probably didn't want to drink, or maybe he'd sworn never to drink again. But a drunk's oaths don't hold, you know.

INTERVIEWER: And where did you live in Paris when you came back from America in 1912?

CENDRARS: Avenue Montaigne. It's a wonderful quarter and I know it well. I've lived at numbers 12, 60, 51, 33, 5, and finally I went back to 12. I could write a book on this quarter, apparently so tranquil, comfortable even, and where plenty takes place, but plenty! I'd even found a title for the book: *Voyage Autour de l'Alma*. But I'll probably never write it, like so many other books I've daydreamed about during the years.

INTERVIEWER: What is your best memory of that neighborhood?

CENDRARS: I don't know, I have too many. It's there that the rat terriers are trained by my good friends the sewer workers of the City of Paris, in a subterranean "ratodrome." Also there was a streetsweeper-Don Juan who bowled over all the housemaids along the avenue and used to lock himself up with them in the interior of a Morris column, where he had installed a red-velvet pouf. It was just in front of the Brazilian Embassy, where I would end the night drinking *cafesinhos*, smoking cigars, and talking away like a madman with dear old Souza-Dantas, called the Bohemian Ambassador because he didn't have a bed—when he was sleepy, he turned up his collar, pulled a hat down on his head and stretched himself out on a Russian leather *canapé*, closed his eyes and slept like a baby, without caring whether you had left or not.

I even wrote a little book in 1913 on Russian music for the inauguration of the Grand-Théâtre des Champs-Élysées, and the evening of the *première* of *Petrouchka*, a woman covered with diamonds, driven mad by the music of Stravinsky, tore loose a brand new theater seat in order to break it over my head, which she did so well that I passed the rest of the night drinking champagne in Montmartre with Stravinsky, Diaghilev, and some of the dancers of the Ballet Russe, wearing this seat like a collar and my face streaked with blood and scratches. I've seen the quarter evolve, the *grands couturiers*—from Madeleine Vionnet to Boyd—come to establish themselves there . . . taxis replace the fiacres . . . Jouvet open the Comédie, Batbedat the Studio, Hébertot turn the Salle de Perret—which had been built to produce Parsifal when the Richard Wagner opera should enter the public domain and have it all over Bayreuth, with the aid of steam-making machinery installed under the stage at a cost of millions and which has never been used—into a music hall of grand luxe where all high-style Paris came running, to say nothing of the Swedish Ballets of Rolf de Maré who mounted my Negro ballet, *La Création du Monde*, with music by Darius Milhaud and décors by Fernand Léger, *Les Mariés de la Tour Eiffel* of Cocteau, *Relâche* by Eric Satie, for which I had written the argument for old Satie and Francis Picabia swiped the idea of it from me, the subject and the cinematic interlude of *Entre-Acte*, thanks to which René Clair was able to make his debut as a director, Picabia having profited by the fact that I had gone to Brazil. You see, it was quite an epoch.

INTERVIEWER: Among the strange people you've liked, which ones have you found in Paris?

CENDRARS: The strangest being I came across on the Avenue Montaigne was the madwoman from whom Giraudoux drew his *Madwoman of Chaillot*. She wasn't the "brat with diamonds" in Montmartre as the newspapers of the period captioned a picture of her. Madame Leffray was an Englishwoman, the widow of a true cockney coachman. She lived on the rue Lauriston. I often followed her: every day she came from Chaillot to the Avenue Montaigne, where she sat on a bench facing the Hôtel Plaza-Athénée. She stayed there in an ecstasy, just like the actress Moreno, but much thinner; decked out in velvet hat with dirty ostrich feathers; dirty trinkets; a long dress full of holes and lace; a filthy ermine scarf of which nothing was left but the little black tails; wild high-heeled shoes; gloves; grotesque jewels; a lorgnette; a handbag dragging on the ground. Everyone in the neighborhood knew her and made fun of her. She was really insane; she never spoke to anyone and never answered questions. She had her dignity, was haughty, self-sufficient. It was there, sitting on that bench which no longer exists, that Giraudoux could have seen her as often as I, because Jean came to the neighborhood practically every day.

INTERVIEWER: What do you do when you're traveling? Do you write in your cabin on board or do you wait until you've returned?

CENDRARS: I like long sea voyages, and the unique life at sea, too much to ever dream of working. It's the apotheosis of idleness; a triumph—to do nothing while the deck rocks, the boat moves, the engines knock, the ocean rolls, the wind blows, the earth revolves with the heavens and the stars, and the entire universe rushes to open for you to pass. I'm never in a hurry to arrive, and I've tried dozens of times to seduce the captain into taking his boat elsewhere than the designated port. "There's no way, alas!" an old Dutchman told me. "For thirty years I've been making the trip between Rotterdam and Buenos Aires, as if I was the engineer of a train. Impossible to change anything, the route is set in advance, the timetable fixed, I must get there on such a day at such a time, it's outlined in advance by the company, who are masters after God. But the most annoying thing is that it's always the same people who get on, always the same heads I'm obliged to have at my table—the same chargés d'affaires, the same diplomats, the same nabobs, the same big bankers. After thirty years, I know them too well! If only I had the courage to follow your infernal ideas, swing the helm and point elsewhere, to the east or the west, no matter . . . pass the Cape, dive into the southern seas."

All that to tell you that on board, I don't write.

INTERVIEWER: Haven't you said that you fortify yourself in love and solitude?

CENDRARS: In truth, artists live alongside, on the margin of life and of humanity; that's why they're very great or very small.

INTERVIEWER: On the margin of humanity? You don't then consider yourself as an artist?

CENDRARS: No. I've already had thirty-six professions, and I'm ready to start something entirely different tomorrow morning.

INTERVIEWER: You've never had trouble earning your living. During the occupation, you lived for the most part on the sale of herbs and plants which you grew in your garden at Aix-en-Provence.

CENDRARS: Some green plants, some medicinal plants.

INTERVIEWER: You're interested in bees?

CENDRARS: I'm interested in bees because they make me a lot of money, I wouldn't have Maeterlinck's interest—to study the habits of bees and draw absurd moral conclusions applicable to man. One meets thousands of similar people throughout the world, who study the lives of bees or ants passionately and then cite their social organization as an example, entirely wrongly I think, because insects have no ethics or sense of justice. I made honey because it was easy work, well paid. All you need are good customers.

INTERVIEWER: You've said that unlike many writers, you didn't go to war to write, that at that time you were a soldier, you had a gun.

CENDRARS: That's why I've never been one of those writer-soldiers. One is a fighter or one is a writer. When one writes, one isn't shooting, and when one's shooting one isn't writing, one writes afterward. One would have done better to write before and prevent all that.

INTERVIEWER: And what do you think of Jean-Paul Sartre?

CENDRARS: I have no opinion of him, Sartre doesn't send me his books. Existentialism? As for its philosophical doctrine, it was Schopenhauer who put us on guard against the professors of philosophy who, after completing the official course of studies, meditate, write, think, draw up manifestoes—and Sartre is a professor. Philosophical plays are boring in the theater, and Sartre displays his theses on the stage. The novels of the school are well written or badly written, those of Sartre are neither one nor the other. The young writers today—I've seen a great deal of them since my return to Paris and I ask myself where and in what they are specifically existentialist? Is it because they disguise themselves each evening to go to Saint-Germain-des-Prés the way their fathers dressed up each evening to go out in society or to their club? It's a fashion which will pass, which has already passed. I don't get carried away by the noise of a parade. But the world gets bored with itself. The cinema, radio, television. . . . The truth is, few enough people know how to live and those who accept life as it is are still more rare.

INTERVIEWER: I don't know what can be said exactly of this invasion of literature by the professors, but one thing certain is that Jean-Paul Sartre's movement hasn't produced any poets. It's not made up of poets. No poet has come out of it.

CENDRARS: You're probably right. For the surrealists, I would make a single exception: Robert Desnos. Robert was a good guy and very sharp indeed. I've laughed much and drunk much with him in a bar where we used to meet and which I baptized "L'Œil de Paris" because it was in the rue de Rivoli, under the arcades, a couple of steps from the Concorde and where you could see all Paris pass by without moving from your table, and that Robert maliciously named "Chez Madame Zyeux" because of the ladies who came in to go down to the toilet and came back out, eyes strictly front, so as not to ruffle their dignity by admitting they had been to piss.

INTERVIEWER: You've said that you envy Mayakovsky because of the illuminated signboard he had charge of over Red Square in Moscow.

CENDRARS: I don't know any other poet anywhere who had the luck and the opportunity to use an illuminated newspaper to pub-lish—or rather, stick up—his poems in the street. It wasn't advertis-ing or propaganda. Perhaps part of it, yes, simple propaganda of a party member, but Mayakovsky had too great a love of the people and of poetry. Think of the millions of illiterates there were in Russia. Nothing less than the genius of a Mayakovsky could stir such a crowd. And that's where I envy Mayakovsky—his poems weren't spoken, his poems weren't written, they were designed. Even illiterates can understand drawings. I can only compare him with Walt Disney, who is also a fine inventor, perhaps less pure, and the greatest poet in America, although commercialized. I'm sure that today Mayakovsky would shout his poems in Red Square over a loudspeaker, and that he'd improvise them every night on the radio in order that they might be heard in every corner of the world—more and more new poems, revolutionary in form and spirit.

INTERVIEWER: You say that there are other things in life to do besides writing books, but you are, all the same, an extraordinary worker.

CENDRARS: It's you others who are extraordinary! You all want us to write books without ever stopping. Where does that lead? Tell me . . . go take a walk through the Bibliothèque Nationale and you will see where that leads, that route. A cemetery. A submerged continent. Millions of volumes delivered over to the worms. No one knows any longer whose they are. No one ever asks. Terra incognita. It's rather discouraging.

No, I'm not an extraordinary worker, I'm an extraordinary daydreamer. I exceed all my fantasies—even that of writing.

MICHEL MANOLL
(*Translated by William Brandon*)

3. Jean Cocteau

Jean Cocteau was born on July 5, 1891. From the end of the First World War (in which he served in an ambulance unit), volumes of his poetry appeared at regular intervals: *Le Cap de Bonne Espérance* (1919), *Plain-Chant* (1923), *Poésie 1916–23* (1924), *Opéra* (1925–27), *Énigme* (1931), *Mythologie* (1934), *Allégories* (1941), *Poésies* (1948), and *Poèmes 1916–55* (1956). His first novel, *Le Potomak*, was published in 1919 and was followed by many others: *Le Grand Écart* (1923), *Thomas l'Imposteur* (1923), *Le Livre Blanc* (1928), *Les Enfants Terribles* (1929), *Le Fantôme de Marseille* (1933). He worked not only in the five traditional arts but also in the cinema, the ballet, the circus, and jazz. "Art must satisfy the nine muses," he said. Cocteau frequently collaborated with Apollinaire, Picasso, Stravinsky, and Diaghilev, among others, and his association with Satie, Bakst, Diaghilev, and "Les Six" resulted in the ballets *Parade* (1917—music by Satie), *Les Mariés de la Tour Eiffel* (1924 —music by "Les Six"), and *Le Pauvre Matelot* (1927—music by Honegger). Cocteau wrote opera libretti for Stravinsky (*Oedipus Rex* [1928]) and Honegger (*Antigone* [1928]). His work for the theater includes: *La Voix Humaine*, a one-act monologue; *La Machine Infernale* (1934); and *Les Parents Terribles*, the Paris stage hit of 1939. He also wrote and directed many films: *Le Sang d'un Poète* (1932), *Les Enfants Terribles* (1948), and *Orphée* (1949). In addition, he distinguished himself as a skilled graphic artist and as an articulate critic and essayist (*Le Coq et l'Arléquin* [1918], *Lettre à Jacques Maritain* [1926], *Opium* [1930], *Mon Premier Voyage* [1936], and *Lettre aux Américains* [1946]).

Cocteau died on October 11, 1963, hours after hearing of the death of his lifelong friend Edith Piaf.

Borgia, et dont les peintres maudits, Van Gogh e
tile, furent les premiers martyrs.

malheur au jeune peintre dont la force s'exprime
par un charme et qui devra subir la malédiction
~~sous les pas...~~ de plaire à ceux
qui estiment qu'il importe de ~~leur~~ déplaire et
qui poussent la modestie jusqu'à suspecter ce
qu'il leur plaît.

mais en musique les choses ne suivent point
la même pente. La musique est sournoise.
Elle ~~se~~ pénètre l'âme par des pentes qu'on
n'ajusterait pas. Elle traverse, semble-t-il, des
cloisons étanches et je me demande si de
farouches adeptes du Jazz ~~font~~ guettant
d'une oreille ~~attentive~~ la moindre ~~...~~ note qui
trahirait la cause, s'irriterait ~~...~~ des règles et
chercherait les routes du cœur, je me
demande, dis-je, si certains prêtres du culte
ne trahissent pas eux-mêmes et ne se

Manuscript page by Jean Cocteau

Jean Cocteau

A collector had a house full of horrible things. "Do you like these?" Cocteau finally asked. "No. But my parents missed the chance of buying the Impressionists cheap because they didn't like them. I buy only what I don't like."—A young Netherlander, said Cocteau, was the first to buy the Impressionists and take them home. Locked in an insane asylum for fifteen years, he died there. In his trunk were found some of the masterpieces of impressionism, which had by then acquired considerable value. His parents went to the head of the asylum and accused him of having kept a sane man incarcerated.

Cocteau's vivacity of intelligence caused him to live in a world of accelerated images, as if a film were run in fast motion. One thinks of a different time stage as a real possibility: differing human beings apparently all on the same physical ground living *actually at different accelerations. In Cocteau's case, there was no doubt that a rapidity of intelligence accounted for the multiplication, juxtaposition, proliferation, and mixing of experience and its exterior face, behavior—as well as for what was often called a certain superficiality or légèreté. "He who sees further renders less of what he sees, however much he renders."*

First met on the set of Orphée *in 1959 among the lime rocks, tortured as they are into Cocteauan shapes by the wind, at Les Baux in Provence—significantly on the day he filmed the death of the poet, himself—Cocteau treated the interviewer to a glimpse into a life that bridges two epochs* (*Proust and Rostand to Picasso and Stravinsky*). *He chatted with eminent grace between takes, then went over to stretch out again* (*upon a tarpaulin laid down out of camera range*) *on the floor of the quarried-out cavern in rock, lit up eerily by the floodlights, to be the transpierced poet—a spear through his breast* (*actually built around his breast under his jacket on an iron hoop*). *The hands gripped the spear; the talc-white face from the age of Diderot became anguished.*

The taped interview took place in the Riviera villa of Mme. Alec Weisweiller a few months before Cocteau's death in the fall of 1963. The villa entrance was framed by facsimiles of two great Etruscan masks from his staging of his Oedipus Rex—*a kind of static opera in scenes which he wrote after music by Stravinsky— masks worked in mosaic into the cement walk that winds through gardenia bushes and lilies to the portal out on the point of Cap Ferrat. You saw the schooner-form yacht of Niarchos out on the water toward Villefranche, where Cocteau lived in the Hotel Welcome in 1925 with Christian Bérard and wrote* Orphée; *the poet was framed by his own tapestry of Judith and Holofernes which covers the whole of one of Mme. Weisweiller's dining terrace walls, and provokes strange reminiscences of the slumbering Roman soldiery in the "Resurrection" of Piero della Francesca. Lunch was preceded by a cocktail, mixed by the famous hands, which Cocteau said he had learned to make from a novel by Peter Cheyney: "white rum, curaçao, and some other things." Lunch finished, the recorder was plugged in.*

COCTEAU: After you have written a thing and you reread it, there is always the temptation to fix it up, to improve it, to remove its poison, blunt its sting. No—a writer prefers, usually, in his work the *resemblances*—how it accords with what he has read. His originality—himself—is not *there*, of course.

INTERVIEWER: When I brought forward your resemblance to Voltaire at lunch you were—I had better say "highly displeased." But you share Voltaire's rapidity of thought.

COCTEAU: I am very French—like him. Very, very French.

INTERVIEWER: My thought was Voltaire isn't as dry-sharp as is supposed: that this is a miscalculation owing to imputing to him what would be a thought-out hypercleverness in a more lethargic mind. But in fact Voltaire wrote very fast—*Candide* in three days. That holocaust of sparks was simply thrown off. Whether or not this is true of Voltaire, it is certainly true of you.

COCTEAU: *Tiens!* I am the antipode of Voltaire! He is all thought—intellect. I am nothing—"another" speaks in me. This force takes the *form* of intelligence, and this is my tragedy—and it always has been from the beginning.

INTERVIEWER: It takes us rather far to think you are *victimized* by intelligence, especially since for a half century you have been thought of as one of the keenest critical and critical-poetical intelligences in France; but doesn't this bear on something you told me about yourself and Proust—that you both got started wrong?

COCTEAU: We both came out of the dandyism of the end of the nineteenth century. I turned my vest, eventually, toward 1912, but in the proper sense—in the right direction. Yet I am afraid the taint has persisted even to today. I suppressed all my earlier books of poems—from before 1913—and they are not in my collected works. Though I suppose that, after all, something from that epoch has always . . .

Marcel combated those things in his own way. He would circle among his victims collecting his "black honey," his *miel noir*—he asked me once, "I beg of you, Jean, since you live in the rue d'Anjou in the same building with Mme. de Chevigné, of whom I've made the Duchesse de Guermantes; I entreat you to get her to read my book. She won't read me; and she says she stubs her foot in my sentences. I beg you—" I told him that was as if he asked an ant to read Fabre. You don't ask an insect to read entomology.

INTERVIEWER: Strictly statistically, you were born in 1889. How could it have happened that you entered into this child-protégé phase, so very like Voltaire, taken up by all Paris? Did you have some roots in the arts—in your family, for example?

COCTEAU: No. We lived at Maisons-Laffitte a few miles outside Paris; played tennis at this house and that, and were divided into two camps over the Dreyfus affair. My father painted a little, an amateur—my grandfather had collected Stradivariuses and some excellent paintings.

INTERVIEWER: Excuse me. Do you think the loss of your father in your first year bears on your accomplishment? There is a whole theory that genius is only-childism and you were brought up by women, by your mother. An exceedingly beautiful one, from her pictures.

COCTEAU: I can only reply to that that I have never felt any connection with my family. There is—I must say simply—something in me that is not in my family. That was not visible in my father or mother. I do not know its origin.

INTERVIEWER: What happened in those days after you were launched?

COCTEAU: I had met Edouard de Max, the theater manager and actor, and Sarah Bernhardt, and others then called the "sacred monsters" of Paris, and in 1908 de Max and Sarah Bernhardt hired the Théâtre Fémina in the Champs-Élysées for an evening of reading of my poems.

INTERVIEWER: How old were you then?

COCTEAU: Seventeen. It was the fourth of April, 1908. I became eighteen three months later. I then came to know Proust, the Comtesse de Noailles, the Rostands. The next year, with Maurice Rostand, I became director of the deluxe magazine *Schéhérazade*.

INTERVIEWER: Sarah Bernhardt. Edmond—the Rostand who wrote *Cyrano*. It seems like another century. Then?

COCTEAU: I was on a slope that led straight toward the Académie Française (where, incidentally, I have finally arrived; but for inverse reasons); and then, at about that time, I met Gide. I was pleasing myself by tracing arabesques; I took my youth for audacity, and mistook witticism for profundity. But something from Gide, not very clearly then, made me ashamed.

INTERVIEWER: I recall something particularly scintillating you wrote in your first novel, *Potamak*, begun in 1914—though I think you didn't finish and publish it until after the war—which must have been ironically autobiographical of that stage.

COCTEAU: Yes, *Potomak* was published in 1919 and 1924.

INTERVIEWER: You wrote something to the effect of: a chameleon has a master who places it on a Scotch plaid. It is first frenzied, and then dies of fatigue.

COCTEAU: *C'était malheureusement comme ça!* Yes, I thought literature gay and amusing. But the Ballet Russe had come to Paris; had had to leave Russia, I believe. There are these strange conjunctures. I often wonder if much would have eventuated if Diaghilev had not come to Paris. He would say, "I do not like Paris. But if it were not for Paris, I believe I would not be staged." Everything began, finally, you see, with Stravinsky's *Sacre*. The *Sacre du Printemps* reversed everything. Suddenly, we saw that art was a terrible *sacerdoce*—the Muses could have frightful aspects, as if they were she-devils. One had to enter into art as one went into monastic orders; little it mattered if one pleased or not, the point wasn't in that. Ha!—Nijinsky. He was a simple, you know; not in the least intelligent, and rather stupid. His body knew; his limbs had the intelligence. He, too, was infected by something happening then—when was it? It must have been in the May or April of 1913. Nijinsky was taller than the ordinary, with a Mongol monkey face, and blunted fingers that looked like they'd been cut off short; it seemed unbelievable he was the idol of the public. When he invented his famous leap—in *Le Spectre de la Rose*—and sailed off the scene—Dimitri, his valet, would spew water from his lips into his face, and they would engulf him in hot towels. Poor fellow, he could not comprehend when the public hissed the choreography of *Sacre du Printemps* when he had himself—poor devil—seen they applauded *Le Spectre de la Rose*. Yet he was—manikin of a total professional deformation that he was—caught in the strange thing that was happening. Put the foot *there*; simply because it had always been put somewhere else before. I recall the night after the *première* of *Sacre*—Diaghilev, Nijinsky, Stravinsky, and I went for a drive in a fiacre in the Bois de Boulogne, and that was when the first idea of *Parade* was born.

INTERVIEWER: But it wasn't presented then?

COCTEAU: A year or two later, listening to music of Satie, it took further form in my mind. Then, in 1917, to Satie's music, Léonide Massine, who did the choreography, I who wrote it, Diaghilev, and Picasso—in Rome—worked it out.

INTERVIEWER: Picasso?

COCTEAU: I had induced him to try set designs; he did the stage settings: the housefronts of Paris, a Sunday. It was put on by the Ballet Russe in Paris; and we were hissed and hooted. Fortunately, Apollinaire was back from the front and in uniform, and it was 1917, and so he saved Picasso and me from the crowd, or I am afraid we might have been hurt. It was new, you see—not what was expected.

INTERVIEWER: Aren't you really positing a kind of passion of anti-conformism in the ferment of those days?

COCTEAU: Yes. That's right. It was Satie who said, later, the great thing is not to refuse the Legion of Honor—the great thing is not to have deserved it. Everything was turning about. All the old traditional order was reversing. Satie said Ravel may have refused the Legion of Honor but that all his work accepted it! If you receive academic honors you must do so with lowered head—as punishment. You have disclosed yourself; you have committed a *fault*.

INTERVIEWER: Do you think this liberty can go too far?

COCTEAU: There is a total rupture between the artist and public since about 1914. But it will cause its opposite, of necessity, and there will be a new conformism. The new great painter will be a figurative—but with something mysterious. Undoubtedly, Marcel —Proust—was stronger because he hid his crimes (and he *lived* those crimes) behind an apparent classicism, not saying, "I am a nasty man of bad habits and I am going frankly to recount them to you."

INTERVIEWER: You make me think of Hemingway, in that. His whole school—

COCTEAU: He told me a very interesting thing. He said: "France is impossible. The people are impossible. But you have luck. In America a writer is considered a trained seal, a clown. But you respect artists so much here that when you said, 'Careful; Genet is a genius,' when you said Genet is a great writer he wasn't condemned; the judges took fright and let him off." And it is true, the thing Hemingway said. The French are inattentive and the worst public in the world—yet the artist is still respected. In America the theater audiences are very respectful, I am afraid.

INTERVIEWER: Who would you name as fundamental to this conversion?

COCTEAU: Oh—Satie, Stravinsky, Picasso.

INTERVIEWER: If you had to name the chief architect of this revolt?

COCTEAU: Oh—for me—Stravinsky. But you see I met Picasso only in 1916. And of course he had painted the *Demoiselles d'Avignon* nearly a decade before. And Satie was a great innovator. I can tell you something about him that will perhaps seem only amusing. But it is very significant. He had died, and we all went to his apartment, and under his blotter on his desk we all found our letters to him—unopened.

INTERVIEWER: Some moments ago, you spoke of this "other." I

think we would do well to try to pin down what you mean by that. Picasso has spoken of it—said it is the real doer of his creation—and you have during our earlier talks. How would you define it?

COCTEAU: I feel myself inhabited by a force or being—very little known to me. *It gives* the orders; I follow. The conception of my novel *Les Enfants Terribles* came to me from a friend, from what he told me of a circle: a family closed from societal life. I commenced to write: exactly seventeen pages per day. It went well. I was pleased with it. Very. There was in the original life story some connection with America, and I had something I wanted to say about America. Poof! The being in me did not want to write that! Dead halt. A month of stupid staring at paper unable to say *any*thing. One day it commenced again in its own way.

INTERVIEWER: Do you mean the unconscious creates?

COCTEAU: I long said art is a marriage of the conscious and the unconscious. Latterly, I have begun to think: Is genius an at-present undiscovered form of the memory?

INTERVIEWER: Now bearing on that, you once wrote a long time ago that the idea is born of the sentence as the dream of the positions of the dreamer. And Picasso says a creation has to be an accident or fault or misstep, for otherwise it has to come out of conscious experience, which is observed from what pre-exists. And you've averred: the poet doesn't invent, he listens.

COCTEAU: Yes, but it may be much more complex than that. There's Satie, who didn't want to receive outside messages. And to *what* do we listen?

INTERVIEWER: Simply banally, how do you manage such things as names of characters?

COCTEAU: Dargelos, of course, was a real person. He is the one who throws the fatal snowball in *The Blood of a Poet*; again the same, a snowball, in my novel *Les Enfants Terribles*, which Rosamond Lehmann has translated (with obsessive difficulty, she wrote me); and this time, also, the black globule of poison—sent Paul to provoke his suicide, I found I had to use the name of the actual person, with whom I was in school. The name is mythical, but somehow it had to remain that of the lad. There are strange things that enter into these origins. Radiguet said to me: "In three days, I am going to be shot by the soldiers of God." And three days later he died. There was that, too. The name of the Angel Heurtebise, in the book of poems *L'Ange Heurtebise,* which was written in an unbroken automatism from start to finish, was taken from the name of an elevator stop where I happened to pause once. And I have named characters after designations on those great old-fashioned glass jars in a pharmacy in Normandy.

INTERVIEWER: What about the mechanism of translation? I think you once wrote in German?

COCTEAU: I had a German nurse. Apart from a few dozen words of yours, it is the only language I know aside from French. But my vocabulary was very limited. From this handicap I extracted obstacle—difficulty which I thought I could use to advantage, and I wrote some poems in German. But that is another matter and touches on the whole question of the necessity of obstacle.

INTERVIEWER: Well, what is this question of the necessity of obstacle?

COCTEAU: Without resistance you can do nothing.

INTERVIEWER: You were telling some story about the Impressionists and a Netherlander who bought them—which I think expressed one of your prime convictions: about the mutability of taste, or, really, the nonexistence of bad-good in any real objective sense. And about that time I believe you suggested poetry does not translate. Rilke—

COCTEAU: Yes, Rilke was translating my *Orphée* when he died. He wrote me that all poets speak a common language, but in different fashion. I am always badly translated.

INTERVIEWER: What I have read of your poetry in English does you no justice whatever.

COCTEAU: I write with an apparent simplicity—which is really a ferocious mathematical calculation—the language and not the content. Which is to say the after-the-fact work, for, regrettably, our vehicles of communication in writing are conventions. If Picasso displaces an eye to make a portrait jump into life, or provoke collision which gives the sense of multi-view, that is one thing; if I displace a word to restore some of its freshness, that is a far, far more difficult thing. Translators, mistaking my simplicity for insubstantiality, render me superficial I am told. Miss Rosamond Lehmann tells me I am badly translated in English. *Tiens*, in German they thought to make my *La Difficulté d'Être* "the difficulty to *Leben*"; no! "the difficulty *zu sein*." The difficulty to live is another thing: taxes, complications, and all the rest. But the difficulty to *be*—ah! to be here; to exist.

INTERVIEWER: Well, of course, if I may put in here, it seems you are writing a language of considerable contraction out of a world in which there is a very substantial amount of changing light and shade. You have got to say a very great deal in a little space if you are to convey simultaneity. You write somewhere that you mustn't look back (on your own product) for "might you not turn into a column of sugar if you looked back?" It is easy to take the surface of this joke; slide off. But it seems to me you evoke facetedness, glint, crystallization, perhaps even the cube, because you were intimately connected with the origins of Cubism; I don't want to go too far. I know from what you have told me that you do not "work these things up"—they jump into your mind. What are you to do, then? "De-apt" them? Make them less apt and water them down? But that would be false. It is possible to think that here *is* a reaching for more mysterious truths, truths that issue from juxtaposition, on the part of a delicate and in its special way quite modest mind.

COCTEAU: Story, of course, translates very well. Shakespeare translates in part because of his high *relief*—the immense relief of the tale derived from chronicles ordinarily, which one may read as one might read Braille.

INTERVIEWER: But surely the world doesn't read Shakespeare for just a kind of Lamb's tales approximation?

COCTEAU: No. Truly. There is something else. Madame Colette once said to me one needn't *read* the great poets, for they give off an atmosphere. It is truly very strange, too, that we poets can read one another, as Rilke says. With a friend to help with the words, I can read Shakespeare in English, but not the newspaper.

INTERVIEWER: Your own definition of poetry seems relevant here. You have said somewhere that when you love a piece of theater, others say it is not theater but something else; and if you love a film, your friends say that is not film but it is something else; and if you admire something in sport, they say that is not sport but it is something else. And finally you have arrived at realizing that that "something else" is poetry.

COCTEAU: You see, you do not know what you *do*. It is not possible to do what one *intends*. The mechanism is too subtle for that, too secret. Apollinaire set out to duplicate Anatole France, his model, and failed magnificently. He created a new poetry, small, but valid. Some do a very small thing, like Apollinaire, and have a large reward, as he did finally; others, a great thing, as did Max Jacob, who was the true poet of Cubism, and not Apollinaire, and the result—one's gain and reputation—is minute. Baudelaire writes much fabricated verse and then—*tout à coup!*—poetry.

INTERVIEWER: Isn't it the same in Shelley?

COCTEAU: Shelley. Keats. One single phrase, and the whole of the poem carried into the sky! Or Rimbaud commences writing poetry right from the start, and then simply gives it up because it is very evident the audience doesn't care.

INTERVIEWER: Is that really true?

COCTEAU: Yours and mine is a dreadful métier, my friend. The public is never pleased with what we do, wanting always a copy of what we have done. Why do we write—above all, publish? I posed this to my friend Genet. "We do it because some force unknown to the public and also to us pushes us to," he said. And that is very true. When you speak of these things to one who works systematically—one such as Mauriac—they think you jest. Or that you are lazy and use this as an excuse. Put yourself at a desk and write! You are a writer, are you not? *Violà!* I have tried this. What comes is no good. *Never any good.* Claudel at his desk from nine to twelve. It is unthinkable to work like that!

INTERVIEWER: Why, then, bother?

COCTEAU: When it goes well, the euphoria of such moments has been much the most intense and joyous of my life experience.

INTERVIEWER: What finally worked out between you and Gide? I read once in a French critic that his work always tended to keep to the surface, but yours plunged for the depths, with—sometimes —a considerable fracture of the waves, as well as sounding.

COCTEAU: We commenced to dispute in the press toward 1919. Gide always wanted to be *visible*; for me, the poet is invisible. One who walks naked with impunity. Gide was the architect of his labyrinth, by which he negated the character of poet.

INTERVIEWER: Do you keep a sort of abstract potential reader or viewer in mind when you work?

COCTEAU: You are always concentrated on the inner thing. The moment one becomes aware of the crowd, performs for the crowd, it is spectacle. It is *fichu*.

INTERVIEWER: Can you say something about inspiration?

COCTEAU: It is not *in*spiration; it is expiration. [*The gaunt, fine hands on the thorax; evacuation of the chest; a great breathing out from himself.*]

INTERVIEWER: Are there any artificial helps—stimulants or drugs? You resorted to opium after the death of Radiguet, wrote your book about it, *Opium*, and were, I believe, in a period of disintoxication from it when you wrote *Les Enfants Terribles*.

COCTEAU: It is very useful to have some depressant, perhaps. Extreme fatigue can serve. Filming *Beauty and the Beast* on the Loire in 1945 immediately at the end of the war, I was very ill. Everything went wrong. Electricity failures nearly every day; planes passing over just at the moment of a scene. Jean Marais' horses made difficulties, and he persisted in vaulting onto them himself out of second-floor windows, refusing a double, and risking his bones. And the sunlight changes every minute on the Loire. All these things contributed to the virtue of the film. And in *The Blood of a Poet* Man Ray's wife played a role; she had never acted. Her exhaustion and fear paralyzed her and she passed before the cameras so stunned she remembered nothing afterward. In the rushes we saw she was splendid; with the outer part suppressed, she had been let perform.

INTERVIEWER: We have these great difficulties of communication in print. All our readers are not John Gielgud or Louis Jouvet, and unfortunately when they read a novel they must play the parts. How are we to get across the shadings? I pose this because I know you have experimented with this technical dilemma. I hope you will let me reproduce eight lines of your *Le Cap de Bonne Espérance*.

COCTEAU: Yes.

INTERVIEWER: I will not need to translate. That will not be the point.

> Mon œuvre encoche
> et là
> et là
> et là [*Sudden discovery.*]
> et
> là [*Descent inward, with a note of
>   grief almost.*]
> dort
> la profonde poésie.

Whatever else, I am sure few readers would supply that phrasing if your words were printed on a straight line.

COCTEAU: Very difficult.

INTERVIEWER: Rossellini, in Rome, told me that if he were to put down in a script all his imagination casts up for the scene he would have to write a novel; but in fiction we must put it down, or it is lost.

COCTEAU: And the public is lazy! You ask them to enter into habits of thinking other than their own, and they don't want to. And then . . . what you have written in autograph changes in typewriting, and again in print. Painting is more satisfying because it is more direct; you work directly on the surface.

INTERVIEWER: We are struggling with imponderables here.

COCTEAU: But of course. The Cubists had to get rid of the whole question of subject, which is a *thing*, to express the poetry —or art—which is a thing also. And that was the meaning of Cubism, and not the accident that Matisse noticed the forms were cubic.

INTERVIEWER: You are the greatest expositor of Pablo Picasso, I should think very likely including Picasso. Your testimony is invaluable because you have been with him side by side through the whole art revolution from 1916 onward and because you have said his principle of permanent revolution and refreshment in art is the chief single influence in your own creative universe.

COCTEAU: He has no theory. He cannot have, because the creation ends at his wrists. Here. (*Cocteau touches two beautiful thin coupled wrists, quite different from the* costaud *wrists of Picasso.*) His mind does not enter in; there is an insulation, a defense, which he has formalized over years. It is the hand—*la main de gloire*— one thinks of the sacred mummy hand capable of opening any door, but severed at the wrist. An essential problem is that one cannot know, questions of formulation and art are too complicated for it to be possible for one to foresee, and one *simply does not know*. Perhaps for this reason Picasso says of painting—that it is the art of the blind. He never reflects; never halts; makes no attempt to concentrate his expression in a given work . . . to produce a *chef-d'œuvre*. With him, nothing is superfluous and nothing is of capital importance.

INTERVIEWER: Could this be another way of saying that everything is of capital importance for the total *œuvre*—but spread or diffused, not compacted—as in a Da Vinci?

COCTEAU: He has done that once or twice. Formulated "Guernica." And the *"Demoiselles d'Avignon"*—which it must be recognized was the beginning of Picassan art, before which there is no "Picasso" though there are Picassos. He finds first, and afterwards researches. Not, as is sometimes said, surfacing that given by intuition—but rather accommodating to the discoveries of his hand. It is important to know that this puts one in constant flight from oneself; from one's "experience." Like Orpheus, Picasso pipes and the objects fall in line after him, the most diverse, and submit to his will. But what that will is—?

INTERVIEWER: I wonder if you recall what you wrote about him in 1923?

COCTEAU: If you would recall for me—

INTERVIEWER: You wrote: "He contents himself with painting, acquiring an incomparable métier, and placing it at the service of hazard. I have often seen Picasso seek to quit his muse—that's to say, attempt to paint like everyone else. He quickly returns, eyes blindfolded. . . ."

COCTEAU: Yes. One day in 1917—the year I induced him to attempt stage design; the settings for "Parade"—the company was on stage rehearsing when we noticed a *vide*—a space—in the stage design. Picasso caught up a pot of ink and, with a few strokes, instantly, caused lines to explode into Grecian columns—so spontaneously, abruptly, and astonishingly that everyone applauded. I asked him afterward, "Did you know beforehand what you were going to do?" He said, "Yes and no. The unconscious must work without our knowing it." You see, art *is* a marriage of the conscious and the unconscious. The artist must not interfere. Picasso, too, does not want to be interfered with. When we were at dinner at D.C.'s the first satellite passed over. "*Ça m'emmerde*," he said—"That sullies me. What has it to do with me?" He is wholly concentrated on his work—more than any other man I know—inhumanly! He needs nothing outside his own closed universe. He rebuffs his friends—but sees nonentities—why? Because, he says, he does not want to nurture feelings of resentment against those few he loves: who, alone, can disorient him. He does not want to resent their intrusion—on the permanent gestation. Yet—how strange it is that this art—so completely "closed," that is, personal and isolate—has the great popular success. It entirely contradicts the shibboleth of the artist's contact with his audience.

INTERVIEWER: Is it possible to penetrate this closed universe and get his (undoubtedly partial and biased) opinion on him?

Cocteau: He would tell you nothing! He *never* discusses the rationale. How can he, for it is a process of the hands—manual, plastic. He would reply with *boutades*, jokes and absurdities: he lives behind them, in the protection of them, as if they were quills of the hedgehog. His tremendous work—he works more than any other man alive—is flight from the emptiness of life, and from any kind of formalism of anything. Expressionism has gone on and on knotting the cord—till it seems likely there is nothing left to knot but the void. But if the Montparnasse revolution has come to its end Picasso seems able to go on. Believe me—he does not know what to *do* but he knows unerringly what not to do. His hand knows where not to go, to avoid the stroke of the slightest banality, the least bit academic—a *constant* renewal—but where it does go, where the line does go, is merely the only place left.

Interviewer: Why does he deify the ugly? The effect on his psyche of the Spanish War?

Cocteau: Do you know he made the first sketches in the direction of "Guernica" *before* the Spanish War? The real inspiration of "Guernica" was Goya.

Interviewer: Even so, Picasso was turned to the late Goya by the Civil War? It seems as if Picasso is transported "bodily" more than altered by an influence, even if remaining in a frame of art reference.

Cocteau: Art is but an extension of the life process for him, not differentiated. Buffet criticized him publicly, and when he was asked to retort by judging Buffet's art he said, "I do not look at his art. I do not like the way he lives." When he had been particularly heartless and inaccessible in a human situation, I confronted him with it. "I am as I paint," he said. *Tiens, mon ami*, it takes great courage to be original! The *first* time a thing appears it disconcerts everyone, the artist too. But you have to leave it—not retouch it. *Of course* you must then canonize the "bad." For the good is the familiar. The new arrives only by mischance. As Picasso says, it is a *fault*. And by sanctifying our *faults* we create. "It is too easy when you have a certain proficiency to be right," he says.

INTERVIEWER: Does Picasso consciously try to displease—reserve to himself the right to displease like his *torero* friend Luis Miguel Dominguin? You told me how pleasant the original sketches for his chapel of "*La Guerre et La Paix*" were, and how he progressively deformed them until we have the final work—which is pretty frightening—and which you tell me made Matisse so terrified of being caught at producing conventional beauty that he deformed *his* chapel at Vence.

COCTEAU: He thinks neither of pleasing nor displeasing. He doesn't think of that at all.

INTERVIEWER: What do you think of the French new-novelists who are beginning to abandon subject—Robbe-Grillet? Nathalie Sarraute?

COCTEAU: I must make a disagreeable confession. I read nothing within the lines of my work. I find it very disconcerting; I disorient "the other." I have not looked at a newspaper in twenty years; if one is brought into the room, I flee. This is not because I am indifferent but because one cannot follow every road. And nevertheless such a thing as the tragedy of Algeria undoubtedly enters into one's work, doubtless plays its role in the fatigued and useless state in which you find me. Not that "I do not wish to lose Algeria!" but the useless killing, killing for the sake of killing. In fear of the police, men keep to a certain conduct; but when they become the police they are terrible. No, one feels shame at being a part of the human race. About novels: I read detective fiction, espionage, science fiction.

INTERVIEWER: Do you recommend, then, to writers they read nothing serious at all?

COCTEAU [*shrugs*]: I myself do not.

INTERVIEWER [*a few moments later*]: To get back to that about Algeria, and so on—as a point of clarification—I gather you mean the writer can't escape his world but oughtn't to let his detail memory be too much interfered with?

[*And here Cocteau did something odd. He stood—rather tiredly —he was very slight, quite small—his photographs belie and do not really convey him; Picasso, for one, is wholly portrayed by his photos and if you have seen them you know him—and he went with slow steps to an end table. And he took up a tube of silver cardboard or foil, which made a cylinder mirror upon its outside. And he placed it down carefully in the exact center of an indecipherable photograph which was spread flat on this table, that I would learn was Rubens's "Crucifixion" taken with a camera that shot in round. Masses of fog blurred out in the photo; elongations without sense. Upon the tube, which corresponded in some unseen fashion with the camera, the maker, the photograph was restored—swirls became men. Nevertheless, the objective photograph remained insane.*

He didn't say anything. Later on, he did remark, seated wearily, "I feel sorry for the young. It is not at all as it was in the Paris of sixteen. Paris has become an automobile garage. Neon, jazz—condition everything. And it is not at all as it was, a young man sitting writing by a candle. In Montparnasse, we never thought of a 'public.' It was all between ourselves. A great scientist came here the other day; he said, 'There is almost nothing left to be discovered.' And we know nothing about the mind! Nothing! Yevtushenko came to me. We had absolutely nothing to say to each other. Do you know why? There were twenty or thirty photographers and journalists there to snap and misrepresent it all. And the young are in a limbo that hasn't a future. Their auto accidents—to express their sense of the shortness of tenure. The world is very tired; we go back to the Charleston, the clothes of the twenties. And speleology—that is a rage here—burrowing down to the most primitive caves."]

INTERVIEWER: You wrote one of your novels in three weeks; one of your theater pieces in a single night. What does this tell us about the act of composition?

COCTEAU: If the force functions, it goes well. If not, you are helpless.

INTERVIEWER: Is there no way to get it started, crank it up?

COCTEAU: In painting, yes. By application to all the mechanical details one commences to begin. For writing "one receives an order. . . ."

INTERVIEWER: Françoise Sagan—others—describe how writing begins to flow with the use of the pen. I thought this was rather general experience.

COCTEAU: If the ideas come, one must hurry to set them down out of fear of forgetting them. They come once; once only. On the other hand, if I am obliged to do some little task—such as writing a preface or notice—the labor to give the appearance of easiness to the few lines is excruciating. I have no facility whatever. Yes, in one respect what you say is true. I had written a novel, then fallen silent. And the editors at the publishing house of Stock, seeing this, said, You have too great a fear of not writing a masterpiece. Write something, anything. Merely to begin. So I did—and wrote the first lines of *Les Enfants Terribles*. But that is only for beginnings—in fiction. I have never written unless deeply moved about something. The one exception is my play *La Machine à Écrire*. I had written the play *Les Parents Terribles* and it was very successful, and something was wanted to follow. *La Machine à Écrire* exists in several versions, which is very telling, and was an *enormous* amount of work. It is no good at all. Of course, it is one of the most popular of my works. If you make fifty designs and one or two please you least, these will nearly surely be the ones most liked. No doubt because they resemble something. People love to recognize, not venture. The former is so much more comfortable and self-flattering.

It seems to me nearly the whole of your work can be read as indirect spiritual autobiography.

INTERVIEWER: The wound in the hand of the poet in your film *The Blood of a Poet*—the wound in the man's hand out of which the poetry speaks—certainly this reproduces the "wound" of your experience in poetry around 1912–1914? "The horse of Orpheus" —without which he remains terrestrial—is surely that poetic and invisible "other" in you of which you speak.

COCTEAU: *En effet!* The work of every creator is autobiography, even if he does not know it or wish it, even if his work is "abstract." It is why you cannot redo your work.

INTERVIEWER: Not rewrite? Is that absolutely precluded?

COCTEAU: Very superficially. Simply the syntax and orthography. And even there— My long poem—*Requiem*—has just come out from Gallimard. I leave repetitions, *maladresses*, words badly placed quite unchanged, and there is no punctuation. It would be artificial to impose punctuation on a black river of ink. A hundred seventy pages—yes—and no punctuation. None. I was finishing staging one of my things in Nice; I said to the leading woman, "When the curtain is to come down, fall as if you had lost all your blood." After the *première* next night, I collapsed. And it was found I had been unknowingly hemorrhaging within for days, and had almost no blood. Hurrah!—my conscious self at lowest ebb, the being within me exults. I commence to write—difficultly above my head in bed, with a *stylo Bic*,* as a fly walks on the ceiling. It took me three years to decipher the script; I finally change nothing. One must fire on the target, after all, as Stendhal does. What matter how it is said? I have told you I dislike Pascal because I dislike his skepticism, but I like his style! He repeats the same word five times in a sentence. What has *Salammbô* to say to me? Nothing. Flaubert is simply bad. Montaigne is the best writer in French. Simply out of the language, almost argot. Almost slang. Straight out. It is so nearly always.

[*At this one point in the tape recording we have now reached, and as I remember only here, his voice loses its vibrant timbre—it "bleeds out." His voice was exceptionally young; here it becomes faded. One feels sure he recognizes the imputations for the art of writing in the decision not to correct; I recall that if* La Machine à Écrire *was a disaster clearly because it was intentional effort, then the successful* Parents Terribles *was dicté in a state of near somnambulism; there is the temptation to rerun the tape many times*

* *Ball-point pen.*

at this point, and ponder. That dicté—*combined with "retouch nothing, not even orthography"—frightens; Picasso seen at first-hand too touches this terror; for it is certain that it is his line which writes, through all his later art, a living line, which he merely watches; a dilemma of the Montparnasse generation; one feels Cocteau has looked into this chasm inwardly many times, and that here is his courage.*]

INTERVIEWER: By *refaire*, a moment ago, I think you did not quite mean "rewrite."

COCTEAU [*resignedly*]: What is wanted is only what one has already done. Another *Blood of a Poet* . . . another *Orphée* . . . It is not even possible. Picasso remarked the other day that the bump on the bridge of my nose is that of my grandfather, but that I did not have it when I was forty. My nose was straight. One changes, and is not what one was.

INTERVIEWER: Radiguet?

COCTEAU: Oh, he was very young. There was an enormous creative liberation in Paris. It was stopped—guillotined—by the Aristotelian rule of Cubism. Radiguet was fifteen when he first appeared. His father was a cartoonist, and Raymond used to bring in his work to deliver it to the papers. If his father didn't produce, then Radiguet did the sketches himself. One day, in the rue d'Anjou, the maid announced that there was "a young man with a cane" downstairs. Raymond came up—he was fifteen—and commenced to tell me all about art. We were his whole history, you see, and he'd been used to lie on the bank of the Seine out of Paris and read us. He had decided we were all wrong.

INTERVIEWER: How?

COCTEAU: He said that an *avant-garde* commences standing, and ends seated soon enough. He meant, in the academic chair.

INTERVIEWER: What did he propose?

COCTEAU: He said we should imitate the great classics. We would miss; and that miss would be our originality. So later on he set out to imitate *La Princesse de Clèves* and wrote *Le Bal du*

Comte d'Orgel and I sought to imitate *The Charterhouse of Parma* and wrote *Thomas l'Imposteur*.

INTERVIEWER: How old was he when he wrote *The Devil in the Flesh?* One still sees that novel in so many of the bookshop windows of Paris.

COCTEAU: Oh, he was very young. He died at the end of his teens. That was—in twenty-one—yes—two years before. He was remarkable in that he began perfectly from the beginning, without error.

INTERVIEWER: How is that possible?

COCTEAU: Ah. Answer that! He slept on the floor or on a table from house to house of the various painters. Then in the summer vacation with me on the Bay of Arcachon he wrote *The Devil in the Flesh*; *Bal du Comte d'Orgel* he did not even write, but sat and dictated to Georges Auric, who tapped it out on the machine as they went. I looked on, and he simply talked it all out. Rapidly and effortlessly. And it is flawless style. He was a Chinese Mandarin with the naïveté of a child.

INTERVIEWER: Those were certainly very remarkable days. Modigliani. Yourself. Apollinaire.

COCTEAU: I will recount one thing; then you must let me rest. You perhaps know the work of the painter Domergue? The long girls; calendar art, I am afraid. He had a *domestique* in those days —a "housemaid" who would make the beds, fill the coal scuttles. We all gathered in those days at the Café Rotonde. And a little man with a bulging forehead and black goatee would come there sometimes for a glass, and to hear us talk. And to "look at the painters." This was the "housemaid" of Domergue, out of funds. We asked him once (he said nothing and merely listened) what he did. He said he meant to overthrow the government of Russia. We all laughed, because of course we did too. That is the kind of time it was! It was Lenin.

INTERVIEWER: Your position as by far the most celebrated literary figure in France is crowned by the Académie Française, Belgian

Royal Academy, Oxford *honoris causa,* and so on. Yet I suppose that these are "faults"?

Cocteau: It is necessary always to oppose. The *avant-garde*—if that is enthroned.

Cocteau at dinner in Paris, a little restaurant in the 16th arrondissement.

Cocteau: Critics? A critic severely criticized my lighting at a Saturday evening opening in Munich. I thanked him but there was no time to change anything for the Sunday matinee. He felicitated me on the improvement. "You see how my suggestions helped?" he said. No, there will always be a conflict between creators and the technicians of the métier.

Interviewer: I was struck by the banality of Alberto Moravia in an interview with a movie actress recently in the French press.

Cocteau: I saw him on television and he was very mediocre. But that is the difficulty. That is the kind of thing that goes down with the public. And all they want are names.

Cocteau: Appreciation of art is a moral erection; otherwise mere dilettantism. I believe sexuality is the basis of all friendship.

Cocteau: This sickness, to express oneself. What is it?

William Fifield

4. Louis-Ferdinand Céline

Louis-Ferdinand Destouches (Céline is a pen name) was born in Paris on May 27, 1894, the son of a poor clerk and a lace seamstress. After receiving an elementary education, Destouches worked at various occupations until 1912, when he joined the cavalry. In the first year of World War I, he was wounded in the head and shell-shocked in an action for which he was decorated for bravery. The suffering, mental and physical, caused by these wounds pursued him to the end of his life.

After being invalided out, he earned a medical degree; he eventually became staff surgeon at the Ford plant in Detroit. Next he went to Africa, and then, after a period with the League of Nations, he settled down to ill-paid medical work among the poor of Paris.

The first Céline novel was *Voyage au Bout de la Nuit* (*Journey to the End of Night*—1932), which soon became an international success. His second novel, *Mort à Crédit* (*Death on the Installment Plan*—1936), enhanced his reputation. Céline's colloquial language, his insights into life in the lower depths, his mockery—all coupled with compassion—influenced Sartre, Queneau, and Bernanos, and among Americans Henry Miller, Burroughs, Ginsberg, and Kerouac.

In the late thirties Céline began to move toward Fascist political views and proclaimed his anti-Semitism. During the German occupation his record was ambiguous. After the liberation he had to flee to Denmark, his identity disguised by his real name. He was tried *in absentia*, but the sentence was later reversed and he was permitted to return to France, where he spent his last years—partially paralyzed and on the border of insanity. Céline nevertheless continued to write, producing two novels—*D'un Château à l'Autre* (1957) and *Nord* (1960) —considered by some critics to rank with his two great books of the thirties. He died in Paris on July 1, 1961.

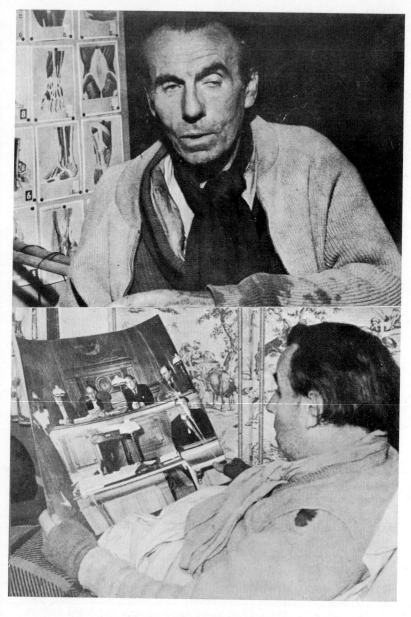

Top: Céline in Meudon, France, 1960
Below: Denmark, 1959, internment camp: Céline with report of his own in-absentia *trial*,
in Paris (Photos: Michel Bernard)

Louis-Ferdinand Céline

(*Interview, June 1, 1960*)

CÉLINE: So what can I say to you? I don't know how to please your readers. Those're people with whom you've got to be gentle. . . . You can't beat them up. They like us to amuse them without abusing them. Good . . . Let's talk. An author doesn't have so many books in him. *Journey to the End of Night, Death on the Installment Plan*—that should've been enough . . . I got into it out of curiosity. Curiosity, that's expensive. I've become a tragical chronicler. Most authors are looking for tragedy without finding it. They remember personal little stories which aren't tragedy. You'll say: The Greeks. The tragic Greeks had the impression of speaking with the gods. . . . Well, sure . . . Christ, it's not everyday you have a chance to telephone the gods.

INTERVIEWER: And for you the tragic in our times?

CÉLINE: It's Stalingrad. How's that for catharsis! The fall of Stalingrad is the finish of Europe. *There* was a cataclysm. The core of it all was Stalingrad. There you can say it was finished and well finished, the White civilization. So all that, it made some noise, some boiling, the guns, the waterfalls. I was in it . . . I profited off it. I used this stuff. I sell it. Evidently I've been mixed up in situations—the Jewish situation—which were none of my business, I had no business being there. Even so I described them . . . after my fashion.

INTERVIEWER: A fashion that caused a scandal with the appearance of *Journey*. Your style shook a lot of habits.

CÉLINE: They call that inventing. Take the impressionists. They took their painting one fine day and went to paint outside. They saw how you really lunch on the grass. The musicians worked at it too. From Bach to Debussy there's a big difference. They've caused some revolutions. They've stirred the colors, the sounds.

For me it's words, the positions of words. Where French literature's concerned, there I'm going to be the wise man, make no mistake. We're pupils of the religions—Catholic, Protestant, Jewish. . . . Well, the Christian religions. Those who directed French education down through the centuries were the Jesuits. They taught us how to make sentences translated from the Latin, well balanced, with a verb, a subject, a complement, a rhythm. In short—here a speech, there a preach, everywhere a sermon! They say of an author, "He knits a nice sentence!" Me, I say, "It's unreadable." They say, "What magnificent theatrical language!" I look, I listen. It's flat, it's nothing, it's nil. Me, I've slipped the spoken word into print. In one sole shot.

INTERVIEWER: That's what you call your "little music," isn't it?

CÉLINE: I call it "little music" because I'm modest, but it's a very hard transformation to achieve. It's work. It doesn't seem like anything the way it is, but it's quality. To do a novel like one of mine you have to write eighty thousand pages in order to get eight hundred. Some people say when talking about me, "There's natural eloquence. . . . He writes like he talks. . . . Those are everyday words. . . . They're practically identical. . . . You recognize them." Well, there, that's "transformation." That's just not the word you're expecting, not the situation you're expecting. A word used like that becomes at the same time more intimate and more exact than what you usually find there. You make up your style. It helps to get out what you want to show of yourself.

INTERVIEWER: What are you trying to show?

CÉLINE: Emotion. Savy, the biologist, said something appropriate: In the beginning there was emotion, and the verb wasn't there at all. When you tickle an amoeba she withdraws, she has emotion, she doesn't speak but she does have emotion. A baby cries, a horse gallops. Only us, they've given us the verb. That gives you the politician, the writer, the prophet. The verb's horrible. You can't smell it. But to get to the point where you can translate this emotion, that's a difficulty no one imagines. . . . It's ugly. . . . It's superhuman. . . . It's a trick that'll kill a guy.

INTERVIEWER: However, you've always approved of the need to write.

CÉLINE: You don't do anything for free. You've got to pay. A story you make up, that isn't worth anything. The only story that counts is the one you pay for. When it's paid for, then you've got the right to transform it. Otherwise it's lousy. Me, I work. . . . I have a contract, it's got to be filled. Only I'm sixty-six years old today, I'm seventy-five per cent mutilated. At my age most men have retired. I owe six million to Gallimard . . . so I'm obliged to keep on going. . . . I already have another novel in the works: always the same stuff. . . . It's chicken feed. I know a few novels. But novels are a little like lace . . . an art that disappeared with the convents. Novels can't fight cars, movies, television, booze. A guy who's eaten well, who's escaped the big war, in the evenings gives a peck to the old lady and his day's finished. Done with.

(Interview, later in 1960)

INTERVIEWER: Do you remember having had a shock, a literary explosion, which marked you?

CÉLINE: Oh, never, no! Me, I started in medicine and I wanted medicine and certainly not literature. Jesus Christ, no! If there are any people who seem to me gifted, I've seen it in—always the same —Paul Morand, Ramuz, Barbusse, the guys who were made for it.

INTERVIEWER: In your childhood you didn't think you'd be a writer?

CÉLINE: Oh, not at all, oh, no, no, no. I had an enormous admiration for doctors. Oh, that seemed extraordinary, that did. Medicine was my passion.

INTERVIEWER: In your childhood, what did a doctor represent?

CÉLINE: Just a fellow who came to the Passage Choiseul to see my sick mother, my father. I saw a miraculous guy, I did, who cured, who did surprising things to a body which didn't feel like working. I found that terrific. He looked very wise. I found it absolutely magical.

INTERVIEWER: And today, what does a doctor represent for you?

CÉLINE: Bah! Now he's so mistreated by society he has competition from everybody, he has no more prestige, no more prestige. Since he's dressed up like a gas-station attendant, well, bit by bit, he becomes a gas-station attendant. Eh? He doesn't have much to say any more, the housewife has *Larousse Médical*, and then diseases themselves have lost their prestige, there are fewer of them, so look what's happened: no syph, no gonorrhea, no typhoid. Antibiotics have taken a lot of the tragedy out of medicine. So there's no more plague, no more cholera.

INTERVIEWER: And the nervous, mental diseases, are there more of those instead?

CÉLINE: Well, there we can't do anything at all. Some madnesses kill, but not many. But as for the half-mad, Paris is full of them. There's a natural need to look for excitement, but obviously all the bottoms you see around town inflame the sex drive to a degree . . . drive the teen-agers nuts, eh?

INTERVIEWER: When you were working at Ford's, did you have the impression that the way of life imposed on people who worked there risked aggravating mental disturbances?

CÉLINE: Oh, not at all. No. I had a chief doctor at Ford's who used to say, "They say chimpanzees pick cotton. I say it'd be better to see some working on the machines." The sick are preferable, they're much more attached to the factory than the healthy, the healthy are always quitting, whereas the sick stay at the job very well. But the human problem, now, is not medicine. It's mainly women who consult doctors. Woman is very troubled, because clearly she has every kind of known weakness. She needs . . . she wants to stay young. She has her menopause, her periods, the whole genital business, which is very delicate, it makes a martyr out of her, doesn't it, so this martyr lives anyway, she bleeds, she doesn't bleed, she goes and gets the doctor, she has operations, she doesn't have operations, she gets re-operated, then in between she gives birth, she loses her shape, all that's important. She wants to stay young, keep her figure, well. She doesn't want to do a thing and she can't do a thing. She hasn't any muscle. It's an immense problem . . . hardly recognized. It supports the beauty parlors, the quacks, and the druggists. But it doesn't present an interesting medical situation, woman's decline. It's obviously a fading rose, you can't say it's a medical problem, or an agricultural problem. In a garden, when you see a rose fade, you accept it. Another one will bloom. Whereas in woman, she doesn't want to die. That's the hard part.

INTERVIEWER: Your profession as a doctor brought you a certain number of revelations and experiences you passed on in your books.

CÉLINE: Oh yes, oh yes, I spent thirty-five years doctoring, so it does count a bit. I ran around a lot in my youth. We climbed a lot of stairs, saw a lot of people. It helped me a lot in all ways, I must say. Yes, enormously. But I didn't write any medical novels, that's an abominable bore . . . like Soubiran.

INTERVIEWER: You got your medical calling very early in life, and yet you started out entirely differently.

CÉLINE: Oh, yes. And how! They wanted to make a buyer out of me. A department store salesman! We didn't have anything, my parents didn't have the means, don't you see. I started in poverty, and that's how I'm finishing.

INTERVIEWER: What was life like for small businesses around 1900?

CÉLINE: Fierce, fierce. In the sense that we hardly had enough to eat, and you had to keep up appearances. For example, we had two shop-fronts in the Passage Choiseul, but there was always only one lit up because the other was empty. And you had to wash the passage before going to work. My father. That was no joke. Well. My mother had earrings. We always took them to the pawn-shop at the end of the month, to pay the gas bill. Oh, no, it was awful.

INTERVIEWER: Did you live a long time in the Passage Choiseul?

CÉLINE: Well, eighteen years. Until I joined up. It was extreme poverty. Tougher than poverty, because in poverty you can let yourself go, degenerate, get drunk, but this was poverty which keeps up, dignified poverty. It was terrible. All my life I ate noodles.

Because my mother used to repair old lacework. And one thing about old lace is that odors stick to it forever. And you can't deliver smelly lace! So what didn't smell? Noodles. I've eaten basinfuls of noodles. My mother made noodles by the basinful. Boiled noodles, oh, yes, yes, all my youth, noodles and mush. Stuff that didn't smell. The kitchen in the Passage Choiseul was on the second floor, as big as a cupboard, you got to the second floor by a corkscrew staircase, like this, and you had to go up and down endlessly to see if it was cooking, if it was boiling, if it wasn't boiling, impossible. My mother was a cripple, one of her legs didn't work, and she had to climb that staircase. We used to climb it twenty-five times a day. It was some life. An impossible life. And my father was a clerk. He came home at five. He had to do the deliveries for her. Oh, no, that was poverty, dignified poverty.

INTERVIEWER: Did you also feel the harshness of poverty when you went to school?

CÉLINE: We weren't rich at school. It was a state school, you know, so there weren't any complexes. Not many inferiority complexes, either. They were all like me, little flea-bitten kids. No, there weren't any rich people in that place. We knew the rich ones. There were two or three. We worshiped them! My parents used to tell me, those people were rich, the local linen merchant. Pru'homme. They'd drifted in by mistake, but we recognized them, with awe. In those days we worshiped the rich man! For his wealth! And at the same time we thought he was intelligent.

INTERVIEWER: When and how did you become aware of the injustice it represented?

CÉLINE: Very late, I must confess. After the war. It happened, you see, when I saw people making money while the others were dying in the trenches. You saw it and you couldn't do anything about it. Then later I was at the League of Nations, and there I saw the light. I really saw the world was ruled by the Ox, by Mammon! Oh, no kidding! Implacably. Social consciousness certainly came to me late. I didn't have it, I was resigned.

INTERVIEWER: Was your parents' attitude one of acceptance?

CÉLINE: It was one of frantic acceptance! My mother always used to tell me, "Poor kid, if you didn't have the rich people (because I already had a few little ideas, as it happened), if there weren't any rich people we wouldn't have anything to eat. Rich people have responsibilities." My mother worshiped rich people, you see. So what do you expect, it colored me too. I wasn't quite convinced. No. But I didn't dare have an opinion, no, no. My mother who was in lace up to her neck would never have dreamed of wearing any. That was for the customers. Never. It wasn't done, you see. Not even the jeweler, he didn't wear jewels, the jeweler's wife never wore jewels. I was one of their errand boys. At Robert's in the rue Royale, at Lacloche's in the rue de la Paix. I was very active in those days. O, la la! I did everything really fast. I'm all gouty now, but in those days I used to beat the Métro. Our feet always hurt. My feet always have hurt. Because we didn't change our shoes very often, you know. Our shoes were too small and we were getting bigger. I ran all my errands on foot. Yes . . . Social consciousness. . . . When I was in the cavalry I went to the hunting parties at Prince Orloff's and the Duchess of Uzès', and we used to hold the officers' horses. That was as far as it went. Absolute cattle, we were. It was clearly understood, of course, that was the deal.

INTERVIEWER: Did your mother have much influence on you?

CÉLINE: I have her character. Much more than anything else. She was so hard, she was impossible, that woman. I must say she had some temperament. She didn't enjoy life, that's all. Always worried and always in a trance. She worked up to the last minute of her life.

INTERVIEWER: What did she call you? Ferdinand?

CÉLINE: No. Louis. She wanted to see me in a big store, at the Hôtel de Ville, the Louvre. Buyer. That was the ideal for her. And my father thought so too. Because he'd had so little success with his degree in literature! And my grandfather had a doctorate! They'd had so little success, they used to say, business, he'll succeed in business.

INTERVIEWER: Couldn't your father have had a better position teaching?

CÉLINE: Yes, poor man, but here's what happened: he needed a teaching degree and he only had a general education degree, and he couldn't go any further because he didn't have any money. His father had died and left a wife and five children.

INTERVIEWER: And did your father die late in life?

CÉLINE: He died when *Journey* came out, in thirty-two.

INTERVIEWER: Before the book came out?

CÉLINE: Yes, just. Oh, he wouldn't have liked it. What's more, he was jealous. He didn't see me as a writer at all. Neither did I, for that matter. We were agreed on at least one point.

INTERVIEWER: And how did your mother react to your books?

CÉLINE: She thought it was dangerous and nasty and it caused trouble. She saw it was going to end very badly. She had a prudent nature.

INTERVIEWER: Did she read your books?

CÉLINE: Oh, she couldn't, it wasn't within her reach. She'd have thought it all coarse, and then she didn't read books, she wasn't the kind of woman who reads. She didn't have any vanity at all. She kept on working till her death. I was in prison. I heard she had died. No, I was just arriving in Copenhagen when I heard of her death. A terrible trip, vile, yes—the perfect orchestration. Abominable. But things are only abominable from one side, don't forget, eh? And, you know . . . experience is a dim lamp which only lights the one who bears it . . . and incommunicable. . . . Have to keep that for myself. For me, you only had the right to die when you had a good tale to tell. To enter in, you tell your story and pass on. That's what *Death on the Installment Plan* is, symbolically, the reward of life being death. Seeing as . . . it's not the good Lord who rules, it's the devil. Man. Nature's disgusting, just look at it, bird life, animal life.

INTERVIEWER: When in your life were you happy?

CÉLINE: Bloody well never, I think. Because what you need, getting old . . . I think if I were given a lot of dough to be free from want—I'd love that—it'd give me the chance to retire and go off somewhere, so I'd not have to work, and be able to watch others. Happiness would be to be alone at the seaside, and then be left in peace. And to eat very little; yes. Almost nothing. A candle. I wouldn't live with electricity and things. A candle! A candle, and then I'd read the newspaper. Others, I see them agitated, above all excited by ambitions, their life's a show, the rich swapping invitations to keep up with the performance. I've seen it, I lived among society people once—"I say, Gontran, hear what he said to you; oh, Gaston, you really were on form yesterday, eh! Told him what was what, eh! He told me about it again last night! His wife was saying, oh, Gaston surprised us!" It's a comedy. They spend their time at it. Chasing each other round, meeting at the same golf clubs, the same restaurants.

INTERVIEWER: If you could have it all over again, would you pick your joys outside literature?

CÉLINE: Oh, absolutely! I don't ask for joy. I don't feel joy. To enjoy life is a question of temperament, of diet. You have to eat well, drink well, then the days pass quickly, don't they? Eat and drink well, go for a drive in the car, read a few papers, the day's soon gone. Your paper, some guests, morning coffee, my God, it's lunchtime when you've had your stroll, eh? See a few friends in the afternoon and the day's gone. In the evening, bed as usual and shut-eye. And there you are. And the more so with age, things go faster, don't they? A day's endless when you're young, whereas when you grow old it's very soon over. When you're retired, a day's a flash, when you're a kid it's very slow.

INTERVIEWER: How would you fill your time if you were retired with income?

CÉLINE: I'd read the paper. I'd take a little walk in a place where no one could see me.

INTERVIEWER: Can you take walks here?

CÉLINE: No, never, no! Better not!

INTERVIEWER: Why not?

CÉLINE: I'd be noticed. I don't want that. I don't want to be seen. In a port you disappear. In Le Havre . . . I shouldn't think they'd notice a fellow on the docks in Le Havre. You don't see a thing. An old sailor, an old fool. . . .

INTERVIEWER: And you like boats?

CÉLINE: Oh, yes! Yes! I love watching them. Watching them come and go. That and the jetty, and me, I'm happy. They steam, they go away, they come back, it's none of your business, eh? No one asks you anything! Yes, and you read the local paper, *Le Petit Havrais,* and . . . and that's it. That's all. Oh, I'd live my life over differently.

INTERVIEWER: Were there ever any exemplary people, for you? People you'd have liked to imitate?

CÉLINE: No, because that's all magnificent, all that, I don't want to be magnificent at all, no desire for all that, I just want to be an ignored old man. Those are the people in the encyclopedias, I don't want that.

INTERVIEWER: I meant people you might have met in daily life.

CÉLINE: Oh, no, no, no, I always see them conning others. They get on my nerves. No. There I have a kind of modesty from my mother, an absolute insignificance, really absolute! What I'm interested in is being completely ignored. I've an appetite, an animal appetite for seclusion. Yes, I'd quite like Boulogne, yes, Boulogne-sur-Mer. I've often been to Saint-Malo, but that's not possible any more. I'm more or less known there. Places people never go. . . .

(*Céline's last interview, June 1, 1961*)

INTERVIEWER: In your novels does love hold much importance?

CÉLINE: None. You don't need any. You've got to have modesty when you're a novelist.

INTERVIEWER: And friendship?

CÉLINE: Don't mention that either.

INTERVIEWER: Well, do you think you should concentrate on unimportant feelings?

CÉLINE: You've got to talk about the job. That's all that counts.

And furthermore, with lots of discretion. It's talked about with much too much publicity. We're just publicity objects. It's repulsive. Time will come for everybody to take a cure of modesty. In literature as well as in everything else. We're infected by publicity. It's really ignoble. There's nothing to do but a *job* and shut up. That's all. The public looks at it, doesn't look at it, reads it, or doesn't read it, and that's its business. The author only has to disappear.

INTERVIEWER: Do you write for the pleasure of it?

CÉLINE: Not at all, absolutely not. If I had money I'd never write. Article number one.

INTERVIEWER: You don't write out of love or hate?

CÉLINE: Oh, not at all! That's my business if I approve of these feelings you're talking about, love and friendship, but it's no business of the public's!

INTERVIEWER: Do your contemporaries interest you?

CÉLINE: Oh, no, not at all. I got interested in them once to try to keep them from running off to war. Anyhow, they didn't go off to the war, but they came back loaded with glory. Well, me, they shoved me in prison. I messed up in bothering with them. I shouldn't have bothered. I had only myself to bother with.

INTERVIEWER: In your latest books there's still a certain number of feelings which reveal you.

CÉLINE: You can reveal yourself no matter what. It's not difficult.

INTERVIEWER: You mean you want to persuade us there's nothing of the intimate you in your latest books?

CÉLINE: Oh, no, intimate, no, nothing. There might be one thing, the only one, which is that I don't know how to play with life. I have a certain superiority over the others who are, after all, rotten, since they're always in the middle of playing with life. To play with life, that's to drink, eat, belch, fuck, a whole pile of things that leave a guy nothing, or a broad. Me, I'm not a player, not at all. So, well, that works out fine. I know how to select. I know how to taste, but as the decadent Roman said, It's not going to the whore house, it's the not leaving that counts, isn't it? Me, I've been in there—all my life in the whore houses, but I got out quick. I don't drink. I don't like eating. All that's for the shits. I have the right, don't I? I've only got one life: It's to sleep and to be left alone.

INTERVIEWER: Who are the writers in whom you recognize a real writing talent?

CÉLINE: There are three characters I felt in the big period who were writers. Morand, Ramuz, Barbusse were writers. They had the feel. They were made for it. But the others aren't made for it. For God's sake, they're impostors, they're bands of impostors, and the impostors are the masters.

INTERVIEWER: Do you think you're still one of the greatest living writers?

CÉLINE: Oh, not at all. The great writers . . . I don't have to screw around with adjectives. First you've got to die and when you're dead, afterwards they classify. First thing you've got to be is dead.

INTERVIEWER: Are you convinced posterity will do you justice?

CÉLINE: But, good God, I'm not convinced! Good God, no! And maybe there won't even be a France then. It'll be the Chinese or the Barbarians doing the inventory and they'll be plenty bugged by my literature, my style of owl plotting, and my three dots. . . . It's not hard. I've finished, since we're talking about "literature." I've finished. After *Death on the Installment Plan* I've said everything, and it wasn't so much.

INTERVIEWER: Do you detest life?

CÉLINE: Well, I can't say I love it, no. I tolerate it because I'm alive and because I've got responsibilities. Without that, I'm pretty much of the pessimist school. I've got to hope for something. I don't hope for nothing. I hope to die as painlessly as possible. Like everyone else. That's all. That no one suffers for me, because of me. Well, to die peacefully, huh? To die if possible from an infection or, well, I'll do myself in. That'd still be by far more simple. What's coming, *that's* what's going to be more and more rugged. I work now much more painfully than I worked just a year ago, and next year it's going to be tougher than this year. That's all.

(*Interview that same year in which Céline imagines the introduction and end to a film adaptation of* Journey to the End of Night)

CÉLINE: Well, here you are. July '14. We're in the Avenue du Bois. And here we have three somewhat nervy Parisiennes. Ladies of the time—time of Gyp. So then, for God's sake, we hear what they're saying. And along the Avenue du Bois, along the *allée cavalière* goes a general, his *aide de camp* bringing up the rear, on horseback, of course, on horseback. So the first of the ladies, for God's sake, "Oh, I say, it's General de Boisrobert, did you see?" "Yes, I saw." "He greeted me, didn't he?" "Yes, yes, he greeted you. I didn't recognize him. I'm really not interested, you know." "But the *aide de camp*, it's little Boilepère, Oh, he was there yesterday, he's impossible, don't show you've seen anything, don't look, don't look. He was telling us all about the big exercises at Mourmelon, you know! Oh, he said, it means war, I'll be leaving, I'm going. . . . He's impossible, isn't he, with his war. . . ."

Then you hear music in the distance, ringing, warlike music.

"D'you think so, really?"

"Oh, yes, darling, they're impossible, with this war of theirs. These military parades in the evenings, what d'you think they look like? It's ludicrous, it's comic opera. Last time at Longchamps I saw all those soldiers with stewpots on their heads, sort of helmets, you'd never believe it, it's so ugly, that's what they call war, making themselves look ugly. It's ridiculous, in my opinion, quite ridiculous. Yes, yes, yes, ridiculous. Oh, do look, there's the attaché, the Spanish Embassy. He's talking war too, darling, it's quite appalling, oh, really I'm quite tired of it, we'd do far better to go on a shoot and kill pheasants. Wars nowadays are ridiculous, for heavens' sake, it's unthinkable, one just can't believe in them any more. They sing those stupid songs, no really, like Maurice Chevalier, actually he's rather funny, he makes everyone laugh."

So there you are, yes, that's all.

"Oh, I'd far rather talk about the flower carnival, yes, the flower carnival, it was so pretty, so lovely everywhere. But now they're going off to war, so stupid, isn't it, it's quite impossible, it can't last."

Good, okay, we've got a curtain-raiser there, we're in the war. Good. At that point you can move into Paris and show a bus, there are plenty of striking shots, a bus going down toward the *Carrefour Drouot*, at one point the bus breaks into a gallop, that's a funny sight to see, the three-horse Madeleine-Bastille bus, yes, get that shot there. Good, right. At that point you go out into the countryside. Take the landscapes in *Journey*. You're going to have to read *Journey* again—what a bore for you. You'll have to find things in *Journey* that still exist. The Passage Choiseul, you're sure to be able to take that. And there'll be Epinay, the climb up to Epinay, that'll still be there for you. Suresnes, you can take that too, though it's not the same as it was. . . . And you can take the Tuileries, and the Square Louvois, the little street, you ought to get a look at that, see what fits in with your ideas.

Then there's mobilization. All right. At that point you begin the *Journey*. This is where the heroes of *Journey* go off to war—part of the big picture. You'll need a pile of dough for that . . .

Then the end.

I'm giving you a dreamy passage here, then maybe you can show a bit of the Meuse countryside, that's where I began in the war, by the way, a bit of Flanders, good, fine, you just need to look at it, it's very evocative, and then very softly you begin to let the rumbling of the guns rise up. What you knew the war by, what the people of '14 knew it by, was the gunfire, from both sides. It was a rolling BLOM BELOLOM BELOM, it was a mill, grinding our epoch down. That's to say, you had the line of fire there in front of you, that was where you were going to be written off, it was where they all died. Yes and what you were supposed to do was climb up there with your bayonet. But for the most part it meant

shooting and flames. First shooting, then burning. Villages burning, everything burning. First shooting, then butchery.

Show that as best you may, it's your problem, work it out. I'm
relying on little Descaves, there. You need music to go with the
sound of the guns. Sinister kind of music, kind of deep Wagner-
ian music, he can get it out of the music libraries. Music that fits
everything. Very few speeches. Very few words. Even for the big
scene, even for the three hundred million. Gunfire. BELOMBELOLOM
BOM, *tactactac.* Machine guns—they had them already. From the
North Sea to Switzerland there was a four-hundred-and-fifty-kilo-
meter strip which never stopped chewing up men from one end to
the other. Yes, oh, yes, whenever a guy got there he said, So this
is where it happens, this is where the chopper is, eh. That was
where we all slaughtered each other. No dreaming there! One million seven hundred thousand died just there. More than a few.
With retreats, advances, retreats, louder and louder BOBOOMS, big
guns, little guns, not many planes, no, you can show a plane
vaguely, but they weren't much, no, what scared us was the gunfire, pure and simple. The Germans had big guns and they were
a big surprise, for the French army, 105's, we didn't have any. Okay.
And bicycles which you bent in half and folded up.

So to end your story, the *Journey,* see, it ends, well, it ends as
best it can, eh, but still, there is one end, a conclusion, a signature
after the *Journey,* a really lifelike one. The book ends in philosophical language, the book does, but not the film. Here's how it is for
the film. This was one way I saw the end, like this: There's an old
fellow—I think of him as Simon—who looks after the cemetery,
the military cemetery. Well, he's old now, he's seventy, he's worn
out. And the director of the military cemetery, the curator, he's
a young man and he's let him know it's time he retired. Ah, he
says, by all means, I'd like nothing better, can't get about any
more. Because you see, they've built him a little hut, not far from
Verdun, you know, a hut, so this hut, this kind of Nissen hut, he's
turned it into a little café bar at the same time, and he's got a

gramophone, but really, a period gramophone, yes! So in this bar
he serves people drinks and he talks, you know, he tells his story,
tells it to lots of people, and you see the bar, and people coming
in, many people used to come, they don't come any more, to visit
the graves of their dear departed, but after all those tombs of the
dear departed he feels pretty old, eh, and it's a lot of trouble getting there, so much trouble he doesn't go any more, himself, because he says, I'm too old, I can't, I can't move. Walk three
kilometers over those furrows, too much bloody trouble, it is, impossible, I'd come back dead, I would, I'm worn out, worn out, I
am. And he has an opportunity to say that because the director
of the cemetery has found someone to take his place. And who is
this someone who'll take his place? I'll tell you. It's . . . they're
Armenians. A family of Armenians. There's a father, a mother,
and five little children. And what are they doing there? Well,
they'd gone to Africa, like all Armenians, and they'd been kicked
out of it, and someone told them they could go and hide up north,
they'd find a cemetery and a fellow just on the point of quitting
and they could take his place. And oh, he says, that's fine, because
the kids are sick, Africa's too hot for them anyway. So Simon takes
them in. The cemetery keeper. He has his peaked cap on and all.
Well, he says, you'll be taking my place. You'll be none too warm,
though. If you want to make a bit of a fire, there's wood for the
fetching, though the wood fire's just an old stove for his pot, and
he says, me, I can't last any longer, because of all this running
around. There used to be the Americans, in the old days. There
still are the Americans, too, down under there, you'll see, you'll
find them. . . . Well, I'll show you the gate where they come in,
it's not far, hardly a kilometer, but I can't do it any more—because
he limps too, you see, he limps too—I'm wounded, I am, disabled
eighty per cent after '14, it makes a difference! I'll be going to live
with my sister. A fine bitch of a woman she was. Lives in Asnières!
Dirty slut, she is! She says I've got to go, she says I've got to but
I don't know that I'll get on with her, haven't seen her for thirty
years now, I haven't, dirty slut she was, must be more of a slut

than ever by now. She's married, she says they've a room, maybe, I don't know what I'll do there, still, can't stay here, can I, can't do the job, I can't do it. There aren't many doing it nowadays, two or three of them still come, there used to be plenty, they used to come in droves, in the old days, in memory of them all, the French and the English, there are all kinds buried down there, but you'll see, like they told me, oh, put the crosses right, yes, some have fallen down, of course they have, time does its work, crosses won't stay up forever, so I put the crosses right as best I could for a long time, but I don't go any more now, no, no, I can't, I have to lie down afterwards, you see, I can't, and lying down here wouldn't be any pleasure, and I've no one with me, so the visitors come and as it happens one good woman, an American, a very old American woman, and she says, "I want to see my old friend John Brown, my dear uncle that died, don't you have him there?" Oh, he says, it's all in the registers, wait a moment, I'll go and have a look, yes, I'll show you the register, there, and he shows her the register and says, I kept it well, you see, there, can't say I didn't do that, eh, now let's see, Brown, Brown, Brown. Oh, yes, yes, yes, yes, yes. Well, you know, it's down in the *Fauvettes* cemetery, down there, lady, hard to find, it is. No, no, please, him over there, with his wife and children, very interesting, the grounds are, they'll put it all in order for you; and I can't, you see, I can't, I've told you I can't, it's no use, madam, and believe me if you try going over there, eh, eh, let me tell you, finding where he is, he's there all right, in my register, but it's a long while since I went to look at it, the American one, it's a long way, two and a half kilometers at least, no, no, let them do it, they'll do it. I can serve you what there is, though, granadilla juice, lemon. Oh, you'd like a cup of coffee, oh, to be sure, we couldn't say no to a cup of coffee, I'll make you a cup of coffee.

And he makes her a cup of coffee, d'you follow, he's got a nose for a wealthy dame. Well, he says, you see, my sister, over in Asnières, here's the coffee, a little coffee? Do you know, that reminds me, I'm not so sure she knows how to make it. A trollop, she is, I say it myself. Eh, I don't know what I'll do, I don't, still, have to go, really have to go. So there it is. Yes. I'm going. Yes, I'm really going, I'm going to leave you with them. Don't be frightened, now (the others are beginning to look scared). Oh, it's none too warm here, but just you put some wood on and it warms up, that's no trouble. Oh, you'll see, it's no joke, here. What about a bit of music. Ah, it was a good one, that gramophone there was, a fine one, ah yes, one from the old days, it was, it was a . . . And he gets out a wind-up thing and they play the old-time records, but really the old-time, eh—"*Viens Poupoule*," "*Ma Tonkinoise*"— there you are, you see, it's better with that on, isn't it, you can play it all summer long, you can, that'll bring them in again, once they've swabbed the place down a bit, just needs doing, eh? Well, madame, going back, are you? Going to Paris, are you? You've got a car? Well, now, I must say, that'd be a help, that would, fancy that, eh, going back in a car. . . .

J. DARRIBEHAUDE
J. GUENOT
ANDRÉ PARINAUD
CLAUDE SARRAUTE

(*Translated by James Sherwood and Patrick Bowles*)

5. Evelyn Waugh

Born in London on October 28, 1903, Evelyn Waugh was the second son of Arthur Waugh, a well-known publisher and critic. He attended Oxford but left without a degree.

A biography of Dante Gabriel Rossetti (1928) was his first published work, but his novel *Decline and Fall*, which appeared later that year, established his reputation. His wit, sophistication, and caustic style led Edmund Wilson to describe Waugh as "the only first-rate comic genius that has appeared in England since Bernard Shaw." *Decline and Fall*, and many of the satirical novels which followed it, continue to be popular works: *Vile Bodies* (1930), *Black Mischief* (1932), *A Handful of Dust* (1934), *Scoop* (1938), *Put Out More Flags* (1942), *Scott-King's Modern Europe* (1947), *The Loved One* (1948), and *The Ordeal of Gilbert Pinfold* (1957).

In the 1930s Waugh was converted to Catholicism. During the Second World War he served as an officer. Religion and military life provided dominant themes for the novel *Brideshead Revisited* (1945) and for the trilogy *Men at Arms* (1952), *Officers and Gentlemen* (1955), and *Unconditional Surrender* (1961). Waugh also wrote a number of travel books, including *Labels* (1930), *Remote People* (1931), *Ninety-Two Days* (1934), *Waugh in Abyssinia* (1936), *Robbery Under Law: The Mexican Object Lesson* (1939), and *When the Going was Good* (1946); two biographies: the strongly Catholic *Edmund Campion* (1935) and *Ronald Knox* (1959); and numerous short stories, collected into three anthologies: *Mr. Loveday's Little Outing and Other Sad Stories* (1936), *Work Suspended* (1942), and *Tactical Exercise* (1954). The first volume of his autobiography, *A Little Learning*, appeared in 1964.

He died at his home in Somerset, England, on April 10, 1966.

Manuscript page by Evelyn Waugh

Evelyn Waugh

The interview which follows is the result of two meetings on successive days at the Hyde Park Hotel, London, during April 1962.

I had written to Mr. Waugh earlier asking permission to interview him and in this letter I had promised that I should not bring a tape recorder with me. I imagined, from what he had written in the early part of The Ordeal of Gilbert Pinfold, *that he was particularly averse to them.*

We met in the hall of the hotel at three in the afternoon. Mr. Waugh was dressed in a dark-blue suit with a heavy overcoat and a black Homburg hat. Apart from a neatly tied small brown paper parcel, he was unencumbered. After we had shaken hands and he had explained that the interview would take place in his own room, the first thing he said was, "Where is your machine?"

I explained that I hadn't brought one.

"Have you sold it?" he continued as we got into the lift. I was

somewhat nonplussed. In fact I had at one time owned a tape recorder and I had indeed sold it three years earlier, before going to live abroad. None of this seemed very relevant. As we ascended slowly, Mr. Waugh continued his cross-questioning about the machine. How much had I bought it for? How much had I sold it for? Whom did I sell it to?

"Do you have shorthand, then?" he asked as we left the lift. I explained that I did not.

"Then it was very foolhardy of you to sell your machine, wasn't it?"

He showed me into a comfortable, soberly furnished room, with a fine view over the trees across Hyde Park. As he moved about the room he repeated twice under his breath, "The horrors of London life! The horrors of London life!"

"I hope you won't mind if I go to bed," he said, going through into the bathroom. From there he gave me a number of comments and directions:

"Go and look out of the window. This is the only hotel with a civilized view left in London. . . . Do you see a brown paper parcel? Open it, please."

I did so.

"What do you find?"

"A box of cigars."

"Do you smoke?"

"Yes. I am smoking a cigarette now."

"I think cigarettes are rather squalid in the bedroom. Wouldn't you rather smoke a cigar?"

He re-entered, wearing a pair of white pajamas and metal-rimmed spectacles. He took a cigar, lit it, and got into bed.

I sat down in an armchair at the foot of the bed, juggling notebook, pen, and enormous cigar between hands and knees.

"I shan't be able to hear you there. Bring up that chair." He indicated one by the window, so I rearranged my paraphernalia as we talked of mutual friends. Quite soon he said, "When is the inquisition to begin?"

I had prepared a number of lengthy questions—the reader will no doubt detect the shadows of them in what follows—but I soon discovered that they did not, as I had hoped, elicit long or ruminative replies. Perhaps what was most striking about Mr. Waugh's conversation was his command of language: his spoken sentences were as graceful, precise, and rounded as his written sentences. He never faltered, nor once gave the impression of searching for a word. The answers he gave to my questions came without hesitation or qualification, and any attempt I made to induce him to expand a reply generally resulted in a rephrasing of what he had said before.

I am well aware that the result on the following pages is unlike the majority of Paris Review *interviews; first it is very much shorter and secondly it is not "an interview in depth." Personally, I believe that Mr. Waugh did not lend himself, either as a writer or as a man, to the form of delicate psychological probing and self-analysis which are characteristic of many of the other interviews. He would consider impertinent an attempt publicly to relate his life and his art, as was demonstrated conclusively when he appeared on an English television program, "Face to Face," some time ago and parried all such probing with brief, flat, and, wherever possible, monosyllabic replies.*

However, I should like to do something to dismiss the mythical image of Evelyn Waugh as an ogre of arrogance and reaction. Although he carefully avoided taking part in the market place of literary life, of conferences, prize-giving, and reputation-building, he was, nonetheless, both well informed and decided in his opinions about his contemporaries and juniors. Throughout the three hours I spent with him he was consistently helpful, attentive, and courteous, allowing himself only minor flights of ironic exasperation if he considered my questions irrelevant or ill-phrased.

INTERVIEWER: Were there attempts at other novels before *Decline and Fall*?

WAUGH: I wrote my first piece of fiction at seven. *The Curse of the Horse Race*. It was vivid and full of action. Then, let's see, there was *The World to Come*, written in the meter of "Hiawatha." When I was at school I wrote a five-thousand-word novel about modern school life. It was intolerably bad.

INTERVIEWER: Did you write a novel at Oxford?

WAUGH: No. I did sketches and that sort of thing for the *Cherwell*, and for a paper Harold Acton edited—*Broom* it was called. The *Isis* was the official undergraduate magazine: it was boring and hearty, written for beer drinkers and rugger players. The *Cherwell* was a little more frivolous.

INTERVIEWER: Did you write your life of Rosetti at that time?

WAUGH: No. I came down from Oxford without a degree, wanting to be a painter. My father settled my debts and I tried to become a painter. I failed as I had neither the talent nor the application—I didn't have the moral qualities.

INTERVIEWER: Then what?

WAUGH: I became a prep-school master. It was very jolly and I enjoyed it very much. I taught at two private schools for a period of nearly two years and during this I started an Oxford novel which was of no interest. After I had been expelled from the second school for drunkenness I returned penniless to my father. I went to see my friend Anthony Powell, who was working with Duckworths, the publishers, at the time, and said, "I'm starving." (This wasn't true: my father fed me.) The director of the firm agreed to pay me fifty pounds for a brief life of Rossetti. I was delighted, as fifty pounds was quite a lot then. I dashed off and dashed it off. The result was hurried and bad. I haven't let them reprint it again. Then I wrote *Decline and Fall*. It was in a sense based on my experiences as a schoolmaster, yet I had a much nicer time than the hero.

INTERVIEWER: Did *Vile Bodies* follow on immediately?

WAUGH: I went through a form of marriage and traveled about Europe for some months with this consort. I wrote accounts of these travels which were bundled together into books and paid for the journeys, but left nothing over. I was in the middle of *Vile Bodies* when she left me. It was a bad book, I think, not so carefully constructed as the first. Separate scenes tended to go on for too long—the conversation in the train between those two women, the film shows of the dotty father.

INTERVIEWER: I think most of your readers would group these two novels closely together. I don't think that most of us would recognize that the second was the more weakly constructed.

WAUGH [*briskly*]: It was. It was secondhand too. I cribbed much of the scene at the customs from Firbank. I popularized a fashionable language, like the beatnik writers today, and the book caught on.

INTERVIEWER: Have you found that the inspiration or starting point of each of your novels has been different? Do you sometimes start with a character, sometimes with an event or circumstance? Did you, for example, think of the ramifications of an aristocratic divorce as the center of *A Handful of Dust*, or was it the character of Tony and his ultimate fate which you started from?

WAUGH: I wrote a story called *The Man Who Liked Dickens*, which is identical to the final part of the book. About two years after I had written it, I became interested in the circumstances which might have produced this character; in his delirium there were hints of what he might have been like in his former life, so I followed them up.

INTERVIEWER: Did you return again and again to the story in the intervening two years?

WAUGH: I wasn't haunted by it, if that's what you mean. Just curious. You can find the original story in a collection got together by Alfred Hitchcock.

INTERVIEWER: Did you write these early novels with ease or—

WAUGH: Six weeks' work.

INTERVIEWER: Including revisions?

WAUGH: Yes.

INTERVIEWER: Do you write with the same speed and ease today?

WAUGH: I've got slower as I grow older. *Men at Arms* took a year. One's memory gets so much worse. I used to be able to hold the whole of a book in my head. Now if I take a walk whilst I am writing, I have to hurry back and make a correction, before I forget it.

INTERVIEWER: Do you mean you worked a bit every day over a year, or that you worked in concentrated periods?

WAUGH: Concentrated periods. Two thousand words is a good day's work.

INTERVIEWER: E. M. Forster has spoken of "flat characters and round characters"; if you recognize this distinction, would you agree that you created no "round" characters until *A Handful of Dust*?

WAUGH: All fictional characters are flat. A writer can give an illusion of depth by giving an apparently stereoscopic view of a character—seeing him from two vantage points; all a writer can do is give more or less information about a character, not information of a different order.

INTERVIEWER: Then do you make no radical distinction between characters as differently conceived as Mr. Prendegast and Sebastian Flyte?

WAUGH: Yes, I do. There are the protagonists and there are characters who are furniture. One gives only one aspect of the furniture. Sebastian Flyte was a protagonist.

INTERVIEWER: Would you say, then, that Charles Ryder was the character about whom you gave most information?

WAUGH: No, Guy Crouchback. [*A little restlessly*] But look, I think that your questions are dealing too much with the creation of character and not enough with the technique of writing. I regard writing not as investigation of character, but as an exercise in the use of language, and with this I am obsessed. I have no technical psychological interest. It is drama, speech, and events that interest me.

INTERVIEWER: Does this mean that you continually refine and experiment?

WAUGH: Experiment? God forbid! Look at the results of experiment in the case of a writer like Joyce. He started off writing very well, then you can watch him going mad with vanity. He ends up a lunatic.

INTERVIEWER: I gather from what you said earlier that you don't find the act of writing difficult.

WAUGH: I don't find it easy. You see, there are always words going round in my head; some people think in pictures, some in ideas. I think entirely in words. By the time I come to stick my pen in my inkpot these words have reached a stage of order which is fairly presentable.

INTERVIEWER: Perhaps that explains why Gilbert Pinfold was haunted by voices—by disembodied words.

WAUGH: Yes, that's true—the word made manifest.

INTERVIEWER: Can you say something about the direct influences on your style? Were any of the nineteenth-century writers an influence on you? Samuel Butler, for example?

WAUGH: They were the basis of my education, and as such of course I was affected by reading them. P. G. Wodehouse affected my style directly. Then there was a little book by E. M. Forster called *Pharos and Pharillon*—sketches of the history of Alexandria. I think that Hemingway made real discoveries about the use of language in his first novel, *The Sun Also Rises*. I admired the way he made drunk people talk.

INTERVIEWER: What about Ronald Firbank?

WAUGH: I enjoyed him very much when I was young. I can't read him now.

INTERVIEWER: Why?

WAUGH: I think there would be something wrong with an elderly man who could enjoy Firbank.

INTERVIEWER: Whom do you read for pleasure?

WAUGH: Anthony Powell. Ronald Knox, both for pleasure and moral edification. Erle Stanley Gardner.

INTERVIEWER: And Raymond Chandler!

WAUGH: No. I'm bored by all those slugs of whisky. I don't care for all the violence either.

INTERVIEWER: But isn't there a lot of violence in Gardner?

WAUGH: Not of the extraneous lubricious sort you find in other American crime writers.

INTERVIEWER: What do you think of other American writers, of Scott Fitzgerald or William Faulkner, for example?

WAUGH: I enjoyed the first part of *Tender Is the Night*. I find Faulkner intolerably bad.

INTERVIEWER: It is evident that you reverence the authority of established institutions—the Catholic Church and the army. Would you agree that on one level both *Brideshead Revisited* and the army trilogy were celebrations of this reverence?

WAUGH: No, certainly not. I reverence the Catholic Church because it is true, not because it is established or an institution. *Men at Arms* was a kind of uncelebration, a history of Guy Crouchback's disillusion with the army. Guy has old-fashioned ideas of honor and illusions of chivalry; we see these being used up and destroyed by his encounters with the realities of army life.

INTERVIEWER: Would you say that there was any direct moral to the army trilogy?

WAUGH: Yes, I imply that there is a moral purpose, a chance of salvation, in every human life. Do you know the old Protestant hymn which goes: "Once to every man and nation/Comes the moment to decide"? Guy is offered this chance by making himself responsible for the upbringing of Trimmer's child, to see that he is not brought up by his dissolute mother. He is essentially an unselfish character.

INTERVIEWER: Can you say something about the conception of the trilogy. Did you carry out a plan which you had made at the start?

WAUGH: It changed a lot in the writing. Originally I had intended the second volume, *Officers and Gentlemen*, to be two volumes. Then I decided to lump them together and finish it off. There's a very bad transitional passage on board the troop ship. The third volume really arose from the fact that Ludovic needed explaining. As it turned out, each volume had a common form because there was an irrelevant ludicrous figure in each to make the running.

INTERVIEWER: Even if, as you say, the whole conception of the trilogy was not clearly worked out before you started to write, were there not some things which you saw from the beginning?

WAUGH: Yes, both the sword in the Italian church and the sword of Stalingrad were, as you put it, there from the beginning.

INTERVIEWER: Can you say something about the germination of *Brideshead Revisited*?

WAUGH: It is very much a child of its time. Had it not been written when it was, at a very bad time in the war when there was nothing to eat, it would have been a different book. The fact that it is rich in evocative description—in gluttonous writing—is a direct result of the privations and austerity of the times.

INTERVIEWER: Have you found any professional criticism of your work illuminating or helpful? Edmund Wilson, for example?

WAUGH: Is he an American?

INTERVIEWER: Yes.

WAUGH: I don't think what they have to say is of much interest, do you? I think the general state of reviewing in England is contemptible—both slovenly and ostentatious. I used to have a rule when I reviewed books as a young man never to give an unfavorable notice to a book I hadn't read. I find even this simple rule is flagrantly broken now. Naturally I abhor the Cambridge movement of criticism, with its horror of elegance and its members mutually encouraging uncouth writing. Otherwise, I am pleased if my friends like my books.

INTERVIEWER: Do you think it just to describe you as a reactionary?

WAUGH: An artist must be a reactionary. He has to stand out against the tenor of the age and not go flopping along; he must offer some little opposition. Even the great Victorian artists were all anti-Victorian, despite the pressures to conform.

INTERVIEWER: But what about Dickens? Although he preached social reform he also sought a public image.

WAUGH: Oh, that's quite different. He liked adulation and he liked showing off. But he was still deeply antagonistic to Victorianism.

INTERVIEWER: Is there any particular historical period, other than this one, in which you would like to have lived?

WAUGH: The seventeenth century. I think it was the time of the greatest drama and romance. I think I might have been happy in the thirteenth century, too.

INTERVIEWER: Despite the great variety of the characters you have created in your novels, it is very noticeable that you have never given a sympathetic or even a full-scale portrait of a working-class character. Is there any reason for this?

WAUGH: I don't know them, and I'm not interested in them. No writer before the middle of the nineteenth century wrote about the working classes other than as grotesques or as pastoral decorations. Then when they were given the vote certain writers started to suck up to them.

INTERVIEWER: What about Pistol . . . or much later, Moll Flanders and—

WAUGH: Ah, the criminal classes. That's rather different. They have always had a certain fascination.

INTERVIEWER: May I ask you what you are writing at the moment?

WAUGH: An autobiography.

INTERVIEWER: Will it be conventional in form?

WAUGH: Extremely.

INTERVIEWER: Are there any books which you would like to have written and have found impossible?

WAUGH: I have done all I could. I have done my best.

JULIAN JEBB

6. Lillian Hellman

Lillian Hellman was born on June 20, 1905, in New Orleans. Except for occasional visits to her Southern relatives, she spent her childhood in New York, where she had moved at the age of five. In 1923 she entered New York University. She did not graduate, however, and after transferring to Columbia for one semester left college for good in 1924 to work as a publisher's assistant for Horace Liveright. In 1925 she married playwright-author Arthur Kober. During their seven years of marriage she worked as a reviewer for the *New York Herald-Tribune* and as a play reader (one of her discoveries was Vicki Baum's *Grand Hotel*). A year after her divorce from Kober in 1932, she began work on what was to be her first produced play. With the guidance of Dashiell Hammett, who remained her lifelong friend, she finished the play in 1934: *The Children's Hour* opened that year on Broadway and ran for six hundred ninety-one performances.

Since then, her plays have been produced regularly: *Days to Come* (1936); *The Little Foxes* (1939); *Watch on the Rhine*, which won the New York Drama Critics' Circle Award in 1941; *The Searching Wind* (1944); *Another Part of the Forest* (1946); *The Autumn Garden* (1951); and *Toys in the Attic* (1960). She has also written a number of adaptations: *Montserrat* (1949), based on Emmanuel Robles's novel; *The Lark* (1955), based on Jean Anouilh's play; and *My Mother, My Father and Me* (1963), based on Burt Blechman's novel *How Much*. She wrote the libretto for the musical *Candide* (1956) and the film script *The Chase* (1966). Among her other screenplays are *Dark Angel* (1935), *These Three* (the first film version of *The Children's Hour*—1935–1936), *Dead End* (1937), *The Little Foxes* (1940), *North Star* (1943), and *The Searching Wind* (1945). She edited *Selected Letters of Anton Chekhov* in 1955.

                              CAL
Miss Zan she had two helpings frozen fruit cream and she tell
that honored guest, she tell him that you make the best frozen
fruit cream in all the south.

                        ADDIE
          (Smiles, pleased)
Did she? Well, save her a little. She like it right before
she go to bed.

                    (Cal nods, exits. After a second the
                    dining room doors are opened and quickly
                    closed again by BIRDIE HUBBARD. Birdie
                    is a woman of about forty, with a pretty,
                    well-bred, faded face. Her movements are
                    usually nervous and timid, but now, as she
                    comes running into the room, she is gay
                    and excited)   Don't understand
                                                              P.H.

                        BIRDIE
          (Running to the bell-cord)
My, Addie. What a good dinner. Just as good as good can be.

                    ADDIE
You look pretty this evening, Miss Birdie, and young. more casual

                        BIRDIE
          (Laughing, pleased)
Me, young!
          (ADDIE looks at her as she rings the
          bell again)
I want one of the kitchen boys to run home for me. He's to   To
look in my desk drawer, the left drawer, and bring my music   much
album right away. Mr. Marshall is very anxious to see it   how
because of his father and the opera in Chicago. Mr. Marshall   college
is such a polite man with his manners, and very educated and
cultured —
          (CAL appears at the door)
Oh, Cal. Tell Simon or one of the boys to run down to our
house and look in my desk, the left drawer, and —

                    (The dining room doors are opened and quickly
                    closed by OSCAR HUBBARD. He is a tall, thin-
                    faced man in his late forties)

                              OSCAR
          (Sharply)
Birdie.

                        BIRDIE
          (Turning, nervously)
Oh. Oscar. I was just sending Simon for my music album.

          (To Cal)   OSCAR
Never mind about Simon. Miss Birdie has changed her mind.

Manuscript page from The Little Foxes

ANNE HOLLANDER

Lillian Hellman

Miss Hellman spends her summers in a comfortable white house at the bottom of a sandbank in the town of Vineyard Haven, Massachusetts, on the island of Martha's Vineyard. There is none of old Cape Cod about it; a modern house, newly built with lots of big windows and a wooden deck facing on the harbor. Miss Hellman observes the ferries of Woods Hole–Martha's Vineyard –Nantucket Steamship Authority, weighted down with passengers and automobiles, push through the harbor on their midsummer schedule and disgorge ever more visitors upon this teeming, heterogeneous resort. It is a measure of Miss Hellman's dedication to her work that she achieves so much in her exposed situation, not half a mile from the ferry dock. Here she stays with her maid, and a big barking poodle that discourages few of the peak-of-the-season visitors who troop through her parlor.

Behind this new house and out of view on top of the sandbank is the old one, which Miss Hellman sold after Dashiell Hammett died. A frame house with yellow painted shingles and climbing roses, plainer and more regional in its architecture, like a Yankee farmhouse of the last century, it had a complex of boxlike rooms where Miss Hellman's guests thronged. Removed from these, on the far east wing of the house, stood a tower formed by the shell of an old Cape Cod windmill. Up in this windmill tower was the room where Dashiell Hammett lived; he always escaped there when company came. He had been an invalid since the war; he became a recluse and at the end of his life talked to almost nobody. Hammett was a thin, finely built man and very tall—when he was seen walking in delicate silence, in the cruel wasting of his illness, down a crowded sidewalk on his way to the library, unrecognized, unknown, forgotten, the proudness of his bearing set him off from the summer people.

Occasionally a stranger would come in the house uninvited and catch Dashiell Hammett off guard. He might be reading in an easy chair. Miss Hellman would introduce him, and he would elegantly rise and shake hands. Like many a famous writer who detests being disturbed in his private self, a million miles from any social confrontation, he had learned to scare off the intruder with his smile. Here he was luckier than most, for rather than looking pained and fraudulent, rather than a predictable Sam Spade/Humphrey Bogart hard-guy leer, the smile Dashiell Hammett produced on his clear-eyed, lean, aristocratic face was so nearly beatific that it disarmed the intruder long enough for Dashiell Hammett, with no more than a how-do-you-do, to vanish from the room. The armchair or the book gave his only evidence. Even the invited dinner guest coming punctually into the room would know the same ectoplasmic presence, when Miss Hellman, the laughter mingled in her greeting, would immediately explain what Dash had said—what his joking exit line had been on, it seemed, the instant of your entrance. He was elusive but never aloof. Through the medium of Miss Hellman it was possible to carry on a running extrasensory conversation. A question to him, put through to her, on one evening (*as how to clean a meerschaum pipe*) or a request for an opinion (on somebody's writing, on something President Eisenhower did) was sure to be answered on another. And five years before the meeting with Miss Hellman, a request had been put in writing for a *Paris Review* interview. He was by then at the end of his tether, often too weak to take his meals at the table. An answer came: "Sorry. Don't think it would work. Lilly will explain." Which she does, though neither by design nor by coincidence, in this interview. On a table in the parlor where she talked was a framed snapshot of Dashiell Hammett as he looked in World War II as a corporal in the Army Service Forces. He is lighting his cigarette on a PX-Zippo lighter and looking every inch a soldier in his impeccably creased suntans and overseas cap tilted toward the right of his head of white hair.

Miss Hellman's voice has a quality, not to be captured on the page, of being at once angry, funny, slyly feminine, sad, affectionate, and harsh. While talking here she often allowed her laughter, like an antidote to bitterness, to break into her thoughts and give a more generous dimension to her comments, which, in print, may seem at first glance merely captious. These pages are compiled from three afternoon conversations in the more than usually harrying conditions of the Labor Day weekend on Martha's Vineyard, while Miss Hellman was driving herself to finish a movie script for Sam Spiegel. There were many interruptions—telephone calls and people coming and going in the room. Such circumstances cannot excuse but may in part explain some of the interviewers' unrehearsed and too eagerly "literary" questions.

INTERVIEWER: Before you wrote plays, did you write anything else?

HELLMAN: Yes, short stories, a few poems. A couple of the stories were printed in a long-dead magazine called *The Paris Comet* for which Arthur Kober worked. Arthur and I were married and living in Paris. Let's see, about 1928, 1929, somewhere in there. They were very lady-writer stories. I reread them a few years ago. The kind of stories where the man puts his fork down and the woman knows it's all over. You know.

INTERVIEWER: Was it Dashiell Hammett who encouraged you to write plays?

HELLMAN: No. He disliked the theater. He always wanted me to write a novel. I wrote a play before *The Children's Hour* with Louis Kronenberger called *The Dear Queen*. It was about a royal family. A royal family who wanted to be bourgeois. They kept running away to be middle class, and Dash used to say the play was no good because Louis would laugh only at his lines and I would laugh only at mine.

INTERVIEWER: Which of your plays do you like best?

HELLMAN: I don't like that question. You always like best the last thing you did. You like to think that you got better with time. But you know it isn't always true. I very seldom reread the plays. The few times I have, I have been pleasantly surprised by things that were better than I had remembered and horrified by other things I had thought were good. But I suppose *Autumn Garden*. I suppose I think it is the best play, if that is what you mean by "like."

INTERVIEWER: Somebody who saw you watch the opening night in Paris of Simone Signoret's adaptation of *The Little Foxes* said that through the performance you kept leaving your seat and pacing the vestibule.

HELLMAN: I jump up and down through most performances. But that particular night I was shaken by what I was seeing. I like *Little Foxes*, but I'm tired of it. I don't think many writers like best their best-known piece of work, particularly when it was written a long time ago.

INTERVIEWER: What prompted you to go back to the theme and the characters of *The Little Foxes*? Only seven years later you wrote *Another Part of the Forest*.

HELLMAN: I always intended to do *The Little Foxes* as a trilogy. Regina in *The Little Foxes* is about thirty-eight years old, and the year is 1900. I had meant to take up with her again in about 1920 or 1925, in Europe. And her daughter, Alexandra, was to have become maybe a spinsterish social worker, disappointed, a rather angry woman.

INTERVIEWER: In the third act of *The Little Foxes* is a speech which carries the burden of the play. It says there are people who eat the earth and all the people on it, like the locusts in the Bible. And there are the people who let them do it. "Sometimes I think it ain't right to stand by and watch them do it." At the end of this play Alexandra decides that she is not going to be one of those passive people. She is going to leave her mother.

HELLMAN: Yes, I meant her to leave. But to my great surprise, the ending of the play was taken to be a statement of faith in Alexandra, in her denial of her family. I never meant it that way. She did have courage enough to leave, but she would never have the force or vigor of her mother's family. That's what I meant. Or maybe I made it up afterward.

INTERVIEWER: These wheelers and dealers in your plays—the gouging, avaricious Hubbards. Had you known many people like that?

HELLMAN: Lots of people thought it was my mother's family.

INTERVIEWER: Might you ever write that third play?

HELLMAN: I'm tired of the people in *The Little Foxes*.

INTERVIEWER: In *Regina*, the opera Marc Blitzstein based on *The Little Foxes*, the badness of Regina is most emphatic.

HELLMAN: Marc and I were close friends but we never collaborated. I had nothing to do with the opera. I never saw Regina that way. You have no right to see your characters as good or bad. Such words have nothing to do with people you write about. Other people see them that way.

INTERVIEWER: You say in your introduction that *The Children's Hour* is about goodness and badness.

HELLMAN: Goodness and badness is different from good and bad people, isn't it? *The Children's Hour*—I was pleased with the results—was a kind of exercise. I didn't know how to write a play and I was teaching myself. I chose, or Dashiell Hammett chose for me, an actual law case, on the theory that I would do better with something that was there, had a foundation in fact. I didn't want to write about myself at the age of twenty-six. The play was based on a law case in a book by William Roughead. I changed it, of course, completely, by the time I finished. The case took place in Edinburgh in the nineteenth century, and was about two old-maid schoolteachers who ran a sort of second-rate private school. A little Indian girl—an India Indian—had been enrolled by her grandmother in the school. She brought charges of Lesbianism against the two teachers. The two poor middle-aged ladies spent the rest of their lives suing, sometimes losing, sometimes winning, until they no longer had any money and no school.

INTERVIEWER: As a rule does the germ of a play come to you abstractly? Do you work from a general conception?

HELLMAN: No, I've never done that. I used to say that I saw a play only in terms of the people in it. I used to say that because I believed that is the way you do the best work. I have come now to think that is it people *and* ideas.

INTERVIEWER: Have characters invented themselves before you write them?

HELLMAN: I don't think characters turn out the way you think they are going to turn out. They don't always go your way. At least they don't go my way. If I wanted to start writing about you, by page ten I probably wouldn't be. I don't think you start with a person. I think you start with the parts of many people. Drama has to do with conflict in people, with denials. But I don't really know much about the process of creation and I don't like talking about it.

INTERVIEWER: Is there something mysterious in what a play evokes as art and the craft of writing it?

HELLMAN: Sure. That is really the only mystery because theories may work for one person and not for another. It's very hard, at least for me, to have theories about writing.

INTERVIEWER: But you had to begin with a clear idea of what the action of the play would be?

HELLMAN: Not always. Not as I got older. It was bright of Hammett to see that somebody starting to write should have a solid foundation to build on. It made the wheels go easier. When I first started to write I used to do two or three page outlines. Afterward, I didn't.

INTERVIEWER: Do you think the kind of play you do—the well-made play, one which runs the honest risk of melodrama for a purpose—is going to survive?

HELLMAN: I don't know what survives and what doesn't. Like everybody else, I hope I will survive. But survival won't have anything to do with well-made or not well-made, or words like "melodrama." I don't like labels and isms. They are for people who raise or lower skirts because that's the thing you do for this year. You write as you write, in your time, as you see your world. One form is as good as another. There are a thousand ways to write, and each is as good as the other if it fits you, if you are any good. If you can break into a new pattern along the way, and it opens things up, and allows you more freedom, that's something. But not everything, maybe even not much. Take any form, and if you're good—

INTERVIEWER: Do you have to do with the casting of your plays?

HELLMAN: Yes.

INTERVIEWER: Do you feel you were well served always?

HELLMAN: Sometimes, sometimes not. *Candide* and *My Mother, My Father and Me* were botched, and I helped to do the botching. You never know with failures who has done the harm. *Days to Come* was botched. The whole production was botched, including my botching. It was an absolute horror of a failure. I mean the curtain wasn't up ten minutes and catastrophe set in. It was just an awful failure. Mr. William Randolph Hearst caused a little excitement by getting up in the middle of the first act and leaving with his party of ten. I vomited in the back aisle. I did. I had to go home and change my clothes. I was drunk.

INTERVIEWER: Have you enjoyed the adaptations you have done of European plays?

HELLMAN: Sometimes, not always. I didn't like Anouilh's *The*

Lark very much. But I didn't discover I didn't like it until I was halfway through. I liked *Montserrat*. I don't seem to have good luck with adaptations. I got nothing but pain out of *Candide*. That's a long story. No, I had a good time on *Candide* when I was working alone. I am not a collaborator. It was a stormy collaboration. But I had a good time alone.

INTERVIEWER: *Candide* was a box-office failure, but obviously it was a success. The record is very popular.

HELLMAN: It has become a cult show. It happens. I'm glad.

INTERVIEWER: Do you think *My Mother, My Father and Me* was a cult show?

HELLMAN: It opened during the newspaper strike, and that was fatal. Yes, I guess we were a cult show. Oddly enough, mostly with jazz musicians. The last week the audience was filled with jazz musicians. Stan Getz had come to see it and liked it, and he must have told his friends about it. I hope it will be revived because I like it. Off Broadway. I had wanted it done off Broadway in the beginning.

INTERVIEWER: Can you comment on your contemporaries—Arthur Miller?

HELLMAN: I like *Death of a Salesman*. I have reservations about it, but I thought it was an effective play. I like best *View from the Bridge*.

INTERVIEWER: *After the Fall*?

HELLMAN: So you put on a stage your ex-wife who is dead from suicide and you dress her up so nobody can mistake her. Her name is Marilyn Monroe, good at any box office, so you cash in on her, and cash in on yourself, which is maybe even worse.

INTERVIEWER: In an important subplot of this play a man who was once briefly a communist names a close friend before a congressional committee.

HELLMAN: I couldn't understand all that. Miller felt differently once upon a time, although I never much liked his House Un-American Committee testimony: a little breast-beating and a little apology. And recently I went back to reread it and liked it even less. I suppose, in the play, he was being tolerant: those who betrayed their friends had a point, those who didn't also had a point. Two sides to every question and all that rot.

INTERVIEWER: And Tennessee Williams?

HELLMAN: I think he is a natural playwright. He writes by sanded fingertips. I don't always like his plays—the last three or four seem to me to have gone off, kind of way out in a conventional way. He is throwing his talent around.

INTERVIEWER: Mary McCarthy wrote in a review that you get the feeling that no matter what happens Mr. Williams will be rich and famous.

HELLMAN: I have the same feeling about Miss McCarthy.

INTERVIEWER: She has accused you of, among other things, a certain "lubricity," of an overfacility in answering complex questions. Being too facile, relying on contrivance.

HELLMAN: I don't like to defend myself against Miss McCarthy's opinions, or anybody else's. I think Miss McCarthy is often brilliant and sometimes even sound. But, in fiction, she is a lady writer, a lady magazine writer. Of course, that doesn't mean that she isn't right about me. But if I thought she was, I'd quit. I would like critics to like my plays because that is what makes plays successful. But a few people I respect are the only ones whose opinions I've worried about in the end.

INTERVIEWER: There is a special element in your plays—of tension rising into violence. In *Days to Come* and *Watch on the Rhine* there are killings directly on stage. Was there possibly, from your association with Dashiell Hammett and his work, some sort of influence, probably indirect, on you?

HELLMAN: I don't think so, I don't think so. Dash and I thought differently and were totally different writers. He frequently objected to my use of violence. He often felt that I was far too held up by how to do things, by the technique. I guess he was right. But he wasn't writing for the theater and I was.

INTERVIEWER: You have written a lot of movies?

HELLMAN: Let's see. I wrote a picture called *The Dark Angel* when I first started. I did the adaptation of *Dead End*. I did the adaptation of *The Little Foxes*. Right now I'm doing a picture called *The Chase*.

INTERVIEWER: Did you ever worry about Hollywood being a dead end for a serious writer?

HELLMAN: Never. I wouldn't have written movies if I'd thought that. When I first went out to Hollywood one heard talk from writers about whoring. But you are not tempted to whore unless you want to be a whore.

INTERVIEWER: The other night when we listened to Pete Seeger sing his folk songs you seemed nostalgic.

HELLMAN: I was moved by seeing a man of conviction again.

INTERVIEWER: We aren't making them like that any more?

HELLMAN: Not too many. Seeger's naïveté and the sweetness, the hard work, the depth of belief I found touching. He reminded me of very different times and people. There were always X number of clowns, X number of simple-minded fools, X number of fashionables who just went along with what was being said and done, but there were also remarkable people, people of belief, people willing to live by their beliefs. Roosevelt gave you a feeling that you had something to do with your government, something to do with better conditions for yourself and for other people. With all its foolishness, the thirties were a good time and I often have regrets for it. Many people of my age make fun of that period, and are bitter about it. A few do so out of a genuine regret for foolish things said or foolish things done—but many do so because belief is unfashionable now and fear comes with middle age.

INTERVIEWER: Do people still mention your statement before the House Un-American Activities Committee: "I can't cut my conscience to fit this year's fashions"?

HELLMAN: Yes.

INTERVIEWER: Did that put you in contempt of Congress?

HELLMAN: No, I never was in contempt. They brought no contempt charges at the end of that day. My lawyer, Joseph Rauh, was so proud and pleased. He was afraid I would be harmed because I might have waived my rights under the Fifth Amendment.

INTERVIEWER: You took the stand that you would tell the committee all they wanted to know about you, but you weren't going to bring bad trouble upon innocent people no matter if they had been fooled?

HELLMAN: We sent a letter* saying that I would come and testify about myself as long as I wasn't asked questions about other people. But the committee wasn't interested in that. I think they knew I was innocent, but they were interested in other people. It was very common in those days, not only to talk about other people, but to make the talk as interesting as possible. Friendly witnesses, so-called, would often make their past more colorful than ever was the case. Otherwise you might turn out to be dull. I thought mine was a good position to take—I still think so.

INTERVIEWER: Was it something of a custom among theater people in those days, when they were going to name some old acquaintance to a committee, to call him beforehand and let him know? Just to be fair and square, as it were?

HELLMAN: Yes. They would telephone around among their friends. In several cases the to-be-injured people actually gave their permission. They understood the motive of their friends' betrayal—money, injury to a career. Oh, yes, there was a great deal of telephoning around. Kind of worse than testifying, isn't it?— the fraternity of the betrayers and the betrayed. There was a man in California who had been barred from pictures because he had been a communist. After a while he was broke, this Mr. Smith, and his mother-in-law, who was getting bored with him—anybody would have been bored with him—said that he could have a little piece of land. So he started to build a two-room house, and he borrowed the tools from his closest friend, his old college roommate, Mr. Jones. He had been working on his house for about seven or eight months and almost had it finished when Mr. Jones arrived to say that he had to have the tools back because, he, Mr.

---

* Following the interview is the text of this letter. The Committee rejected the proposal contained in the letter.

Jones, was being called before the committee the next day and was going to name Mr. Smith and thought it was rather unethical for Mr. Smith to have his tools while he was naming him. I don't know whether the house ever got finished. Clowns, they were.

INTERVIEWER: A little-known aspect of Lillian Hellman is that she was the inspiration for Dashiell Hammett's Nora Charles, the loyal wife of Nick Charles, the detective-hero of *The Thin Man*. That marriage is beautifully evoked in the book and was played by William Powell and Myrna Loy in the movies.

HELLMAN: Yes.

INTERVIEWER: Didn't it give you some gratification?

HELLMAN: It did, indeed.

INTERVIEWER: When Myrna Loy turned into her, then she became the perfect wife.

HELLMAN: Yes. I liked that. But Nora is often a foolish lady. She goes around trying to get Nick into trouble.

INTERVIEWER: And that was about you both?

HELLMAN: Well, Hammett and I had a good time together. Most of it, not all of it. We were amused by each other.

INTERVIEWER: Was it because of that book that Gertrude Stein invited you to dinner?

HELLMAN: Miss Stein arrived in America and said that there were two people that she wanted to meet. They were both in California at that minute—Chaplin and Dash. And we were invited to dinner at the house of a friend of Miss Stein; Charlie Chaplin, Dash and myself, Paulette Goddard, Miss Toklas, our host and hostess, and another man. There was this magnificent china and lace tablecloth. Chaplin turned over his coffee cup, nowhere near Stein, just all over this beautiful cloth, and the first thing Miss Stein said was, "Don't worry, it didn't get on me." She was miles away from him. She said it perfectly seriously. Then she told Dash he was the only American writer who wrote well about women. He was very pleased.

INTERVIEWER: Did he give you any credit for that?

HELLMAN: He pointed to me, but she didn't pay any attention.

She wasn't having any part of me. I was just a girl around the table. I talked to Miss Toklas. We talked about food. It was very pleasant.

INTERVIEWER: Did you know Nathanael West?

HELLMAN: He managed a hotel, the Sutton Hotel. We all lived there half free, sometimes all free. Dash wrote *The Thin Man* at the Sutton Hotel. Pep West's uncle or cousin owned it, I think. He gave Pep a job out of kindness. There couldn't have been any other reason. Pep liked opening letters addressed to the guests. He was writing, you know, and he was curious about everything and everybody. He would steam open envelopes, and I would help him. He wanted to know about everybody.

Dash had the Royal Suite—three very small rooms. And we had to eat there most of the time because we didn't have enough money to eat any place else. It was awful food, almost spoiled. I think Pep bought it extra cheap. But it was the depression and I couldn't get a job. I remember reading the manuscript of *Balso Snell* in the hotel. And I think he was also writing *Lonelyhearts* at that time. Dash was writing *The Thin Man*. The hotel had started out very fancy—it had a swimming pool. I spent a good deal of time in the swimming pool . . . I had nothing else to do with myself.

Then the Perelmans * bought a house in Bucks County. We all went down to see it. There was a dead fish in a closet. I don't know why I remember that fish. Later we would all go down for weekends, to hunt. I have a snapshot of the Perelmans and Dash and me and Pep and Bob Coates.

Even in a fuzzy snapshot you can see that we are all drunk. We used to go hunting. My memory of those hunting trips is of trying to be the last to climb the fence, with the other guns in front of me, just in case. Pep was a good shot. He used to hunt with Faulkner. So was Dash.

INTERVIEWER: Did Faulkner come around a lot in those days?

* S. J. Perelman was West's brother-in-law.

HELLMAN: Faulkner and Dash liked each other. Dash's short stories were selling, the movies were selling. So we had a lot of money, and he gave it away and we lived fine. Always, he gave it away—to the end of his life when there wasn't much, any more. We met every night at some point for months on end, during one of Faulkner's New York visits. We had literary discussions. A constant argument about Thomas Mann. This must have taken up weeks of time.

INTERVIEWER: Was Faulkner quiet?

HELLMAN: He was a gallant man, very Southern. He used to call me Miss Lillian. I never was to see him much after that period, until a few years ago when I saw him a couple of times. We remembered the days with Dash, and he said what a good time in his life that was and what a good time we had had together.

INTERVIEWER: Was any play easy to write?

HELLMAN: *Autumn Garden* was easier than any other.

INTERVIEWER: At the very end of the play, the retired general, Griggs, makes one of the rare speeches in your plays that is of a remotely "philosophic" nature.

HELLMAN: Dash wrote that speech. I worked on it over and over again but it never came right. One night he said, "Go to bed and let me try." Dash comes into this interview very often, doesn't he?

INTERVIEWER: "That big hour of decision, the turning point in your life, the someday you've counted on when you'd suddenly wipe out your past mistakes, do the work you'd never done, think the way you'd never thought, have what you'd never had, it just doesn't come suddenly. You trained yourself for it while you waited —or you've let it all run past you and frittered yourself away."

HELLMAN: Yes, the basic idea was his. Dash was hipped on the subject. I think I believe that speech . . . I know I do. . . . Dash worked at it far harder than I ever have, as his death proved. He wasn't prepared for death, but he was prepared for the trouble and the sickness he had, and was able to bear it—I think, because of this belief—with enormous courage, and quietness.

INTERVIEWER: What is the sensation the writer has when he

hears his own words from the mouth of somebody else? Of even the most gifted actor?

HELLMAN: Sometimes you're pleased and the words take on meanings they didn't have before, larger meanings. But sometimes it is the opposite. There is no rule. I don't have to tell you that speech on the stage is not the speech of life, not even the written speech.

INTERVIEWER: But do you hear dialogue spoken when you are writing it?

HELLMAN: I guess I do. Anyway, I read it to myself. I usually know in the first few days of rehearsals what I have made actors stumble over, and what can or cannot be cured.

INTERVIEWER: Do you have disputes with actors who want their lines changed?

HELLMAN: Not too many. I took a stubborn stand on the first play and now I have a reputation for stubbornness.

INTERVIEWER: Is that because you have written always to be read, even more than to be acted?

HELLMAN: Partly. But I had learned early that in the theater, good or bad, you'd better stand on what you did. In *Candide* I was persuaded to do what I didn't believe in, and I am no good at all at that game. It wasn't that the other people were necessarily wrong, I just couldn't do what they wanted. With age, I guess, I began to want to be agreeable.

INTERVIEWER: Would you mind if your plays were never produced again but only read?

HELLMAN: I wouldn't like it. Plays are there to be acted. I want both.

INTERVIEWER: The famous Hemingway dialogue, the best of it, turns to parody when actors speak it verbatim in adaptations of his work.

HELLMAN: That's right. It shows up, it shows up. That's just what I meant by listening to the actor. Writing for the theater is a totally different form. But then, if you want to be good and hope people will also read the plays, then it becomes a question of making sure the two forms come together. Very often in the printed form, you must recast a sentence. I do it—when I'm not too lazy—for the published version. But in minor ways, like changing the place of a verb, or punctuation. I overpunctuate for theater scripts.

INTERVIEWER: Do you think the political message in some of your plays is more important than the characters and the development?

HELLMAN: I've never been interested in political messages, so it is hard for me to believe I wrote them. Like every other writer, I use myself and the time I live in. The nearest thing to a political play was *The Searching Wind*, which is probably why I don't like it much any more. But even there I meant only to write about nice, well-born people who, with good intentions, helped to sell out a world.

INTERVIEWER: Maybe this was one play in which you were more concerned with a situation of crisis than with your characters?

HELLMAN: Yes. But I didn't know that when I was writing it. I felt very strongly that people had gotten us into a bad situation—gotten us into a war that could have been avoided if fascism had been recognized early enough.

INTERVIEWER: What were you doing in those war years?

HELLMAN: In 1944 I was invited by the Russians to come on a kind of cultural mission. Maybe because they were producing *Watch on the Rhine* and *The Little Foxes* in Moscow.

INTERVIEWER: What were those productions like?

HELLMAN: *The Little Foxes* was an excellent production. *Watch on the Rhine* was very bad. I had thought it would be the other way around. I would go to rehearsals of *Watch on the Rhine* with Serge Eisenstein, and when I made faces or noises, he would say, "Never mind, never mind. It's a good play. Don't pay any attention to what they are doing. They can't ruin it." I saw a great deal of Eisenstein. I was very fond of him.

INTERVIEWER: When did you discover that you could no longer earn money by writing for the movies?

HELLMAN: I learned about the black-listing by accident in 1948. Wyler and I were going to do *Sister Carrie*. Somebody, I think Mr. Balaban, told Wyler that I couldn't be hired. That unwritten, unofficial, powerful black list stayed in effect until two or three years ago.

INTERVIEWER: Weren't you offered clearance if you would sign something? If you made an appropriate act of contrition?

HELLMAN: Later. Shortly after the first black-listing I was offered a contract by Columbia Pictures—a contract that I had always wanted—to direct, produce, and write, all three or any. And a great, great deal of money. But it came at the time of the famous movie conference of top Hollywood producers. They met to face the attacks of the Red-baiters and to appease them down. A new clause went into movie contracts. I no longer remember the legal phrases, but it was a lulu. I didn't sign the contract.

INTERVIEWER: What did you think about what was happening?

HELLMAN: I was so unprepared for it all, so surprised McCarthy was happening in America. So few people fought, so few people spoke out. I think I was more surprised by that than I was by McCarthy.

INTERVIEWER: People in the theater or pictures?

HELLMAN: Yes, and literary people and liberals. Still painful to me, still puzzling. Recently I was asked to sign a protest about Polish writers. I signed it—it was a good protest, I thought—and went out to mail it. But I tore it up when I realized not one of the people protesting had ever protested about any of us.

INTERVIEWER: What did you think was going to happen?

HELLMAN: I thought McCarthy would last longer than he did. I thought the whole period would be worse and longer than it was. You know, I was very worried about Dash. He was a sick man and I was scared that he might go back to prison and get sicker—I lived for a long time in fear that he would go back and not get good medical treatment and be alone and— But jail hadn't worried him much or he pretended it hadn't. It amused him to act as if jail was like college. He talked about going to jail the way people talk about going to college. He used to make me angry. . . .

INTERVIEWER: *The Maltese Falcon* was taken off the shelves of the U.S.I.S. libraries when Roy Cohn and David Schine were riding high. Dashiell Hammett was called before Senator McCarthy's committee.

HELLMAN: Yes. It was on television and I watched it. They called Dash, and Dash was a handsome man, a remarkably handsome man, and he looked nice. One of the senators, I think McCarthy, said to him, "Mr. Hammett, if you were in our position, would you allow your books in U.S.I.S. libraries?" And he said, "If I were you, Senator, I would not allow any libraries." A good remark. McCarthy laughed. Nobody else did, but McCarthy did. Dash had an extremely irritating habit of shrugging his shoulders. For years I would say, "Please don't shrug your shoulders." I don't know why it worried me, but it did. He was shrugging his shoulders like mad at the committee. He'd give an answer, and he'd shrug his shoulders with it. And when he was finished and got to the airport he rang me up and said, "Hey, how did you like it? I was shrugging my shoulders just for you."

INTERVIEWER: Did that period—and its effect on people—appeal to you as a subject?

HELLMAN: I've never known how to do it. It was really a clownish period. It was full of clowns talking their heads off, apologizing, inventing sins to apologize for. And other clowns, liberals, who just took to the hills. Ugly clowning is a hard thing to write about. Few people acted large enough for drama and not pleasant enough for comedy.

INTERVIEWER: Then you went to England to do a movie?

HELLMAN: I used to try to explain that it wasn't as bad as they thought it was. And it wasn't. They were exaggerating it because they don't always like us very much. So much talk about fascism here and how many people were in jail. The only time I ever met Richard Crossman, he didn't know I knew Hammett. Hammett was in jail, and Crossman said what a disgrace that was. "What's the matter with all of you, you don't lift a finger for this man? It couldn't happen here, we'd have raised a row." I told him I had lifted a finger.

INTERVIEWER: Did you ever think of living abroad as other Americans were doing?

HELLMAN: I was tempted to stay in England, but I couldn't. I like this country. This is where I belong. Anyway, I don't much like exiles. But I used to try to persuade Dash to go away, just to save his life. He had emphysema. He caught tuberculosis in the First World War and emphysema in the Second. He had never been to Europe. He used to laugh when I suggested his leaving here. He had a provincial dislike of foreigners, and an amused contempt for Russian bureaucracy. He didn't understand all of our trotting around Europe. Thought it was a waste of time.

INTERVIEWER: Did he laugh at the idea that they admired him over there?

HELLMAN: No. He liked it but it didn't interest him much. When I told him that André Gide admired him, he made a joke which you can't print.

INTERVIEWER: Let's be bold.

HELLMAN: All right. He said, "I wish that fag would take me out of his mouth."

INTERVIEWER: Whom did he want to admire his work?

HELLMAN: Like most writers he wanted to be admired by good writers. He had started off as a pulp writer, you know, and had a wide audience—he wrote a lot for a pulp mystery magazine, *The Black Mask*. But I believe Dash took himself very seriously as a writer from the beginning.

INTERVIEWER: He helped you with your work. Did you help him with his?

HELLMAN: No, no.

INTERVIEWER: Did he show you his novels while he was writing them?

HELLMAN: *The Thin Man* and some stories, and a novel unfinished at his death. The other novels were written before I met him.

INTERVIEWER: But he worked very painstakingly with you, on your work.

HELLMAN: Oh, yes, and was very critical of me. The rules didn't apply the other way. I had many problems writing *The Little Foxes*. When I thought I had got it right, I wanted Dash to read it. It was five o'clock in the morning. I was pleased with this sixth version, and I put the manuscript near his door with a note, "I hope *this* satisfies you." When I got up, the manuscript was outside my door with a note saying, "Things are going pretty well if you will just cut out the liberal blackamoor chitchat."

INTERVIEWER: He meant the Negro servants talking?

HELLMAN: Yes. No other praise, just that.

INTERVIEWER: So you knew you were all right?

HELLMAN: No, I wrote it all over again. He was generous with anybody who asked for help. He felt that you didn't lie about writing and anybody who couldn't take hard words was about to be shrugged off, anyway. He was a dedicated man about writing. Tough and generous.

INTERVIEWER: Was he always reasonably successful?

HELLMAN: Oh, no. He earned a kind of living at first, but pulp magazines didn't pay much. He was not really discovered until shortly before I met him, in 1930. He had been writing for a long time.

INTERVIEWER: He read constantly?

HELLMAN: Enormously. He had little formal education. He quit school at thirteen to work. He was the most widely read person I ever knew. He read anything, just anything. All kinds of science books, farm books, books on making turtle traps, tying knots, novels—he spent almost a year on the retina of the eye. I got very tired of retinas. And there was a period of poisonous plants and Icelandic sagas and how to take the muddy taste from lake bass. I finally made a rule that I would not listen to any more retina-of-the-eye talk or knot talk or baseball talk or football talk.

INTERVIEWER: Do you consider yourself to be closely tied to the theater and to "theater people"?

HELLMAN: In the early days I didn't think it out, but I stayed away from them. I was frightened of competing. I felt that the further I stayed away, the better chance I had. No, I don't know too many theater people.

INTERVIEWER: A man who has known both breeds said that on the whole writers are even more narcissistic and nastier and more competitive than people in show biz.

HELLMAN: Hard to know the more or less. But people in the theater are usually generous with money and often with good will. Maybe the old-troupers world—having to live together and sharing. Writers are interesting people, but often mean and petty. Competing with each other and ungenerous about each other. Hemingway was ungenerous about other writers. Most writers are. Writers can be the stinkers of all time, can't they?

INTERVIEWER: The playwright knows dangers that are different from those the novelists know?

HELLMAN: Yes, because failure is faster in the theater. It is necessary that you not become frightened of failure. Failure in the theater is more dramatic and uglier than in any other form of writing. It costs so much, you feel so guilty. In the production of *Candide*, for the first time in my life, I guess, I was worried by all this. It was bad for me.

INTERVIEWER: Writing about the Lincoln Center Repertory in the *New York Review of Books*, Elizabeth Hardwick said that the trouble with the present theater is that it is all professionalism and is divorced from literature.

HELLMAN: Yes, of course she was right. There shouldn't be any difference between writing for the theater and writing for anything else. Only that one has to know the theater. Know it. To publish a novel or a poem one doesn't have to know print types or the publishing world. But to do a play, no matter how much one wishes to stay away from it, one has to *know* the theater. Playwrights have tried to stay away, including Shaw and Chekhov, but in the end, they were involved. Chekhov used to send letters of instructions and angry notes. A play is not only on paper. It is there to share with actors, directors, scene designers, electricians.

INTERVIEWER: Do you believe there are many talented writers working at present?

HELLMAN: Yes, but nothing like the period when I was very young, in the twenties. That was a wonderfully talented generation, the one before mine. But, you know, I think there's talent around now. Maybe not great talent, but how often does that occur anyway? It is good that we have this much. And there are signs now of cutting up. They are not always to my taste, but that doesn't matter. Cutting up is a form of belief, a negative expression of it, but belief.

INTERVIEWER: The hard professionalism in writers of that generation, like Ring Lardner, Dashiell Hammett, or Dorothy Parker, seems very unfashionable now. Young writers take themselves very seriously as highbrows and artists.

HELLMAN: The writer's intention hasn't anything to do with what he achieves. The intent to earn money or the intent to be famous or the intent to be great doesn't matter in the end. Just what comes out. It is a present fashion to believe that the best writing comes out of a hophead's dream. You pitch it around and paste it up. So sentimental.

INTERVIEWER: Sentimental or romantic?

HELLMAN: Romantic and sentimental. I am surprised, for example, at the sentimentality in much of Genet, and surprised that people are romantic enough not to see its sentimentality. I mean a sentimental way of looking at life, at sex, at love, at the way you live or the way you think. It is interesting that the "way-out" is not the sharpness of a point of view or the toughness, but just tough words and tough actions, masking the romantic. Violence, in space, is a romantic notion. Antibourgeois in an old-fashioned sense.

INTERVIEWER: Philip Rahv said the old idea of *épatisme* is dead. You can no longer scandalize the bourgeois. He may be vicious about defending his property; but as to morality, he is wide open to any and all nihilistic ideas.

HELLMAN: Yes, indeed. He has caught up. That is what words like "the sexual revolution" mean, I guess—the bourgeois sexual revolution. I agree with Philip. "Epataying" is just a sticking out of the tongue now, isn't it? The tongue or other organs.

INTERVIEWER: You have seen a lot of the contemporary theater in Europe. How does it compare with ours?

HELLMAN: The British have more talented young men and women than we have here, but I doubt if they are major talents. Genet and Ionesco are interesting men, but they are not to my taste in the theater. Beckett is the only possibly first-rate talent in the world theater. But he must grow larger, the scale's too small. We don't know much about the Russian theater. Obviously, it hasn't produced good playwrights. Certainly not when I was there. But Russian production, directing, and acting are often wonderful. But that's a dead end. When the major talents are directors, actors, and scene designers—that's dead-end theater. Fine to see, but it ain't going nowhere. You have to turn out good new writers.

INTERVIEWER: What about the revival of Brecht?

HELLMAN: Brecht was the truest talent of the last forty or fifty years. But a great deal of nonsense has been written about Brecht. Brecht himself talked a great deal of nonsense. Deliberately, I think. He was a showman and it is showman-like in the theater to have theories. But that doesn't matter. What a wonderful play *Galileo* is. Writers talk too much.

INTERVIEWER: What do you want to do next?

HELLMAN: I am going to edit that anthology. I had a struggle with myself because Dash would not have wanted it. He didn't want the short stories printed again. But I decided that I was going to have to forget what he wanted. Someday even the second copyrights will expire and the stories will be in public domain. I don't really know why he didn't want them reprinted—maybe because he was too sick to care. It will be a hard job. I have already started the introduction and I find it very difficult to write about so complex a man, and even I knew so little of what he was. I am not sure I can do it in the end, but I am going to have a try. But I don't know his reasons. Probably when you're sick enough you don't care much. He went through a bad time.

JOHN PHILLIPS
ANNE HOLLANDER

May 19, 1952

Honorable John S. Wood
Chairman
House Committee on Un-American Activities

Dear Mr. Wood:

As you know, I am under subpoena to appear before your Committee on May 21, 1952.

I am most willing to answer all questions about myself. I have nothing to hide from your Committee and there is nothing in my life of which I am ashamed. I have been advised by counsel that under the Fifth Amendment I have a constitutional privilege to decline to answer any questions about my political opinions, activities and associations, on the grounds of self-incrimination. I do not wish to claim this privilege. I am ready and willing to testify before representatives of our Government as to my own opinions and my own actions, regardless of any risks or consequences to myself.

But I am advised by counsel that if I answer the Committee's questions about myself, I must also answer questions about other people and that if I refuse to do so, I can be cited for contempt. My counsel tells me that if I answer questions about myself, I will have waived my rights under the Fifth Amendment and could be forced legally to answer questions about others. This is very difficult for a layman to understand. But there is one principle that I do understand: I am not willing, now or in the future, to bring bad trouble to people who, in my past association with them, were completely innocent of any talk or any action that was disloyal or subversive. . . .

But to hurt innocent people whom I knew many years ago in order to save myself is, to me, inhuman and indecent and dishonorable. I cannot and will not cut my conscience to fit this year's fashions, even though I long ago came to the conclusion that I was not a political person and could have no comfortable place in any political group. . . .

I am prepared to waive the privilege against self-incrimination and to tell you anything you wish to know about my views or actions if your Committee will agree to refrain from asking me to name other people. If the Committee is unwilling to give me this assurance, I will be forced to plead the privilege of the Fifth Amendment at the hearing.

A reply to this letter would be appreciated.

Sincerely yours,
LILLIAN HELLMAN

7. William Burroughs

William Burroughs was born into a wealthy family in Saint Louis on February 5, 1914. He was graduated from Harvard, traveled widely in Europe, then returned to the United States, and worked at varied occupations—among them detective work, pest exterminating, and bartending. He has lived in Mexico, Tangier, London, and Paris.

His first book (published under the pseudonym Will Lee) was *Junkie: Confessions of an Unredeemed Drug Addict* (1953). Burroughs's best-known work is *Naked Lunch* (1959), which Robert Lowell called "a completely powerful and serious book, as good as anything in prose or poetry by a beat writer and one of the most alive books written by any American for years." Mary McCarthy described him as "the writer of the century who has most deeply affected the literary *cognoscenti*." Norman Mailer considers him the "only American novelist living today who may conceivably be possessed by genius." Burroughs's other works include *The Exterminator* (with Byron Gysin—1960), *The Soft Machine* (1961), *The Ticket That Exploded* (1962), *The Yage Letters* (with Allen Ginsberg—1963), and *Nova Express* (1964).

Much attention has been given to Burroughs's efforts to apply to his writing the most advanced techniques of painting, music, and film. Marshall McLuhan finds him unique in that "he is attempting to reproduce in prose what we accommodate every day as a commonplace aspect of life in the electric age."

Burroughs in Paris, 1960 (Photo: Charles Henri Ford)

William Burroughs

Firecrackers and whistles sounded the advent of the New Year of 1965 in Saint Louis, and stripteasers ran from the bars in Gaslight Square to dance in the street when midnight came. William Seward Burroughs III, who had watched television alone that night, was asleep in his room at the Chase-Park Plaza Hotel, Saint Louis's most elegant. After an absence of twenty years, he had returned to his birthplace from Tangier.

At noon the next day he was ready for the interview. He wore a gray lightweight Brooks Brothers suit with vest, a blue-striped shirt from Gibraltar cut in the English style, and a deep-blue tie with small white polka dots. His manner was not so much pedagogic as didactic or forensic. He might have been a senior partner in a private bank, charting the course of huge but anonymous fortunes. A friend of the interviewer, spotting him across the lobby, thought he was a British diplomat. At the age of fifty, he is trim; he performs a complex abdominal exercise daily and walks a good deal. His face carries no excess flesh. His expression is taut, and his features are intense and chiseled. He did not smile during the interview and laughed only once, but he gives the impression of being capable of much dry laughter under other circumstances. His voice is sonorous, its tone reasonable and patient; his accent is mid-Atlantic, the kind of regionless inflection Americans acquire after many years abroad. He speaks elliptically, in short, clear bursts.

On the dresser of his room sat a European transistor radio, several science-fiction paperbacks, and Romance *by Joseph Conrad,* The Day Lincoln Was Shot *by Jim Bishop, and* Ghosts in American Houses *by James Reynolds. A Zeiss Ikon camera in a scuffed leather case lay on one of the twin beds beside a copy of* Field & Stream. *On the other bed were a pair of long shears, clippings from*

*newspaper society pages, photographs, and a scrapbook on which
he had been working when the interviewer arrived. He had begun
three scrapbooks several months earlier in Tangier. They consisted
of typed material, photographs, and printed matter en collage in
French ledger books. One was devoted to Gibraltar and the other
two to general subjects. A Facit portable typewriter sat on the desk,
and gradually one became aware that the room, although neat,
contained a great deal of paper.*

*After a brief discussion of the use of the tape recorder to prepare
cut-up interviews, he settled in a chair next to a window. He smoked
incessantly, alternating between a box of English Ovals and a box
of Benson & Hedges. As the interview progressed, the room filled
with smoke. He opened the window. The temperature outside was
seventy degrees, the warmest New Year's Day in Saint Louis history; a yellow jacket flew in and settled on the pane. The twelfth-
story room overlooked the ample roofs of the houses on a series of
private streets with gates at both ends, once the most substantial
neighborhood in Saint Louis. In one of these homes, at 4664 Per-
shing Avenue, he had been born. The bright afternoon deepened.
The faint cries of children rose up from the broad brick alleys in
which he had played as a boy.*

INTERVIEWER: You grew up here?

BURROUGHS: Yes. I went to John Burroughs School and the Taylor School, and was out West for a bit, and then went to Harvard.

INTERVIEWER: Any relation to the adding-machine firm?

BURROUGHS: My grandfather. You see, he didn't exactly invent
the adding machine, but he invented the gimmick that made it
work—namely, a cylinder full of oil and a perforated piston that
will always move up and down at the same rate of speed. Very
simple principle, like most inventions. And it gave me a little
money, not much, but a little.

INTERVIEWER: What did you do at Harvard?

BURROUGHS: Studied English Lit. John Livingston Lowes. Whit-
ing. I sat in on Kittredge's course. Those are the main people I

recall. I lived in Adams House and then I got fed up with the food and I moved to Claverly Hall, where I lived the last two years. I didn't do any writing in college.

INTERVIEWER: When and why did you start to write?

BURROUGHS: I started to write about 1950; I was thirty-five at the time; there didn't seem to be any strong motivation. I simply was endeavoring to put down in a more-or-less straightforward journalistic style something about my experiences with addiction and addicts.

INTERVIEWER: Why did you feel compelled to record these experiences?

BURROUGHS: I didn't feel compelled. I had nothing else to do. Writing gave me something to do every day. I don't feel the results were at all spectacular. *Junkie* is not much of a book, actually. I knew very little about writing at that time.

INTERVIEWER: Where was this?

BURROUGHS: In Mexico City. I was living near Sears, Roebuck, right around the corner from the University of Mexico. I had been in the army four or five months and I was there on the G.I. Bill, studying native dialects. I went to Mexico partly because things were becoming so difficult with the drug situation in America. Getting drugs in Mexico was quite easy, so I didn't have to rush around, and there wasn't any pressure from the law.

INTERVIEWER: Why did you start taking drugs?

BURROUGHS: Well, I was just bored. I didn't seem to have much interest in becoming a successful advertising executive or whatever, or living the kind of life Harvard designs for you. After I became addicted in New York in 1944, things began to happen. I got in some trouble with the law, got married, moved to New Orleans and then went to Mexico.

INTERVIEWER: There seems to be a great deal of middle-class voyeurism in this country concerning addiction, and in the literary world, downright reverence for the addict. You apparently don't share these points of view.

BURROUGHS: No, most of it is nonsense. I think drugs are interesting principally as chemical means of altering metabolism and thereby altering what we call reality, which I would define as a more-or-less constant scanning pattern.

INTERVIEWER: What do you think of the hallucinogens and the new psychedelic drugs—LSD-25?

BURROUGHS: I think they're extremely dangerous, much more dangerous than heroin. They can produce overwhelming anxiety states. I've seen people try to throw themselves out of windows, whereas the heroin addict is mainly interested in staring at his own toe. Other than deprivation of the drug, the main threat to him is an overdose. I've tried most of the hallucinogens, without an anxiety reaction, fortunately. LSD-25 produced results for me similar to mescaline. Like all hallucinogens, LSD gave me an increased awareness, more a hallucinated viewpoint than any actual hallucination. You might look at a doorknob and it will appear to revolve, although you are conscious that this is the result of the drug. Also, Van Goghish colors, with all those swirls, and the crackle of the universe.

INTERVIEWER: Have you read Henri Michaux's book on mescaline?

BURROUGHS: His idea was to go into his room and close the door and hold in the experiences. I had my most interesting experiences with mescaline when I got outdoors and walked around—colors, sunsets, gardens. It produces a terrible hangover, though, nasty stuff. It makes one ill and interferes with coordination. I've had all the interesting effects I need, and I don't want any repetition of those extremely unpleasant physical reactions.

INTERVIEWER: The visions of drugs and the visions of art don't mix?

BURROUGHS: Never. The hallucinogens produce visionary states, sort of, but morphine and its derivatives decrease awareness of inner processes, thoughts and feelings. They are painkillers, pure and simple. They are absolutely contra-indicated for creative work, and I include in the lot alcohol, morphine, barbiturates, tranquilizers—the whole spectrum of sedative drugs. As for visions and heroin, I had a hallucinatory period at the very beginning of addiction, for instance, a sense of moving at high speed through space, but as soon as addiction was established, I had no visions—vision—at all and very few dreams.

INTERVIEWER: Why did you stop taking drugs?

BURROUGHS: I was living in Tangier in 1957, and I had spent a month in a tiny room in the Casbah staring at the toe of my foot. The room had filled up with empty Eukodol cartons; I suddenly realized I was not doing *anything*. I was dying. I was just apt to be finished. So I flew to London and turned myself over to Dr. John Yerbury Dent for treatment. I'd heard of his success with the apomorphine treatment. Apomorphine is simply morphine boiled in hydrochloric acid; it's nonaddicting. What the apomorphine did was to regulate my metabolism. It's a metabolic regulator. It cured me physiologically. I'd already taken the cure once at Lexington, and although I was off drugs when I got out, there was a physiological residue. Apomorphine eliminated that. I've been trying to get people in this country interested in it, but without much luck. The vast majority—social workers, doctors—have the cop's mentality toward addiction. A probation officer in California wrote me recently to inquire about the apomorphine treatment. I'll answer him at length. I always answer letters like that.

INTERVIEWER: Have you had any relapses?

BURROUGHS: Yes, a couple. Short. Both were straightened out with apomorphine and now heroin is no temptation for me. I'm just not interested. I've seen a lot of it around. I know people who are addicts. I don't have to use any will power. Dr. Dent always said there is no such thing as will power. You've got to reach a state of mind in which you don't want it or need it.

INTERVIEWER: You regard addiction as an illness, but also a central human fact, a drama?

BURROUGHS: Both, absolutely. It's as simple as the way in which anyone happens to become an alcoholic. They start drinking, that's all. They like it, and they drink, and then they become alcoholic. I was exposed to heroin in New York—that is, I was going around with people who were using it; I took it; the effects were pleasant. I went on using it and became addicted. Remember that if it can be readily obtained, you will have any number of addicts. The idea that addiction is somehow a psychological illness is, I think, totally ridiculous. It's as psychological as malaria. It's a matter of exposure. People, generally speaking, will take any intoxicant or any drug that gives them a pleasant effect if it is available to them. In Iran, for instance, opium was sold in shops until quite recently, and they had three million addicts in a population of twenty million. There are also all forms of spiritual addiction. Anything that can be done chemically can be done in other ways—that is, if we have sufficient knowledge of the processes involved. Many policemen and narcotics agents are precisely addicted to power, to exercising a certain nasty kind of power over people who are helpless. The nasty sort of power: white junk I call it—rightness; they're right, right, right—and if they lost that power, they would suffer excruciating withdrawal symptoms. The picture we get of the whole Russian bureaucracy, people who are exclusively preoccupied with power and advantage, this must be an addiction. Suppose they lose it? Well, it's been their whole life.

INTERVIEWER: Can you amplify your idea of junk as image?

BURROUGHS: It's only a theory and, I feel, an inadequate one. I don't think anyone really understands what a narcotic is or how it works, how it kills pain. My idea is sort of a stab in the dark. As I see it, what has been damaged in pain is, of course, the image, and morphine must in some sense replace this. We know it blankets the cells and that addicts are practically immune to certain viruses, to influenza and respiratory complaints. This is simple, because the influenza virus has to make a hole in the cell receptors. When those are covered, as they are in morphine addiction, the virus can't get in. As soon as morphine is withdrawn, addicts will immediately come down with colds and often with influenza.

INTERVIEWER: Certain schizophrenics also resist respiratory disease.

BURROUGHS: A long time ago I suggested there were similarities in terminal addiction and terminal schizophrenia. That was why I made the suggestion that they addict these people to heroin, then withdraw it and see if they could be motivated; in other words, find out whether they'd walk across the room and pick up a syringe. Needless to say, I didn't get very far, but I think it would be interesting.

INTERVIEWER: Narcotics, then, disturb normal perception—

BURROUGHS:—and set up instead a random craving for images. If drugs weren't forbidden in America, they would be the perfect middle-class vice. Addicts would do their work and come home to consume the huge dose of images awaiting them in the mass media. Junkies love to look at television. Billie Holiday said she knew she was going off drugs when she didn't like to watch TV. Or they'll sit and read a newspaper or magazine, and by God, read it all. I knew this old junkie in New York, and he'd go out and get a lot of newspapers and magazines and some candy bars and several packages of cigarettes and then he'd sit in his room and he'd read those newspapers and magazines right straight through. Indiscriminately. Every word.

INTERVIEWER: You seem primarily interested in bypassing the conscious, rational apparatus to which most writers direct their efforts.

BURROUGHS: I don't know about where fiction ordinarily directs itself, but I am quite deliberately addressing myself to the whole area of what we call dreams. Precisely what is a dream? A certain juxtaposition of word and image. I've recently done a lot of experiments with scrapbooks. I'll read in the newspaper something that reminds me of or has relation to something I've written. I'll cut out the picture or article and paste it in a scrapbook beside the words from my book. Or, I'll be walking down the street and I'll suddenly see a scene from my book and I'll photograph it and put it in a scrapbook. I'll show you some of those.* I've found that when preparing a page, I'll almost invariably dream that night something re-

* See pages 151, 152, 155.

lating to this juxtaposition of word and image. In other words, I've been interested in precisely how word and image get around on very, very complex association lines. I do a lot of exercises in what I call time travel, in taking coordinates, such as what I photographed on the train, what I was thinking about at the time, what I was reading and what I wrote; all of this to see how completely I can project myself back to that one point in time.

INTERVIEWER: In *Nova Express* you indicate that silence is a desirable state.

BURROUGHS: The *most* desirable state. In one sense a special use of words and pictures can conduce silence. The scrapbooks and time travel are exercises to expand consciousness, to teach me to think in association blocks rather than words. I've recently spent a little time studying hieroglyph systems, both the Egyptian and the Mayan. A whole block of associations—boonf!—like that! Words—at least the way we use them—can stand in the way of what I call nonbody experience. It's time we thought about leaving the body behind.

INTERVIEWER: Marshall McLuhan said that you believed heroin was needed to turn the human body into an environment that includes the universe. But from what you've told me, you're not at all interested in turning the body into an environment.

BURROUGHS: No, junk narrows consciousness. The only benefit to me as a writer (aside from putting me into contact with the whole carny world) came to me after I went off it. What I want to do is to learn to see more of what's out there, to look outside, to achieve as far as possible a complete awareness of surroundings. Beckett wants to go inward. First he was in a bottle and now he is in the mud. I am aimed in the other direction: outward.

INTERVIEWER: Have you been able to think for any length of time in images, with the inner voice silent?

BURROUGHS: I'm becoming more proficient at it, partly through my work with scrapbooks and translating the connections between words and images. Try this: Carefully memorize the meaning of a passage, then read it; you'll find you can actually read it without

From the address book and memory of Mr. Rives Matthews of St. Louis Mo. and Tangier Morocco.

PHOTOGRAPHS BY
WALTER WIRTHLIN

Happy New year Comte
Hector Perrone de San
Martine Mrs Edge at home
last Thursday in May
Fete Dieu,Principe de
La Tour,Gentilhomo di
Palazzo,your a long
way from St.Louis..I
had not thought death
has undone so many..

Richard Halliburton,Tommy
Elliot this music on the
waters (off stage the
Vieled Prophet Ball in
St.Louis..Clock ticking
away to a Victorian house

UNDER
3
FLAGS.

DESIGNED IN AMERICA

NORCROSS

A. REPORTER

Page from Burroughs' St. Louis journal

ESPAÑA
Sucesos

son cuatro los militares muertos, Hubo cuatro muertos

you are reading the fut-
ure on (5) formulae (6) to
record in writing our worn
out film dim jerky far
away. You will see days
run backwards again in
four days like the train
did. distant band couldn't
time guesses to the last
broadcast. Record in the
history of the radio you
are reading the future fro
me today arrange a meet-
ing for four well known
people home by train.

The NOVA EXPRESS

place dim jerky far away the
dorm playground 1920 ponda in
vacant lots adios marks this
long ago MEMORY address the
porch noise home from work used
to be me Mister mouth and nose

By train

Lighthouse keeper as I am in
a policeman's bed sitter record
in the history of radio you
are reading the future from me
today arrange a meeting for
four well known people home by
train Mr. and Mrs. Mortimer
Burroughs and their two sons
sons Mortimer Jr. and William
Seward Burroughs of 4664 Berlin

Page from Burroughs' St. Louis journal

the words' making any sound whatever in the mind's ear. Extraordinary experience, and one that will carry over into dreams. When you start thinking in images, without words, you're well on the way.

INTERVIEWER: Why is the wordless state so desirable?

BURROUGHS: I think it's the evolutionary trend. I think that words are an around-the-world, ox-cart way of doing things, awkward instruments, and they will be laid aside eventually, probably sooner than we think. This is something that will happen in the space age. Most serious writers refuse to make themselves available to the things that technology is doing. I've never been able to understand this sort of fear. Many of them are afraid of tape recorders and the idea of using any mechanical means for literary purposes seems to them some sort of a sacrilege. This is one objection to the cutups. There's been a lot of that, a sort of a superstitious reverence for the word. My God, they say, you can't cut up these words. Why *can't* I? I find it much easier to get interest in the cutups from people who are not writers—doctors, lawyers, or engineers, any open-minded, fairly intelligent person—than from those who are.

INTERVIEWER: How did you become interested in the cutup technique?

BURROUGHS: A friend, Brion Gysin, an American poet and painter, who has lived in Europe for thirty years, was, as far as I know, the first to create cutups. His cutup poem, "Minutes to Go," was broadcast by the BBC and later published in a pamphlet. I was in Paris in the summer of 1960; this was after the publication there of *Naked Lunch*. I became interested in the possibilities of this technique, and I began experimenting myself. Of course, when you think of it, "The Waste Land" was the first great cutup collage, and Tristan Tzara had done a bit along the same lines. Dos Passos used the same idea in "The Camera Eye" sequences in *U.S.A.* I felt I had been working toward the same goal; thus it was a major revelation to me when I actually saw it being done.

INTERVIEWER: What do cutups offer the reader that conventional narrative doesn't? .

BURROUGHS: Any narrative passage or any passage, say, of poetic images is subject to any number of variations, all of which may be interesting and valid in their own right. A page of Rimbaud cut up and rearranged will give you quite new images. Rimbaud images —real Rimbaud images—but new ones.

INTERVIEWER: You deplore the accumulation of images and at the same time you seem to be looking for new ones.

BURROUGHS: Yes, it's part of the paradox of anyone who is working with word and image, and after all, that is what a writer is still doing. Painter too. Cutups establish new connections between images, and one's range of vision consequently expands.

INTERVIEWER: Instead of going to the trouble of working with scissors and all those pieces of paper, couldn't you obtain the same effect by simply free-associating at the typewriter?

BURROUGHS: One's mind can't cover it that way. Now, for example, if I wanted to make a cutup of this [*picking up a copy of the* Nation], there are many ways I could do it. I could read crosscolumn; I could say: "Today's men's nerves surround us. Each technological extension gone outside is electrical involves an act of collective environment. The human nervous environment system itself can be reprogrammed with all its private and social values because it is content. He programs logically as readily as any radio net is swallowed by the new environment. The sensory order." You find it often makes quite as much sense as the original. You learn to leave out words and to make connections. [*Gesturing*] Suppose I should cut this down the middle here, and put this up here. Your mind simply could not manage it. It's like trying to keep so many chess moves in mind, you just couldn't do it. The mental mechanisms of repression and selection are also operating against you.

INTERVIEWER: You believe that an audience can be eventually trained to respond to cutups?

BURROUGHS: Of course, because cutups make explicit a psycho-

REGISTER C··ELVE·RD

1 2 3 4 5 6 7 8

REPORTS

Some displacements of a sedate and celebrated rose garden but ideal for the processes of a quiet riverview restaurant—

THREE FLAGS Interstate 70 & 5th St. in St. Charles on the banks of the Missouri. An all-glassed-in room overlooks the river. Featuring American, Spanish and French Foods. RA 3-0330.

Best Wishes on Your Retirement

| 1 | 2 | 3 |

What in Horton Hotel Rue
Vernet Gen-San Martine
Zapiola The Swan Last Day
de Cobo Principe di Castel
Hose it Chicale von Koepen
Countess Gay Gudewill
Count Randy Anne Fuzz Rose
Mary Griesedick Wieled
Miguel Garcia de Gordon
Hell does that mean?????
On the scene photographs
by William Born Field
Retarded Children Project
Inc Famous Barr Post St.
Louis Magasine 52 just
outside the barbecue corr
all mes cheries Guggenheim
Theresa Riley Nance Roger
sponsored from top to
bottom excitingly randy
young St.Louis citizen's
Bicentennial salute :

(His Eminence John,all mes
cheries Guggenheim,St.Loui
Louis Cardinal Designate
Glennon Theresa Riley
Nance Roger **thanks** for
you gracious (sponsored
from top) ticking message
looked 8 minutes **bottom**
excitedly randy Victorian
younger with such hair
to too two young St.Louis
citizens gay happy goats
and monkey's XXXXXXXXXX
bicentennial salute randy
at home,
Miguel de Gorden waters
last Thursday in Hell
(does that mean off
stage Fete Dieu,Principe
di Hell on the scene
photographs The Swan
La Tour??) William born
last day field,your a long
retarded children project
vieled way from St.Louis.
I Inc, Famous Barr Post St.
Prophet had not thought

4

Richard
Halliburt
what in
Hotel rue
Elliot
this music
on the
Martine
waters
(off stage
The Swan
Last Day)
vieled
phophet
in di
castle
St.Louis
clock
ticking
Victorian
gay happy
randy at
home

Meet me in
the shooting
gallery/hick/
Quiet the
roses/hick/
Ship scenes
necessary/
hick/
Signed

Death Magasine 52 had
undone so many outside the
barbecue Castle

tharnks for your gracious
message..looked 8 minutes
younger with such hair too
goats and monkeys

A REPORTER

Page from Burroughs' St. Louis journal

sensory process that is going on all the time anyway. Somebody is reading a newspaper, and his eye follows the column in the proper Aristotelian manner, one idea and sentence at a time. But subliminally he is reading the columns on either side and is aware of the person sitting next to him. That's a cutup. I was sitting in a lunchroom in New York having my doughnuts and coffee. I was thinking that one *does* feel a little boxed in New York, like living in a series of boxes. I looked out the window and there was a great big Yale truck. That's cutup—a juxtaposition of what's happening outside and what you're thinking of. I make this a practice when I walk down the street. I'll say, When I got to here I saw that sign, I was thinking this, and when I return to the house I'll type these up. Some of this material I use and some I don't. I have literally thousands of pages of notes here, raw, and I keep a diary as well. In a sense it's traveling in time.

Most people don't see what's going on around them. That's my principal message to writers: For Godsake, keep your *eyes* open. Notice what's going on around you. I mean, I walk down the street with friends. I ask, "Did you see him, that person who just walked by?" No, they didn't notice him. I had a very pleasant time on the train coming out here. I haven't traveled on trains in years. I found there were no drawing rooms. I got a bedroom so I could set up my typewriter and look out the window. I was taking photos, too. I also noticed all the signs and what I was thinking at the time, you see. And I got some extraordinary juxtapositions. For example, a friend of mine has a loft apartment in New York. He said, "Every time we go out of the house and come back, if we leave the bathroom door open, there's a rat in the house." I look out the window, there's Able Pest Control.

INTERVIEWER: The one flaw in the cutup argument seems to lie in the linguistic base on which we operate, the straight declarative sentence. It's going to take a great deal to change that.

BURROUGHS: Yes, it is unfortunately one of the great errors of Western thought, the whole either-or proposition. You remember Korzybski and his idea of non-Aristotelian logic. Either-or thinking just is not accurate thinking. That's not the way things occur, and I feel the Aristotelian construct is one of the great shackles of Western civilization. Cutups are a movement toward breaking this down. I should imagine it would be much easier to find acceptance of the cutups from, possibly, the Chinese, because you see already there are many ways that they can read any given ideograph. It's already cut up.

INTERVIEWER: What will happen to the straight plot in fiction?

BURROUGHS: Plot has always had the definite function of stage direction, of getting the characters from here to there, and that will continue, but the new techniques, such as cutup, will involve much more of the total capacity of the observer. It enriches the whole aesthetic experience, extends it.

INTERVIEWER: *Nova Express* is a cutup of many writers?

BURROUGHS: Joyce is in there. Shakespeare, Rimbaud, some writers that people haven't heard about, someone named Jack Stern. There's Kerouac. I don't know, when you start making these foldins and cutups you lose track. Genet, of course, is someone I admire very much. But what he's doing is classical French prose. He's not a verbal innovator. Also Kafka, Eliot, and one of my favorites is Joseph Conrad. My story, "They Just Fade Away," is a foldin (instead of cutting, you fold) from *Lord Jim*. In fact, it's almost a retelling of the *Lord Jim* story. My Stein is the same Stein as in *Lord Jim*. Richard Hughes is another favorite of mine. And Graham Greene. For exercise, when I make a trip, such as from Tangier to Gibraltar, I will record this in three columns in a notebook I always take with me. One column will contain simply an account of the trip, what happened: I arrived at the air terminal, what was said by the clerks, what I overheard on the plane, what hotel I checked into. The next column presents my memories: that is, what I was thinking of at the time, the memories that were activated by my encounters. And the third column, which I call my reading column, gives quotations from any book that I take with me. I have practically a whole novel alone on my trips to Gibraltar. Besides Graham Greene, I've used other books. I used *The Wonderful Country* by Tom Lea on one trip. Let's see . . . and Eliot's *The Cocktail Party*; *In Hazard* by Richard Hughes. For example, I'm reading *The Wonderful Country* and the hero is just crossing the frontier into Mexico. Well, just at this point I come to the Spanish frontier, so I note that down in the margin. Or I'm on a boat or a train and I'm reading *The Quiet American*; I look around and see if there's a quiet American aboard. Sure enough, there's a quiet sort of young American with a crew cut, drinking a bottle of beer. It's extraordinary, if you really keep your eyes open. I was reading Raymond Chandler, and one of his characters was an albino gunman. My God, if there wasn't an albino in the room. He wasn't a gunman.

Who else? Wait a minute, I'll just check my coordinate books to see if there's anyone I've forgotten—Conrad, Richard Hughes, science fiction, quite a bit of science fiction. Eric Frank Russell has written some very, very interesting books. Here's one, *The Star Virus*; I doubt if you've heard of it. He develops a concept here of what he calls Deadliners who have this strange sort of seedy look. I read this when I was in Gibraltar, and I began to find Deadliners all over the place. The story has a fish pond in it, and quite a flower garden. My father was always very interested in gardening.

INTERVIEWER: In view of all this, what will happen to fiction in the next twenty-five years?

BURROUGHS: In the first place, I think there's going to be more and more merging of art and science. Scientists are already studying the creative process, and I think the whole line between art and science will break down and that scientists, I hope, will become more creative and writers more scientific. And I see no reason why the artistic world can't absolutely merge with Madison Avenue. Pop art is a move in that direction. Why can't we have advertisements with beautiful words and beautiful images? Already some of the very beautiful color photography appears in

whisky ads, I notice. Science will also discover for us how association blocks actually form.

INTERVIEWER: Do you think this will destroy the magic?

BURROUGHS: Not at all. I would say it would enhance it.

INTERVIEWER: Have you done anything with computers?

BURROUGHS: I've not done anything, but I've seen some of the
computer poetry. I can take one of those computer poems and
then try to find correlatives of it—that is, pictures to go with it;
it's quite possible.

INTERVIEWER: Does the fact that it comes from a machine
diminish its value to you?

BURROUGHS: I think that any artistic product must stand or
fall on what's there.

INTERVIEWER: Therefore, you're not upset by the fact that a
chimpanzee can do an abstract painting?

BURROUGHS: If he does a good one, no. People say to me, "Oh,
this is all very good, but you got it by cutting up." I say that has
nothing to do with it, how I got it. What is any writing but a
cutup? Somebody has to program the machine; somebody has to
do the cutting up. Remember that I first made selections. Out
of hundreds of possible sentences that I might have used, I chose
one.

INTERVIEWER: Incidentally, one image in *Nova Express* keeps
coming back to me and I don't quite understand it: the gray room,
"breaking through to the gray room."

BURROUGHS: I see that as very much like the photographic darkroom where the reality photographs are actually produced. Implicit
in *Nova Express* is a theory that what we call reality is actually a
movie. It's a film—what I call a biologic film. What has happened
is that the underground and also the nova police have made a
break-through past the guards and gotten into the darkroom where
the films are processed, where they're in a position to expose nega-
tives and prevent events from occurring. They're like police anywhere. All right, you've got a bad situation here in which the nova

mob is about to blow up the planet. So the Heavy Metal Kid calls in the nova police. Once you get them in there, by God, they begin acting like any police. They're always an ambivalent agency. I recall once in South America that I complained to the police that a camera had been stolen and they ended up arresting me. I hadn't registered or something. In other words, once you get them on the scene they really start nosing around. Once the law starts asking questions, there's no end to it. For "nova police," read "technology," if you wish.

INTERVIEWER: Mary McCarthy has commented on the carnival origins of your characters in *Naked Lunch*. What are their other derivations?

BURROUGHS: The carny world was the one I exactly intended to create—a kind of Midwestern, small-town, cracker-barrel, pratfall type of folklore, very much my own background. That world was an integral part of America and existed nowhere else, at least not in the same form. My family was Southern on my mother's side. My grandfather was a circuit-riding Methodist minister with thirteen children. Most of them went up to New York and became quite successful in advertising and public relations. One of them, an uncle, was a master image-maker, Ivy Lee, Rockefeller's publicity manager.

INTERVIEWER: Is it true that you did a great deal of acting out to create your characters when you were finishing *Naked Lunch*?

BURROUGHS: Excuse me, there is no accurate description of the creation of a book, or an event. Read Durrell's "Alexandria" novels for four different ways of looking at the same thing. Gysin saw me pasting pictures on the wall of a Paris hotel room and using a tape recorder to act out several voices. Actually, it was written mainly in Tangier, after I had taken the cure with Dr. Dent in London in 1957. I came back to Tangier and I started working on a lot of notes that I had made over a period of years. Most of the book was written at that time. I went to Paris about 1959, and I had a great pile of manuscripts. Girodias was interested, and he asked if I could get the book ready in two weeks. This is the period that Brion is referring to when, from manuscripts collected over a period of years, I assembled what became the book from some thousand pages, something like that.

INTERVIEWER: But did you actually leap up and act out, say, Dr. Benway?

BURROUGHS: Yes, I have. Dr. Benway dates back to a story I wrote in 1938 with a friend of mine, Kells Elvins, who is now dead. That's about the only piece of writing I did prior to *Junkie*. And we did definitely act the thing out. We decided that was the way to write. Now here's this guy, what does he say, what does he do? Dr. Benway sort of emerged quite spontaneously while we were composing this piece. Something I've been meaning to do with my scrapbooks is to have files on every character, almost like police files: habits, idiosyncrasies, where born, pictures. That is, if I ever see anyone in a magazine or newspaper who looks like Dr. Benway (and several people have played Dr. Benway, sort of amateur actors), I take their photographs. Many of my characters first come through strongly to me as voices. That's why I use a tape recorder. They also carry over from one book to another.

INTERVIEWER: Do any have their origins in actual persons?

BURROUGHS: Hamburger Mary is one. There was a place in New York called Hamburger Mary's. I was in Hamburger Mary's when a friend gave me a batch of morphine syrettes. That was my first experience with morphine, and then I built up a whole picture of Hamburger Mary. She is also an actual person. I don't like to give her name for fear of being sued for libel, but she was a Scientologist who started out in a hamburger joint in Portland, Oregon, and now has eleven million dollars.

INTERVIEWER: What about the Heavy Metal Kid?

BURROUGHS: There again, quite complicated origins, partly based on my own experience. I felt that heavy metal was sort of the ultimate expression of addiction, that there's something actually metallic in addiction, that the final stage reached is not so much vegetable as mineral. It's increasingly inanimate, in any case. You see, as Dr. Benway said, I've now decided that junk is not green, but blue. Some of my characters come to me in dreams, Daddy Long Legs, for instance. Once, in a clinic, I had a dream in which I saw a man in this run-down clinic and his name in the dream was Daddy Long Legs. Many characters have come to me like that in a dream, and then I'll elaborate from there. I always write down all my dreams. That's why I've got that notebook beside the bed there.

INTERVIEWER: Earlier you mentioned that if junk had done nothing else, it at least put you in contact with the carny world.

BURROUGHS: Yes, the underworld, the old-time thieves, pickpockets, and people like that. They're a dying race; very few of those old-timers left. Yeah, well, they were show business.

INTERVIEWER: What's the difference between the modern junkie and the 1944 junkie?

BURROUGHS: For one thing, all these young addicts; that was quite unknown in 1944. Most of the ones I knew were middle-aged men or old. I knew some of the old-time pickpockets and sneak thieves and short-change artists. They had something called The Bill, a short-change deal. I've never been able to figure out how it works. One man I knew beat all the cashiers in Grand Central with this thing. It starts with a twenty-dollar bill. You give them a twenty-dollar bill and then when you get the change you say, "Well, wait a minute, I must have been dreaming, I've got the change after all." First thing you know, the cashier's short ten dollars. One day this short-change artist went to Grand Central, even though he knew it was burned down, but he wanted to change twenty dollars. Well, a guy got on the buzzer, and they arrested him. When they got up in court and tried to explain what had happened, none of them could do it. I keep stories like this in my files.

INTERVIEWER: In your apartment in Tangier?

BURROUGHS: No, all of it is right here in this room.

INTERVIEWER: In case Tangier is blown up, it's all safe?

BURROUGHS: Well, more than that. *I need it all.* I brought everything. That's why I have to travel by boat and by train, because, well, just to give you an idea, that's a photographic file. [*Thud*]

Those are all photographs and photographs. When I sit down to write, I may suddenly think of something I wrote three years ago which should be in this file over here. It may not be. I'm always looking through these files. That's why I need a place where I can really spread them out, to see what's what. I'm looking for one particular paper, it often takes me a long time and sometimes I don't find it. Those dresser drawers are full of files. All those drawers in the closets are full of files. It's pretty well organized. Here's a file, THE 1920 MOVIE, which partly contains some motion picture ideas. Here's ALL THE SAD OLD SHOWMEN; has some business about bank robbers in it. Here's THE NOVA POLICE GAZETTE. This is ANALOG, which contains science-fiction material. This is THE CAPTAIN'S LOGBOOK. I've been interested in sea stories, but I know so little about the sea, I hesitate to do much. I collect sea disasters such as the *Mary Celeste*. Here's a file on Mr. Luce.

INTERVIEWER: Do you admire Mr. Luce?

BURROUGHS: I don't admire him at all. He has set up one of the greatest word-and-image banks in the world. I mean, there are thousands of photos, thousands of words about anything and everything, all in his files. All the best pictures go into the files. Of course, they're reduced to microphotos now. I've been interested in the Mayan system, which was a control calendar. You see, their calendar postulated really how everyone should feel at a given time, with lucky days, unlucky days, et cetera. And I feel that Luce's system is comparable to that. It is a control system. It has nothing to do with reporting. *Time-Life-Fortune* is some sort of a police organization.

INTERVIEWER: You've said your next book will be about the American West and a gunfighter.

BURROUGHS: Yes, I've thought about this for years and I have hundreds of pages of notes on the whole concept of the gunfighter. The gun duel was a sort of Zen contest, a real spiritual contest like Zen swordsmanship.

INTERVIEWER: Would this be cutup, or more a conventional narrative?

BURROUGHS: I'd use cutups extensively in the preparation, because they would give me all sorts of facets of character and place, but the final version would be straight narrative. I wouldn't want to get bogged down in too much factual detail, but I'd like to do research in New Mexico or Arizona, even though the actual towns out there have become synthetic tourist attractions. Occasionally I have the sensation that I'm repeating myself in my work, and I would like to do something different—almost a deliberate change of style. I'm not sure if it's possible, but I want to try. I've been thinking about the western for years. As a boy, I was sent to school in New Mexico, and during the war I was stationed in Coldspring, Texas, near Conroe. That's genuine backwoods country, and I picked up some real characters there. For instance, a fellow who actually lived in east Texas. He was always having trouble with his neighbors, who suspected him of rustling their cattle, I think with good reason. But he was competent with a gun and there wasn't anyone who would go up against him. He finally was killed. He got drunk and went to sleep under a tree by a campfire. The fire set fire to the tree, and it fell on him. I'm interested in extending newspaper and magazine formats to so-called literary materials. Here, this is one of my attempts. This is going to be published in a little magazine, *The Sparrow.*

INTERVIEWER [*reading*]: "The Coldspring News, All the News That Fits We Print, Sunday, September 17, 1899, William Burroughs, Editor." Here's Bradley Martin again.

BURROUGHS: Yes, he's the gunfighter. I'm not sure yet what's going to happen after Clem accuses him of rustling cattle. I guess Clem goes into Coldspring and there's gunplay between him and the gunfighter. He's going to kill Clem, obviously. Clem is practically a dead man. Clem is going to get "likkered up" and think he can tangle with Bradley Martin, and Bradley Martin is going to kill him, that's for sure.

INTERVIEWER: Will your other characters reappear? Dr. Benway?

BURROUGHS: He'd be the local doctor. That's what I'd like to do, you see, use all these characters in a straight western story. There would be Mr. Bradley Mr. Martin, whose name is Bradley Martin; there would be Dr. Benway; and we'd have the various traveling carny-and-medicine shows that come through with the Subliminal Kid and all of the con men. That was the heyday for those old joes.

INTERVIEWER: Do you think of the artist at all as being a con man?

BURROUGHS: In a sense. You see, a real con man is a creator. He creates a set. No, a con man is more a movie director than a writer. The Yellow Kid created a whole set, a whole cast of characters, a whole brokerage house, a whole bank. It was just like a movie studio.

INTERVIEWER: What about addicts?

BURROUGHS: Well, there will be a lot of morphine addiction. Remember that there were a great many addicts at that time. Jesse James was an addict. He started using morphine for a wound in his lung, and I don't know whether he was permanently addicted, but he tried to kill himself. He took sixteen grains of morphine and it didn't kill him, which indicates a terrific tolerance. So he must have been fairly heavily addicted. A dumb, brutal hick—that's what he was, like Dillinger. And there were so many genteel old ladies who didn't feel right unless they had their Dr. Jones mixture every day.

INTERVIEWER: What about the Green Boy, Izzy the Push, Green Tony, Sammy the Butcher, and Willie the Fink?

BURROUGHS: See, all of them could be western characters except Izzy the Push. The buildings weren't high enough in those days. Defenestration, incidentally, is a very interesting phenomenon. Some people who are prone to it will not live in high buildings. They get near a window, someone in the next room hears a cry, and they're gone. "Fell or jumped" is the phrase. I would add, "or was pushed."

INTERVIEWER: What other character types interest you?

BURROUGHS: Not the people in advertising and television, nor the American postman or middle-class housewife; not the young man setting forth. The whole world of high finance interests me, the men such as Rockefeller who were specialized types of organisms that could exist in a certain environment. He was really a money-making machine, but I doubt that he could have made a dime today because he required the old laissez-faire capitalism. He was a specialized monopolistic organism. My uncle Ivy created images for him. I fail to understand why people like J. Paul Getty have to come on with such a stuffy, uninteresting image. He decides to write his life history. I've never read anything so dull, so absolutely devoid of any spark. Well, after all, he was quite a playboy in his youth. There must have been something going on. None of it's in the book. Here he is, the only man of enormous wealth who operates alone, but there's nobody to present the image. Well, yes, I wouldn't mind doing that sort of job myself. I'd like to take somebody like Getty and try to find an image for him that would be of some interest. If Getty wants to build an image, why doesn't he hire a first-class writer to write his story? For that matter, advertising has a long way to go. I'd like to see a story by Norman Mailer or John O'Hara which just makes some mention of a product, say, Southern Comfort. I can see the O'Hara story. It would be about someone who went into a bar and asked for Southern Comfort; they didn't have it, and he gets into a long, stupid argument with the bartender. It shouldn't be obtrusive; the story must be interesting in itself so that people read this just as they read any story in *Playboy*, and Southern Comfort would be guaranteed that people will look at that advertisement for a certain number of minutes. You see what I mean? They'll read the story. Now, there are many other ideas; you could have serialized comic strips, serial stories. Well, all we have to do is have James Bond smoking a certain brand of cigarettes.

INTERVIEWER: Didn't you once work for an advertising agency?

BURROUGHS: Yes, after I got out of Harvard in 1936. I had done some graduate work in anthropology. I got a glimpse of academic life and I didn't like it at all. It looked like there was too much faculty intrigue, faculty teas, cultivating the head of the department, and so on and so forth. Then I spent a year as a copy writer in this small advertising agency, since defunct, in New York. We had a lot of rather weird accounts. There was some device called the Cascade for giving high colonics, and something called Endo-creme. It was supposed to make women look younger, because it contained some female sex hormones. The Interstate Commerce Commission was never far behind. As you can see, I've recently thought a great deal about advertising. After all, they're doing the same sort of thing. They are concerned with the precise manipulation of word and image. Anyway, after the ad game I was in the army for a bit. Honorably discharged and then the usual strange wartime jobs—bartender, exterminator, reporter, and factory and office jobs. Then Mexico, a sinister place.

INTERVIEWER: Why sinister?

BURROUGHS: I was there during the Alemán regime. If you walked into a bar, there would be at least fifteen people in there who were carrying guns. Everybody was carrying guns. They got drunk and they were a menace to any living creature. I mean, sitting in a cocktail lounge, you always had to be ready to hit the deck. I had a friend who was shot, killed. But he asked for it. He was waving his little .25 automatic around in a bar and some Mexican blasted him with a .45. They listed the death as natural causes, because the killer was a political big shot. There was no scandal, but it was really as much as your life was worth to go into a cocktail lounge. And I had that terrible accident with Joan Vollmer, my wife. I had a revolver that I was planning to sell to a friend. I was checking it over and it went off—killed her. A rumor started that I was trying to shoot a glass of champagne from her head, William Tell style. Absurd and false. Then they had a big depistolization. Mexico City had one of the highest per-capita homicide rates in the world. Another thing, every time you turned around there was some Mexican cop with his hand out, finding some fault with your papers, or something, just anything he could latch onto. "Papers very bad, señor." It really was a bit much, the Alemán regime.

INTERVIEWER: From Mexico?

BURROUGHS: I went to Colombia, Peru, and Ecuador, just looking around. I was particularly interested in the Amazon region of Peru, where I took a drug called yage, *Bannisteria caapi*, a hallucinogen as powerful as mescaline, I believe. The whole trip gave me an awful lot of copy. A lot of these experiences went into *The Ticket That Exploded*, which is sort of midway between *Naked Lunch* and *The Soft Machine*. It's not a book I'm satisfied with in its present form. If it's published in the United States, I would have to rewrite it. *The Soft Machine*, which will come out here in due time, is an expansion of my South American experiences, with surreal extensions. When I rewrote it recently, I included about sixty-five pages of straight narrative concerning Dr. Benway, and the Sailor, and various characters from *Naked Lunch*. These people pop up everywhere.

INTERVIEWER: Then from South America you went to Europe. Is the geographic switch as important as it once was to American writing?

BURROUGHS: Well, if I hadn't covered a lot of ground, I wouldn't have encountered the extra dimensions of character and extremity that make the difference. But I think the day of the expatriate is definitely over. It's becoming more and more uncomfortable, more and more expensive, and less and less rewarding to live abroad, as far as I'm concerned. Now I'm particularly concerned with quiet writing conditions—being able to concentrate—and not so much interested in the place where I am. To me, Paris is now one of the most disagreeable cities in the world. I just hate it. The food is uneatable. It's either very expensive, or you just can't eat it. In order to get a good sandwich at three o'clock in the afternoon, I have to get into a taxi and go all the way over to the Right Bank. Here all I have to do is pick up the phone. They send me up a club sandwich and a glass of buttermilk, which is all I want for lunch anyway. The French have gotten so nasty and they're getting nastier and nastier. The Algerian war and then all those millions of people dumped back into France and all of them thoroughly dissatisfied. I don't know, I think the atmosphere there is unpleasant and not conducive to anything. You can't get an apartment. You can't get a quiet place to work. Best you can do is a dinky hotel room somewhere. If I want to get something like this, it costs me thirty dollars a day. The main thing I've found after twenty years away from Saint Louis is that the standard of service is much better than New York. These are Claridge's or Ritz accommodations. If I could afford it, keep it, this would be an ideal place for me. There's not a sound in here. It's been very conducive to work. I've got a lot of room here to spread out all my papers in all these drawers and shelves. It's quiet. When I want something to eat, I pick up the phone. I can work right straight through. Get up in the morning, pick up the phone about two o'clock and have a sandwich, and work through till dinner time. Also, it's interesting to turn on the TV set every now and then.

INTERVIEWER: What do you find on it?

BURROUGHS: That's a *real* cutup. It flickers, just like the old movies used to. When talkies came in and they perfected the image, the movies became as dull as looking out the window. A bunch of Italians in Rabat have a television station and we could get the signal in Tangier. I just sat there openmouthed looking at it. What with blurring and contractions and visual static, some of their westerns became very, very odd. Gysin has been experimenting with the flicker principle in a gadget he calls a Dreamachine. There used to be one in the window of The English Bookshop on the Rue de Seine. Helena Rubenstein was so fascinated she bought a couple, and Harold Matson, the agent, thinks it's a million-dollar idea.

INTERVIEWER: Describe a typical day's work.

BURROUGHS: I get up about nine o'clock and order breakfast; I hate to go out for breakfast. I work usually until about two o'clock or two-thirty, when I like to have a sandwich and a glass of milk, which takes about ten minutes. I'll work through until six or seven o'clock. Then, if I'm seeing people or going out, I'll go out, have a few drinks, come back and maybe do a little reading and go to bed.

I go to bed pretty early. I don't make myself work. It's just the thing I want to do. To be completely alone in a room, to know that there'll be no interruptions and I've got eight hours is just exactly what I want—yeah, just paradise.

INTERVIEWER: Do you compose on the typewriter?

BURROUGHS: I use the typewriter and I use scissors. I can sit down with scissors and old manuscripts and paste in photographs for hours; I have hundreds of photographs. I usually take a walk every day. Here in Saint Louis I've been trying to take 1920 photographs, alleys and whatnot. This [*pointing*] is a ghostly photograph of the house in which I grew up, seen back through forty-five years. Here's a photo of an old ashpit. It was great fun for children to get out there in the alley after Christmas and build a fire in the ashpit with all the excelsior and wrappings. Here, these are stories and pictures from the society columns. I've been doing a cutup of society coverage. I had a lot of fun piling up these names; you get some improbable names in the society columns.

INTERVIEWER: You recently said you would like to settle in the Ozarks. Were you serious?

BURROUGHS: I would like to have a place there. It's a very beautiful area in the fall, and I'd like to spend periods of time, say every month or every two months, in complete solitude, just working, which requires an isolated situation. Of course, I'd have to buy a car, for one thing, and you run into considerable expense. I just have to think in terms of an apartment. I thought possibly an apartment here, but most likely I'll get one in New York. I'm not returning to Tangier. I just don't like it any more. It's become just a small town. There's no life there, and the place has no novelty for me at all. I was sitting there, and I thought, My God, I might as well be in Columbus, Ohio, as here, for all the interest that the town has for me. I was just sitting in my apartment working. I could have a better apartment and better working conditions somewhere else. After ten o'clock at night, there's no one on the streets. The old settlers like Paul Bowles and those people who have been there for years and years are sort of hanging on desperately asking,

"Where could we go if we left Tangier?" I don't know, it just depresses me now. It's not even cheap there. If I travel anywhere, it will be to the Far East, but only for a visit. I've never been east of Athens.

INTERVIEWER: That reminds me, I meant to ask you what's behind your interest in the more exotic systems such as Zen, or Dr. Reich's orgone theories?

BURROUGHS: Well, these nonconventional theories frequently touch on something going on that Harvard and M.I.T. can't explain. I don't mean that I endorse them wholeheartedly, but I am interested in any attempt along those lines. I've used these orgone accumulators and I'm convinced that something occurs there, I don't know quite what. Of course, Reich himself went around the bend, no question of that.

INTERVIEWER: You mentioned Scientology earlier. Do you have a system for getting on, or are you looking for one?

BURROUGHS: I'm not very interested in such a crudely three-dimensional manipulative schema as L. Ron Hubbard's, although it's got its points. I've studied it and I've seen how it works. It's a series of manipulative gimmicks. They tell you to look around and see what you would have. The results are much more subtle and more successful than Dale Carnegie's. But as far as my living by a system, no. At the same time, I don't think anything happens in this universe except by some power—or individual—making it happen. Nothing happens of itself. I believe all events are produced by will.

INTERVIEWER: Then do you believe in the existence of God?

BURROUGHS: God? I wouldn't say. I think there are innumerable gods. What we on earth call God is a little tribal god who has made an awful mess. Certainly forces operating through human consciousness control events. A Luce writer may be an agent of God knows what power, a force with an insatiable appetite for word and image. What does this force propose to do with such a tremendous mound of image garbage? They've got a regular casting office. To interview Mary McCarthy, they'll send a shy Vassar girl who's just trying to get along. They had several carny people for me. "Shucks, Bill, you got a reefer?" *Reefer,* my God! "Certainly not," I told them. "I don't know what you're talking about." Then they go back and write a nasty article for the files.

INTERVIEWER: In some respects, *Nova Express* seems to be a prescription for social ailments. Do you see the need, for instance, of biologic courts in the future?

BURROUGHS: Certainly. Science eventually will be forced to establish courts of biologic mediation, because life forms are going to become more incompatible with the conditions of existence as man penetrates further into space. Mankind will have to undergo biologic alterations ultimately, if we are to survive at all. This will require biologic law to decide what changes to make. We will simply have to use our intelligence to plan mutations, rather than letting them occur at random. Because many such mutations— look at the sabertooth tiger—are bound to be very poor engineering designs. The future, decidedly, yes. I think there are innumerable possibilities, literally innumerable. The hope lies in the development of nonbody experience and eventually getting away from the body itself, away from three-dimensional coordinates and concomitant animal reactions of fear and flight, which lead inevitably to tribal feuds and dissension.

INTERVIEWER: Why did you choose an interplanetary war as the conflict in *Nova Express*, rather than discord between nations? You seem fascinated with the idea that a superterrestrial power is exercising an apparatus of control, such as the death dwarfs—

BURROUGHS: They're parasitic organisms occupying a human host, rather like a radio transmitter, which direct and control it. The people who work with encephalograms and brain waves point out that technically it will someday be possible to install at birth a radio antenna in the brain which will control thought, feeling, and sensory perceptions, actually not only control thought, but make certain thoughts impossible. The death dwarfs are weapons of the nova mob, which in turn is calling the shots in the Cold War. The nova mob is using that conflict in an attempt to blow up the planet, because when you get right down to it, what are America and Russia really arguing about? The Soviet Union and the United States will eventually consist of interchangeable social parts and neither nation is morally "right." The idea that anyone can run his own factory in America is ridiculous. The government and the unions—which both amount to the same thing: control systems—tell him who he can hire, how much he can pay them, and how he can sell his goods. What difference does it make if the state owns the plant and retains him as manager? Regardless of how it's done, the same kind of people will be in charge. One's ally today is an enemy tomorrow. I have postulated this power—the nova mob—which forces us to play musical chairs.

INTERVIEWER: You see hope for the human race, but at the same time you are alarmed as the instruments of control become more sophisticated.

BURROUGHS: Well, whereas they become more sophisticated they also become more vulnerable. *Time-Life-Fortune* applies a more complex, effective control system than the Mayan calendar, but it also is much more vulnerable because it is so vast and mechanized. Not even Henry Luce understands what's going on in the system now. Well, a machine can be redirected. One technical sergeant can fuck up the whole works. Nobody can control the whole operation. It's too complex. The captain comes in and says, "All right, boys, we're moving up." Now, who knows what buttons to push? Who knows how to get the cases of Spam up to where they're going, and how to fill out the forms? The sergeant does. The captain doesn't know. As long as there're sergeants around, the machine can be dismantled, and we may get out of all this alive yet.

INTERVIEWER: Sex seems equated with death frequently in your work.

BURROUGHS: That is an extension of the idea of sex as a biologic weapon. I feel that sex, like practically every other human manifestation, has been degraded for control purposes, or really for antihuman purposes. This whole puritanism. How are we ever going to find out anything about sex scientifically, when a priori the subject cannot even be investigated? It can't even be thought about or written about. That was one of the interesting things about Reich. He was one of the few people who ever tried to investigate sex—sexual phenomena, from a scientific point of view. There's this prurience and this fear of sex. We know nothing about sex. What is it? Why is it pleasurable? What is pleasure? Relief from tension? Well, possibly.

INTERVIEWER: Are you irreconcilably hostile to the twentieth century?

BURROUGHS: Not at all, although I can imagine myself as having been born under many different circumstances. For example, I had a dream recently in which I returned to the family home and I found a different father and a different house from any I'd ever seen before. Yet in a dream sense, the father and the house were quite familiar.

INTERVIEWER: Mary McCarthy has characterized you as a soured utopian. Is that accurate?

BURROUGHS: I do definitely mean what I say to be taken literally, yes, to make people aware of the true criminality of our times, to wise up the marks. All of my work is directed against those who are bent, through stupidity or design, on blowing up the planet or rendering it uninhabitable. Like the advertising people we talked about, I'm concerned with the precise manipulation of word and image to create an action, not to go out and buy a Coca-Cola, but to create an alteration in the reader's consciousness. You know, they ask me if I were on a desert island and knew nobody would ever see what I wrote, would I go on writing. My answer is most emphatically yes. I would go on writing for company. Because I'm creating an imaginary—it's always imaginary—world in which I would like to live.

CONRAD KNICKERBOCKER

8. Saul Bellow

Born the youngest of four children in Lachine, Quebec, on June 10, 1915, Saul Bellow spent his youth in Chicago, where his family had moved when he was nine. Later, enrolled at the University of Chicago, he found that the "dense atmosphere of learning, of cultural effort oppressed me; I felt that wisdom and culture were immense and that I was hopelessly small." In 1935 he transferred to Northwestern University and graduated with honors in anthropology and sociology in 1937. He started graduate school at the University of Wisconsin, but during Christmas vacation of his first year he married and left the university: "In my innocence, I had decided to become a writer."

His first two novels, *Dangling Man* (1944) and *The Victim* (1947), won him a small but devoted group of readers. Wider recognition came with the publication of *The Adventures of Augie March*, which won the National Book Award in 1954. A series of highly successful novels has followed: *Seize the Day* (1956), *Henderson the Rain King* (1959), and, most notably, *Herzog*, which won the National Book Award in 1964. Bellow's fiction and essays have appeared in *The New Yorker*, *The New Republic*, *Encounter*, *The New Leader*, and many literary quarterlies. A play, *The Last Analysis*, was produced in New York in 1964, and *Under the Weather*, three one-act plays, was produced in the fall of 1966.

Bellow has twice been a Guggenheim Fellow (1948–49 and 1955–56) and has taught at Princeton University (1952–53) and at Bard College (1953–54). He lives in Chicago, where he is a Fellow of the Committee on Social Thought at the University of Chicago.

What did he call it?

"We're all right."

"Comfortably settled? Liking Chicago? Little Ephraim still in the Lab School?"

"Yes."

Still the Buber kick!

"And the Temple? I see that Val taped a program with Rabbi Itzkowitz—Hasidic Judaism, Martin Buber, *I and Thou.* He's very thick with these rabbis. Maybe he wants to swap wives with a rabbi. He'll work his way round from 'I and Thou' to 'Me and You'— 'You and Me, Kid!' I suppose you wouldn't go along with everything."

But

*I'd draw the line there*①

you

Phoebe made no answer and remained standing.

"Maybe you think I'll leave sooner if you don't sit. Come, Phoebe, sit down. I promise you I haven't come to make scenes. I have only one purpose here, in addition to wanting to see an old friend. . . ."

"We're not really old friends."

"Not by calendar years. But we were so close out in Ludeyville. That is true. You have to think of duration—Bergsonian duration. We have known each other in duration. Some people are *sentenced* to certain relationships." *Maybe every relationship is either a joy or a sentence.*

Say what you think, Phoebe, that's what I want.

"You earned your own sentence, if that's how you want to think about it. We had a quiet life till you and Madeleine descended on Ludeyville and forced yourself on me." Phoebe, her face thin but hot, eyelids unmoving, sat down on the edge of the chair Herzog had drawn forward for her.

"Good. Sit back. Don't be afraid. I'm not looking for trouble. We've got a problem in common."

Phoebe denied this. She shook her head, with a stubborn look, all too vigorously. "I'm a plain woman. Valentine is from upstate New York."

Didn't know how to deal a number.

"Just a rube. Yes. Knows nothing about fancy vices from the big city. Had to be led step by step into degeneracy by me—Moses E. Herzog."

She came to a

Stiff and hesitant, she turned her body aside in her abrupt way, then, ~~her decision reached,~~ turned just as abruptly to him again. "You never understood a thing about him. He fell for you. Adored you. Tried to become an intellectual because he wanted to help you—saw what a terrible thing you had done in giving up your respectable university position and how reckless you were, rushing out to the country with Madeleine. He thought she was ruining you and tried to set you on the right track again. He read all those books so you'd have somebody to talk to, out in the sticks, Moses. Because you needed help, praise, flattery, support, affection. It never was enough. You wore him out." *It nearly killed him.*

"Yes .   ? What else? Go on," said Herzog. *trying to back you up.*

"It's still not enough. What do you want from him now? What are you here for? More excitement? Are you still greedy for ~~it~~ *excitement?*"

Herzog no longer smiled. "Some of what you say is right enough, Phoebe. I was certainly floundering in Ludeyville. But you take the wind out of me when you say you were leading a perfectly

ROSALIE SEIDLER

Saul Bellow

The interview "took place" over a period of several weeks. Beginning with some exploratory discussions during May of 1965, it was shelved during the summer, and actually accomplished during September and October. Two recording sessions were held, totaling about an hour and a half, but this was only a small part of the effort Mr. Bellow gave to this interview. A series of meetings, for over five weeks, was devoted to the most careful revision of the original material. Recognizing at the outset the effort he would make for such an interview, he had real reluctance about beginning it at all. Once his decision had been reached, however, he gave a remarkable amount of his time freely to the task—up to two hours a day, at least twice and often three times a week throughout the entire five-week period. It had become an opportunity, as he put it, to say some things which were important but which weren't being said.

Certain types of questions were ruled out in early discussions.

Mr. Bellow was not interested in responding to criticisms of his work which he found trivial or stupid. He quoted the Jewish proverb that a fool can throw a stone into the water which ten wise men cannot recover. Nor did he wish to discuss what he considered his personal writing habits, whether he used a pen or typewriter, how hard he pressed on the page. For the artist to give such loving attention to his own shoelaces was dangerous, even immoral. Finally, there were certain questions that led into too "wide spaces" for this interview, subjects for fuller treatment on other occasions.

The two tapes were made in Bellow's University of Chicago office on the fifth floor of the Social Sciences Building. The office, though large, is fairly typical of those on the main quadrangles: much of it rather dark with one brightly lighted area, occupied by his desk, immediately before a set of three dormer windows; dark-green metal bookcases line the walls, casually used as storage for a miscellany of books, magazines, and correspondence. A set of The Complete Works of Rudyard Kipling ("it was given to me") shares space with examination copies of new novels and with a few of Bellow's own books, including recent French and Italian translations of Herzog. A table, a couple of typing stands, and various decrepit and mismatched chairs are scattered in apparently haphazard fashion throughout the room. A wall rack just inside the door holds his jaunty black felt hat and his walking cane. There is a general sense of disarray, with stacks of papers, books, and letters lying everywhere. When one comes to the door, Bellow is frequently at his typing stand, rapidly pounding out on a portable machine responses to some of the many letters he gets daily. Occasionally a secretary enters and proceeds to type away on some project at the far end of the room.

During the two sessions with the tape recorder, Bellow sat at his desk, between the eaves which project prominently into the room, backlighted by the dormer windows which let in the bright afternoon sun from the south. Four stories below lie Fifty-ninth Street and Chicago's Midway, their automobile and human noises continually penetrating the office. As the questions were asked,

Bellow listened carefully and often developed an answer slowly, pausing frequently to think out the exact phrasing he sought. His answers were serious, but full of his special quality of humor. He took obvious pleasure in the amusing turns of thought with which he often concluded an answer. Throughout, he was at great pains to make his ideas transparent to the interviewer, asking repeatedly if this was clear or if he should say more on the subject. His concentration during these sessions was intense enough to be tiring, and both tapes were brought to a close with his confessing to some exhaustion.

Following each taping session, a typescript of his remarks was prepared. Bellow worked over these typed sheets extensively with pen and ink, taking as many as three separate meetings to do a complete revision. Then another typescript was made, and the process started over. This work was done when the interviewer could be present, and again the changes were frequently tested on him. Generally these sessions occured at Bellow's office or at his apartment, overlooking the Outer Drive and Lake Michigan. Once, however, revisions were made while he and the interviewer sat on a Jackson Park bench on a fine October afternoon, and one typescript was worked on along with beer and hamburgers at a local bar.

Revisions were of various sorts. Frequently there were slight changes in meaning: "That's what I really meant to say." Other alterations tightened up his language or were in the nature of stylistic improvements. Any sections which he judged to be excursions from the main topic were deleted. Most regretted by the interviewer were prunings that eliminated certain samples of the characteristic Bellow wit: in a few places he came to feel he was simply "exhibiting" himself, and these were scratched out. On the other hand, whenever he could substitute for conventional literary diction an unexpected colloquial turn of phrase—which often proved humorous in context—he did so.

INTERVIEWER: Some critics have felt that your work falls within the tradition of American naturalism, possibly because of some things you've said about Dreiser. I was wondering if you saw yourself in a particular literary tradition?

BELLOW: Well, I think that the development of realism in the nineteenth century is still the major event of modern literature. Dreiser, a realist of course, had elements of genius. He was clumsy, cumbersome, and in some respects a poor thinker. But he was rich in a kind of feeling which has been ruled off the grounds by many contemporary writers—the kind of feeling that every human being intuitively recognizes as primary. Dreiser has more open access to primary feelings than any American writer of the twentieth century. It makes a good many people uncomfortable that his emotion has not found a more developed literary form. It's true his art may be too "natural." He sometimes conveys his understanding by masses of words, verbal approximations. He blunders, but generally in the direction of truth. The result is that we are moved in an unmediated way by his characters, as by life, and then we say that his novels are simply torn from the side of life, and therefore not novels. But we can't escape reading them. He somehow conveys, without much refinement, depths of feeling that we usually associate with Balzac or Shakespeare.

INTERVIEWER: This realism, then, is a particular kind of sensibility, rather than a technique?

BELLOW: Realism specializes in *apparently* unmediated experiences. What stirred Dreiser was simply the idea that you could bring unmediated feeling to the novel. He took it up naïvely without going to the trouble of mastering an art. We don't see this because he makes so many familiar "art" gestures, borrowed from the art-fashions of his day, and even from the slick magazines, but he is really a natural, a primitive. I have great respect for his simplicities and I think they are worth more than much that has been praised as high art in the American novel.

INTERVIEWER: Could you give me an example of what you mean?

BELLOW: In a book like *Jennie Gerhardt* the delicacy with which Jennie allows Lester Kane to pursue his conventional life while she herself lives unrecognized with her illegitimate daughter, the depth of her understanding, and the depth of her sympathy and of her truthfulness impress me. She is not a sentimental figure. She has a natural sort of honor.

INTERVIEWER: Has recent American fiction pretty much followed this direction?

BELLOW: Well, among his heirs there are those who believe that clumsiness and truthfulness go together. But cumbersomeness does not necessarily imply a sincere heart. Most of the "Dreiserians" lack talent. On the other hand, people who put Dreiser down, adhering to a "high art" standard for the novel, miss the point.

INTERVIEWER: Aside from Dreiser, what other American writers do you find particularly of interest?

BELLOW: I like Hemingway, Faulkner, and Fitzgerald. I think of Hemingway as a man who developed a significant manner as an artist, a life-style which is important. For his generation, his language created a life-style, one which pathetic old gentlemen are still found clinging to. I don't think of Hemingway as a great novelist. I like Fitzgerald's novels better, but I often feel about Fitzgerald that he couldn't distinguish between innocence and social climbing. I am thinking of *The Great Gatsby*.

INTERVIEWER: If we go outside American literature, you've mentioned that you read the nineteenth-century Russian writers with a good deal of interest. Is there anything particular about them that attracts you?

BELLOW: Well, the Russians have an immediate charismatic appeal—excuse the Max Weberism. Their conventions allow them to express freely their feelings about nature and human beings. We have inherited a more restricted and imprisoning attitude toward the emotions. We have to work around puritanical and stoical restraints. We lack the Russian openness. Our path is narrower.

INTERVIEWER: In what other writers do you take special interest?

BELLOW: I have a special interest in Joyce; I have a special interest in Lawrence. I read certain poets over and over again. I can't say where they belong in my theoretical scheme; I only know that I have an attachment to them. Yeats is one such poet. Hart Crane is another. Hardy and Walter de la Mare. I don't know what these have in common—probably nothing. I know that I am drawn repeatedly to these men.

INTERVIEWER: It's been said that one can't like *both* Lawrence and Joyce, that one has to choose between them. You don't feel this way?

BELLOW: No. Because I really don't take Lawrence's sexual theories very seriously. I take his art seriously, not his doctrine. But he himself warned us repeatedly not to trust the artist. He said trust the work itself. So I have little use for the Lawrence who wrote *The Plumed Serpent* and great admiration for the Lawrence who wrote *The Lost Girl*.

INTERVIEWER: Does Lawrence at all share the special feeling you find attractive in Dreiser?

BELLOW: A certain openness to experience, yes. And a willingness to trust one's instinct, to follow it freely—that Lawrence has.

INTERVIEWER: You mentioned before the interview that you would prefer not to talk about your early novels, that you feel you are a different person now from what you were then. I wonder if this is all you want to say, or if you can say something about how you have changed.

BELLOW: I think that when I wrote those early books I was timid. I still felt the incredible effrontery of announcing myself to the world (in part I mean the WASP world) as a writer and an artist. I had to touch a great many bases, demonstrate my abilities, pay my respects to formal requirements. In short, I was afraid to let myself go.

INTERVIEWER: When do you find a significant change occurring?

BELLOW: When I began to write *Augie March*. I took off many of these restraints. I think I took off too many, and went too far, but I was feeling the excitement of discovery. I had just increased my freedom, and like any emancipated plebeian I abused it at once.

INTERVIEWER: What were these restraints that you took off in *Augie March*?

BELLOW: My first two books are well made. I wrote the first quickly but took great pains with it. I labored with the second and tried to make it letter-perfect. In writing *The Victim* I accepted a Flaubertian standard. Not a bad standard, to be sure, but one which, in the end, I found repressive—repressive because of the circumstances of my life and because of my upbringing in Chicago as the son of immigrants. I could not, with such an instrument as I developed in the first two books, express a variety of things I knew intimately. Those books, though useful, did not give me a form in which I felt comfortable. A writer should be able to express himself easily, naturally, copiously in a form which frees his mind, his energies. Why should he hobble himself with formalities? With a borrowed sensibility? With the desire to be "correct"? Why should I force myself to write like an Englishman or a contributor to *The New Yorker*? I soon saw that it was simply not in me to be a mandarin. I should add that for a young man in my position there were social inhibitions, too. I had good reason to fear that I would be put down as a foreigner, an interloper. It was made clear to me when I studied literature in the university that as a Jew and the son of Russian Jews I would probably never have the right *feeling* for Anglo-Saxon traditions, for English words. I realized even in college that the people who told me this were not necessarily disinterested friends. But they had an effect on me, nevertheless. This was something from which I had to free myself. I fought free because I had to.

INTERVIEWER: Are these social inhibitors as powerful today as they were when you wrote *Dangling Man*?

BELLOW: I think I was lucky to have grown up in the Middle West, where such influences are less strong. If I'd grown up in the East and attended an Ivy League university, I might have been damaged more badly. Puritan and Protestant America carries less weight in Illinois than in Massachusetts. But I don't bother much with such things now.

INTERVIEWER: Did another change in your writing occur between *Augie March* and *Herzog*? You've mentioned writing *Augie March* with a great sense of freedom, but I take it that *Herzog* was a very difficult book to write.

BELLOW: It was. I had to tame and restrain the style I developed in *Augie March* in order to write *Henderson* and *Herzog*. I think both those books reflect that change in style. I wouldn't really know how to describe it. I don't care to trouble my mind to find an exact description for it, but it has something to do with a kind of readiness to record impressions arising from a source of which we know little. I suppose that all of us have a primitive prompter or commentator within, who from earliest years has been advising us, telling us what the real world is. There is such a commentator in me. I have to prepare the ground for him. From this source come words, phrases, syllables; sometimes only sounds, which I try to interpret, sometimes whole paragraphs, fully punctuated. When E. M. Forster said, "How do I know what I think until I see what I say?" he was perhaps referring to his own prompter. There is that observing instrument in us—in childhood at any rate. At the sight of a man's face, his shoes, the color of light, a woman's mouth or perhaps her ear, one receives a word, a phrase, at times nothing but a nonsense syllable from the primitive commentator.

INTERVIEWER: So this change in your writing—

BELLOW:—was an attempt to get nearer to that primitive commentator.

INTERVIEWER: How do you go about getting nearer to him, preparing the way for him?

BELLOW: When I say the commentator is primitive, I don't mean that he's crude; God knows he's often fastidious. But he won't talk until the situation's right. And if you prepare the ground for him with too many difficulties underfoot, he won't say anything. I must be terribly given to fraud and deceit because I sometimes have great difficulty preparing a suitable ground. This is why I've had so much trouble with my last two novels. I appealed directly to my prompter. The prompter, however, has to find the occasion perfect—that is to say, truthful, and necessary. If there is any superfluity or inner falsehood in the preparations, he is aware of it. I have to stop. Often I have to begin again, with the first word. I can't remember how many times I wrote *Herzog*. But at last I did find the acceptable ground for it.

INTERVIEWER: Do these preparations include your coming to some general conception of the work?

BELLOW: Well, I don't know exactly how it's done. I let it alone a good deal. I try to avoid common forms of strain and distortion.

For a long time, perhaps from the middle of the nineteenth century, writers have not been satisfied to regard themselves simply as writers. They have required also a theoretical framework. Most often they have been their own theoreticians, have created their own ground as artists, and have provided an exegesis for their own works. They have found it necessary to take a position, not merely to write novels. In bed last night I was reading a collection of articles by Stendhal. One of them amused me very much, touched me. Stendhal was saying how lucky writers were in the age of Louis XIV not to have anyone take them very seriously. Their obscurity was very valuable. Corneille had been dead for several days before anyone at court considered the fact important enough to mention. In the nineteenth century, says Stendhal, there would have been several public orations, Corneille's funeral covered by all the papers. There are great advantages in not being taken *too* seriously. Some writers are excessively serious about themselves. They accept the ideas of the "cultivated public." There is such a thing as overcapitalizing the A in artist. Certain writers and musicians understand this. Stravinsky says the composer should practice his trade exactly as a shoemaker does. Mozart and Haydn accepted commissions—wrote to order. In the nineteenth century, the artist loftily waited for Inspiration. Once you elevate yourself to the rank of a cultural institution, you're in for a lot of trouble.

Then there is a minor modern disorder—the disease of people who live by an image of themselves created by papers, television, Broadway, Sardi's, gossip, or the public need for celebrities. Even buffoons, prize fighters, and movie stars have caught the bug. I avoid these "images." I have a longing, not for downright obscurity—I'm too egotistical for that—but for peace, and freedom from meddling.

INTERVIEWER: In line with this, the enthusiastic response to *Herzog* must have affected your life considerably. Do you have any thoughts as to why this book became and remained the bestseller it did?

BELLOW: I don't like to agree with the going view that if you write a bestseller it's because you betrayed an important principle or sold your soul. I know that sophisticated opinion believes this. And although I don't take much stock in sophisticated opinion, I have examined my conscience. I've tried to find out whether I had unwittingly done wrong. But I haven't yet discovered the sin. I do think that a book like *Herzog*, which ought to have been an obscure book with a total sale of eight thousand, has such a reception because it appeals to the unconscious sympathies of many people. I know from the mail I've received that the book described a common predicament. *Herzog* appealed to Jewish readers, to those who have been divorced, to those who talk to themselves, to college graduates, readers of paperbacks, autodidacts, to those who yet hope to live awhile, etc.

INTERVIEWER: Do you feel there were deliberate attempts at lionizing by the literary tastemakers? I was thinking that the recent deaths of Faulkner and Hemingway have been seen as creating a vacuum in American letters, which we all know is abhorrent.

BELLOW: Well, I don't know whether I would say a vacuum. Perhaps a pigeonhole. I agree that there is a need to keep the pigeonholes filled and that people are uneasy when there are vacancies. Also the mass media demand material—grist—and literary journalists have to create a major-league atmosphere in literature. The writers don't offer to fill the pigeonholes. It's the critics who want figures in the Pantheon. But there are many people who assume that every writer must be bucking for the niche. Why should writers wish to be rated—seeded—like tennis players? Handicapped like racehorses? What an epitaph for a novelist: "He won all the polls"!

INTERVIEWER: How much are you conscious of the reader when you write? Is there an ideal audience that you write for?

BELLOW: I have in mind another human being who will understand me. I count on this. Not on perfect understanding, which is Cartesian, but on approximate understanding, which is Jewish. And on a meeting of sympathies, which is human. But I have no ideal reader in my head, no. Let me just say this, too. I seem to have the blind self-acceptance of the eccentric who can't conceive that his eccentricities are not clearly understood.

INTERVIEWER: So there isn't a great deal of calculation about rhetoric?

BELLOW: These are things that can't really be contrived. People who talk about contrivance must think that a novelist is a man capable of building a skyscraper to conceal a dead mouse. Skyscrapers are not raised simply to conceal mice.

INTERVIEWER: It's been said that contemporary fiction sees man as a victim. You gave this title to one of your early novels, yet there seems to be very strong opposition in your fiction to seeing man as simply determined or futile. Do you see any truth to this claim about contemporary fiction?

BELLOW: Oh, I think that realistic literature from the first has been a victim literature. Pit any ordinary individual—and realistic literature concerns itself with ordinary individuals—against the external world, and the external world will conquer him, of course. Everything that people believed in the nineteenth century about determinism, about man's place in nature, about the power of productive forces in society, made it inevitable that the hero of the realistic novel should not be a hero but a sufferer who is eventually overcome. So I was doing nothing very original by writing another realistic novel about a common man and calling it *The Victim*. I suppose I was discovering independently the essence of much of modern realism. In my innocence, I put my finger on it. Serious realism also contrasts the common man with aristocratic greatness. He is overborne by fate, just as the great are in Shakespeare or Sophocles. But this contrast, inherent in literary tradition, always damages him. In the end the force of tradition carries realism into parody, satire, mock-epic—Leopold Bloom.

INTERVIEWER: Haven't you yourself moved away from the suggestion of plebeian tragedy toward a treatment of the sufferer that has greater comic elements? Although the concerns and difficulties are still fundamentally serious, the comic elements in *Henderson*, in *Herzog*, even in *Seize the Day* seem much more prominent than in *Dangling Man* or *The Victim*.

BELLOW: Yes, because I got very tired of the solemnity of complaint, altogether impatient with complaint. Obliged to choose between complaint and comedy, I choose comedy, as more energetic, wiser, and manlier. This is really one reason why I dislike my own early novels. I find them plaintive, sometimes querulous. *Herzog* makes comic use of complaint.

INTERVIEWER: When you say that you are obliged to choose between complaint and comedy, does it mean this is the only choice —that you are limited to choosing between just these two alternatives?

BELLOW: I'm not inclined to predict what will happen. I may feel drawn to comedy again, I may not. But modern literature was dominated by a tone of elegy from the twenties to the fifties, the atmosphere of Eliot in "The Waste Land" and that of Joyce in *A Portrait of the Artist as a Young Man*. Sensibility absorbed this sadness, this view of the artist as the only contemporary link with an age of gold, forced to watch the sewage flowing in the Thames, every aspect of modern civilization doing violence to his (artist-patrician) feelings. This went much farther than it should have been allowed to go. It descended to absurdities, of which I think we have had enough.

INTERVIEWER: I wonder if you could say something about how important the environments are in your works. I take it that for the realist tradition the context in which the action occurs is of vital importance. You set your novels in Chicago, New York, as far away as Africa. How important are these settings for the fiction?

BELLOW: Well, you present me with a problem to which I think no one has the answer. People write realistically but at the same time they want to create environments which are somehow desirable, which are surrounded by atmospheres in which behavior becomes significant, which display the charm of life. What is literature without these things? Dickens's London is gloomy, but also cozy. And yet realism has always offered to annihilate precisely such qualities. That is to say, if you want to be ultimately realistic you bring artistic space itself in danger. In Dickens, there is no void beyond the fog. The environment is human, at all times. Do you follow me?

INTERVIEWER: I'm not sure I do.

BELLOW: The realistic tendency is to challenge the human significance of things. The more realistic you are the more you threaten the grounds of your own art. Realism has always both accepted and rejected the circumstances of ordinary life. It accepted the task of writing about ordinary life and tried to meet it in some extraordinary fashion. As Flaubert did. The subject might be common, low, degrading; all this was to be redeemed by art. I really do see those Chicago environments as I represent them. They suggest their own style of presentation. I elaborate it.

INTERVIEWER: Then you aren't especially disturbed by readers of *Henderson*, for example, who say that Africa really isn't like that? One sort of realist would require a writer to spend several years on location before daring to place his characters there. You're not troubled by him, I take it?

BELLOW: Perhaps you should say "factualist" rather than "realist." Years ago, I studied African ethnography with the late Professor Herskovits. Later he scolded me for writing a book like *Henderson*. He said the subject was much too serious for such fooling. I felt that my fooling was fairly serious. Literalism, factualism, will smother the imagination altogether.

INTERVIEWER: You have on occasion divided recent American fiction into what you call the "cleans" and the "dirties." The former, I gather, tend to be conservative and easily optimistic, the latter the eternal nay-sayers, rebels, iconoclasts. Do you feel this is still pretty much the picture of American fiction today?

BELLOW: I feel that both choices are rudimentary and pitiful, and though I know the uselessness of advocating any given path to other novelists, I am still inclined to say, Leave both these extremes. They are useless, childish. No wonder the really powerful men in our society, whether politicians or scientists, hold writers and poets in contempt. They do it because they get no evidence from modern literature that anybody is thinking about any significant question. What does the radicalism of radical writers nowadays amount to? Most of it is hand-me-down bohemianism, sentimental populism, D. H. Lawrence-and-water, or imitation Sartre. For American writers radicalism is a question of honor.

They must be radicals for the sake of their dignity. They see it as their function, and a noble function, to say Nay, and to bite not only the hand that feeds them (and feeds them with comic abundance, I might add) but almost any other hand held out to them. Their radicalism, however, is contentless. A genuine radicalism, which truly challenges authority, we need desperately. But a radicalism of posture is easy and banal. Radical criticism requires knowledge, not posture, not slogans, not rant. People who maintain their dignity as artists, in a small way, by being mischievous on television, simply delight the networks and the public. True radicalism requires homework—thought. Of the cleans, on the other hand, there isn't much to say. They seem faded.

INTERVIEWER: Your context is essentially that of the modern city, isn't it? Is there a reason for this beyond the fact that you come out of an urban experience?

BELLOW: Well, I don't know how I could possibly separate my knowledge of life, such as it is, from the city. I could no more tell you how deeply it's gotten into my bones than the lady who paints radium dials in the clock factory can tell you.

INTERVIEWER: You've mentioned the distractive character of modern life. Would this be most intense in the city?

BELLOW: The volume of judgments one is called upon to make depends upon the receptivity of the observer, and if one is very receptive, one has a terrifying number of opinions to render— "What do you think about this, about that, about Viet Nam, about city planning, about expressways, or garbage disposal, or democracy, or Plato, or pop art, or welfare states, or literacy in a 'mass society'?" I wonder whether there will ever be enough tranquillity under modern circumstances to allow our contemporary Wordsworth to recollect anything. I feel that art has something to do with the achievement of stillness in the midst of chaos. A stillness which characterizes prayer, too, and the eye of the storm. I think that art has something to do with an arrest of attention in the midst of distraction.

INTERVIEWER: I believe you once said that it is the novel which must deal particularly with this kind of chaos, and that as a consequence certain forms appropriate to poetry or to music are not available to the novelist.

BELLOW: I'm no longer so sure of that. I think the novelist can avail himself of similar privileges. It's just that he can't act with the same purity or economy of means as the poet. He has to traverse a very muddy and noisy territory before he can arrive at a pure conclusion. He's more exposed to the details of life.

INTERVIEWER: Is there anything peculiar about the *kind* of distractions you see the novelist having to confront today? Is it just that there are more details, or is their quality different today from what it used to be?

BELLOW: The modern masterpiece of confusion is Joyce's *Ulysses*. There the mind is unable to resist experience. Experience in all its diversity, its pleasure and horror, passes through Bloom's head like an ocean through a sponge. The sponge can't resist; it has to accept whatever the waters bring. It also notes every microorganism that passes through it. This is what I mean. How much of this must the spirit suffer, in what detail is it obliged to receive this ocean with its human plankton? Sometimes it looks as if the power of the mind has been nullified by the volume of experiences. But of course this is assuming the degree of passivity that Joyce assumes in *Ulysses*. Stronger, more purposeful minds can demand order, impose order, select, disregard, but there is still the threat of disintegration under the particulars. A Faustian artist is unwilling to surrender to the mass of particulars.

INTERVIEWER: Some people have felt your protagonists are seeking the answer to a question that might be phrased, How is it possible today for a good man to live? I wonder if you feel there is any single recurring question like this in the novels?

BELLOW: I don't think that I've represented any really good men; no one is thoroughly admirable in any of my novels. Realism has restrained me too much for that. I should *like* to represent good men. I long to know who and what they are and what their condition might be. I often represent men who desire such qualities but seem unable to achieve them on any significant scale. I criticize this in myself. I find it a limitation.

INTERVIEWER: I'm sorry; what exactly is this limitation?

BELLOW: The fact that I have not discerned those qualities or that I have not shown them in action. Herzog wants very much to have effective virtues. But that's a source of comedy in the book. I think I am far more concerned with another matter, and I don't approach this as a problem with a ready answer. I see it rather as a piece of research, having to do with human characteristics or qualities which have no need of justification. It's an odd thing to do, it shouldn't be necessary to "justify" certain things. But there are many skeptical, rebellious, or simply nervous writers all around us, who, having existed a full twenty or thirty years in this universe, denounce or reject life because it fails to meet their standards as philosophical intellectuals. It seems to me that they can't know enough about it for confident denial. The mystery is too great. So when they knock at the door of mystery with the knuckles of cognition it is quite right that the door should open and some mysterious power should squirt them in the eye. I think a good deal of *Herzog* can be explained simply by the implicit assumption that existence, quite apart from any of our judgments, has value, that existence is worth-ful. Here it is possible, however, that the desire to go on with his creaturely career vulgarly betrays Herzog. He wants to live? What of it! The clay that frames him contains this common want. Simple *aviditas vitae*. Does a man deserve any credit for this?

INTERVIEWER: Would this help to explain, then, why many of the difficulties which Herzog's mind throws up for him throughout the novel don't ever seem to be *intellectually* resolved?

BELLOW: The book is not anti-intellectual, as some have said. It simply points to the comic impossibility of arriving at a synthesis that can satisfy modern demands. That is to say, full awareness of all major problems, together with the necessary knowledge of history, of science and philosophy. That's why Herzog paraphrases Thomas Marshall, Woodrow Wilson's Vice-President, who said what this country needs is a good five-cent cigar. (I think it was Bugs Baer who said it first.) Herzog's version: what this country needs is a good five-cent synthesis.

INTERVIEWER: Do you find many contemporary writers attempting to develop such syntheses or insisting that significant fiction provide them?

BELLOW: Well, I don't know that too many American novelists, young or old, are tormenting their minds with these problems. Europeans do. I don't know that they can ever reach satisfactory results on the grounds they have chosen. At any rate, they write few good novels. But that leads us into some very wide spaces.

INTERVIEWER: Do the ideas in *Herzog* have any other major roles to play? The "anti-intellectual" charge seems to come from people who don't feel the ideas are essential either in motivating the action, the decisions Herzog makes, or in helping him to come through at the end.

BELLOW: To begin with, I suppose I should say something about the difference in the role ideas play in American literature. European literature—I speak now of the Continent—is intellectual in a different sense from ours. The intellectual hero of a French or a German novel is likely to be a philosophical intellectual, an ideological intellectual. We here, intellectuals—or the educated public—know that in our liberal democracy ideas become effective within an entirely different tradition. The lines are less clearly drawn. We do not expect thought to have results, say, in the moral sphere, or in the political, in quite the way a Frenchman would. To be an intellectual in the United States sometimes means to be immured in a private life in which one thinks, but thinks with some humiliating sense of how little thought can accomplish. To call therefore for a dramatic resolution in terms of ideas in an American novel is to demand something for which there is scarcely any precedent. My novel deals with the humiliating sense that results from the American mixture of private concerns and intellectual interests. This is something which most readers of the book seem utterly to have missed. Some, fortunately, have caught it. But in part *Herzog* is intended to bring to an end, under blinding light, a certain course of development. Many people feel a "private life" to be an affliction. In some sense it is a genuine affliction; it cuts one off from a common life. To me, a significant theme of *Herzog* is the imprisonment of the individual in a shameful and impotent privacy. He feels humiliated by it; he struggles comically with it; and he comes to realize at last that what he considered his intellectual "privilege" has proved to be another form of bondage. Anyone who misses this misses the point of the book. So that to say that Herzog is not motivated in his acts by ideas is entirely false. Any *Bildungsroman*—and *Herzog* is, to use that heavy German term, a *Bildungsroman*—concludes with the first step. The first *real* step. Any man who has rid himself of superfluous ideas in order to take that first step has done something significant. When people complain of a lack of ideas in novels, they may mean that they do not find familiar ideas, fashionable ideas. Ideas outside the "canon" they don't recognize. So, if what they mean is ideas à la Sartre or ideas à la Camus, they are quite right: there are few such in *Herzog*. Perhaps they mean that the thoughts of a man fighting for sanity and life are not suitable for framing.

INTERVIEWER: Herzog rejects certain of these fashionable ideas, doesn't he—the ideas à la Sartre or à la Camus?

BELLOW: I think he tests them first upon his own sense of life and against his own desperate need for clarity. With him these thoughts are not a game. Though he may laugh as he thinks them, his survival depends upon them. I didn't have him engage in full combat with figures like Sartre. If he had chosen to debate with Sartre in typical Herzogian fashion he would perhaps have begun with Sartre's proposition that Jews exist only because of anti-Semitism, that the Jew has to choose between authentic and inauthentic existence, that authentic existence can never be detached from this anti-Semitism which determines it. Herzog might have remembered that for Sartre, the Jew exists because he is hated, not because he has a history, not because he has origins of his own—but simply because he is designated, created, in his Jewishness by an outrageous evil. Sartre offers a remedy for those Jews who are prepared to make the authentic choice: he extends to them the invitation to become Frenchmen. If this great prince of contemporary European philosophy offers Herzog ideas such as this to embrace (or dispute), who can blame him for his skepticism toward what is called, so respectfully, Thought, toward contemporary intellectual fare? Often Herzog deals with ideas in negative fashion. He needs to dismiss a great mass of irrelevancy and nonsense in order to survive. Perhaps this was what I meant earlier when I said that we were called upon to make innumerable judgments. We can be consumed simply by the necessity to discriminate between multitudes of propositions. We have to dismiss a great number of thoughts if we are to have any creaturely or human life at all. It seems at times that we are on trial seven days a week answering the questions, giving a clear account of ourselves. But when does one live? How does one live if it is necessary to render ceaseless judgments?

INTERVIEWER: Herzog's rejection of certain ideas has been widely recognized, but—

BELLOW:—why he rejects them is not at all clear. Herzog's skepticism toward ideas is very deep. Though Jews are often accused of being "rootless" rationalists, a man like Herzog knows very well that habit, custom, tendency, temperament, inheritance, and the power to recognize real and human facts have equal weight with ideas.

INTERVIEWER: You've spoken also of the disabling effects of basing a novel on ideas. Does this mean structuring a novel according to a philosophical conception?

BELLOW: No, I have no objection to that, nor do I have any objection to basing novels on philosophical conceptions or anything else that works. But let us look at one of the dominant ideas of the century, accepted by many modern artists—the idea that humankind has reached a terminal point. We find this terminal assumption in writers like Joyce, Céline, Thomas Mann. In *Doktor Faustus* politics and art are joined in the destruction of civilization. Now here is an idea, found in some of the greatest novelists of the twentieth century. How good is this idea? Frightful things have happened, but is the apocalyptic interpretation true? The terminations did not fully terminate. Civilization is still here. The prophecies have not been borne out. Novelists are wrong to put an interpretation of history at the base of artistic creation—to speak "the last word." It is better that the novelist should trust his own sense of life. Less ambitious. More likely to tell the truth.

INTERVIEWER: Frequently in your fiction the hero strives to avoid being swallowed up by other people's ideas or versions of reality. On occasion you seem to present him with something like the whole range of contemporary alternatives—say, in *Augie March* or *Herzog*. Was this one of your intentions?

BELLOW: All these matters are really so complicated. Of course these books are somewhat concerned with free choice. I don't think that they pose the question successfully—the terms are not broad enough. I think I have let myself off easily. I seem to have asked in my books, How can one resist the controls of this vast society *without* turning into a nihilist, avoiding the absurdity of empty rebellion? I have asked, Are there other, more good-natured forms of resistance and free choice? And I suppose that, like most Americans, I have involuntarily favored the more comforting or melioristic side of the question. I don't mean that I ought to have been more "pessimistic," because I have found "pessimism" to be in most of its forms nearly as empty as "optimism." But I am obliged to admit that I have not followed these questions to the necessary depth. I can't blame myself for not having been a stern moralist; I can always use the excuse that I'm after all nothing but a writer of fiction. But I don't feel satisfied with what I have done to date, except in the comic form. There is, however, this to be added—that our French friends invariably see the answers to such questions, and all questions of truth, to be overwhelmingly formidable, uncongenial, hostile to us. It may be, however, that truth is not always so punitive. I've tried to suggest this in my books. There may be truths on the side of life. I am quite prepared to admit that being habitual liars and self-deluders, we have good cause to fear the truth, but I'm not at all ready to stop hoping. There may be some truths which are, after all, our friends in the universe.

GORDON LLOYD HARPER

9. Arthur Miller

Arthur Miller was born on October 17, 1915, in New York City. During spring vacation of his freshman year at the University of Michigan he wrote his first play, *Honors at Dawn*. As he remembers, "the play won several prizes and made me confident I could go ahead from there." Under the tutelage of Kenneth Rowe, Miller wrote two plays a year until he was graduated from the University in 1938.

He returned to New York and wrote for radio until 1944—the year he published his first book, *Situation Normal* (a series of impressions of army life), and saw his first play, *The Man Who Had All the Luck*, produced on Broadway. It ran for four days. In 1945 his novel *Focus* became a best seller, but it was soon overshadowed by the success of his play *All My Sons*, winner of the New York Drama Critics' Circle Award in 1947. The play attracted the attention of Elia Kazan, who later directed *Death of a Salesman*, which won both the Critics' Circle Award and the Pulitzer Prize for Drama in 1949.

Since then a steady succession of plays has followed: *The Crucible* (1953), *A View from the Bridge* (1955), *After the Fall* (1963), and *Incident at Vichy* (1964). In 1951 Miller wrote an adaptation of Ibsen's *An Enemy of the People*; in 1961, he adapted his own story *The Misfits* (1960) into a film which starred his second wife, Marilyn Monroe. A volume of stories, *I Don't Need You Any More*, was published in 1967. In 1966–67 Arthur Miller served as international president of P.E.N.

I

Solomon's Antiques. Solomon, buried in
his junk, is reading the paper, drinking
coffee from a container, smoking. Enter
Martin.

        Martin
Excuse me.

        Solomon
Yes, sir.

        Martin
I'm looking for a Christmas present.

        Solomon
 Well that depends which Christmas.

        Martin
(Smiles) Well, let's say this Christmas.

        Solomon *(lighting a half-burned cigarette)*
For this Christmas is very difficult. What're you got in mind?

        Martin
(Looking around)
I don't know. I went to all the department stores, walked down
all the streets. Everything is either junk or unnecessary.

        Solomon   *(he coughs, blows his nose.) excuse me*
My boy, you're not in the swim. Sit down, take it easy. There..
there's a nice Louis ~~the~~ Fourteen ~~th~~ chair, sit down.

        Martin
I'm exhausted.

        Solomon
So is everybody. ~~The~~ The first step to wisdom is to stop. Whatever
it is, stop it. Then maybe you'll find out. For who is the present?

        Martin
My wife.

        Solomon
For a wife is difficult.
                    (Looks around) *points his thumb — to a silver chandelier*
I got here a nice harp.

        Martin
What the hell would she do with a harp?

        Solomon
She'll have it. What do you mean?--what does she do with anything?

        Martin
No, you got me wrong. I love her.

Manuscript page of an unpublished Miller play

Arthur Miller

Arthur Miller's white farmhouse is set high on the border of the roller-coaster hills of Roxbury and Woodbury, in Connecticut's Litchfield County. The author, brought up in Brooklyn and Harlem, is now a country man. His house is surrounded by the trees he has raised—native dogwood, exotic katsura, Chinese scholar, tulip, and locust. Most of them were flowering as we approached his house for our interview in spring 1966. The only sound was a rhythmic hammering echoing from the other side of the hill. We walked to its source, a stately red barn, and there found the playwright, hammer in hand, standing in dim light, amid lumber, tools, and plumbing equipment. He welcomed us, a tall, rangy, good-looking man with a weathered face and sudden smile, a scholar-farmer in horn-rimmed glasses and high work shoes. He invited us in to judge his prowess: he was turning the barn into a guest house (partitions here, cedar closets there, shower over there . . .). Car-

*pentry, he said, was his oldest hobby—he had started at the age of
five.*

We walked back past the banked iris, past the hammock, and
entered the house by way of the terrace, which was guarded by a
suspicious basset named Hugo. Mr. Miller explained as we went
in that the house was silent because his wife, photographer Inge
Morath, had driven to Vermont to do a portrait of Bernard Mala-
mud, and that their three-year-old daughter Rebecca was napping.
The living room, glassed-in from the terrace, was eclectic, charming: white walls patterned with a Steinberg sketch, a splashy painting by neighbor Alexander Calder, posters of early Miller plays,
photographs by Mrs. Miller. It held colorful modern rugs and sofas,
an antique rocker, oversized black Eames chair, glass coffee table
supporting a bright mobile, small peasant figurines—souvenirs of
a recent trip to Russia—unique Mexican candlesticks and strange
pottery animals atop a very old carved Spanish table, these last
from their Paris apartment; and plants, plants everywhere.

The author's study was in total contrast. We walked up a green
knoll to a spare single-roomed structure with small louvered windows. The electric light was on—he could not work by daylight, he
confided. The room harbors a plain slab desk fashioned by the
playwright, his chair, a rumpled gray day bed, another webbed
chair from the thirties, and a bookshelf with half a dozen jacket-
less books. This is all, except for a snapshot of Inge and Rebecca,
thumbtacked to the wall. Mr. Miller adjusted a microphone he
had hung crookedly from the arm of his desk lamp. Then, quite
casually, he picked up a rifle from the day bed and took a shot
through the open louvers at a woodchuck who, scared but reprieved,
scurried across the far slope. We were startled—he smiled at our
lack of composure. He said that his study was also an excellent
duckblind.

The interview began. His tone and expression were serious, interested. Often a secret grin surfaced, as he reminisced. He is a
storyteller, a man with a marvelous memory, a simple man with a

capacity for wonder, concerned with people and ideas. We listened at our ease at he responded to questions.

INTERVIEWER: Vosnessensky, the Russian poet, said when he was here that the landscape in this part of the country reminded him of his Sigulda*—that it was a "good microclimate" for writing. Do you agree?

MILLER: Well, I enjoy it. It's not such a vast landscape that you're lost in it, and it's not so surburban a place that you feel you might as well be in a city. The distances—internal and external—are exactly correct, I think. There's a *foreground* here, no matter which way you look.

INTERVIEWER: After reading your short stories, especially "The Prophecy" and "I Don't Need You Any More," which have not only the dramatic power of your plays but also the description of place, the *foreground*, the intimacy of thought hard to achieve in a play, I wonder: is the stage much more compelling for you?

MILLER: It is only very rarely that I can feel in a short story that I'm right on top of something, as I feel when I write for the stage. I am then in the ultimate place of vision—you can't back me up any further. Everything is inevitable, down to the last comma. In a short story, or any kind of prose, I still can't escape the feeling of a certain arbitrary quality. Mistakes go by—people consent to them more—more than mistakes do on the stage. This may be my illusion. But there's another matter; the whole business of my own role in my own mind. To me the great thing is to write a good play, and when I'm writing a short story it's as though I'm saying to myself, Well, I'm only doing this because I'm not writing a play at the moment. There's guilt connected with it. Naturally I do enjoy writing a short story; it is a form that has a certain strictness. I think I reserve for plays those things which take a kind of excruciating effort. What comes easier goes into a short story.

* A resort in Lithuania.

INTERVIEWER: Would you tell us a little about the beginning of your writing career?

MILLER: The first play I wrote was in Michigan in 1935. It was written on a spring vacation in six days. I was so young that I dared do such things, begin it and finish it in a week. I'd seen about two plays in my life, so I didn't know how long an act was supposed to be, but across the hall there was a fellow who did the costumes for the University theater and he said, "Well, it's roughly forty minutes." I had written an enormous amount of material and I got an alarm clock. It was all a lark to me, and not to be taken too seriously . . . that's what I told myself. As it turned out, the acts were longer than that, but the sense of the timing was in me even from the beginning, and the play had a form right from the start.

Being a playwright was always the maximum idea. I'd always felt that the theater was the most exciting and the most demanding form one could try to master. When I began to write, one assumed inevitably that one was in the mainstream that began with Aeschylus and went through about twenty-five hundred years of playwriting. There are so few masterpieces in the theater, as opposed to the other arts, that one can pretty well encompass all of them by the age of nineteen. Today, I don't think playwrights care about history. I think they feel that it has no relevance.

INTERVIEWER: Is it just the young playwrights who feel this?

MILLER: I think the young playwrights I've had any chance to talk to are either ignorant of the past or they feel the old forms are too square, or too cohesive. I may be wrong, but I don't see that the whole tragic arch of the drama has had any effect on them.

INTERVIEWER: Which playwrights did you most admire when you were young?

MILLER: Well, first the Greeks, for their magnificent form, the symmetry. Half the time I couldn't really repeat the story because the characters in the mythology were completely blank to me. I had no background at that time to know really what was involved in these plays, but the architecture was clear. One looks at some building of the past whose use one is ignorant of, and yet it has a modernity. It had its own specific gravity. That form has never left me; I suppose it just got burned in.

INTERVIEWER: You were particularly drawn to tragedy, then?

MILLER: It seemed to me the only form there was. The rest of it was all either attempts at it, or escapes from it. But tragedy was the basic pillar.

INTERVIEWER: When *Death of a Salesman* opened, you said to *The New York Times* in an interview that the tragic feeling is evoked in us when we're in the presence of a character who is ready to lay down his life, if need be, to secure one thing—his sense of personal dignity. Do you consider your plays modern tragedies?

MILLER: I changed my mind about it several times. I think that to make a direct or arithmetical comparison between any contemporary work and the classic tragedies is impossible because of the question of religion and power, which was taken for granted and is an a priori consideration in any classic tragedy. Like a religious ceremony, where they finally reached the objective by the sacrifice. It has to do with the community sacrificing some man whom they both adore and despise in order to reach its basic and fundamental laws and, therefore, justify its existence and feel safe.

INTERVIEWER: In *After the Fall*, although Maggie was "sacrificed," the central character, Quentin, survives. Did you see him as tragic or in any degree potentially tragic?

MILLER: I can't answer that, because I can't, quite frankly, separate in my mind tragedy from death. In some people's minds I know there's no reason to put them together. I can't break it—for one reason, and that is, to coin a phrase: there's nothing like death. Dying isn't like it, you know. There's no substitute for the impact on the mind of the spectacle of death. And there is no possibility, it seems to me, of speaking of tragedy without it. Because if the total demise of the person we watch for two or three hours doesn't occur, if he just walks away, no matter how damaged, no matter how much he suffers—

INTERVIEWER: What were those two plays you had seen before you began to write?

MILLER: When I was about twelve, I think it was, my mother took me to a theater one afternoon. We lived in Harlem and in Harlem there were two or three theaters that ran all the time and many women would drop in for all or part of the afternoon performances. All I remember was that there were people in the hold of a ship, the stage was rocking—they actually rocked the stage—and some cannibal on the ship had a time bomb. And they were all looking for the cannibal: it was thrilling. The other one was a morality play about taking dope. Evidently there was much excitement in New York then about the Chinese and dope. The Chinese were kidnaping beautiful blond, blue-eyed girls who, people thought, had lost their bearings morally; they were flappers who drank gin and ran around with boys. And they inevitably ended up in some basement in Chinatown, where they were irretrievably lost by virtue of eating opium or smoking some pot. Those were the two masterpieces I had seen. I'd read some others, of course, by the time I started writing. I'd read Shakespeare and Ibsen, a little, not much. I never connected playwriting with our theater, even from the beginning.

INTERVIEWER: Did your first play have any bearing on *All My Sons,* or *Death of a Salesman?*

MILLER: It did. It was a play about a father owning a business in 1935, a business that was being struck, and a son being torn between his father's interests and his sense of justice. But it turned into a near-comic play. At that stage of my life I was removed somewhat. I was not Clifford Odets: he took it head on.

INTERVIEWER: Many of your plays have that father-son relationship as the dominant theme. Were you very close to your father?

MILLER: I was. I still am, but I think, actually, that my plays don't reflect directly my relationship to him. It's a very primitive thing in my plays. That is, the father was really a figure who incorporated both power and some kind of a moral law which he had either broken himself or had fallen prey to. He figures as an immense shadow. . . . I didn't expect that of my own father, literally, but of his position, apparently I did. The reason that I was able to write about the relationship, I think now, was because it had a mythical quality to me. If I had ever thought that I was writing about my father, I suppose I never could have done it. My father is, literally, a much more realistic guy than Willy Loman, and much more successful as a personality. And he'd be the last man in the world to ever commit suicide. Willy is based on an individual whom I knew very little, who was a salesman; it was years later that I realized I had only seen that man about a total of four hours in twenty years. He gave one of those impressions that is basic, evidently. When I thought of him, he would simply be a mute man: he said no more than two hundred words to me. I was a kid. Later on, I had another of that kind of a contact, with a man whose fantasy was always overreaching his real outline. I've always been aware of that kind of an agony, of someone who has some driving, implacable wish in him which never goes away, which he can never block out. And it broods over him, it makes him happy sometimes or it makes him suicidal, but it never leaves him. Any hero whom we even begin to think of as tragic is obsessed, whether it's Lear or Hamlet or the women in the Greek plays.

INTERVIEWER: Do any of the younger playwrights create heroes —in your opinion?

MILLER: I tell you, I may be working on a different wave length, but I don't think they are looking at character any more, at the documentation of facts about people. All experience is looked at now from a schematic point of view. These playwrights won't let the characters escape for a moment from their preconceived scheme of how dreadful the world is. It is very much like the old strike plays. The scheme then was that someone began a play with a bourgeois ideology and got involved in some area of experience which had a connection to the labor movement—either it was actually a strike or, in a larger sense, it was the collapse of capitalism—and he ended the play with some new positioning vis-à-vis that collapse. He started without an enlightenment and he ended with some kind of enlightenment. And you could predict that in the first five minutes. Very few of those plays could be done any more, because they're absurd now. I've found over the years that a similar thing has happened with the so-called absurd theater. Predictable.

INTERVIEWER: In other words, the notion of tragedy about which you were talking earlier is absent from this preconceived view of the world.

MILLER: Absolutely. The tragic hero was supposed to join the scheme of things by his sacrifice. It's a religious thing, I've always thought. He threw some sharp light upon the hidden scheme of existence, either by breaking one of its profoundest laws, as Oedipus breaks a taboo, and therefore proves the existence of the taboo, or by proving a moral world at the cost of his own life. And that's the victory. We need him, as the vanguard of the race. We need his crime. That crime is a civilizing crime. Well, *now* the view is that it's an inconsolable universe. Nothing is proved by a crime excepting that some people are freer to produce crime than others, and usually they are more honest than the others. There is no final reassertion of a community at all. There isn't the kind of communication that a child demands. The best you could say is that it is intelligent.

INTERVIEWER: Then it's aware—

MILLER: It's aware, but it will not admit into itself any moral universe at all. Another thing that's missing is the positioning of the author in relation to power. I always assumed that underlying any story is the question of who should wield power. See, in *Death of a Salesman* you have two viewpoints. They show what would happen if we all took Willy's viewpoint toward the world, or if we all took Biff's. And took it seriously, as almost a political fact. I'm debating really which way the world ought to be run; I'm speaking of psychology and the spirit, too. For example, a play that isn't usually linked with this kind of problem is Tennessee Williams's *Cat on a Hot Tin Roof*. It struck me sharply that what is at stake there is the father's great power. He's the owner, literally, of an empire of land and farms. And he wants to immortalize that power, he wants to hand it on, because he's dying. The son has a much finer appreciation of justice and human relations than the father. The father is rougher, more Philistine; he's cruder; and when we speak of the fineness of emotions, we would probably say the son has them and the father lacks them. When I saw the play I thought, This is going to be simply marvelous because the person with the sensitivity will be presented with power and what is he going to do about it? But it never gets to that. It gets deflected onto a question of personal neurosis. It comes to a dead end. If we're talking about tragedy, the Greeks would have done something miraculous with that idea. They would have stuck the son with the power, and faced him with the racking conflicts of the sensitive man having to rule. And then you would throw light on what the tragedy of power is.

INTERVIEWER: Which is what you were getting at in *Incident at Vichy*.

MILLER: That's exactly what I was after. But I feel today's stage turns away from any consideration of power, which always lies at the heart of tragedy. I use Williams's play as an example because he's that excellent that his problems are symptomatic of the time —*Cat* ultimately came down to the mendacity of human relations. It was a most accurate personalization but it bypasses the issue which the play seems to me to raise, namely the mendacity in social relations. I still believe that when a play questions, even threatens, our social arrangement, that is when it really shakes us profoundly and dangerously, and that is when you've got to be great; good isn't enough.

INTERVIEWER: Do you think that people in general now rationalize so, and have so many euphemisms for death, that they can't face tragedy?

MILLER: I wonder whether there isn't a certain—I'm speaking now of all classes of people—you could call it a softness, or else a genuine inability to face the tough decisions and the dreadful results of error. I say that only because when *Death of a Salesman* went on again recently, I sensed in some of the reaction that it was simply too threatening. Now there were probably a lot of people in the forties, when it first opened, who felt the same way. Maybe I just didn't hear those people as much as I heard other people— maybe it has to do with my own reaction. You need a certain amount of confidence to watch tragedy. If you yourself are about to die, you're not going to see that play. I've always thought that the Americans had, almost inborn, a primordial fear of falling, being declassed—you get it with your driver's license, if not earlier.

INTERVIEWER: What about Europeans?

MILLER: Well, the play opened in Paris again only last September; it opened in Paris ten years earlier, too, with very little effect. It wasn't a very good production, I understand. But now suddenly they discovered this play. And I sensed that their reaction was quite an American reaction. Maybe it comes with having . . . having the guilt of wealth; it would be interesting if the Russians ever got to feel that way!

INTERVIEWER: *Death of a Salesman* has been done in Russia, hasn't it?

MILLER: Oh, many times.

INTERVIEWER: When you were in Russia recently did you form any opinion about the Russian theater public?

MILLER: First of all, there's a wonderful naïveté that they have; they're not bored to death. They're not coming in out of the rain, so to speak, with nothing better to do. When they go to the theater, it has great weight with them. They come to see something that'll change their lives. Ninety per cent of the time, of course, there's nothing there, but they're open to a grand experience. This is not the way we go to the theater.

INTERVIEWER: What about the plays themselves?

MILLER: I think they do things on the stage which are exciting and deft and they have marvelous actors, but the drama itself is not adventurous. The plays are basically a species of naturalism; it's not even realism. They're violently opposed to the theater of the absurd because they see it as a fragmenting of the community into perverse individuals who will no longer be under any mutual obligation at all, and I can see some point in their fear. Of course, these things should be done if only so one can rebut them. I know that I was very moved in many ways by German expressionism when I was in school: yet there too something was perverse in it to me. It was the end of man, there are no people in it any more; that was especially true of the real German stuff: it's the bitter end of the world where man is a voice of his class function, and that's it. Brecht has a lot of that in him, but he's too much of a poet to be enslaved by it. And yet, at the same time, I learned a great deal from it. I used elements of it that were fused into *Death of a Salesman*. For instance, I purposefully would not give Ben any character, because for Willy he *has* no character—which is, psychologically, expressionist because so many memories come back with a simple tag on them: somebody represents a threat to you, or a promise.

INTERVIEWER: Speaking of different cultures, what is your feeling about the French Théâtre National Populaire?

MILLER: I thought a play I saw by Corneille, *L'Allusion Comique*, one of the most exciting things I've ever seen. We saw something I never thought I could enjoy—my French is not all that good. But I had just gotten over being sick, and we were about to leave France, and I wanted to see what they did with it. It was just superb. It is one of Corneille's lesser works, about a magician who takes people into the nether regions. What a marvelous mixture of satire, and broad comedy, and characterizations! And the acting was simply out of this world. Of course, one of the best parts about the whole thing was the audience. Because they're mostly under thirty, it looked to me; they pay very little to get in; and I would guess there are between twenty-five hundred and three thousand seats in that place. And the vitality of the audience is breathtaking. Of course the actors' ability to speak that language so beautifully is just in itself a joy. From that vast stage, to talk quietly, and make you *feel* the voice just wafting all over the house . . .

INTERVIEWER: Why do you think we haven't been able to do

such a thing here? Why has Whitehead's Lincoln Center Repertory Theater failed as such?

MILLER: Well, that is a phenomenon worthy of a sociological study. When I got into it, *After the Fall* was about two-thirds written. Whitehead came to me and said, "I hear you're writing a play. Can we use it to start the Lincoln Center Repertory Company?" For one reason or another I said I would do it. I expected to take a financial beating (I could hope to earn maybe twenty per cent of what I normally earn with a play, but I assumed that people would say, "Well, it's a stupid but not idiotic action"). What developed, before any play opened at all, was a hostility which completely dumfounded me. I don't think it was directed against anybody in particular. For actors who want to develop their art, there's no better place to do it than in a permanent repertory company, where you play different parts and you have opportunities you've never had in a lifetime on Broadway. But the actors seemed to be affronted by the whole thing. I couldn't dig it! I could understand the enmity of commercial producers who, after all, thought they were threatened by it. But the professional people of every kind greeted it as though it were some kind of an insult. The only conclusion I can come to is that an actor was now threatened with having to put up or shut up. He had always been able to walk around on Broadway, where conditions were dreadful, and say, "I'm a great actor but I'm unappreciated," but in the back of his mind he could figure, "Well, one of these days I'll get a starring role and I'll go to Hollywood and get rich." This he couldn't do in a repertory theater where he signed up for several years. So the whole idea of that kind of quick success was renounced. He didn't want to face an opportunity which threatened him in this way. It makes me wonder whether there is such a profound alienation among artists that any organized attempt to create something that is not based upon commerce, that has sponsorship, automatically sets people against it. I think that's an interesting facet. I also spoke to a group of young playwrights. Now, if it had been me, I would have been knocking at the door, demanding that they read my play, as I did unsuccessfully when the Group Theatre was around. Then every playwright was banging on the door and furious and wanted the art theater to do what *he* thought they should do. We could do that because it belonged to us all—you know—we thought of the Group Theatre as a public enterprise. Well, that wasn't true at all here. Everyone thought the Lincoln Theater was the property of the directors, of Miller and Whitehead and Kazan and one or two other people. Of course, what also made it fail was, as Laurence Olivier suggested, that it takes years to do anything. But he also made the point that with his English repertory theater he got encouragement from the beginning. There were people who pooh-poohed the whole thing, and said it was ridiculous, but basically the artistic community was in favor of it.

INTERVIEWER: How about the actors themselves? Did Lee Strasberg influence them?

MILLER: I think Strasberg is a symptom, really. He's a great force, and (in my unique opinion, evidently) a force which is not for the good in the theater. He makes actors secret people and he makes acting secret, and it's the most communicative art known to man; I mean, that's what the actor's *supposed* to be doing. But I wouldn't blame the Repertory Theater failures on him, because the people in there were not Actors Studio people at all; so he is not responsible for that. But the Method is in the air: the actor is defending himself from the Philistine, vulgar public. I had a girl in my play I couldn't hear, and the acoustics in that little theater we were using were simply magnificent. I said to her, "I can't hear you," and I kept on saying, "I can't hear you." She finally got furious and said to me, in effect, that she was acting the truth, and that she was not going to prostitute herself to the audience. That was the living end! It reminded me of Walter Hampden's comment—because we had a similar problem in *The Crucible* with some actors —he said they play a cello with the most perfect bowing and the fingering is magnificent but there are no strings on the instrument. The problem is that the actor is now working out his private fate through his role, and the idea of communicating the meaning of the play is the last thing that occurs to him. In the Actors Studio, despite denials, the actor is told that the text is really the framework for his emotions; I've heard actors change the order of lines in my work and tell me that the lines are only, so to speak, the libretto for the music—that the actor is the main force that the audience is watching and that the playwright is his servant. They are told that the analysis of the text, and the rhythm of the text, the verbal texture, is of no importance whatever. This is Method, as they are teaching it, which is, of course, a perversion of it, if you go back to the beginning. But there was always a tendency in that direction. Chekhov, himself, said that Stanislavsky had perverted *The Seagull*.

INTERVIEWER: What about Method acting in the movies?

MILLER: Well, in the movies, curiously enough, the Method works better. Because the camera can come right up to an actor's nostrils and suck out of him a communicative gesture; a look in the eye, a wrinkle of his grin, and so on, which registers nothing on the stage. The stage is, after all, a verbal medium. You've got to make large gestures if they're going to be seen at all. In other words, you've got to be unnatural. You've got to say, I am out to move into that audience; that's my job. In a movie you don't do that; as a matter of fact, that's bad movie acting, it's overacting. Movies are wonderful for private acting.

INTERVIEWER: Do you think the movies helped bring about this private acting in the theater?

MILLER: Well, it's a perversion of the Chekhovian play and of the Stanislavsky technique. What Chekhov was doing was eliminating the histrionics of his actors by incorporating them in the writing: the internal life was what he was writing about. And Stanislavsky's direction was also internal: for the first time he was trying to motivate every move from within instead of imitating an action; which is what acting should be. When you eliminate the vital element of the actor in the community and simply make a psychiatric figure on the stage who is thinking profound thoughts which he doesn't let anyone know about, then it's a perversion.

INTERVIEWER: How does the success of Peter Weiss's *Marat/Sade* play fit into this?

MILLER: Well, I would emphasize its production and direction. Peter Brook has been trying for years, especially through productions of Shakespeare, to make the bridge between psychological acting and theater, between the private personality, perhaps, and its public demonstration. *Marat/Sade* is more an oratorio than a play; the characters are basically thematic relationships rather than human entities, so the action exemplified rather than characterized.

INTERVIEWER: Do you think the popularity of the movies has had any influence on playwriting itself?

MILLER: Yes. Its form has been changed by the movies. I think certain techniques, such as the jumping from place to place, although it's as old as Shakespeare, came to us not through Shakespeare, but through the movies, a telegraphic, dream-constructed way of seeing life.

INTERVIEWER: How important is the screenwriter in motion pictures?

MILLER: Well, you'd be hard put to remember the dialogue in some of the great pictures that you've seen. That's why pictures are so international. You don't have to hear the style of the dialogue in an Italian movie or a French movie. We're watching the film, so that the vehicle is not the ear or the word, it's the eye. The director of a play is nailed to words. He can interpret them a little differently, but he has limits: you can only inflect a sentence in two or three different ways, but you can inflect an image on the screen in an infinite number of ways. You can make one character practically fall out of the frame; you can shoot it where you don't even see his face. Two people can be talking, and the man talking cannot be seen, so the emphasis is on the reaction to the speech rather than on the speech itself.

INTERVIEWER: What about television as a medium for drama?

MILLER: I don't think there is anything that approaches the theater. The sheer presence of a living person is always stronger than his image. But there's no reason why TV shouldn't be a terrific medium. The problem is that the audience watching TV shows is always separated. My feeling is that people in a group, en masse, watching something, react differently, and perhaps more profoundly, than they do when they're alone in their living rooms. Yet it's not a hurdle that couldn't be jumped by the right kind of material. Simply, it's hard to get good movies, it's hard to get good novels, it's hard to get good poetry—it's *impossible* to get good television because in addition to the indigenous difficulties there's the whole question of it being a medium that's controlled by big business. It took TV seventeen years to do *Death of a Salesman* here. It's been done on TV in every country in the world at least once, but it's critical of the business world and the content is downbeat.

INTERVIEWER: A long time ago, you used to write radio scripts. Did you learn much about technique from that experience?

MILLER: I did. We had twenty-eight and a half minutes to tell a whole story in a radio play, and you had to concentrate on the words because you couldn't see anything. You were playing in a dark closet, in fact. So the economy of words in a good radio play was everything. It drove you more and more to realize what the power of a good sentence was, and the right phrase could save you a page you would otherwise be wasting. I was always sorry radio didn't last long enough for contemporary poetic movements to take advantage of it, because it's a natural medium for poets. It's pure voice, pure words. Words and silence; a marvelous medium. I've often thought, even recently, that I would like to write another radio play, and just give it to someone and let them do it on WBAI. The English do radio plays still, very good ones.

INTERVIEWER: You used to write verse drama too, didn't you?

MILLER: Oh yes, I was up to my neck in it.

INTERVIEWER: Would you ever do it again?

MILLER: I might. I often write speeches in verse, and then break them down. Much of *Death of a Salesman* was originally written in verse, and *The Crucible* was all written in verse, but I broke it up. I was frightened that the actors would take an attitude toward the material that would destroy its vitality. I didn't want anyone standing up there making speeches. You see, we have no tradition of verse, and as soon as an American actor sees something printed like verse, he immediately puts one foot in front of the other—or else he mutters. Then you can't hear it at all.

INTERVIEWER: Which of your own plays do you feel closest to now?

MILLER: I don't know if I feel closer to one than another. I suppose *The Crucible* in some ways. I think there's a lot of myself in it. There are a lot of layers in there that I know about that nobody else does.

INTERVIEWER: More so than in *After the Fall*?

MILLER: Yes, because although *After the Fall* is more psychological it's less developed as an artifice. You see, in *The Crucible* I was completely freed by the period I was writing about—over three centuries ago. It was a different diction, a different age. I had great joy writing that, more than with almost any other play I've written. I learned about how writers felt in the past when they were dealing almost constantly with historical material. A dramatist writing history could finish a play Monday and start another Wednesday, and go right on. Because the *stories* are all prepared for him. Inventing the story is what takes all the time. It takes a year to invent the story. The historical dramatist doesn't have to invent anything, except his language, and his characterizations. Oh, of course, there's the terrific problem of condensing history, a lot of reshuffling and bringing in characters who never lived, or who died a hundred years apart—but basically if you've got the story, you're a year ahead.

INTERVIEWER: It must also be tempting to use a historical figure whose epoch was one of faith.

MILLER: It is. With all the modern psychology and psychiatry and the level of literacy higher than it ever was, we get less perspective on ourselves than at almost any time I know about. I have never been so aware of clique ideas overtaking people—fashions, for example—and sweeping them away, as though the last day of the world had come. One can sometimes point to a week or month in which things changed abruptly. It's like women's clothing in a certain issue of *Vogue* magazine. There is such a wish to be part of that enormous minority that likes to create new minorities. Yet people are desperately afraid of being alone.

INTERVIEWER: Has our insight into psychology affected this?

MILLER: It has simply helped people rationalize their situation, rather than get out of it, or break through it. In other words—you've heard it a hundred times—"Well, I am this type of person, and this type doesn't do anything but what I'm doing."

INTERVIEWER: Do you think the push toward personal success dominates American life now more than it used to?

MILLER: I think it's far more powerful today than when I wrote *Death of a Salesman*. I think it's closer to a madness today than it was then. Now there's no perspective on it at all.

INTERVIEWER: Would you say that the girl in *After the Fall* is a symbol of that obsession?

MILLER: Yes, she is consumed by what she does, and instead of it being a means of release, it's a jail. A prison which defines her, finally. She can't break through. In other words, success, instead of giving freedom of choice, becomes a way of life. There's no country I've been to where people, when you come into a room and sit down with them, so often ask you, "What do you do?" And, being American, many's the time I've almost asked that question, then realized it's good for my soul not to know. For a while! Just to let the evening wear on and see what I think of this person without knowing what he does and how successful he is, or what a failure. We're *ranking* everybody every minute of the day.

INTERVIEWER: Will you write about American success again?

MILLER: I might, but you see, as a thing in itself, success is self-satirizing; it's self-elucidating, in a way. That's why it's so difficult to write about. Because the very people who are being swallowed up by this ethos nod in agreement when you tell them, "You are being swallowed up by this thing." To really wrench them and find them another feasible perspective is therefore extremely difficult.

INTERVIEWER: In your story "The Prophecy," the protagonist

says this is a time of the supremacy of personal relations, that there are no larger aims in our lives. Is this your view too?

MILLER: Well, that story was written under the pall of the fifties, but I think there's been a terrific politicalization of the people these past four or five years. Not in the old sense, but in the sense that it is no longer gauche or stupid to be interested in the fate of society and in injustice and in race problems and the rest of it. It now becomes aesthetic material once again. In the fifties it was *out* to mention this. It meant you were really not an artist. That prejudice seems to have gone. The Negroes broke it up, thank God! But it has been an era of personal relations—and now it's being synthesized in a good way. That is, the closer you get to any kind of political action among young people, the more they demand that the action have a certain fidelity to human nature, and that pomposity, and posing, and role-taking not be allowed to strip the movement of its veracity. What they suspect most is gesturing, you know, just making gestures, which are either futile, or self-serving, or merely conscientious. The intense personal-relations concentration of the fifties seems now to have been joined to a political consciousness, which is terrific.

INTERVIEWER: Do you feel politics in any way to be an invasion of your privacy?

MILLER: No, I always drew a lot of inspiration from politics, from one or another kind of national struggle. You live in the world even though you only vote once in a while. It determines the extensions of your personality. I lived through the McCarthy time, when one saw personalities shifting and changing before one's eyes, as a direct, obvious result of a political situation. And had it gone on, we would have gotten a whole new American personality—which in part we have. It's ten years since McCarthy died, and it's only now that powerful Senators dare to suggest that it might be wise to learn a little Chinese, to talk to some Chinese. I mean, it took ten years, and even those guys who are thought to be quite brave and courageous just now dare to make these suggestions. Such a pall of fright was laid upon us that it truly deflected the American mind. It's part of a paranoia which we haven't escaped yet. Good God, people still give their lives for it; look what we're doing in the Pacific.

INTERVIEWER: Yet so much of the theater these last few years has had nothing to do with public life.

MILLER: Yes, it's got so we've lost the technique of grappling with the world that Homer had, that Aeschylus had, that Euripides had. And Shakespeare. How amazing it is that people who adore the Greek drama fail to see that these great works are works of a man confronting his society, the illusions of the society, the faiths of the society. They're social documents, not little piddling private conversations. We just got educated into thinking this is all "a story," a myth for its own sake.

INTERVIEWER: Do you think there'll be a return to social drama now?

MILLER: I think there will be, if theater is to survive. Look at Molière. You can't conceive of him except as a social playwright. He's a social critic. Bathes up to his neck in what's going on around him.

INTERVIEWER: Could the strict forms utilized by Molière appear again?

MILLER: I don't think one can repeat old forms as such, because they express most densely a moment of time. For example, I couldn't write a play like *Death of a Salesman* any more. I couldn't really write any of my plays now. Each is different, spaced sometimes two years apart, because each moment called for a different vocabulary and a different organization of the material. However, when you speak of a strict form, I believe in it for the theater. Otherwise you end up with anecdotes, not with plays. We're in an era of anecdotes, in my opinion, which is going to pass any minute. The audience has been trained to eschew the organized climax because it's corny, or because it violates the chaos which we all revere. But I think that's going to disappear with the first play of a new kind which will once again pound the boards and shake people out of their seats with a deeply, intensely organized climax. It can

only come from a strict form: you can't get it except as the culmi-
nation of two hours of development. You can't get it by raising
your voice and yelling, suddenly—because it's getting time to get
on the train for Yonkers.

INTERVIEWER: Have you any conception of what your own evolution has been? In terms of form and themes?

MILLER: I keep going. Both forward and backward. Hopefully,
more forward than backward. That is to say, before I wrote my
first *successful* play, I wrote, oh, I don't know, maybe fourteen or
fifteen other full-length plays and maybe thirty radio plays. The
majority of them were nonrealistic plays. They were metaphorical
plays, or symbolistic plays; some of them were in verse, or in one
case—writing about Montezuma—I turned out a grand historical
tragedy, partly in verse, rather Elizabethan in form. Then I began
to be known really by virtue of the single play I had ever tried to
do in completely realistic Ibsen-like form, which was *All My Sons*.
The fortunes of a writer! The others, like *Salesman*, which are a
compound of expressionism and realism, or even *A View from the
Bridge*, which is realism of a sort (though it's broken up severely),
are more typical of the bulk of the work I've done. *After the Fall*
is really down the middle, it's more like most of the work I've done
than any other play—excepting that what has *surfaced* has been
more realistic than in the others. It's really an impressionistic kind
of a work. I was trying to create a total by throwing many small
pieces at the spectator.

INTERVIEWER: What production of *After the Fall* do you think
did it the most justice?

MILLER: I saw one production which I thought was quite marvelous. That was the one Zeffirelli did in Italy. He understood that
this was a play which reflected the world as one man saw it.
Through the play the mounting awareness of this man was the
issue, and as it approached agony the audience was to be enlarged
in its consciousness of what was happening. The other productions that I've seen have all been really *realistic* in the worst sense.
That is to say, they simply played the scenes without any attempt

to allow the main character to develop this widened awareness. He has different reactions on page ten than he does on page one, but it takes an actor with a certain amount of brains to see that evolution. It isn't enough to feel them. And as a director, Zeffirelli had an absolutely organic viewpoint toward it. The play is about someone desperately striving to obtain a viewpoint.

INTERVIEWER: Do you feel in the New York production that the girl allegedly based on Marilyn Monroe was out of proportion, entirely separate from Quentin?

MILLER: Yes, although I failed to foresee it myself. In the Italian production this never happened; it was always in proportion. I suppose, too, that by the time Zeffirelli did the play, the publicity shock had been absorbed, so that one could watch Quentin's evolution without being distracted.

INTERVIEWER: What do you think happened in New York?

MILLER: Something I never thought could happen. The play was never judged as a play at all. Good or bad, I would never know what it was from what I read about it, only what it was supposed to have been.

INTERVIEWER: Because they all reacted as if it were simply a segment of your personal life?

MILLER: Yes.

INTERVIEWER: Do you think contemporary American critics tend to regard the theater in terms of literature rather than theater?

MILLER: Yes, for years theatrical criticism was carried on mainly by reporters. Reporters who, by and large, had no references in the aesthetic theories of the drama, except in the most rudimentary way. And off in a corner, somewhere, the professors, with no relation whatsoever to the newspaper critics, were regarding the drama from a so-called academic viewpoint—with its relentless standards of tragedy, and so forth. What the reporters had very often was a simple, primitive love of a good show. And if nothing else, you could tell whether that level of mind was genuinely interested or not. There was a certain naïveté in the reportage. They could destroy plays which dealt on a level of sensibility that was beyond them. But by and large, you got a playback on what you put in. They knew how to laugh, cry, at least a native kind of reaction, stamp their feet—they loved the theater. Since then, the reporter-critics have been largely displaced by academic critics or graduates of that school. Quite frankly, two-thirds of the time I don't know what they really feel about the play. They seem to feel that the theater is an intrusion on literature. The theater as theater—as a place where people go to be swept up in some new experience—seems to antagonize them. I don't think we can really do away with *joy*: the joy of being distracted altogether in the service of some aesthetic. That seems to be the general drift, but it won't work: sooner or later the theater outwits everybody. Someone comes in who just loves to write, or to act, and who'll sweep the audience, and the critics, with him.

INTERVIEWER: Do you think these critics influence playwrights?

MILLER: Everything influences playwrights. A playwright who isn't influenced is never of any use. He's the litmus paper of the arts. He's got to be, because if he isn't working on the same wave length as the audience, no one would know what in hell he was talking about. He is a kind of psychic journalist, even when he's great; consequently, for him the total atmosphere is more important in this art than it is probably in any other.

INTERVIEWER: What do you think of a certain critic's statement that the success of a really contemporary play, like *Marat/Sade*, makes Tennessee Williams and his genre obsolete?

MILLER: Ridiculous. No more than that Tennessee's remarkable success made obsolete the past before him. There are some biological laws in the theater which can't be violated. It should not be made into an activated chess game. You can't have a theater based upon anything other than a mass audience if it's going to succeed. The larger the better. It's the law of the theater. In the Greek audience fourteen thousand people sat down at the same time, to see a play. Fourteen thousand people! And nobody can tell me that those people were all readers of the *New York Review of Books*! Even Shakespeare was smashed around in his time by university people. I think for much the same reasons—because he was reaching for those parts of man's make-up which respond to melodrama, broad comedy, violence, dirty words, and blood. Plenty of blood, murder, and not very well motivated at that.

INTERVIEWER: What is your feeling about Eugene O'Neill as a playwright?

MILLER: O'Neill never meant much to me when I was starting. In the thirties, and for the most part in the forties, you would have said that he was a finished figure. He was not a force any more. *The Iceman Cometh* and *The Long Day's Journey into Night,* so popular a few years ago, would not have been successful when they were written. Which is another example of the psychic journalism of the stage. A great deal depends upon when a play is produced. That's why playwriting is such a fatal profession to take up. You can have everything, but if you don't have that sense of timing, nothing happens. One thing I always respected about O'Neill was his insistence on his vision. That is, even when he was twisting materials to distortion and really ruining his work, there was an image behind it of a possessed individual, who, for good or ill, was himself. I don't think there is anything in it for a young man to learn technically; that was probably why I wasn't interested in it. He had one virtue which is not technical, it's what I call "drumming"; he repeats something up to and past the point where you say, "I know this, I've heard this ninety-three different ways," and suddenly you realize you are being swept up in something that you thought you understood and he has drummed you over the horizon into a new perception. He doesn't care if he's repeating. It's part of his insensitivity. He's a very insensitive writer. There's no finesse at all: he's the Dreiser of the stage. He writes with heavy pencils. His virtue is that he insists on his climax, and not the one you would want to put there. His failing is that so many of his plays are so distorted that one no longer knows on what level to receive them. His people are not symbolic; his lines are certainly not verse; the prose is not realistic—his is the never-never land of a quasi-Strindberg writer. But where he's wonderful, it's superb.

The last play is really a masterpiece. But, to give you an example of timing: *The Iceman Cometh* opened, it happened, the same year that *All My Sons* opened. It's an interesting sociological phenomenon. That was in forty-seven, soon after the war. There was still in the air a certain hopefulness about the organization of the world. There was no depression in the United States. McCarthyism had not yet started. There was a kind of . . . one could almost speak of it as an atmosphere of good will, if such a term can be used in the twentieth century. Then a play comes along which posits a world *really* filled with disasters of one kind or another. A cul-de-sac is described, a bag with no way out. At that time it didn't corroborate what people had experienced. It corroborated what they were *going* to experience, and pretty soon after, it became very timely. We moved into the bag that he had gotten into first! But at the time it opened, nobody went to see *Iceman*. In a big way, nobody went. Even after it was cut, the thing took four or five hours to play. The production was simply dreadful. But nobody made any note that it was dreadful. Nobody perceived what this play was. It was described simply as the work of a sick old man of whom everybody said, "Isn't it wonderful that he can still spell?" When I went to see that play not long after it opened, there must have been thirty people in the audience. I think there were a dozen people left by the end of the play. It was quite obviously a great piece of work which was being mangled on the stage. It was obvious to me. And to a certain number of directors who saw it. Not all of them. Not all directors can tell the difference between the production and the play. I can't do it all the time, either, though *Iceman* was one where I could. But as for the critics I don't think there is anybody alive today, with the possible exception of Harold Clurman, whom I would trust to know the difference between production and play. Harold can do it—not always, but a lot of the time —because he has directed a good deal.

INTERVIEWER: Could this question of timing have affected the reaction here to *After the Fall?*

MILLER: Look, *After the Fall* would have been altogether different if by some means the hero was killed, or shot himself. Then we would have been in business. I knew it at the time. As I was saying before, there's nothing like death. Still, I just wasn't going to do it. The ironical thing to me was that I heard cries of indignation from various people who had in the lifetime of Marilyn Monroe either exploited her unmercifully, in a way that would have subjected them to peonage laws, or mocked her viciously, or refused to take any of her pretensions seriously. So consequently, it was impossible to credit their sincerity.

INTERVIEWER: They were letting you get them off the hook.

MILLER: That's right. That's exactly right.

INTERVIEWER: And they didn't want Quentin to compromise.

MILLER: I think Günter Grass recently has said that art is uncompromising and life is full of compromises. To bring them together is a near impossibility, and that is what I was trying to do. I was trying to make it as much like life as it could possibly be and as excruciating—so the relief that we want would not be there: I denied the audience the relief. And of course all these hard realists betrayed their basic romanticism by their reaction.

INTERVIEWER: Do you think if you had done it in poetry that would have removed the threat more?

MILLER: Yes, I suppose so. But I didn't want to remove it. It would have seduced people in a way I didn't want to. Look, I know how to make 'em go with me—it's the first instinct of a writer who succeeds in the theater at all. I mean by the time you've written your third play or so you know which buttons to push; if you want an easy success there's no problem that way once you've gotten a story. People are pretty primitive—they really want the thing to turn out all right. After all, for a century and a half *King Lear* was played in England with a happy ending. I wrote a radio play about the boy who wrote that version—William Ireland—who forged Shakespeare's plays, and edited *King Lear* so that it conformed to a middle-class view of life. They thought, including all but Malone, who was the first good critic, that this was the real Shakespeare. He was an expert forger. He fixed up several of the other plays, but this one he really rewrote. He was seventeen years old. And they produced it—it was a big success—and Boswell thought it was the greatest thing he'd ever seen, and so did all the others. The only one was Malone, who on the basis of textual impossibilities—aside from the fact that he sensed it was a bowdlerization—proved that it couldn't have been Shakespeare. It's what I was talking about before: the litmus paper of the playwright: you see, Ireland sensed quite correctly what these people really wanted from *King Lear*, and he gave it to them. He sentimentalized it; took out any noxious references.

INTERVIEWER: And did it end with a happy family reunion?

MILLER: Yes, kind of like a Jewish melodrama. A family play.

INTERVIEWER: To go back to *After the Fall*. Did the style in which this play was presented in New York affect its reception?

MILLER: Well, you've hit it right on the head. You see, what happened in Italy with Zeffirelli was— I can describe it very simply: there was a stage made up of steel frames; it is as though one were looking into the back of a bellows camera—you know, concentric oblong steel frames receding toward a center. The sides of these steel frames were covered, just like a camera is, but the actors could enter through openings in these covers. They could appear or disappear on the stage at any depth. Furthermore, pneumatic lifts silently and invisibly raised the actors up, so that they could appear for ten seconds—then disappear. Or a table would be raised or a whole group of furniture, which the actors would then use. So that the whole image of all this happening inside a man's head was there from the first second, and remained right through the play. In New York the difficulty was partly due to the stage which was open, rounded. Such a stage has virtues for certain kinds of plays, but it is stiff—there is no place to hide at all. If an actor has to *appear* stage center, he makes his appearance twenty feet off the left or right. The laborious nature of these entrances and exits is insuperable. What is supposed to "appear" doesn't appear, but lumbers on stage toward you.

INTERVIEWER: Did that Italian production have a concentration camp in the background? I remember a piece by Jonathan Miller complaining of your use of the concentration camp in New York.

MILLER: Oh yes. You see in Italy the steel frame itself *became* the concentration camp, so that the whole play in effect was taking place in the *ambiance* of that enclosure. This steel turned into a jail, into a prison, into a camp, into a constricted mechanical environment. You could light those girders in such a way that they were forbidding—it was a great scenic idea.

INTERVIEWER: Why did you choose to use a concentration camp in the first place?

MILLER: Well, I have always felt that concentration camps, though they're a phenomenon of totalitarian states, are also the logical conclusion of contemporary life. If you complain of people being shot down in the streets, of the absence of communication or social responsibility, of the rise of everyday violence which people have become accustomed to, and the dehumanization of feelings, then the ultimate development on an organized social level is the concentration camp. Camps didn't happen in Africa where people had no connection with the basic development of Western civilization. They happened in the heart of Europe, in a country, for example, which was probably less anti-Semitic than other countries, like France. The Dreyfus case did not happen in Germany. In this play the question is, what is there between people that is indestructible? The concentration camp is the final expression of human separateness and its ultimate consequence. It is organized abandonment . . . one of the prime themes of *After the Fall*.

Even in *Salesman* what's driving Willy nuts is that he's trying to establish a connection, in his case, with the world of power; he is trying to say that if you behave in a certain way, you'll end up in the catbird seat. That's your connection; then life is no longer dangerous, you see. You are safe from abandonment.

INTERVIEWER: What is the genesis of *The Crucible*?

MILLER: I thought of it first when I was at Michigan. I read a lot about the Salem witch trials at that time. Then when the

McCarthy era came along, I remembered these stories and I used to tell them to people when it started. I had no idea that it was going to go as far as it went. I used to say, you know, McCarthy is actually saying certain lines that I recall the witch-hunters saying in Salem. So I started to go back, not with the idea of writing a play, but to refresh my own mind because it was getting eerie. For example, his holding up his hand with cards in it, saying, "I have in my hand the names of so-and-so." Well, this was a standard tactic of seventeenth-century prosecutors confronting a witness who was reluctant or confused, or an audience in a church which was not quite convinced that this particular individual might be guilty. He wouldn't say, "I have in my hand a list"; he'd say, "We possess the names of all these people who are guilty. But the time has not come yet to release them." He had nothing at all—he simply wanted to secure in the town's mind the idea that he saw everything, that everyone was transparent to him. It was a way of inflicting guilt on everybody, and many people responded genuinely out of guilt; some would come and tell him some fantasy, or something that they had done or thought that was evil in their minds. I had in my play, for example, the old man who comes and reports that when his wife reads certain books, *he* can't pray. He figures that the prosecutors would know the reason, that they can see through what to him was an opaque glass. Of course he ends up in a disaster because they prosecuted his wife. Many times completely naïve testimony resulted in somebody being hanged. And it was because they originally said, "We really know what's going on."

INTERVIEWER: Was it the play, *The Crucible* itself, do you think, or was it perhaps that piece you did in the *Nation*—"A Modest Proposal"—that focused the Un-American Activities Committee on you?

MILLER: Well, I had made a lot of statements and I had signed a great many petitions. I'd been involved in organizations, you know, putting my name down for fifteen years before that. But I don't think they ever would have bothered me if I hadn't married

Marilyn. Had they been interested, they would have called me earlier. And, in fact, I was told on good authority that the then chairman, Francis Walter, said that if Marilyn would take a photograph with him, shaking his hand, he would call off the whole thing. It's as simple as that. Marilyn would get them on the front pages right away. They had been on the front page for years, but the issue was starting to lose its punch. They ended up in the back of the paper or on the inside pages, and here they would get right up front again. These men would time hearings to meet a certain day's newspaper. In other words, if they figured the astronauts were going up, let's say, they wouldn't have a hearing that week; they'd wait until they'd returned and things had quieted down.

INTERVIEWER: What happened at the committee hearing?

MILLER: Well, I was indicted for contempt for having refused to give or confirm the name of a writer, whether I had seen him in a meeting of communist writers I had attended some eight or ten years earlier. My legal defense was not on any of the Constitutional amendments but on the contention that Congress couldn't drag people in and question them about anything on the Congressman's mind; they had to show that the witness was likely to have information relevant to some legislation then at issue. The committee had put on a show of interest in passport legislation. I had been denied a passport a couple of years earlier. Ergo, I fitted into their vise. A year later I was convicted after a week's trial. Then about a year after that the Court of Appeals threw out the whole thing. A short while later the committee's chief counsel, who had been my interrogator, was shown to be on the payroll of a racist foundation and was retired to private life. It was all a dreadful waste of time and money and anger, but I suffered very little, really, compared to others who were driven out of their professions and never got back, or who did get back after eight and ten years of black-listing. I wasn't in TV or movies, so I could still function.

INTERVIEWER: Have your political views changed much since then?

MILLER: Nowadays I'm certainly not ready to advocate a tightly organized planned economy. I think it has its virtues, but I'm in deadly fear of people with too much power. I don't trust people that much any more. I used to think that if people had the right idea they could make things move accordingly. Now it's a day-to-day fight to stop dreadful things from happening. In the thirties it was, for me, inconceivable that a socialist government could be really anti-Semitic. It just could not happen, because their whole protest in the beginning was against anti-Semitism, against racism, against this kind of inhumanity; that's why I was drawn to it. It was accounted to Hitler; it was accounted to blind capitalism. I'm much more pragmatic about such things now, and I want to know those I'm against and who it is that I'm backing and what he is like.

INTERVIEWER: Do you feel whatever Jewish tradition you were brought up in has influenced you at all?

MILLER: I never used to, but I think now that, while I hadn't taken over an ideology, I did absorb a certain viewpoint. That there is tragedy in the world but that the world must continue: one is a condition for the other. Jews can't afford to revel too much in the tragic because it might overwhelm them. Consequently, in most Jewish writing there's always the caution, "Don't push it too far toward the abyss, because you're liable to fall in." I think it's part of that psychology and it's part of me, too. I have, so to speak, a psychic investment in the continuity of life. I couldn't ever write a totally nihilistic work.

INTERVIEWER: Would you care to say anything about what you're working on now?

MILLER: I'd better not. I do have about five things started—short stories, a screenplay, et cetera. I'm in the process of collecting my short stories. But I tell myself, What am I doing. I should be doing a play. I have a calendar in my head. You see, the theater season starts in September, and I have always written plays in the summertime. Almost always—I did write *View from the Bridge* in the winter. So, quite frankly, I can't say. I have some interesting beginnings, but I can't see the end of any of them. It's usually that way:

I plan something for weeks or months and suddenly begin writing dialogue which begins in relation to what I had planned and veers off into something I hadn't even thought about. I'm drawing down the lightning, I suppose. Somewhere in the blood you have a play, and you wait until it passes behind the eyes. I'm further along than that, but I'd rather leave it at that for now.

OLGA CARLISLE
ROSE STYRON

10. James Jones

James Jones was born in Robinson, Illinois, on November 6, 1921, into a family that had been well established in the county for several generations. When Jones was a junior at Robinson High School the family fortunes collapsed, and he joined the Army in 1939, immediately after his graduation. He was soon shipped to Hawaii, and it was there, while taking courses at the university, that he first became interested in writing: "I was stationed at Hickman Field in Hawaii when I stumbled upon the work of Thomas Wolfe, and his home life seemed so similar to my own, his feelings about himself so similar to mine about myself, that I realized that I had been a writer without knowing it or without having written."

Jones was serving at Scofield Barracks on the morning of the Japanese attack on Pearl Harbor. He was wounded on Guadalcanal and returned to the United States in 1944. For the next ten years he lived in Illinois. There he wrote his first novel, *From Here to Eternity*, which was an immediate success, winning the National Book Award in 1951. He has since published four more novels: *Some Came Running* (1957), *The Pistol* (1959), *The Thin Red Line* (1962), and *Go to the Widow-Maker* (1967).

In 1957 Jones married Gloria Mosolino of New York City. They have two children and live in Paris.

Chapter 2

Off through the coconut trees there was a long
line of jungle about a hundred and fifty yards from the
bivouac. Through the steaming, chill curtain of the
tropical rain it looked more like a wall than anything
else. Solid and dense, sweeping away to the foothills
in the distance, it might have been an ancient avalanche
of green lava, ~~which had~~ rolled down ~~from~~ some volcano
to form this flat-topped plateau a hundred feet high;
and up the steep green slope of which one might have
climbed, ~~or so it seemed,~~ to walk away over the top
on a surface at least as solid as the wet earth on
which they stood. Almost invisible in the rain at
times, it loomed there, making them aware of it even
when they couldn't see it, a fact of nature like a
mountain or an ocean and equally as ~~deflating to the~~
~~human ego.~~

In the coconut grove they worked doggedly to set
up their camp. The rain came straight down, unaccompanied
by any wind. A quarter of a mile away they could see
the humid sun shining brightly down into the apparently
endless cocopalms. But here it came down in bucketsful
--in huge, fat drops so close together that it actually
seemed as though it were a solid sheet of water which

Manuscript page by James Jones

BIRNKRANT

James Jones

James Jones was interviewed in the sitting room of his rented apart-
ment on the Île de la Cité, where he lives with his lovely wife,
Gloria, and a Burmese cat called Hortense who was any moment
expecting an expensive (a hundred and fifty dollars per kitten)
litter of her kind. The sitting room is furnished with an overstuffed
day bed; an old wooden table littered with half-empty bottles of
Scotch, Haut-Brion, and quarterly magazines; and an odd assort-
ment of straight-backed chairs variously upholstered in bright red,
blue, and royal purple. Although the Joneses are quick to deny re-
sponsibility for the discord of color which plays about the room,
they are proud of the many paintings which they have bought since
coming to Paris. One of these is a delightful representation of the
view from the window, which Jones commissioned from a ten-year-
old boy whom he had seen the previous summer painting along the
Seine. This view is of the quai, the river, and, across the river, the

Hôtel de Ville. Barges churn by under the window, and to the right, upstream, one sees the water swirling under the stern of the Île Saint-Louis. It is what Jones looks out upon as he sits each morning over the typewriter, chain-smoking, writing in bursts of stenographic speed.

Although it was evening when we began and Jones had left his desk some hours before, he was still dressed for work. Tight khaki pants and a loose green sweater set off his slim hips, heavy round-shouldered torso, and thick neck. From time to time as he talked, Jones would get up and pace the room with a peculiar rolling gait which spoke more of the former Golden Gloves contender than of the ex-soldier who had loved close-order drill. He speaks with slow concentration, the Illinois drawl very evident; and one has the impression that he prefers an Anglo-Saxon obscenity to a word with a Latin root. But if violence is always near the surface of Jones's talk, his voice and manner are warm and gentle; the violence is in his own struggle with language itself. One feels finally that he is happier in questioning and listening, which he does with an intensity that is almost disconcerting. Though increasingly wary of interviews, Jones was on this occasion as generous with his time and thoughts as he is always with his whisky. By way of a warm-up he suggested a game of darts, but in spite of Jones's anxious coaching, the interviewer proved an indifferent player, and the session was quickly elevated to a discussion of less serious matters.

INTERVIEWER: For a starter, let's talk about why you have come to Paris. I understand you have sold the house you had built in Illinois and have moved here more or less permanently.

JONES: Well, I suppose my prime excuse, at least in the beginning, was a novel I've had planned to write about Americans in Paris, Americans of *my* generation as distinct from Americans in the twenties. That in itself is fascinating: the difference in flavor between the two generations. It's a lot more complicated than that, but essentially it will have to do with jazzmen, some French and some American, and writers too. But the original idea was to build it around the life and character of Django Reinhardt, the gypsy guitarist.

INTERVIEWER: Yes, I remember that you wrote something about him in *From Here to Eternity*.

JONES: That's the guy. I've always loved his music, better than any other single jazz musician I've heard. Because of that, I got fascinated by what I read and heard about him. He seems to have been a really total individualist, in the sense that gypsies often are: without loyalty of any sort to any country; I mean totally amoral in any political sense. And the jazz part of it fits in here too, you see, because jazz and the jazz life are, after all, semi-illegal. Always have been—from the early days of Storyville and the riverboats: I mean, whorehouses, boozing, bars, dope, even crime, all that stuff. I think that's one of the reasons jazz has attracted each succeeding generation of young Americans. It's a pretty amoral sort of life really, and is one way of escaping the increasingly encroaching controls of a bureaucratic government. Jazz and jazzmen live pretty much on the edge of the law—no matter how the propagandists of any country try to drag them by the hair into the national morality. They are never really outlaws, or outlawed, but they can always be found somewhere on that amorphous fringe. So what I want to explore in this novel is whether Django's type of individuality can exist today in any form. And I think that if it can survive it will be there, in jazz and that type of life, in near-illegality if you will, that we will have to look for it.

INTERVIEWER: Having left America as you have, do you think of the move as a political gesture, a cutting off of national affiliation?

JONES: Oh no. Not at all. I'm an American, and always will be. I happen to love that big, awkward, sprawling country very much— and its big, awkward, sprawling people. Anyway, I don't like politics; and I don't make "political gestures," as you call it. I don't even believe in politics. To me politics is like one of those annoying, and potentially dangerous, but generally just painful, chronic diseases that you just have to put up with in your life if you happen to have contracted it. Politics is like having diabetes. It's a science, a catch-as-catch-can science, which has grown up out of simple animal necessity more than anything else. If I were twice as big as I am, and twice as physically strong, I think I'd be a total anarchist. As it is, since I'm physically a pretty little guy . . . no; in fact, one reason I left was because I believe it is good for an American writer to get outside his country—outside his *continent*—and see it from a vantage point outside its pervading emotional climate.

INTERVIEWER: Do you mean to imply that the American climate of opinion is essentially hostile to the kind of individuality that Reinhardt, and this kind of life, expressed?

JONES: I think any national climate of opinion would be, in the world of today. My grandfather had a saying he used to say to me when I was a kid: "Bodder," he would say (that was a nickname he had for me), "always remember that I'm always for you, but I'd rather be for you when you're right than when you're wrong." Well, that's the way I feel about America. There's no use trying to say we haven't done a lot of things that were bad. We have. Like McCarthy, and the subcommittee hearings, forcing Americans to rat on their friends, putting Ring Lardner and those others in jail for refusing to, forcing still others to abscond, refusing others the right to work and black-listing them. That's a pretty black mark to have to live down. But those things are changing some now. And guys like Arthur Miller can still get up and fight back, and make it stick. And at least in America a writer can still write pretty much what he wants to say—at least, he can say more of it than anywhere else in the world today. Except maybe England.

INTERVIEWER: Incidentally, did you have any difficulty in getting *Eternity* published?

JONES: Well, some, I guess. But it was all sexual, not political. My editor and I went over it with the lawyers beforehand, and we had to cut some scenes and a lot of four-letter words. Then about two years after it came out there was some talk about banning it from the mails. Some devout Catholic postal inspector had discovered it. But it never was. We had to cut some of the sex in

Some Came Running, too. I find it a curious comment on the world we live in that we make such a distinction between what we can say, and do, and be, in private—and in public. My two books and what we had to cut from them are a good example of this.

INTERVIEWER: Well, now that you're settled here in Paris, do you ever plan to go back to America to live?

JONES: Oh, sure. Eventually. But I've also got a book I want to do with an Italian background before we go home. Both of these novels, the Paris one and the Italian one, will be really major novels. Or I hope they will. Both are pretty big bites to chew, if they come off like I am planning them. I've been making notes on both for several years. So it'll be a pretty long time before we go back.

INTERVIEWER: Do you feel that your attitude toward your work has changed since your living here?

JONES: No, no. I find it easy enough to work anywhere . . . that is, if I don't get *too* drunk every night. Although it was not very long ago that I discovered this. In getting married, leaving Illinois for New York and then Paris, I sort of resolved a question in my own mind, which was whether I could live from day to day with a family and friends around me and continue to do the kind of work I want to achieve. I was afraid I couldn't; I was afraid I had to be isolated in order to write.

INTERVIEWER: Was it to provide this isolation for other writers that you built (largely with the profits of *Eternity,* I believe) a writers' colony in Marshall, Illinois?

JONES: Well, that idea was part of my own make-up at the time, yeah. But it wasn't for isolation so much. A colony like that had always been one of my dreams. I honestly believed that if you gave guys who wanted to write a place to do it where they could live and eat free, then they *would* write. Take away the economic-worry factor. But it didn't work. It cost me a lot of dough, too. To learn that there was a lot more to it than that. It just doesn't work. I guess we all want to believe people are better than they are. But most of those guys there, even though they all wanted desperately to write, even though they had food and no rent and their utilities, still didn't write. I guess you just can't pick up any Joe off the street and turn him into a writer by setting him down to copying the great books. And besides, if you are young (and most of them out there were), twenty-five or so, that's not going to be enough to write about all the rest of your life. Anyway, they just wouldn't work, most of them. You have to really work at it to write. I guess there has to be talent first; but even with talent you still have to *work* at it, to write. Anyway, three pretty good novels came out of that thing; and two of the guys have finished second novels.

INTERVIEWER: Could you tell me something about your own work habits?

JONES: They're pretty normal, I guess. I get up earlier than most guys—between seven and eight—but only because I like to go out in the afternoons while there's still sun. After I get up it takes me an hour and a half of fiddling around before I can get up the courage and nerve to go to work. I smoke half a pack of cigarettes, drink six or seven cups of coffee, read over what I wrote the day before. Finally there's no further excuse. I go to the typewriter. Four to six hours of it. Then I quit and we go out. Or stay home and read.

INTERVIEWER: How much do you get done in a day?

JONES: It all depends. It might be two typescript pages, or it might be even less. Or, if it's a dialogue or a scene I had well fixed in my mind, I might get as much as ten or twelve. Usually though, it's a lot less. Three pages maybe. And then I often have to go back over it all the next day because I'm still dissatisfied. I guess I've got some neurotic compulsion to make everything as perfect as I can before I go on.

INTERVIEWER: You do a great deal of revision, then?

JONES: Oh, yes. For instance, take this scene—this chapter, or section, really—that I've been working on lately. You see, because of the nature of the book I'm working on now, I'm doing it in . . . well, in sections, very long chapters of around a hundred pages, which will be interlarded with what I call interchapters, very short pieces from another time and viewpoint. It just has to be done that way, or in some similar way. I won't go into details but actually I've been working for two months now on about forty pages—which I now think are good enough to let go. Well, out of those forty pages there are maybe six, maybe seven pages of dialogue which I wrote in about half an hour. Half an hour out of two months' work, but I haven't changed a word of it. It's good.

INTERVIEWER: You find, then, that writing dialogue is easier than straight narrative?

JONES: Yes. That's what I'm saying. But I have a reservation. Dialogue is almost too easy. For me. So much so that it makes me suspicious of it, so I have to be careful with it. I *could* find myself evading problems of true expression because dialogue's so easy for me to do. There are many important issues and points of subtlety about people, about human behavior, that I want to make in writing, and it's easy to evade these—or do them superficially, do them halfway—by simply writing good dialogue. And it becomes increasingly easy as I get to know the people better. But good dialogue just isn't enough to explain the subtler ramifications of the characters and incidents which I'm trying to work out now. Not *realistic* dialogue, anyway. Perhaps if you used some kind of surrealistic dialogue, but then it would read like a dream episode. It wouldn't be real talk. For instance, it's obvious enough that in almost any conversation things are happening to the people in the conversation which they do not and cannot express. In a play it is possible for a good actor to imply that he is thinking something other than what he is saying. But it's pretty slipshod and half-assed, because he cannot convey what he's thinking *explicitly*. In prose, and especially in the novel form, this can be done. If the man is using a subterfuge, it can be explained explicitly, and why. Actually, in life, conversation is more often likely to be an attempt at deliberate evasion, deliberate confusion, rather than communication. We're all cheats and liars, really. And the novelist can show just how and why we are.

INTERVIEWER: I have heard you say that *Some Came Running*

was the best novel you have written to date. Do you have favorites among your characters as well?

JONES: It's true that I think *Running* is my best work. It was—among a lot of other things, of course—an experiment, an experiment in the use of colloquial forms in expositional and narrative writing. I think that a classic style in writing tends to remove the reader one level from the immediacy of the experience. For any normal reader, I think a colloquial style makes him feel more as though he is within the action, instead of just reading about it. And—

INTERVIEWER: Do you always keep a sort of abstract potential reader in mind, when you write?

JONES: I think one has to. I know there are a lot of writers who say to hell with "the reader"; if he has to work to read me then let him work, if he wants to read me. I don't know what I feel, myself. I guess I would fall somewhere in between the two extremes. I think the writer ought to help the reader as much as he can without damaging what he wants to say; and I don't think it ever hurts the writer to sort of stand back now and then and look at his stuff as if he were reading it instead of writing it.

INTERVIEWER: What were you saying about *Some Came Running*?

JONES: Another reason I like *Running* so much is because of the characters. They are much more like real people, more subtle and devious than the characters in *Eternity*. And that's why I think it is much better writing. *Running* gets down deeper into its people than *Eternity*. But as for my preference for any one of the characters in my books, I have two kinds. One is sentimental and the other is professional. For instance, old Jane Staley is one of my favorites sentimentally, but from a professional point of view I'm more fond of Dave Hirsh than any character in *Eternity*. Largely because my study of Dave Hirsh reaches much deeper levels, gets down much closer to that self-delusive deviousness we humans all labor under.

INTERVIEWER: Do you draw your characters from life?

JONES: I guess so, yes. But by the time I'm done with them, they're not like anybody else but themselves. It would be better to say I use them as springboards. It's funny; I've been accused by various reviewers or critical writers of portraying myself—autobiographically—in nearly all of my characters. It's been said that I was Prewitt; it's been said that I was Warden; it's been said that I was Dave Hirsh. I couldn't be them all. I've actually had people, who of course romanticized Prewitt as a hero, flatly refuse to believe I didn't draw Prewitt from myself, even when I told them I hadn't. I guess it's true that when I was younger and more romantic, I would have liked to be Prewitt, and Warden too for that matter. On the other hand, I certainly wouldn't want to be Dave Hirsh. But by and large, I guess I take my characters from people I've known at one time or another. Sometimes, though, it's simply an event which strikes me and then I try to imagine a character who would fit into that event. For instance, the man who was killed by Fatso Judson in the stockade, Blues Berry, I never knew him at all.

INTERVIEWER: Were you ever in the stockade?

JONES: You mean the post stockade at Scofield Barracks? No, I never was personally. But more than that I wouldn't like to say.

INTERVIEWER: Let me ask you a more abstract question, then. Novels as long as *Eternity* and *Running* must have presented enormous organizational problems. Can you describe how you go about building the structure of a novel?

JONES: I don't "go about it." I work it out as I go along. I begin with a problem that interests or excites me, like that of individualism and the fringe-society of jazz which we were talking about a while ago. Then I take a character who, to some extent, represents the abstract idea of the problem. Not as a symbol, though; I don't like making symbols out of characters. No human being is really a symbol. In *The Pistol*, Mast and the other characters are deliberately symbolic of various aspects of humanity, all hunting for some kind of salvation, which is symbolized by the pistol itself, and the story itself is a symbol of all the ridiculous, outrageous cruelties people will perpetrate upon each other when they think they can acquire salvation for themselves by doing so. The whole thing of *The Pistol* is an experiment in writing a deliberately symbolic little novella. It's okay, for an easy job, an easy out. But human beings themselves are never that easy to symbolize; they're never all black or all white like that; they aren't really any longer human at all. That's why it's so easy to kill real people in the name of some damned ideology or other; once the killer can abstract them in his own mind into being symbols, then he needn't feel guilty for killing them since they're no longer real human beings. And symbolizing characters like that is just as easy an out for the writer as for the ideological killer. I prefer to write about characters who aren't that easily categorized. In this type of novel, the problem is there, and I can actually give it a concrete written definition. I always try to do that. But instead of laying out the abstract idea —if A is put against B then C will result—I take the people, one of whom will more or less represent A (but who has the right to not represent A, if he so chooses), and one of whom will more or less represent B. Then when I set A against B, maybe Z or X will result, instead of C. Because by allowing that unknown to exist in there, I won't actually be able to know what will happen until it writes its own answer. Because after all, this problem, whatever it is, is a question which I haven't answered, and a question which I don't feel qualified to answer, wouldn't presume to answer, for myself or anybody else. And by doing it that way I'm letting the people write their own story themselves. For example, I had written three hundred pages of *Eternity* before I realized that Warden was going to have an affair with Karen Holmes. So I had to go back and bring that about. But even then I didn't know how it would end. I knew only that because of their situation it wouldn't, *couldn't*, work out. And in *Running*, I guess I worked on that book for three years before I knew whether Dave Hirsh would actually marry that slob, Ginnie Moorehead, and then it was another year before I was able to find out whether he would leave her or not after he did marry her. But as for the *structure* of

Running, I think it is sound. If I may flatter myself a little in this interview without making too many enemies, I would like to say that I believe I have a knack, or whatever you want to call it, for structural organization. I'll grant much of the—

INTERVIEWER:—criticism?

JONES: Hell! Criticism is hardly strong enough a word for what was said about me. I'll grant it *is* too long perhaps in places; but I feel I have the right to overwrite now and then if it's something that interests me and I want to put it in—as long as it is accurate within the framework of the characterization. So anyway, I think it could have been cut a little more than we actually did. Maybe even as much as another hundred pages plus the hundred-fifty which we did take out of the original twenty-five hundred typescript pages. But a good case in point is the "road-driving" episode where 'Bama teaches Dave how to drive well, which has been bombed and strafed and shot off at the ankles by so many critics. Sure, it could have been cut without damaging the essential story; but it is an American phenomenon which I, anyway, have never seen written about, and I think it's interesting and I'm glad I left it in. If I hadn't, this facet of American life on that long, flat continent might never have been written about in just that way. So what the hell?

INTERVIEWER: Another critic, Leslie Fiedler, has written a more ambitious essay on *From Here to Eternity.* He entitled it "The Bum as American Culture Hero," and his point was that the Ishmael figure, which is almost constant in American literature, was recast in the novels of Steinbeck and Dos Passos as the man on the bum. He goes on to say that with Prewitt the bum turns up again, this time at the end of his wandering, in the army. But in the army he is recognized as an artist. The army gave him his bugle, but it was being on the bum that made him an artist.

JONES: Well, okay. But so what? I mean what's his conclusion from all this? I don't say I especially disagree with him, at least not yet—except on one point. I don't agree that it was being on the bum that made Prewitt an "artist." What made Prewitt an artist, in my interpretation, was that his old man used to beat up his old lady, as well as himself; and that his old man, like so many human male animals, didn't give a damn about him one way or the other. He was always competing, in a sense, with this image of his father which he was always trying to please. . . . But as for the bum-heroes of Steinbeck and Dos Passos, whether they're the inheritors of Ishmael or not—and I guess they are—the main point about them is that they were all involved in the social revolution that came in the thirties. What's interesting is that if Prewitt is *their* heir, Prewitt as the wanderer had no place left to go *except* into the army—where he became, artist or not, a ward of the government. Which is what is happening everywhere, today, even with businessmen. A government ward who, whatever else he is, is first of all at the call of government to fight for it, or what have you. But the army which Prewitt entered in the late thirties was not then the same total tool of government that the army of today is. It was not, in actual effect, the army which Dewey Cole and Hubie Murson went back to after four years of meaningless civil life after World War II, in *Some Came Running*. And that makes it even more grim.

But I would like to make the point here, also, that if it is true that what Fiedler calls a "bum" is a culture hero of some modern American writers, I think it is because these writers are tired of the phoniness of superficial culture and the shallow kind of relationships which this makes for. Another critic, Edmund Fuller, says somewhat the same thing as Fiedler, but much more complainingly. He calls it the "slob philosophy." And he calls *them* slobs: the "hero-bums." I don't think Prewitt is a slob, but to a man of Mr. Fuller's caliber he probably is a slob. He is crude, vulgar, and Fuller probably thinks he's insensitive as well. The same would be true of Dave Hirsh.

INTERVIEWER: I think Dave Hirsh is a slob.

JONES: Well, in many ways he is; but that's part of the point of the book, the end of which is when he ceases to be a slob. And this has been a very painful thing for him to learn.

But these fellows like Fuller take an unfair advantage of my characters, with their superficial social categorizing. I think of a slob as someone who has an inordinate ego which makes him close his mind down around his small beliefs and prejudices. By that definition even an intellectual like Mr. Fuller might qualify. I don't give a damn whether Dave Hirsh has a Ph.D. or whether he has even gone to school or not. I don't think education can make a man more sensitive. I think only the experiences in his life, if he is able to face and accept them, can do that. In that sense, education can even help make a man a "slob," by my definition, because he can take refuge in it by pretending to be sensitive when in fact he is not.

INTERVIEWER: Do you feel that an academic education can injure a writer?

JONES: I think it can very easily. Though it doesn't necessarily have to. Most of the desultory courses that I've taken in literature have had a peculiar snobbism about them. An adulation of certain writers is inculcated in the student by the instructor (who is probably a frustrated writer anyway), to the point where the student finds himself asking whether he has anything to say that Tolstoy or James haven't already said better. Moreover, most of the instruction seems to be concerned with writings rather than with how to write, which is impossible to teach anyway.

INTERVIEWER: What authors have most influenced your own writing?

JONES: I guess the same writers that have influenced most of my generation: Faulkner, Hemingway, Fitzgerald, Dos Passos, Steinbeck. The older writers, too: James, Hawthorne, Thoreau, Emerson. What do you want, a list? Joyce too, of course. In a more profound way, I think first Stendhal and secondly Dostoevski have influenced me a great deal in the direction I've taken and my idea of what I'd like to accomplish. More than anybody else. Everybody has talked about the influence Wolfe has had on me as a writer, because I once admitted publicly that it was reading Wolfe that first decided me I wanted to be a writer. I have been accused of taking up all of Wolfe's flaws (if they are flaws), such as lack of selectivity and stylistic overwriting and a number of others. All of which I don't think is true. Wolfe actually did influence me a great deal toward becoming a writer, and I am not one of those people who indulge the current fashion of knocking Wolfe. I think he was a great writer. But I think I've moved a long way from him in viewpoint and style and even in selectivity; certainly I have in structuring novels. [*Jones takes a penknife from his pocket and flicks it open.*]

INTERVIEWER: Do you carry that for protection?

JONES: No. I guess you saw that damned picture of me in *Time* magazine. No. I just carry it to clean my nails with. Look. See? It's got scissors, too. As well as a nail file. And a screwdriver, and a bottle opener—which doesn't work well, incidentally.

INTERVIEWER: Well, I was just wondering. There is so much physical violence in your novels.

JONES: Yes, that's true: there is. But then physical violence does exist in life, and theoretically a man ought to be able to protect himself against it. I mean that the perfect ideal would be that a man who is essentially nonviolent would be able to defend himself against any form of violence. But this is very rare in life. But this raises one of the most important themes in *Eternity*, why Prewitt does not shoot back at the MPs who kill him as he tries to get back to his unit after his murder of Fatso Judson. You see, when Prewitt kills Fatso he is carrying the theory of vengeance by violence to its final logical end. But the thing is that Fatso doesn't even know why he is being killed; and when Prewitt sees that, he realizes what a fruitless thing he has done. Then at the end, when he does not fire on the men who are going to kill him, it is because he has accepted the ultimate logical end of passive resistance, which is death.

INTERVIEWER: Are you a pacifist?

JONES: Well, I would like to be. You see, as I go along I've come to consider bravery as just about the most pernicious of virtues. Bravery is a horrible thing. The human race has it left over from the animal world and we can't get rid of it. Take any situation in which a man is attacked; the natural thing for him to do is to fight back. But that's an animal reaction, and I'm about convinced that in the end the only measure by which human beings will be judged as human—by themselves or by others—will be according to what they will do in this situation. If he were truly human, a man would not fight back. But then you get the paradox of such a situation, in that he would be concurring in his own destruction. It's the rebel's suicide in Camus.

There're so many young guys, you know—young Americans and, yes, young men everywhere—a whole generation of people younger than me who have grown up feeling inadequate as men because they haven't been able to fight in a war and find out whether they are brave or not. Because it is in an effort to prove this bravery that we fight—in wars or in bars—whereas if a man were truly brave he wouldn't have to be always proving it to himself. So therefore I am forced to consider bravery suspect, and ridiculous, and dangerous. Because if there are enough young men like that who feel strongly enough about it, they can almost bring on a war, even when none of them want it, and are in fact struggling against having one. (And as far as modern war is concerned I *am* a pacifist. Hell, it isn't even war any more, as far as that goes. It's an industry, a big business complex.) And it's a ridiculous thing because this bravery myth is something those young men should be able to laugh at. Of course the older men like me, their big brothers, and uncles, and maybe even their fathers, we don't help them any. Even those of us who don't openly brag. Because all the time we are talking about how scared we were in the war, we are implying tacitly that we were brave enough to stay. Whereas in actual fact we stayed because we were afraid of being laughed at, or thrown in jail, or *shot*, as far as that goes.

As a matter of fact, I am at the moment trying to write a novel, a combat novel,* which, in addition to being a work which tells the truth about warfare as I saw it, would free all these young men from the horseshit which has been engrained in them by my generation. I don't think that combat has ever been written about truthfully; it has always been described in terms of bravery and

* *The Thin Red Line.*

cowardice. I won't even accept these words as terms of human reference any more. And anyway, hell, they don't even apply to what, in actual fact, modern warfare has become. And I would like to try to write about combat from outside this framework entirely. I say "try" because I have this fear of being thought a coward, too, you see, myself. I don't know if I can actually be truthful to the spirit of what I actually felt. But I've made some strides in trying to understand myself, I think. And I think that in my life I'm less afraid of being thought a coward than I used to be.

INTERVIEWER: Your speaking of this combat novel which "will tell the truth" as you saw it reminds me of a question you make the young novelist, Wally Dennis, ask of himself in *Some Came Running*. He says, "I wonder if a guy could really write a book about people as they *really* are and still make it interesting enough to read?"

JONES: Yes. But I guess I should have said "intelligible" instead of "interesting," though. I have always had the feeling that each character I've created has been made into a better human being than he or she would really have been under any set of circumstances, or than the more-or-less model was in real life. Wally Dennis, you remember, goes on about that, about his own mother, what a stupid slob and selfish old bat his mother really is. I don't think people like to read about themselves or about others as they really are. It would be too horrifying. After all, we have to give ourselves a little of the feeling that we're human beings with a capital H and B. So we do that, and every now and then the real truth surges up to plague us from that limbo to which we've suppressed it—in that violence you were speaking about before, some form of it or other.

INTERVIEWER: So in the past you consciously romanticized your heroes?

JONES: I don't know how much was conscious and how much wasn't. What I'm trying to do now is deliberately romanticize them less. I am wondering if you can create a hero—I don't like that word—a *protagonist* without romanticizing him at all. I think it might be almost unintelligible. I don't believe anyone would believe human beings were that bad, and yet we are all that bad.

INTERVIEWER: Bad? In what ways?

JONES: Bad according to the various moral codes we profess to live by. I mean that everyone's actions and thoughts are so entirely contrary to that code of ethics which we all try to set up for ourselves that people would recoil in horror if this were shown to them.

INTERVIEWER: But you are now trying to write just such a completely realistic novel?

JONES: Yes, I am. But I don't like that word "realism" much. I have been called a realist and a naturalist but I don't know what I am. What the hell is a realist or a naturalist anyway? Edmund Fuller's definition of a realistic writer is someone who is essentially dirty—under the arms as well as in his mind. You know, not very gentlemanly.

INTERVIEWER: Let's go back to the contents of your novels for a minute. I was struck as I read them by the number of games— poker, chess, boxing, surfboarding, et cetera—which figure very prominently in your work. How do you account for this, other than by the fact that games do exist?

JONES: Well, yes, of course games do exist. And it is true that I have been and still am fascinated by them. Last Sunday, for instance, I spent eight hours straight playing English darts with some friends. We would have gone on all night if our wives hadn't stopped us. Why did we do it? I think one reason is that we got completely lost in it, in competing, and for a time thus were able to forget everything else: bills, atom bombs, can I write? am I mad? is humanity mad? And if you win, it's great for your ego; but if you lose, well, it isn't really so bad after all. It's like dope, or getting blind drunk, or gambling. But beyond that I think games are significant in people's lives because in a game everything is clearly defined. You've got the rules and a given period of time in which to play; you've got boundaries and a beginning and an end.

And whether you win, lose, or draw, at least something is sure. But life ain't like that at all. So I think that people invent and play games in order to kid themselves, at least for a time, into thinking that *life* is a game; in order to forget that at the end of life there is nothing but a big blank wall.

INTERVIEWER: Well, I guess in winding up I should ask you that one great question put to every author: Why do you want to write?

JONES: Well, I suppose you could say that I want to impose my personality upon the world. Or, you could say that I want people to know that I have lived—all depends on your viewpoint and the mood you're in. Both are true, I guess. But I do think that the quality which makes a man want to write and be read is essentially a desire for self-exposure and is masochistic. Like one of those guys who has a compulsion to take his thing out and show it on the street. I guess I wrote that somewhere. Stendhal understood this very well, and Dostoevski. But Tolstoy did not operate this way, and that is why I think he is less great than these other two. You must really want to tell the truth about yourself (and no matter what any writer says, every character he creates is a part of himself, romanticized or unromanticized), but in order to do this you have to get down into yourself and try to find out what it is that makes us desire certain things and be afraid of certain other things. But then to write what you have found is essentially masochistic. I'm sure that some damned psychiatrist who doesn't write could probably show you how this is all tied in with what I feel about violence and the need for passive resistance but I don't know how useful that would be in telling you how a man becomes a writer. This is all getting pretty high-flown and pompous, don't you think? Let's go somewhere and have a drink. I should make it plain, though, that boozing does not necessarily have to go hand in hand with being a writer, as seems to be the concept in America. I therefore solemnly declare to all young men trying to become writers that they do not actually have to become drunkards first.

NELSON W. ALDRICH, JR.

11. Norman Mailer

Norman Mailer was born on January 31, 1923, in Long Branch, New Jersey. A few years later his family moved to Brooklyn, where his father worked as an accountant. He attended Brooklyn schools and graduated from Boys' High in 1939. He entered Harvard intending to be an aeronautical engineer, but became increasingly interested in writing, and won *Story* magazine's college writing contest in 1941 with "The Greatest Thing in the World."

In 1944, shortly after graduation from Harvard, he was drafted into the Army and served as a rifleman in the Philippine campaign. Discharged in May 1946, he returned "with the paramount obsession of writing a novel about the war." The result was *The Naked and the Dead* (1948), which received universal acclaim. Since then he has published three novels—*Barbary Shore* (1951), *The Deer Park* (1955), and *An American Dream* (1965)—and a volume of poems, *Death for the Ladies and Other Disasters* (1962). His remarkable and characteristic articles, reviews, and essays have appeared in various periodicals, including *Commentary*, *Esquire*, *Dissent*, and *The Village Voice*. Many of these have been collected in *Advertisements for Myself* (1959), *The Presidential Papers of Norman Mailer* (1963), and *Cannibals and Christians* (1966). His first play, *The Deer Park*, an adaptation of his novel, was produced in 1967.

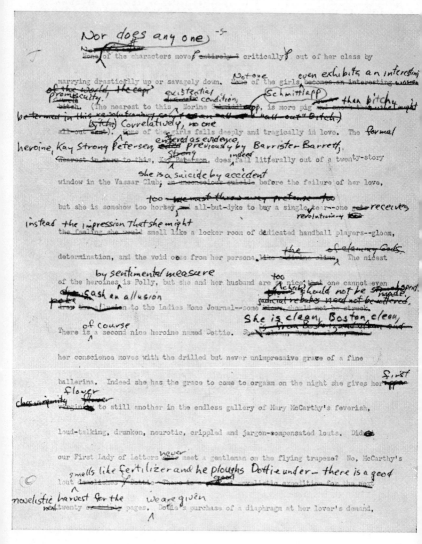

~~Nor~~ does any one) -5-

~~None of the characters move~~ ~~entirely~~ ~~critically~~ out of her class by

marrying drastically up or savagely down. ~~None of the girls~~ Not one even exhibits an interesting ~~becomes an interesting~~ ~~of the world, the cap~~ ex~~is~~tential ~~promiscuity,~~ ~~dramatic~~ condition, (Schmittlapp) then bitchy ~~bitch.~~ (The nearest to this, ~~Norine~~ Schmittlapp, is more pig ~~or~~ ~~be~~ ~~termed in this revolutionary~~ ~~all-out "bitch")~~ ~~(bitch)~~ Correlatively, no one ~~all-out~~). ~~None~~ of the girls falls deeply and tragically in love. The formal entered as evidence heroine, Kay Strong ~~Petersen,~~ ~~and~~ previously by Barrister Barrett, ~~Nearest in~~ ~~Kay Petersen,~~ Strong does indeed fall lit~~t~~erally out of a twenty-story she is a suicide by accident window in the Vassar Club, ~~an unconscious suicide~~ before the failure of her love,

too but she is somehow too horsey, ~~and~~ all-but-dyke to buy a single ~~tear~~-one ~~who~~ receives revolutionary instead the impression that she might ~~the feeling she would~~ smell like a locker room of dedicated handball players--gloom, the ~~of clammy~~ determination, and the void ~~oss~~ from her persona. ~~His~~ ~~clean~~ ~~skin,~~ The nicest by sentimental measure of the heroines is Polly, but she and her husband are ~~so~~ nice, ~~but~~ one cannot even too ~~spend~~ ~~plan~~ ~~should not be struck~~ made ~~cash an allusion~~ ~~make~~ ~~them~~ ~~listen~~ to the Ladies Home Journal--some ~~them~~ ~~should not be uttered.~~ She is clean, Boston, clean, of course There is a second nice heroine named Dottie. ~~She~~ ~~comes~~ ~~from Boston, and~~ her conscience moves with the drilled but never unimpressive grace of a fine First ballerina. Indeed she has the grace to come to orgasm on the night she gives her ~~upper~~ class virginity flower ~~clinging~~ to still another in the endless gallery of Mary McCarthy's feverish, loud-talking, drunken, neurotic, crippled and jargon-~~compensated~~ louts. Did ~~she~~ never our First Lady of Letters ~~ever~~ meet a gentleman on the flying trapeze? No, McCarthy's smells like fertilizer and he ploughs Dottie under— there is a good lout ~~demolishes~~ ~~Dottie.~~ ~~There is a~~ good ~~novelistic ambition for the next~~ novelistic harvest for the we are given next twenty ~~ordinary~~ pages. Dottie's purchase of a diaphragm at her lover's demand,

Manuscript page by Norman Mailer

Norman Mailer

The interview took place on the afternoon of Saturday, July 6, 1963. The setting was Norman Mailer's Brooklyn Heights apartment, whose living room commands a panoramic view of lower Manhattan, the East River, and the New York harbor. The living room is fitted out with nautical or maritime furnishings and decorations, and Mailer, his curls unshorn, seemed at odd moments during the afternoon the novelist-as-ship-captain, though less Ahab than Captain Vere, and less both than Captain Shotover in ripe middle age. Mailer had recently stopped smoking, and the absence of nicotine had caused him to put on weight, which he carries gracefully and with vigor; the new amplitude of flesh seems to have influenced his spirit in the direction of benignity.

Shortly after the interviewer arrived, Mailer excused himself for a few moments. He wanted to change, he said, into his writer's costume. He emerged wearing faded dungarees and an open-necked

*sport shirt. His sharp blue eyes sparkled as he suggested that the
interviewer keep this fashion note in mind. Lunch was then prepared and served by Mailer in what must be called lordly fashion.
In general, he conducts himself without affectation as a kind of
secular prince. The interviewer was repeatedly struck during the
course of a long afternoon's work by Mailer's manners, which were
exquisite. The role of novelist-being-interviewed suits him very well.*

INTERVIEWER: Do you need any particular environment in which
to write?

MAILER: I like a room with a view, preferably a long view. I dislike looking out on gardens. I prefer looking at the sea, or ships,
or anything which has a vista to it. Oddly enough, I've never
worked in the mountains.

INTERVIEWER: Do you need seclusion?

MAILER: I don't know if I need seclusion, but I do like to be
alone in a room.

INTERVIEWER: When did you first think of becoming a writer?

MAILER: That's hard to answer. I did a lot of writing when I
was young.

INTERVIEWER: How young?

MAILER: Seven.

INTERVIEWER: A real novel?

MAILER: Well, it was a science-fiction novel about people on
Earth taking a rocket ship to Mars. The hero had a name which
sounded like Buck Rogers. His assistant was called Dr. Hoor.

INTERVIEWER: Doctor . . . ?

MAILER: Dr. Hoor. *Whore*, pronounced *H-o-o-r*. That's the way
we used to pronounce "whore" in Brooklyn. He was patterned
directly after Dr. Huer in Buck Rogers, who was then appearing
on radio. This novel filled two and a half paper notebooks. You
know the type, about seven by ten. They had soft shiny blue covers
and they were, oh, only ten cents in those days, or a nickel. They
ran to perhaps a hundred pages each, and I used to write on both
sides. My writing was remarkable for the way I hyphenated words.

I loved hyphenating, so I would hyphenate "the" and make it th-e if it came at the end of the line. Or "they" would become the-y. Then I didn't write again for a long time. I didn't even try out for the high-school literary magazine. I had friends who wrote short stories, and their short stories were far better than the ones I would write for assignments in high-school English, and I felt no desire to write. When I got to college I started again. The jump from Boys' High School in Brooklyn to Harvard came as a shock. I started reading some decent novels for the first time.

INTERVIEWER: You mentioned in *Advertisements for Myself* that reading *Studs Lonigan* made you want to be a writer.

MAILER: Yes. It was the best single literary experience I had had because the background of *Studs* was similar to mine. I grew up in Brooklyn, not Chicago, but the atmosphere had the same flatness of affect. Until then I had never considered my life or the life of the people around me as even remotely worthy of—well, I didn't believe they could be treated as subjects for fiction. It had never occurred to me. Suddenly I realized you could write about your own life.

INTERVIEWER: When did you feel that you were started as a writer?

MAILER: When I first began to write again at Harvard. I wasn't very good. I was doing short stories all the time, but I wasn't good. If there were fifty people in the class, let's say I was somewhere in the top ten. My teachers thought I was fair, but I don't believe they ever thought for a moment that I was really talented. Then in the middle of my sophomore year I started getting better. I got on the *Harvard Advocate*, and that gave me confidence, and about this time I did a couple of fairly good short stories for English A-1, one of which won *Story* magazine's college contest for that year. I must say that Robert Gorham Davis, who was my instructor then, picked the story to submit for the contest and was confident it would win.

INTERVIEWER: Was that the story about Al Groot?

MAILER: Yes. And when I found out it had won—which was at the beginning of the summer after my sophomore year (1941)—

well, that fortified me, and I sat down and wrote a novel. It was a very bad novel. I wrote it in two months. It was called *No Percentage*. It was just terrible. But I never questioned any longer whether I was *started* as a writer.

INTERVIEWER: What do you think were some of the early influences in your life? What reading, as a boy, do you recall as important?

MAILER: *The Amateur Gentleman* and *The Broad Highway* were glorious works. So was *Captain Blood*. I think I read every one of Farnol's books and there must be twenty of them. And every one of Sabatini's.

INTERVIEWER: Did you ever read any of them again?

MAILER: No, now I have no real idea of their merit. But I never enjoyed a novel more than *Captain Blood*. Nor a movie. Do you remember Errol Flynn as Captain Blood? Some years ago I was asked by a magazine what were the ten most important books in my development. The book I listed first was *Captain Blood*. Then came *Das Kapital*. Then *The Amateur Gentleman*.

INTERVIEWER: You wouldn't say that *Das Kapital* was boyhood reading?

MAILER: Oh, no, I read that many years later. But it had its mild influence.

INTERVIEWER: It's been said often that novelists are largely nostalgic for their boyhood, and in fact most novelists draw on their youthful experiences a great deal. In your novels, however, the evocation of scenes from boyhood is rare or almost absent.

MAILER: It's difficult to write about childhood. I never felt I understood it in any novel way. I never felt other authors did either. Not particularly. I think the portrait of childhood which is given by most writers is rarely true to anything more than the logic of their novel. Childhood is so protean.

INTERVIEWER: What about Twain, or Hemingway—who drew on their boyhoods successfully?

MAILER: I must admit they created some of the psychological reality of my own childhood. I wanted, for instance, to be like Tom Sawyer.

INTERVIEWER: Not Huck Finn?

MAILER: The magic of Huck Finn seems to have passed me by, I don't know quite why. *Tom Sawyer* was the book of Twain's I always preferred. I remember when I got to college I was startled to find that *Huckleberry Finn* was the classic. Of course I haven't looked at either novel in thirty years.

INTERVIEWER: Can you say something about your methods of working?

MAILER: They vary with each book. I wrote *The Naked and the Dead* on the typewriter. I used to write four days a week: Mondays, Tuesdays, Thursdays, and Fridays.

INTERVIEWER: Definite hours?

MAILER: Yes, very definite hours. I'd get up about eight or eight-thirty and I'd be at work by ten. And I'd work till twelve-thirty; then I'd have lunch. I'd get back to work about two-thirty or three, and work for another two hours. In the afternoon I usually needed a can of beer to prime me. But I'd write for five hours a day. And I wrote a great deal. The average I tried to keep was seven type-written pages a day, twenty-eight pages a week. The first draft took seven months, the second draft—which really was only half a draft—took four months. The part about the platoon went well from the beginning, but the Lieutenant and the General in the first draft were stock characters. If it had been published at that point the book would have been considered an interesting war novel with some good scenes, no more. The second draft was the bonus. Cummings and Hearn were done in the second draft. If you look at the book you can see that the style shifts, that the parts about Cummings and Hearn are written in a somewhat more developed vein. Less forceful but more articulated. And you can see something of the turn my later writing would take in the scenes between Cummings and Hearn.

INTERVIEWER: What methods did you pursue in your next books?

MAILER: Well, with *Barbary Shore*, I began to run into trouble. I started it in Paris about six months after I finished *The Naked and the Dead*, and did about fifty pages. It was then called *Mrs. Guinevere* and was influenced by Sally Bowles in Isherwood's *Ber-*

lin Stories. Mrs. Guinevere never went anywhere. It stopped, just ground down after those first fifty pages. My novelistic tanks ran out of gas. I dropped it completely, thought I'd never pick it up again, and started to work on another novel. Did all the research, went to Indiana to do research.

INTERVIEWER: On what?

MAILER: On a labor novel. There was a union in Evansville with which I had connections. So I stayed for a few days in Indiana, and then went to Jamaica, Vermont, to write the novel. I spent four to six weeks getting ready to begin. I made a great push on the beginning, worked for two weeks, and quit cold. I didn't have the book. I didn't know a damned thing about labor unions. In desperation (I was full of second-novel panic) I picked up *Mrs. Guinevere* and looked at it. And found something there I could go on with. So I worked on it all through the spring of 1949, and then I moved out to Hollywood for the summer. I finished the second half in Hollywood. *Barbary Shore* is really a Hollywood novel. I think it reflected the impact of Hollywood on me in some subterranean fashion. Certainly the first draft is the wildest draft of the three; it's almost insane, and the most indigestible portions were written in the first couple of months I was in Hollywood. I never knew where the book was going, I had no idea where it was going to move from day to day. I'd wake up and push the typewriter in great dread, in literal terror, wondering when this curious and doubtful inspiration was going to stop. It never quite did. It ground along at the rate of three pages, three difficult pages, a day. But I'd get it out. I got a first draft done, and was quite unhappy with it; it was a very bad book at that point. When I rewrote it later, in Provincetown, a summer later, again it went at the rate of three pages a day. This revision was different from the first draft, and I think much better. But working on *Barbary Shore* I always felt as if I were not writing the book myself, but rather as if I were serving as a subject for some intelligence which had decided to use me to write the book. It had nothing to do with whether the work was good or bad. It just had to do with the fact that I had absolutely no conscious control of it; if I hadn't heard about the unconscious I would have had to postulate one to explain this phenomenon. For the first time I became powerfully aware of the fact that I had an unconscious which seemed to have little to do with me.

INTERVIEWER: What about *The Deer Park?*

MAILER: For *The Deer Park* I didn't have much of a method. It was agony; it was far and away the most difficult of my three novels to write. The first and second drafts were written with the idea that they were only the first part of an eight-part novel. I think I used that enormous scheme as a pretext to get into the work. Apparently I just couldn't sit down and write a nice modest Hollywood novel. I had to have something grandiose, in conception, anyway. I started *The Deer Park* with "The Man Who Studied Yoga." That was supposed to be a prologue to all eight novels. It went along nicely and was done in a few weeks. And then I got into *The Deer Park*, and I forget what my methods were exactly; I think they varied. In the revisions of *Barbary Shore* I had started working in longhand; as soon as I found myself blocked on the typewriter I'd shift to longhand. By the time I got to *The Deer Park* I was writing in longhand all the time. I'd write in longhand in the morning, and type up what I'd written in the afternoon. I was averaging about four-five pages a day, I think, three days a week; about fifteen pages a week. But I found it an unendurable book to write because I'd finish each day in the most profound depression; as I found out later it was even a physical depression. I was gutting my liver.

INTERVIEWER: It wasn't alcohol?

MAILER: No, I wasn't much of a drinker in those days. The liver, you see, is not unlike a car battery, and I was draining mine. I was writing with such anxiety and such fear and such distaste, and such gloom and such dissatisfaction that . . .

INTERVIEWER: Dissatisfaction with what?

MAILER: Oh, everything. My work, my life, myself. The early draft of *The Deer Park* was terrible. It had a few good things in it, but it was slow to emerge, it took years, and was stubborn. It still emerges. I mean, I could sit down today and rewrite *The Deer Park.* Of course, what was happening was that this work, such as it was, was continuing to move in a direction which was completely against the grain of my intellect—insofar as my intellect was developed, and had standards and tastes and attitudes toward the novel. I was working toward a novel utterly outrageous to my notion of things.

INTERVIEWER: Say it again?

MAILER: Well, I was a socialist after all, and I believed in large literary works which were filled with characters, and were programmatic, and had large theses, and were developed, let's say, like the Tolstoyan novel. It's as if, all proportion naturally being kept, as if Tolstoy had sat down with the intention of writing *Anna Karenina* and instead came out with *Crime and Punishment*. Obviously, it would have been intolerable for him, and he would have disliked *Crime and Punishment* very much. That was what was going on with me at a much lower level.

INTERVIEWER: How does the idea of a novel come to you?

MAILER: I don't know that it comes. A more appropriate image for me might be that I start with the idea of constructing a treehouse and end with a skyscraper made of wood.

INTERVIEWER: Well, how did the idea of *The Naked and the Dead* come to you?

MAILER: I wanted to write a short novel about a long patrol. All during the war I kept thinking about this patrol. I even had the idea before I went overseas. Probably it was stimulated by a few war books I had read: John Hersey's *Into the Valley*, Harry Brown's *A Walk in the Sun*, and a couple of others I no longer remember. Out of these books came the idea to do a novel about a long patrol. And I began to create my characters. All the while I was overseas a part of me was working on this long patrol. I even ended up in a reconnaissance outfit which I had asked to get into. A reconnaissance outfit, after all, tends to take long patrols. Art kept traducing life. At any rate, when I started writing *The Naked and the Dead* I thought it might be a good idea to have a preliminary chapter or two in which to give the reader a chance to meet my characters before they went on patrol. But the next six months and the first five hundred pages went into that, and I remember in the early days I was annoyed at how long it was taking me to get to the patrol.

INTERVIEWER: Do you keep notes, or a journal, or diaries, or write scenarios? What's your preparatory material?

MAILER: That also varies with each of the books. For *The Naked and the Dead* I had a file full of notes, and a long dossier on each man. Many of these details never got into the novel, but the added knowledge made me feel more comfortable with each character. Indeed I even had charts to show which characters had not yet had scenes with other characters. For a book which seems spontaneous on its surface, *The Naked and the Dead* was written mechanically. I studied engineering at Harvard, and I suppose it was the book of a young engineer. The structure is sturdy, but there's no fine filigree to the joints. Just spot-welding and riveting. And the working plan was very simple. I devised some preliminary actions for the platoon in order to give the reader an opportunity to get to know the men, but this beginning, as I said, took over two-thirds of the book. The patrol itself is also simple, but I did give more thought to working it out ahead of time.

INTERVIEWER: People have commented on the pleasure you seem to take in the military detail of *The Naked and the Dead*.

MAILER: Compared to someone like James Jones, I'm an amateur at military detail. But at that time I did like all those details. I even used to enjoy patrols, or at least I did when I wasn't sick with jungle rot and viruses or atabrine poisoning. I was one of the few men in the platoon who could read a map. I was the only enlisted man I know who really cared about reading a map and once I gave myself away. We used to have classes after a campaign was over; we'd come back to garrison—one of those tent cities out in a rice paddy—and they would teach us all over again how to read maps and read compasses, or they would drill us on the nomenclature of the machine gun for the eighth time. One day, very bored, I was daydreaming, and the instructor pointed to a part of the map and said, "Mailer, what are these coordinates?" If I had had a moment to think I would never have answered, it was bad form to be bright in my outfit, but I didn't think: he caught me in a daze, and I looked up and said, "320.017 dash 146.814" and everyone's mouth dropped. It was the first time anybody ever answered such a question thus briskly in the history of infantry map reading. At any rate, that was the fun for me, the part about the patrol. I suppose it had something to do with *Captain Blood* and *The Amateur Gentleman*.

INTERVIEWER: How much of a plan did you have for *Barbary Shore*?

MAILER: None. As I indicated earlier, *Barbary Shore* just birthed itself slowly. The book came out sentence by sentence. I literally never knew where the next day's work was coming from.

INTERVIEWER: You don't mention (in your description of writing *Barbary Shore*) any relationship to politics. Wasn't your *engagement* at the time a considerable part of the plan?

MAILER: I think it was the unspoken drama in the working-up of the book. I started *Barbary Shore* as some sort of fellow-traveler and finished with a political position which was a far-flung mutation of Trotskyism. And the drafts of the book reflected these ideological changes so drastically that the last draft of *Barbary Shore* is a different novel altogether and has almost nothing in common with the first draft but the names.

INTERVIEWER: Did Jean Malaquais (to whom the book is dedicated) have much to do with this?

MAILER: Yes. He had an enormous influence on me. He's the only man I know who can combine a powerfully dogmatic mind with the keenest sense of nuance, and he has a formidable culture which seems to live in his veins and capillaries. Since he also had a most detailed vision of the Russian Revolution—he was steeped in it the way certain American families are imbued with the records of their clan—I spent a year living more closely in the history of Russia from 1917 to 1937 than in the events of my own life. I doubt if I would even have gone back to rewrite *Barbary Shore* if I didn't know Malaquais. Certainly I could never have conceived McLeod. Malaquais, of course, bears no superficial resemblance whatsoever to McLeod—indeed Malaquais was never even a communist, he started as an anti-Stalinist, but he had a quality when

I first met him which was pure Old Bolshevik. One knew that if he had been born in Russia, a contemporary of Lenin's, he would have been one of the leaders of the Revolution and would doubtless have been executed in the trials. So his personality—as it filtered through the contradictory themes of my unconscious—inhibits *Barbary Shore*.

INTERVIEWER: Would you care to discuss what you mean by the "contradictory themes" of your unconscious? Is that related to what you said a little while ago about becoming aware of your unconscious while writing *Barbary Shore*?

MAILER: *Barbary Shore* was built on the division which existed then in my mind. My conscious intelligence, as I've indicated, became obsessed by the Russian Revolution. But my unconscious was much more interested in other matters: murder, suicide, orgy, psychosis, all the themes I discuss in *Advertisements*. Since the gulf between these conscious and unconscious themes was vast and quite resistant to any quick literary coupling, the tension to get a bridge across resulted in the peculiar feverish hothouse atmosphere of the book. My unconscious felt one kind of dread, my conscious mind another, and *Barbary Shore* lives somewhere between. That's why its focus is so unearthly. And of course this difficulty kept haunting me from then on in all the work I did afterward. But it was a book written without any plan.

INTERVIEWER: And *The Deer Park*?

MAILER: That was different. There I had an idea of what I was going to do. I knew it was going to be a story about a most unhappy love. The problem was getting to the affair: I could hardly wait to reach it, especially because the early parts of the novel were so difficult to write. It is truly difficult to trap Hollywood in a novel. Only in the last draft did I finally get the setting the way I wanted it. I think now the setting is probably the best part. In fact I would judge that the first fifty pages of *The Deer Park* are the best writing I have ever done in fiction. But they were the hardest fifty pages of the book to write and certainly took the longest time.

INTERVIEWER: Do you have any superstitions about your methods of work?

MAILER: I wouldn't call them superstitions exactly. I just think it's bad to talk about one's present work, for it spoils something at the root of the creative act. It discharges the tension.

INTERVIEWER: What writers have you learned the most from, technically?

MAILER: E. M. Forster, I suppose. I wouldn't say he is necessarily one of the novelists I admire most. But I have learned a lot from him. You remember in *The Longest Journey* somewhere about the fourth chapter, you turn the page and read, "Gerald was killed that day. He was beaten to death in a football game." It was quite extraordinary. Gerald had been very important through the beginning of the book. But now that he was suddenly and abruptly dead, everyone else's character began to shift. It taught me that personality was more fluid, more dramatic and startling, more inexact than I had thought. I was brought up on the idea that when you wrote a novel you tried to build a character who could be handled and walked around like a piece of sculpture. Suddenly character seemed related more closely to the paintings of the new realists. For instance, I saw one recently which had a painted girl reclining on a painted bed, and there was a television set next to her in the canvas, a real one which you could turn on. Turning on the literal factual set changes the girl and the painting both. Well, Forster gives you something of that sensation in his novels. I played with such a concept a great deal in *Barbary Shore* and I began to play with it in *The Deer Park* in an altogether different way. I suppose the concept was parallel to the "Alexandria Quartet" in its preoccupations. When you tell the same story through the eyes of different characters, you have not only a different novel but a different reality. I think I could sit down today and write *The Deer Park* through Charles Francis Eitel's eyes, and if I changed the names and the place, no one might know the new book had anything to do with *The Deer Park*. I suppose what I realized, after reading Forster, was that a novel written in the third person was now impossible for me for many years.

INTERVIEWER: Forster has never written a novel in the first person.

MAILER: I know he hasn't, but in some funny way Forster gave my notion of personality a sufficient shock that I could not manage to write in the third person. Forster, after all, had a developed view of the world; I did not. I think I must have felt at that time as if I would never be able to write in the third person until I developed a coherent view of life. I don't know that I've been able to altogether.

INTERVIEWER: You know, Thackeray says at one point that the novelist knows everything. He is like God, and this may be why he could write in the third person.

MAILER: God can write in the third person only so long as He understands His world. But if the world becomes contradictory or incomprehensible to Him, then God begins to grow concerned with his own nature. It's either that, or borrow notions from other Gods.

INTERVIEWER: Have you ever cribbed anything from other writers?

MAILER: Oh, you know, I have such a—what shall I say?—such a stuffy view of myself that I could never *conceive* of cribbing. But I have been *influenced* by—well, Farrell to begin with. Dos Passos, Steinbeck (I am trying to do it chronologically), Hemingway, and later Fitzgerald—much, much later. And Thomas Wolfe, of course.

INTERVIEWER: But back to cribbing. Shakespeare cribs, for example. He never invented a plot.

MAILER: No, but my plots are always rudimentary. Whatever I've accomplished certainly does not depend on my virtuosity with plot. Generally I don't even have a plot. What happens is that my characters engage in an action, and out of that action little bits of plot sometimes adhere to the narrative. I never have to worry about lifting a plot, because I don't conceive of a book that way.

INTERVIEWER: In connection with plot, when did the idea of using a hornet's nest to thwart the climbers in *The Naked and the Dead* come to you?

MAILER: That idea was there before I wrote the first sentence of the book. Actually that incident happened to my reconnaissance platoon on the most ambitious patrol I ever took with them. They sent out thirty of us to locate and destroy one hundred Japanese marines who had gotten behind our lines. Well, we never found the marines, but we did get stuck climbing one hell of an enormous hill with a mean slimy trail, and when we were almost up to the ridge, somebody kicked over a hornet's nest. Half the platoon went tearing up the hill, and the machine-gun squad went flying down to the valley. We never did find each other again that day. We just slunk back to our bivouac.

INTERVIEWER: Apart from the fact that it happened, do you think in fact it was a satisfactory device? It seems to have bothered some people.

MAILER: I think I'd do it the same way again. War is disproportions, and the hornet's nest seemed a perfect disproportion to me. We were ready to lose our lives but we weren't up to getting stung by a hornet.

INTERVIEWER: Would you say something about style, prose style, in relation to the novel?

MAILER: A really good style comes only when a man has become as good as he can be. Style is character. A good style cannot come from a bad, undisciplined character. Now a man may be evil, but I believe that people can be evil in their essential natures and still have good characters. Good in the sense of being well-tuned. They can have characters which are flexible, supple, adaptable, principled in relation to their own good or their own evil—even an evil man can have principles—he can be true to his own evil, which is not always so easy, either. I think good style is a matter of rendering out of oneself all the cupidities, all the cripplings, all the velleities. And then I think one has to develop one's physical grace. Writers who are possessed of some physical grace may tend to write better than writers who are physically clumsy. It's my impression this is so. I don't know that I'd care to attempt to prove it.

INTERVIEWER: Well, how would you describe your own style? I ask this question because certain critics have pointed to deficiencies in it, or what they think of as deficiencies. Didn't Diana Trilling, for instance, criticize certain flatnesses in your style?

MAILER: I think that flatness comes out of certain flatnesses in me. And in trying to overcome that flatness I may push too hard in the other direction. Alfred Kazin once said something very funny about the way I write: "Mailer is as fond of his style as an Italian tenor is of his vocal cords."

INTERVIEWER: Have you ever written to merely improve your writing, practiced your writing as an athlete would work out?

MAILER: No. I don't think it's a proper activity. That's too much like doing a setting-up exercise; any workout which does not involve a certain minimum of danger or responsibility does not improve the body—it just wears it out.

INTERVIEWER: In writing your novels, has any particular formal problem given you trouble—let's say a problem of joining two parts of a narrative together, getting people from point A to point B?

MAILER: You mean like getting them out of a room? I think formal problems exist in inverse proportion to one's honesty. You get to the problem of getting someone out of the room when there's something false about the scene.

INTERVIEWER: Do you do any research or special reading to prepare for writing a novel, or while you're writing a novel?

MAILER: Occasionally I have to look something up. But I'm always unhappy about that and mistrust the writing which comes out of it. I feel in a way that one's ignorance is part of one's creation, too. I don't know quite how to put it, but for instance if I, as a Jew, am writing about other Jews, and if my knowledge of Jewish culture is exceptionally spotty, as indeed it is, I am not so sure that that isn't an advantage in creating a modern American Jew. Because *his* knowledge of Jewish culture is also extremely spotty, and the way in which his personality is composed may be more in accordance with my ignorance than with a cultivated Jew's immersion in the culture. So in certain limited ways one's ignorance can help to buttress the validity of a novel.

INTERVIEWER: Have you ever written about a situation of which you have had no personal experience or knowledge?

MAILER: I don't know. Let's see . . . *Barbary Shore*, for example, is the most imaginative of my novels. But I did live in a rooming house for a short period while I was writing *The Naked and the Dead*. I certainly didn't live in it the way Lovett lived in it. I never met an F.B.I. agent—at least I had no sense of having met one at the time I was writing *Barbary Shore*. I am sure I have met a great many since. They didn't necessarily introduce themselves to me. I had never met an Old Bolshevik, either, although ironically, writing about F.B.I. agents and Old Bolsheviks in *Barbary Shore*, the greatest single difficulty with the book was that my common sense thought it was impossible to have all these agents and impossible heroes congregating in a rooming house in Brooklyn Heights. Yet a couple of years later I was working in a studio on Fulton Street at the end of Brooklyn Heights, a studio I have had for some years. It was a fine old studio building and they're tearing it down now to make room for a twenty-story building which will look like a Kleenex box. At any rate, on the floor below me, worked one Colonel Rudolph Abel, who was the most important spy for the Russians in this country for a period of about eight or ten years, and I am sure we used to be in the elevator together many times. I think he literally had the room beneath me. I have always been overcome with that. It made me decide there's no clear boundary between experience and imagination. Who knows what glimpses of reality we pick up unconsciously, telepathically.

INTERVIEWER: To what extent are your characters modeled on real people?

MAILER: I think half of them might have a point of departure from somebody real. Up to now I've not liked writing about people who are close to me, because they're too difficult to do. Their private reality obviously interferes with the reality one is trying to create. They become alive not as creatures in your imagination but as actors in your life. And so they seem real while you work but you're not working *their* reality into your book. For example, it's not a good idea to try to put your wife into a novel. Not your latest wife, anyway. In practice, I prefer to draw a character from someone I hardly know. Hollingsworth came from someone I met in Paris, a vapid young American who inveigled me to have a cup of coffee with him in a café and asked a lot of dull questions. *The Naked and the Dead* had just come out and I think he was impressed with that. Yet, there was something sinister about him. I had met him at the Sorbonne a week or two before and I saw him again just for this afternoon for no more than an hour, but he stayed in my memory and became Leroy Hollingsworth in *Barbary Shore*.

INTERVIEWER: How do you name your characters?

MAILER: I try to let the name emerge, because I've found out that the names of my characters usually have roots in the book. I try to avoid quick or cheap symbolisms. Although I contradict myself, for much is made in *The Deer Park* of the way the name "Eitel" is pronounced Eye-tell.

INTERVIEWER: *I*-tell?

MAILER: Eye-tell. But I became aware of that, believe it or not, only when the book was half done. The original title of *The Deer Park* was *The Idol and the Octopus*. The book was going to be about Charles Francis Eitel, the Director, and Herman Teppis, the Producer, and the underlying theme was the war between those who wished to make an idol out of art, the artists, and the patron who sued art for power, the octopus.

INTERVIEWER: You also called him "Idell."

MAILER: Frankie Idell in "The Man Who Studied Yoga," yes, but there again, I was obviously getting ready for some, shall we say, hanky-panky, in the eight novels.

INTERVIEWER: Can you describe how you turn a real person into a fictional one?

MAILER: I try to put the model in situations which have very little to do with his real situations in life. Very quickly the model disappears. His private reality can't hold up. For instance, I might take somebody who is a professional football player, a man, let's say, whom I know slightly, and make him a movie star. In a transposition of this sort, everything which relates particularly to the professional football player quickly disappears, and what is left, curiously, is what is *exportable* in his character. But this process, while interesting in the early stages, is not as exciting as the more creative act of allowing your characters to grow once they're separated from the model. It's when they become almost as complex as one's own personality that the fine excitement begins. Because then they are not really characters any longer—they're beings, which is a distinction I like to make. A character is someone you can grasp as a whole, you can have a clear idea of him, but a being is someone whose nature keeps shifting. Like a character of Forster's. In *The Deer Park* Lulu Myers is a being rather than a character. If you study her closely you will see that she is a different person in every scene. Just a little different. I don't know whether initially I did this by accident or purposefully, but at a certain point I made the conscious decision *not* to try to straighten her out, she seemed right in her changeableness.

INTERVIEWER: Is Marion Faye a character or a—

MAILER: No, he's a being. Everybody in *The Deer Park* is a being except the minor characters like Herman Teppis.

INTERVIEWER: Do specific characters reappear in different guises as the novels appear?

MAILER: To a mild degree. Actually it's easier for me to create a new character than to drag along one of the old ones. No, I think it's more that certain themes reappear in my novels, but I'd rather not get into this just yet.

INTERVIEWER: How did Marion Faye emerge?

MAILER: The book needed something which wasn't in the first draft, some sort of evil genius. One felt a dark pressure there in the inner horizon of the book. But even as I say this I know it's not true to the grain of my writing experience. I violate that experience by talking in these terms. I am not sure it's possible to describe the experience of novel-writing authentically. It may be that it is not an experience.

INTERVIEWER: What is it, then?

MAILER: It may be more like a relation, if you will—a continuing relation between a man and his wife. You can't necessarily speak of that as an experience because it may consist of several experiences which are braided together; or it may consist of many experiences which are all more or less similar; or indeed it may consist of two kinds of experiences which are antagonistic to one another. Throughout all of this I've spoken of characters' *emerging*. Quite often they don't emerge; they fail to emerge. And what one's left with is the dull compromise which derives from two kinds of experiences' warring with one another within oneself. A character who should have been brilliant is dull. Or even if a character does prove to be first-rate, it's possible you should have done twice as much with him, three times as much.

INTERVIEWER: You speak of character as emerging, and I gather by that that you mean emerging from yourself and emerging from your idea?

MAILER: They are also emerging from the book. A book takes on its own life in the writing. It has its laws, it becomes a creature to you after a while. One feels a bit like a master who's got a fine animal. Very often I'll feel a certain shame for what I've done with a novel. I won't say it's the novel that's bad; I'll say it's I who was bad. Almost as if the novel did not really belong to me, as if it was something raised by me like a child. I know what's potentially beautiful in my novel, you see. Very often after I've done the novel I realize that that beauty which I recognize in it is not going to be recognized by the reader. I didn't succeed in bringing it out. It's very odd—it's as though I had let the novel down, owed it a duty which I didn't fulfill.

INTERVIEWER: Would you say that there was any secret or hidden pattern being worked out in your novels?

MAILER: I'd rather leave that to others. If I answer the question badly, nothing is accomplished. If I answer too well, it's going to discourage critics. I can imagine nothing more distressing to a critic than to have a writer see accurately into his own work. But I will say one thing, which is that I have some obsession with how God exists. Is He an essential god or an existential god; is He all-powerful or is He, too, an embattled existential creature who may succeed or fail in His vision? I think this theme may become more apparent as the novels go on.

INTERVIEWER: When did this obsession begin?

MAILER: I think it began to show itself while I was doing the last draft of *The Deer Park*. Then it continued to grow as a private theme during all the years I was smoking marijuana.

INTERVIEWER: You have spoken so often of the existential view. What reading or individuals brought you to this?

MAILER: The experience came first. One's condition on marijuana is always existential. One can feel the importance of each moment and how it is changing one. One feels one's being, one becomes aware of the enormous apparatus of nothingness—the hum of a hi-fi set, the emptiness of a pointless interruption, one becomes aware of the war between each of us, how the nothingness in each of us seeks to attack the being of others, how our being in turn is attacked by the nothingness in others. I'm not speaking now of violence or the active conflict between one being and another. That still belongs to drama. But the war between being and nothingness is the underlying illness of the twentieth century. Boredom slays more of existence than war.

INTERVIEWER: Then you didn't come to existentialism because it was a literary influence?

MAILER: No. I'd hardly read anything by Sartre at this time, and nothing by Heidegger. I've read a bit since, and have to admire their formidable powers, but I suspect they are no closer to the buried continent of existentialism than were medieval cartographers near to a useful map of the world. The new continent which shows on our psychic maps as intimations of eternity is still to be discovered.

INTERVIEWER: What do you feel about the other kinds of writing you have done and are doing? How do they stand in relation to your work as a novelist?

MAILER: The essays?

INTERVIEWER: Yes: journalism, essays.

MAILER: Well, you know, there was a time when I wanted very much to belong to the literary world. I wanted to be respected the way someone like Katherine Anne Porter used to be respected.

INTERVIEWER: How do you think she was respected?

MAILER: The way a cardinal is respected—weak people get to their knees when the cardinal goes by.

INTERVIEWER: As a master of the craft, do you mean?

MAILER: As a master of the craft, yes. Her name is invoked in an argument. "Well, Katherine Anne Porter would not do it *that* way." But by now I'm a bit cynical about craft. I think there's a natural mystique in the novel which is more important than craft. One is trying, after all, to capture reality, and that is extraordinarily and exceptionally difficult. I think craft is merely a series of way stations. I think of craft as being like a Saint Bernard dog with that little bottle of brandy under his neck. Whenever you get into *real* trouble the thing that can save you as a novelist is to have enough craft to be able to keep warm long enough to be rescued. Of course this is exactly what keeps good novelists from becoming great novelists. Robert Penn Warren might have written a major novel if he hadn't had just that little extra bit of craft to get him out of all the trouble in *All the King's Men*. If Penn Warren hadn't known anything about Elizabethan literature, the true Elizabethan in him might have emerged. I mean, he might have written a fantastic novel. As it was, he knew enough about craft to—

INTERVIEWER: —to use it as an escape hatch?

MAILER: Yes. And his plot degenerated into a slam-bang of exits and entrances, confrontations, tragedies, quick wits, and woe. But he was really forcing an escape from the problem.

INTERVIEWER: Which was?

MAILER: Oh, the terror of confronting a reality which might open into more and more anxiety and so present a deeper and deeper view of the abyss. Craft protects one from facing those endless expanding realities of deterioration and responsibility.

INTERVIEWER: Deterioration in what sense?

MAILER: The terror, let's say, of being reborn as something much less noble or something much more ignoble. I think this sort of terror depresses us profoundly. Which may be why we throw up our enormous evasions—such as craft. Indeed, I think this adoration of craft, this specific respect for craft makes a church of literature for that vast number of writers who are somewhere on the spectrum between mediocrity and talent. But I think it's fatal for somebody who has a large ambition and a chance of becoming a great writer. I know, for myself, if I am going to make this attempt —that the only way to do it is to keep in shape in a peculiar way.

INTERVIEWER: Can you explain what you mean by that?

MAILER: It's hard to talk about. Harry Greb, for example, was a fighter who used to keep in shape. He was completely a fighter, the way one might wish to be completely a writer. He always did the things which were necessary to him as a fighter. Now, some of these things were extremely irrational, that is, extremely irrational from a prize-fight manager's point of view. That is, before he had a fight he would go to a brothel, and he would have two prostitutes, not one, taking the two of them into the same bed. And this apparently left him feeling like a wild animal. Don't ask me why. Perhaps he picked the two meanest whores in the joint and so absorbed into his system all the small, nasty, concentrated evils which had accumulated from carloads of men. Greb was known as the dirtiest fighter of his time. He didn't have much of a punch but he could spoil other fighters and punish them, he knew more dirty tricks than anyone around. This was one of his training methods and he did it over and over again until he died at a relatively early age of a heart attack, on an operating table. I think he died before he was thirty-eight or so. They operated on him, and bang, he went. Nothing could be done. But the point I make is that he stayed in training by the way he lived his life. The element which was paramount in it was to keep in shape. If he were drinking, you see, the point was to keep in shape *while* drinking. I'm being a touch imprecise about this.

INTERVIEWER: Well . . . what?

MAILER: He would not just drink to release his tension. Rather, what went on was that there was tension in him which was insupportable, so he had to drink. But reasoning as a professional, he felt that if he had to drink, he might as well use that too. In the sense that the actor uses everything which happens to him, so Greb as a fighter used everything which happened to him. As he drank he would notice the way his body moved. One of the best reasons one drinks is to become aware of the way his mind and body move.

INTERVIEWER: Well, how do you keep in shape?

MAILER: Look, before we go on, I want to say a little more about craft. It is a grab bag of procedures, tricks, lore, formal gymnastics, symbolic superstructures—methodology, in short. It's the compendium of what you've acquired from others. And since great writers communicate a vision of existence, one can't usually borrow their methods. The method is married to the vision. No, one acquires craft more from good writers and mediocre writers with a flair. Craft, after all, is what you can take out whole from their work. But keeping in shape is something else. For example, you can do journalism, and it can be terrible for your style. Or it can temper your style . . . in other words, you can become a *better* writer by doing a lot of different kinds of writing. Or you can deteriorate. There's a book came out a few years ago which was a sociological study of some Princeton men—I forget the name of it. One of them said something which I thought was extraordinary. He said he wanted to perform the sexual act under every variety of condition, emotion, and mood available to him. I was struck with this not because I ever wanted necessarily to have that kind of sexual life, but because it seemed to me that was what I was trying to do with my writing. I try to go over my work in every conceivable mood. I edit on a spectrum which runs from the high clear manic impressions of a drunk which has made one electrically alert all the way down to the soberest reaches of depression where I can hardly bear my words. By the time I'm done with writing I care about I usually have worked on it through the full gamut of my consciousness. If you keep yourself in this peculiar kind of shape, the craft will take care of itself. Craft is very little finally. But if you're continually worrying about whether you're growing or deteriorating as a man, whether your integrity is turning soft or firming itself, why then it's in that slow war, that slow rear-guard battle you fight against diminishing talent that you stay in shape as a writer and have a consciousness. You develop a consciousness as you grow older which enables you to write about anything, in effect, and write about it well. That is, provided you keep your consciousness in shape and don't relax into the flabby styles of thought which surround one everywhere. The moment you borrow other writers' styles of thought, you need craft to shore up the walls. But if what you write is a reflection of your own consciousness, then even journalism can become interesting. One wouldn't want to spend one's life at it, and I wouldn't want ever to be caught justifying journalism as a major activity (it's obviously less interesting than to write a novel), but it's better, I think, to see journalism as a venture of one's ability to keep in shape than to see it as an essential betrayal of the chalice of your literary art. Temples are for women.

INTERVIEWER: Temples are for women?

MAILER: Temples are for women.

INTERVIEWER: Well, Faulkner once said that nothing can injure a man's writing if he's a first-rate writer.

MAILER: Faulkner said more asinine things than any other major American writer. I can't remember a single interesting remark Faulkner ever made.

INTERVIEWER: He once called Henry James a "nice old lady."

MAILER: Faulkner had a mean small Southern streak in him, and most of his pronunciamentos reflect that meanness. He's a great writer, but he's not at all interesting in most of his passing remarks.

INTERVIEWER: Well, then, what can ruin a first-rate writer?

MAILER: Booze, pot, too much sex, too much failure in one's private life, too much attrition, too much recognition, too little recognition, frustration. Nearly everything in the scheme of things works to dull a first-rate talent. But the worst probably is cowardice —as one gets older, one becomes aware of one's cowardice, the desire to be bold which once was a joy gets heavy with caution and duty. And finally there's apathy. About the time it doesn't seem to be important any more to be a great writer you know you've slipped far enough to be doing your work now on the comeback trail.

INTERVIEWER: Would you say that is where you are now?

MAILER: Let others say it. I don't know that I choose to. The hardest thing for a writer to decide is whether he's burned out or merely lying fallow. I was ready to think I was burned out before I even started *The Naked and the Dead*.

INTERVIEWER: What kind of an audience do you keep in mind when you write?

MAILER: I suppose it's that audience which has no tradition by which to measure their experience but the intensity and clarity of their inner lives. That's the audience I'd like to be good enough to write for.

INTERVIEWER: Do you feel under any obligation to them?

MAILER: Yes. I have a consciousness now which I think is of use to them. I've got to be able to get it out and do it well, to transmit it in such a way that their experience can rise to a higher level. It's exactly . . . I mean, one doesn't want one's children to make one's own mistakes. Let them make better mistakes, more exceptional mistakes.

INTERVIEWER: What projects do you have for the future?

MAILER: I've got a very long novel I want to do. And beyond that I haven't looked. Some time ahead I'd like to be free of responsibilities so I could spend a year just taking on interesting assignments—cover the World Series, go to report a war. I can't do that now. I have a feeling I've got to come to grips with myself, with my talent, with what I've made of it and what I've spoiled of it. I've got to find out whether I really can write a large novel or not.

INTERVIEWER: What have you spoiled?

MAILER: All sorts of potentialities. I've burned them out—squandered them, wasted them. I think everybody does. It's a question of whether I've spoiled more than my share.

INTERVIEWER: You once said that you wished to become consecutively more disruptive, more dangerous, and more powerful, and you felt this sentence was a description of your function as a novelist. I wonder if you still think that?

MAILER: I might take out "disruptive." It's an unhappy word to use. It implies a love of disruption for the sake of disruption. Actually, I have a fondness for order.

INTERVIEWER: Do you enjoy writing, or is such a term irrelevant to your experience?

MAILER: Oh, no. No, no. You set me thinking of something Jean Malaquais once said. He always had a terrible time writing. He once complained with great anguish about the unspeakable difficulties he was having with a novel. And I asked him, "Why do you do it? You can do many other things well. Why do you bother with it?" I really meant this. Because he suffered when writing like no one I know. He looked up in surprise and said, "Oh, but this is the only way one can ever find the truth. The only time I know that something is true is at the moment I discover it in the act of writing." I think it's that. I think it's this moment when one knows it's true. One may not have written it well enough for others to know, but you're in love with the truth when you discover it at the point of a pencil. That, in and by itself, is one of the few rare pleasures in life.

INTERVIEWER: How do you feel when you aren't working?

MAILER: Edgy. I get into trouble. I would say I'm wasting my substance completely when I'm not writing.

INTERVIEWER: And to be writing . . . to be a writer?

MAILER: Well, at best you affect the consciousness of your time, and so indirectly you affect the history of the time which succeeds you. Of course, you need patience. It takes a long time for sentiments to collect into an action and often they never do. Which is why I was once so ready to conceive of running for Mayor of New York. I wanted to make actions rather than effect sentiments. But I've come to the middle-aged conclusion that I'm probably better as a writer than a man of action. Too bad. Still it's no little matter to be a writer. There's that godawful *Time*-magazine world out there, and one can make raids on it. There are palaces and prisons to attack. One can even succeed now and again in blowing holes in the line of the world's communications. Sometimes I feel as if there's a vast guerrilla war going on for the mind of man, communist against communist, capitalist against capitalist, artist against artist. And the stakes are huge. Will we spoil the best secrets of life or will we help to free a new kind of man? It's intoxicating to think of that. There's something rich waiting if one of us is brave enough and good enough to get there.

STEVEN MARCUS

12. Allen Ginsberg

Allen Ginsberg was born on June 3, 1926, in Paterson, New Jersey, the son of Louis Ginsberg, a poet and schoolteacher. He finished high school in Paterson and was graduated from Columbia in 1948. During the late forties and early fifties he held innumerable jobs: dishwasher in Manhattan, spot-welder in the Brooklyn Navy Yard, night porter with the May Company in Denver, book reviewer for *Newsweek*.

His long, angry, and influential poem "Howl," published in San Francisco in 1956, was seized by U.S. Customs and the local police and was the subject of an obscenity trial. After poets and critics testified in its behalf, the poem was released for distribution. As the acknowledged leader of the Beat Generation poets, Ginsberg traveled widely, reading his poetry and writing. He described his travels in the late fifties: "West coast 3 years. Later Arctic Sea Trip, Tangier, Venice, Amsterdam, Paris, read at Oxford Harvard Columbia Chicago."

Ginsberg has since spent extended periods of time in London, Havana, Calcutta, and Prague, and his appearances have frequently involved him in legal controversies. His work has been translated into many languages: French, Italian, Finnish, Japanese, and Bengali, among others. He has appeared in two films: *Pull My Daisy* (1961) with Jack Kerouac; and Jonas Mekas's *Guns of the Trees* (1962). Ginsberg's recently published works include *Empty Mirror* (1960), *Kaddish* (1960), and *Reality Sandwiches* (1963).

He continues to be an influential figure, and takes a leading role in antiwar protest campaigns and in efforts to alter the laws on obscenity, drugs, and sexual behavior.

Ginsberg in Cuba, with plane shot down at Bay of Pigs (Photo: Tom Maschler)

Manuscript page by Allen Ginsberg

From Journals New York 1961

January N.Y. 1961

```
In bed on my green purple red pink
      yellow orange bolivian blanket,
the tick of the clock, my back against the wall
--staring into black circled eyes magician
      man's bearded glance & story
the kitchen spun in a wheel of virtigo,
the eye in the center of the moving
            mandala--the
            eye in the hand
            the eye in the asshole
            The serpent eating or
                  vomiting its tail
--the blank air a solid wall revolving
      around my retina
The wheel of jewels and fire I saw moving
      vaster than my head in Peru
      Band circling in band and a black
      hole of Calcutta thru which
            I stared at my Atman
                  without a body--
The Giotto window on Boston giving
            to a scene in Bibled Palestine
                  A golden star
            and the flight from Egypt
                  in an instant now
Come true again--the Kabbala sign
      in the vomit on the floor--
On a window in Riverside drive,
      the boat moving slowly
      up the flowing river, small autos
      crawling up Hudson Drive
            a plash of white snow on
                  the Palisades
```

① Sept 28, 1964

E. 2 STREET
HIGH
✴
W/ Harry Smith
✴
OPTICAL
PHENOMENA
✴

REMEMBERING
LEARY'S BEDROOM
HARVARD
JACK HALLUCINATING
✴
OUT ROBT.
LOWELL'S WINDOW

Allen Ginsberg

Allen Ginsberg was elected King of the May by Czech students in Prague on May Day 1965. Soon afterward he was expelled by the Czech government. He had been traveling for several months—in Cuba, Russia, and Poland—and from Prague he flew to London to negotiate the English publication of his poems. I didn't know he was in the country, but one night in Bristol before a poetry reading I saw him in a bar. He read that night; I hadn't heard him read before and was struck that evening by the way he seemed to enter each of his poems emotionally while reading them, the performance as much a discovery for him as for his audience.

Ginsberg and I left Bristol the day after the reading, and hitchhiked to Wells Cathedral and then to Glastonbury, where he picked a flower from King Arthur's grave to send, he said, to Peter Orlovsky. He studied carefully the exhibit of tools and weapons under the huge conical chimney of the ancient Abbot's kitchen, as later in Cambridge he was to study the Fitzwilliam Museum's store of Blake manuscripts; Ginsberg's idea of a Jerusalemic Britain occurring now in the day of long hair and new music meant equally the fulfillment of Blake's predictions of Albion. As we came out of a teashop in Glastonbury (where customers had glanced cautiously at the bearded, prophetic—and unfazed—stranger), Allen, spoke of Life's simulacrum of a report of his Oxford encounter with Dame Edith Sitwell. ("Dope makes me come out all over in spots," she's supposed to have said.)

Leaving the town, we were caught in a rainstorm, and took a bus to Bath. Then, hitchhiking toward London, we were unsuccessful until Ginsberg tried using Buddhist hand signals instead of thumbing; half a minute later a car stopped. Riding through Somerset he talked about notation, *the mode he says he learned from Kerouac and has used in composing his enormous journals; he read from an account he'd made of a recent meeting with the poets Yevtushenko and Vosnessensky in Moscow, and then, looking up at a knot in a withered oak by the road, said,* "The tree has cancer of the breast . . . *that's what I mean.* . . ."

Two weeks later he was in Cambridge for a reading, and I asked him to submit to this interview. He was still busy with Blake, and roaming and musing around the university and countryside in his spare moments; it took two days to get him to sit still long enough to turn on the tape-recorder. He spoke slowly and thoughtfully, tiring after two hours. We stopped for a meal when guests came— when Ginsberg learned one of them was a biochemist he questioned him about viruses and DNA for an hour—then we returned to record the other half of the tape. The words that follow are his, with little alteration save the omission of repetitive matter in half a dozen places.

INTERVIEWER: I think Diana Trilling, speaking about your reading at Columbia, remarked that your poetry, like all poetry in English when dealing with a serious subject, naturally takes on the iambic pentameter rhythm. Do you agree?

GINSBERG: Well, it really isn't an accurate thing, I don't think. I've never actually sat down and made a technical analysis of the rhythms that I write. They're probably more near choriambic— Greek meters, dithyrambic meters—and tending toward de DA de de DA de de . . . what is that? Tending toward dactylic, probably. Williams once remarked that American speech tends toward dactylic. But it's more complicated than dactyl because dactyl is a three, three units, a foot consisting of three parts, whereas the actual rhythm is probably a rhythm which consists of five, six, or seven, like DA de de DA de de DA de de DA DA. Which is more toward the line of Greek dance rhythms—that's why they call them choriambic. So actually, probably it's not really technically correct, what she said. But—and that applies to certain poems, like certain passages of "Howl" and certain passages of "Kaddish"—there are definite rhythms which could be analyzed as corresponding to classical rhythms, though not necessarily *English* classical rhythms; they might correspond to Greek classical rhythms, or Sanskrit prosody. But probably most of the other poetry, like "Aether" or "Laughing Gas" or a lot of those poems, they simply don't fit into that. I think she felt very comfy, to think that that would be so. I really felt quite hurt about that, because it seemed to me that she ignored the main prosodic technical achievements that I had proffered forth to the academy, and they didn't even recognize it. I mean not that I want to stick her with being the academy.

INTERVIEWER: And in "Howl" and "Kaddish" you were working with a kind of classical unit? Is that an accurate description?

GINSBERG: Yeah, but it doesn't do very much good, because I wasn't really working with a classical unit, I was working with my own neural impulses and writing impulses. See, the difference is between someone sitting down to write a poem *in* a definite preconceived metrical pattern and filling in that pattern, and someone working with his physiological movements and *arriving* at a pattern, and perhaps even arriving at a pattern which might even have a name, or might even have a classical usage, but arriving at it organically rather than synthetically. Nobody's got any objection to even iambic pentameter if it comes from a source deeper than the mind—that is to say, if it comes from the breathing and the belly and the lungs.

INTERVIEWER: American poets have been able to break away from a kind of English specified rhythm earlier than English poets have been able to do. Do you think this has anything to do with a peculiarity in English spoken tradition?

GINSBERG: No, I don't really think so, because the English don't speak in iambic pentameter either; they don't speak in the recognizable pattern that they write in. The dimness of their speech and the lack of emotional variation is parallel to the kind of dim diction and literary usage in the poetry now. But you can hear all sorts of Liverpudlian or Gordian—that's Newcastle—you can hear all sorts of variants aside from an upper-tone accent, a high-class accent, that don't fit into the tone of poetry being written right now.

It's not being used like in America—I think it's just that British poets are more cowardly.

INTERVIEWER: Do you find any exception to this?

GINSBERG: It's pretty general, even the supposedly avant-garde poets. They write, you know, in a very toned-down manner.

INTERVIEWER: How about a poet like Basil Bunting?

GINSBERG: Well, he was working with a whole bunch of wild men from an earlier era, who were all breaking through, I guess. And so he had that experience—also he knew Persian, he knew Persian prosody. He was better educated than most English poets.

INTERVIEWER: The kind of organization you use in "Howl," a recurrent kind of syntax—you don't think this is relevant any longer to what you want to do?

GINSBERG: No, but it was relevant to what I wanted to do then, it wasn't even a conscious decision.

INTERVIEWER: Was this related in any way to a kind of music or jazz that you were interested in at the time?

GINSBERG: Mmm . . . the myth of Lester Young as described by Kerouac, blowing eighty-nine choruses of "Lady Be Good," say, in one night, or my own hearing of Illinois Jacquet's *Jazz at the Philharmonic*, Volume 2; I think "Can't Get Started" was the title.

INTERVIEWER: And you've also mentioned poets like Christopher Smart, for instance, as providing an analogy—is this something you discovered later on?

GINSBERG: When I looked into it, yeah. Actually, I keep reading, or earlier I kept reading, that I was influenced by Kenneth Fearing and Carl Sandburg, whereas actually I was more conscious of Christopher Smart, and Blake's Prophetic Books, and Whitman and some aspects of Biblical rhetoric. And a lot of specific prose things, like Genet, Genet's *Our Lady of the Flowers* and the rhetoric in that, and Céline; Kerouac, most of all, was the biggest influence I think—Kerouac's prose.

INTERVIEWER: When did you come onto Burroughs's work?

GINSBERG: Let's see . . . Well, first thing of Burroughs's I ever read was 1946 . . . which was a skit later published and integrated in some other work of his, called *So Proudly We Hail*, describing the sinking of the Titanic and an orchestra playing, a spade orchestra playing "The Star Spangled Banner" while everybody rushed out to the lifeboats and the captain got up in woman's dress and rushed into the purser's office and shot the purser and stole all the money, and a spastic paretic jumped into a lifeboat with a machete and began chopping off people's fingers that were trying to climb into the boat, saying, "Out of the way, you foolth . . . dirty thunthufbithes." That was a thing he had written up at Harvard with a friend named Kells Elvins. Which is really the whole key of all his work, like the sinking of America, and everybody like frightened rats trying to get out, or that was his vision of the time.

Then he and Kerouac later in 1945—forty-five or forty-six—wrote a big detective book together, alternating chapters. I don't know where that book is now—Kerouac has his chapters and Burroughs's are somewhere in his papers. So I think in a sense it was Kerouac that encouraged Burroughs to write really, because Kerouac was so enthusiastic about prose, about writing, about lyricism, about the honor of writing . . . the Thomas Wolfe-ian delights of it. So anyway he turned Burroughs on in a *sense*, because Burroughs found a companion who could write really interestingly, and Burroughs admired Kerouac's perceptions. Kerouac could imitate Dashiell Hammett as well as Bill, which was Bill's natural style: dry, bony, factual. At that time Burroughs was reading John O'Hara, simply for facts, not for any sublime stylistic thing, just because he was a hard-nosed reporter.

Then in Mexico around 1951 he started writing *Junkie*. I've forgotten what relation I had to that—I think I wound up as the agent for it, taking it around New York trying to get it published. I think he sent me portions of it at the time—I've forgotten how it worked out now. This was around 1949 or 1950. He was going through a personal crisis, his wife had died. It was in Mexico or South America . . . but it was a very generous thing of him to do, to start writing all of a sudden. Burroughs was always a very *tender* sort of person, but very dignified and shy and withdrawn, and for him to *commit* himself to a big autobiographical thing like that was . . . at the time, struck me as like a piece of eternity is in love with the . . . what is it, "Eternity is in love with the productions of Time"? So he was making a production of Time then.

Then I started taking that around. I've forgotten who I took that to but I think maybe to Louis Simpson who was then working at Bobbs-Merrill. I'm not sure whether I took it to him—I remember taking it to Jason Epstein who was then working at Doubleday I think. Epstein at the time was not as experienced as he is now. And his reaction to it, I remember when I went back to his office to pick it up, was, well this is all very interesting, but it isn't really interesting, on account of if it were an autobiography of a junkie written by Winston *Churchill* then it'd be interesting, but written by somebody he'd never heard of, well then it's *not* interesting. And anyway I said what about the *prose*, the prose is interesting, and he says, oh, a difference of opinion on that. Finally I wound up taking it to Carl Solomon who was then a reader for A. A. Wynn Company, which was his uncle; and they finally got it through there. But it was finally published as a cheap paperback. With a whole bunch of frightened footnotes; like Burroughs said that marijuana was nonhabit-forming, which is now accepted as a fact, there'd be a footnote by the editor, "Reliable, er, responsible medical opinion does not confirm this." Then they also had a little introduction . . . literally they were afraid of the book being censored or *seized* at the time, is what they said. I've forgotten what the terms of censorship or seizure were that they were worried about. This was about 1952. They *said* that they were afraid to publish it straight for fear there would be a Congressional investigation or something, I don't know what. I think there was some noise about narcotics at the time. Newspaper noise . . . I've forgotten exactly what the arguments were. But anyway they had to write a preface which hedged on the book a lot.

INTERVIEWER: Has there been a time when fear of censorship or similar trouble has made your own expression difficult?

GINSBERG: This is so complicated a matter. The beginning of

the fear with me was, you know, what would my father say to something that I would write. At the time, writing "Howl"—for instance, like I assumed when writing it that it was something that *could* not be published because I wouldn't want my daddy to see what was in there. About my sex life, being fucked in the ass, imagine your father reading a thing like that, was what I thought. Though that disappeared as soon as the thing was real, or as soon as I manifested my . . . you know, it didn't make that much importance finally. That was sort of a help for writing, because I assumed that it wouldn't be published, therefore I could say anything that I wanted. So literally just for myself or anybody that I knew personally well, writers who would be willing to appreciate it with a breadth of tolerance—in a piece of work like "Howl"—who wouldn't be judging from a moralistic viewpoint but looking for evidences of humanity or secret thought or just actual truthfulness.

Then there's later the problem of publication—we had a lot. The English printer refused at first I think, we were afraid of customs; the first edition we had to print with asterisks on some of the dirty words, and then the *Evergreen Review* in reprinting it used asterisks, and various people reprinting it later always wanted to use the *Evergreen* version rather than the corrected legal City Lights version—like I think there's an anthology of Jewish writers, I forgot who edited that, but a couple of the high-class intellectuals from Columbia. I had written asking them specifically to use the later City Lights version, but they went ahead and printed an asterisked version. I forget what was the name of that—something like *New Generation of Jewish Writing*, Philip Roth, et cetera.

INTERVIEWER: Do you take difficulties like these as social problems, problems of communication simply, or do you feel they also block your own ability to express yourself for yourself?

GINSBERG: The problem is, where it gets to literature, is this. We all talk among ourselves and we have common understandings, and we say anything we want to say, and we talk about our assholes, and we talk about our cocks, and we talk about who we fucked last night, or who we're gonna fuck tomorrow, or what kind love affair we have, or when we got drunk, or when we stuck a broom in our ass in the Hotel Ambassador in Prague—anybody tells one's friends about that. So then—what happens if you make a distinction between what you tell your friends and what you tell your Muse? The problem is to break down that distinction: when you approach the Muse to talk as frankly as you would talk with yourself or with your friends. So I began finding, in conversations with Burroughs and Kerouac and Gregory Corso, in conversations with people whom I knew well, whose souls I respected, that the things we were telling each other for real were totally different from what was already in literature. And that was Kerouac's great discovery in *On the Road*. The kinds of things that he and Neal Cassady were talking about, he finally discovered were *the* subject matter for what he wanted to write down. That meant, at that minute, a complete revision of what literature was supposed to be, in *his* mind, and actually in the minds of the people that first read the book. Certainly in the minds of the critics, who had at first attacked it as not being . . . proper structure, or something. In other words, a gang of friends running around in an automobile. Which obviously is like a great picaresque literary device, and a classical one. And was *not* recognized, at the time, as suitable literary subject matter.

INTERVIEWER: So it's not just a matter of themes—sex, or any other one—

GINSBERG: It's the ability to commit to writing, to. *write*, the same way that you . . . are! Anyway! You have many writers who have preconceived ideas about what literature is supposed to be, and their ideas seem to exclude that which makes them most charming in private conversation. Their faggishness, or their campiness, or their neurasthenia, or their solitude, or their goofiness, or their—even—masculinity, at times. Because they think that they're gonna write something that sounds like something else that they've read before, instead of sounds like them. Or comes from their own life. In other words, there's no distinction, there should be no distinction between what we write down, and what we really know, to begin with. As we know it every day, with each other. And the hypocrisy of literature has been—you know like there's supposed to be formal literature, which is supposed to be different from . . . in subject, in diction, and even in organization, from our quotidian inspired lives.

It's also like in Whitman, "I find no fat sweeter than that which sticks to my own bones"—that is to say the self-confidence of someone who knows that he's really alive, and that his existence is just as good as any other subject matter.

INTERVIEWER: Is physiology a part of this too—like the difference between your long breath line, and William Carlos Williams's shorter unit?

GINSBERG: Analytically, ex post facto, it all begins with fucking around and intuition and without any idea of *what* you're doing, I think. Later, I have a tendency to explain it, "Well, I got a longer breath than Williams, or I'm Jewish, or I study yoga, or I sing long lines. . . ." But anyway, what it boils down to is this, it's my *movement*, my feeling is for a big long clanky statement—partly that's something that I share, or maybe that I even got from Kerouac's long prose line; which is really, like he once remarked, an extended poem. Like one long sentence page of his in *Doctor Sax* or *Railroad Earth* or occasionally *On the Road*—if you examine them phrase by phrase they usually have the density of poetry, and the beauty of poetry, but most of all the single elastic rhythm running from beginning to end of the line and ending "mop!"

INTERVIEWER: Have you ever wanted to extend this rhythmic feeling as far as, say, Artaud or now Michael McClure have taken it—to a line that is actually animal noise?

GINSBERG: The rhythm of the long line is also an animal cry.

INTERVIEWER: So you're following that feeling and not a thought or a visual image?

GINSBERG: It's simultaneous. The poetry generally is like a rhythmic articulation of feeling. The feeling is like an impulse that rises within—just like sexual impulses, say; it's almost as definite as that. It's a feeling that begins somewhere in the pit of the stomach and rises up forward in the breast and then comes out through the mouth and ears, and comes forth a croon or a groan or a sigh. Which, if you put words to it by looking around and seeing and trying to describe what's making you sigh—and sigh in words— you simply articulate what you're feeling. As simple as that. Or actually what happens is, at best what happens, is there's a definite body rhythm that has no definite words, or may have one or two words attached to it, one or two key words attached to it. And then, in writing it down, it's simply by a process of association that I find what the rest of the statement is—what can be collected around that word, what that word is connected to. Partly by simple association, the first thing that comes to my mind like "Moloch is" or "Moloch who," and then whatever comes out. But that also goes along with a definite rhythmic impulse, like DA de de DA de de DA de de DA DA. "Moloch whose *eyes* are a *thou*sand blind *windows*." And before I wrote "Moloch whose eyes are a thousand blind windows," I had the word, "Moloch, Moloch, Moloch," and I also had the feeling DA de de DA de de DA de de DA DA. So it was just a question of looking up and seeing a lot of windows, and saying, Oh, windows, of course, but what kind of windows? But not even that—"Moloch whose eyes." "Moloch whose *eyes*"— which is beautiful in itself—but what about it, Moloch whose eyes are *what*? So Moloch whose eyes—then probably the next thing I thought was "thousands." O.K., and then thousands *what*? "Thousands blind." And I had to finish it somehow. So I hadda say "windows." It looked good *afterward*.

Usually during the composition, step by step, word by word and adjective by adjective, if it's at all spontaneous, I don't know whether it even makes sense sometimes. Sometimes I do know it makes complete sense, and I start crying. Because I realize I'm hitting some area which is absolutely true. And in that sense applicable universally, or understandable universally. In that sense able to survive through time—in that sense to be read by somebody and wept to, maybe, centuries later. In that sense prophecy, because it touches a common key . . . what prophecy actually is is not that you actually know that the bomb will fall in 1942. It's that you know and feel something which somebody knows and feels in a hundred years. And maybe articulate it in a hint—concrete way that they can pick up on in a hundred years.

INTERVIEWER: You once mentioned something you had found in Cézanne—a remark about the reconstitution of the *petites sensations* of experience, in his own painting—and you compared this with the method of your poetry.

GINSBERG: I got all hung up on Cézanne around 1949 in my last year at Columbia, studying with Meyer Schapiro. I don't know how it led into it—I think it was about the same time that I was having these Blake visions. So. The thing I understood from Blake was that it was possible to transmit a message through time which could reach the enlightened, that poetry had a definite effect, it wasn't just pretty, or just beautiful, as I had understood pretty beauty before—it was something basic to human existence, or it reached something, it reached the bottom of human existence. But anyway the impression I got was that it was like a kind of time machine through which he could transmit, Blake could transmit, his basic consciousness and communicate it to somebody else after he was dead—in other words, build a time machine.

Now just about that time I was looking at Cézanne and I suddenly got a strange shuddering impression looking at his canvases, partly the effect when someone pulls a Venetian blind, reverses the Venetian—there's a sudden shift, a flashing that you see in Cézanne canvases. Partly it's when the canvas opens up into three dimensions and looks like wooden objects, like solid-space objects, in three dimensions rather than flat. Partly it's the enormous spaces which open up in Cézanne's landscapes. And it's partly that mysterious quality around his figures, like of his wife or the cardplayers or the postman or whoever, the local Aix characters. They look like great huge 3-D wooden dolls, sometimes. Very *uncanny* thing, like a very mysterious thing—in other words, there's a strange sensation that one gets, looking at his canvases, which I began to associate with the extraordinary sensation—cosmic sensation, in fact—that I had experienced catalyzed by Blake's "Sun-flower" and "Sick Rose" and a few other poems. So I began studiously investigating Cézanne's intentions and method, and looking at all the canvases of his that I could find in New York, and all the reproductions I could find, and I was writing at the time a paper on him, for Schapiro at Columbia in the fine-arts course.

And the whole thing opened up, two ways: first, I read a book on Cézanne's composition by Earl Loran, who showed photographs, analyses and photographs of the original motifs, side by side with the actual canvases—and years later I actually went to Aix, with all the postcards, and stood in the spots, and tried to find the places where he painted Mont-Sainte-Victoire from, and got in his studio and saw some of the motifs he used, like his big black hat and his cloak. Well, first of all, I began to see that Cézanne had all sorts of literary symbolism in him, on and off. I was preoccupied with Plotinian terminology, of time and eternity, and I saw it in Cézanne paintings, an early painting of a clock on a shelf which I associated with time and eternity, and I began to think he was a big secret mystic. And I saw a photograph of his studio in Loran's book and it was like an alchemist's studio, because he had a skull, and he had a long black coat, and he had this big black hat. So I began thinking of him as, you know, like a magic character. Like the original version I had thought of him was like this austere dullard from Aix. So I began getting really interested in him as a hermetic type, and then I symbolically read into his canvases things that probably weren't there, like there's a painting of a winding road which turns off, and I saw that as the mystical path: it turns off into a village and the end of the path is hidden. Something he painted I guess when he went out painting with Bernard. Then there was an account of a very fantastic conversation that he had had. It's quoted in Loran's book: there's a long long long paragraph where he says, "By means of squares, cubes, triangles, I try to reconstitute the impression that I have from nature: the means that I use to reconstitute the impression of solidity that I think-feel-see when I am looking at a motif like Victoire is to reduce it to some kind of pictorial language, so I use these squares, cubes, and triangles, but I try to build them together so interknit [*and here in the conversation he held his hands together with his fingers interknit*] so that *no light gets through.*" And I was mystified by that, but it seemed to make sense in terms of the grid of paint strokes that he had on his canvas, so that he produced a solid two-dimensional surface which when you looked *in*to it, maybe from a slight distance with your eyes either unfocused or your eyelids lowered slightly, you could see a great three-dimensional opening, mysterious, stereoscopic, like going into a stereopticon. And I began discovering in "The Cardplayers" all sorts of sinister symbols, like there's one guy leaning against the wall with a stolid expression on his face, that he doesn't want to get involved; and then there's two guys who are peasants, who are looking as if they've just been dealt *Death* cards; and then the *dealer* you look at and he turns out to be a city slicker with a big blue cloak and almost rouge doll-like cheeks and a fat-faced Kafkian-agent impression about him, like he's a cardsharp, he's a cosmic cardsharp dealing out Fate to all these people. This looks like a great big hermetic Rembrandtian portrait in Aix! That's why it has that funny monumentality—aside from the quote plastic values unquote.

Then, I smoked a lot of marijuana and went to the basement of the Museum of Modern Art in New York and looked at his water colors and that's where I began really turning on to space in Cézanne and the way he built it up. Particularly there's one of rocks, I guess "Rocks at Garonne," and you look at them for a while, and after a while they seem like they're rocks, just the rock parts, you don't know where they are, whether they're on the ground or in the air or on top of a cliff, but then they seem to be floating in space like clouds, and then they seem to be also a bit like they're amorphous, like kneecaps or cockheads or faces without eyes. And it has a very mysterious impression. Well, that may have been the result of the pot. But it's a definite thing that I got from that. Then he did some very odd studies after classical statues, Renaissance statues, and they're great gigantesque herculean figures with little tiny pinheads . . . so that apparently was his comment on them!

And then . . . the things were endless to find in Cézanne. Finally I was reading his letters and I discovered this phrase again, *mes petites sensations*—"I'm an old man and my passions are not, my senses are not coarsened by passions like some *other* old men I know, and I have worked for years trying to," I guess it was the phrase, "*reconstitute* the *petites sensations* that I get from nature, and I could stand on a hill and merely by moving my head half an inch the composition of the landscape was totally changed." So apparently he'd refined his optical perception to such a point where it's a real contemplation of optical phenomena in an almost yogic way, where he's standing there, from a specific point studying the optical field, the depth in the optical field, looking, actually looking at his own eyeballs in a sense. The attempting to reconstitute the sensation in his own eyeballs. And what does he say finally—in a very weird statement which one would not expect of the austere old workman—he said, "And this *petite sensation* is nothing other than *pater omnipotens aeterna deus*."

So that was, I felt, the key to Cézanne's hermetic method . . . everybody knows his workman-like, artisan-like, pettified-like painting method which is so great, but the really ro*man*ticistic motif behind it is absolutely marvelous, so you realize that he's really a saint! Working on his form of yoga, all that time, in obvious saintly circumstances of retirement in a small village, leading a relatively nonsociable life, going through the motions of going to church or not, but really containing in his skull these supernatural phenomena, and observations . . . you know, and it's very humble actually, because he didn't know if he was crazy or not—that is a flash of the physical, miracle dimensions of existence, trying to reduce that to canvas in two dimensions, and then trying to do it in such a way as it would look—if the observer looked at it long enough—it would look like as much three dimension as the actual *world* of optical phenomena when one looks through one's eyes. Actually he's *re*constituted the whole fucking universe in his canvases—it's like a fantastic thing!—or at least the appearance of the universe.

So. I used a lot of this material in the references in the last part of the first section of "Howl": "sensation of Pater Omnipotens Aeterna Deus." The last part of "Howl" was really an homage to art but also in specific terms an homage to Cézanne's method, in a sense I adapted what I could to writing; but that's a very complicated matter to explain. Except, putting it very simply, that just as Cézanne doesn't use perspective lines to create space, but it's a juxtaposition of one color against another color (that's one element of his space), so, I had the idea, perhaps overrefined, that by the unexplainable, unexplained nonperspective line, that is, juxtaposition of one *word* against another, a *gap* between the two words —like the space gap in the canvas—there'd be a gap between the two words which the mind would fill in with the sensation of existence. In other words when I say, oh . . . when Shakespeare says, "In the dread vast and middle of the night," something happens between "dread vast" and "middle." That creates like a whole space of, spaciness of black night. How it gets that is very odd, those words put together. Or in the haiku, you have two distinct images, set side by side without drawing a connection, without drawing a logical connection between them: the *mind* fills in this . . . this space. Like

> O *ant*
> *crawl up* Mount Fujiyama,
> *but slowly, slowly.*

Now you have the small ant and you have Mount Fujiyama and you have the slowly, slowly, and what happens is that you feel almost like . . . a cock in your mouth! You feel this enormous space-universe, it's almost a tactile thing. Well, anyway, it's a phenomenon-sensation, phenomenon hyphen sensation, that's created by this little haiku of Issa, for instance.

So, I was trying to do similar things with juxtapositions like "hydrogen jukebox." Or . . . "winter midnight smalltown streetlight rain." Instead of cubes and squares and triangles. Cézanne is reconstituting by means of triangles, cubes, and colors—I have to reconstitute by means of words, rhythms of course, and all that —but say it's words, phrasings. So. The problem is then to reach the different parts of the mind, which are existing simultaneously, the different associations which are going on simultaneously, choosing elements from both, like: jazz, jukebox, and all that, and we have the jukebox from that; politics, hydrogen bomb, and we have the hydrogen of that, you see "hydrogen jukebox." And that actually compresses in one instant like a whole series of things. Or the end of "Sun-flower" with "cunts of wheelbarrows," whatever that all meant, or "rubber dollar bills"—"skin of machinery"; see, and actually in the moment of composition I don't necessarily *know* what it means, but it comes to mean something later, after a year or two, I realize that it meant something clear, unconsciously. Which takes on meaning in time, like a photograph developing slowly. Because we're not really always conscious of the entire depth of our minds—in other words, we just know a lot more than we're able to be aware of, normally—though at moments we're completely aware, I guess.

There's some other element of Cézanne that was interesting . . . oh, his patience, of course. In recording the optical phenomena. Has something to do with Blake: *with* not *through* the eye— "You're led to believe a lie when you see with not through the eye." He's seeing through his eye. One can see *through* his canvas to God, really, is the way it boils down. Or to Pater Omnipotens Aeterna Deus. I could imagine someone not prepared, in a peculiar chemical-physiological state, peculiar mental state, psychic state, someone not prepared who had no experience of eternal ecstasy, passing in front of a Cézanne canvas, distracted and without noticing it, his eye traveling in, to, through the canvas into the space and suddenly stopping with his hair standing on end, dead in his tracks, *see*ing a whole universe. And I think that's what Cézanne really does, to a lot of people.

Where were we now? Yeah, the idea that I had was that gaps in space and time through images juxtaposed, just as in the haiku you get two images which the mind connects in a flash, and so that *flash* is the *petite sensation*; or the *satori*, perhaps, that the Zen haikuists would speak of—if they speak of it like that. So, the poetic experience that Housman talks about, the hair-standing-on-end or the hackles-rising, whatever it is, visceral thing. The interesting thing would be to know if certain combinations of words and rhythms actually had an electrochemical reaction on the body, which could catalyze specific states of consciousness. I think that's what probably happened to me with Blake. I'm *sure* it's what happens on a perhaps lower level with Poe's "Bells" or "Raven," or even Vachel Lindsay's "Congo": that there is a hypnotic rhythm there, which when you introduce it into your nervous system, causes all sorts of electronic changes—permanently alters it. There's a statement by Artaud on that subject, that certain music when introduced into the nervous system changes the molecular composition of the nerve cells or something like that, it permanently alters the being that has experience of this. Well, anyway, this is certainly true. In other words, any experience we have is recorded in the brain and goes through neural patterns and whatnot: so I suppose brain recordings are done by means of shifting around of little electrons—so there is actually an electrochemical effect caused by art.

So . . . the problem is what is the maximum electrochemical effect in the desired direction. That is what I was taking Blake as having done to me. And what I take as one of the optimal possibilities of art. But this is all putting it in a kind of bullshit abstract way. But it's an interesting—toy. To play with. That idea.

INTERVIEWER: In the last five or six months you've been in Cuba, Czechoslovakia, Russia, and Poland. Has this helped to clarify your sense of the current world situation?

GINSBERG: Yeah, I no longer feel—I didn't ever feel that there was any answer in dogmatic Leninism-Marxism—but I feel very definitely now that there's no answer to my desires there. Nor do most of the people in those countries—in Russia or Poland or Cuba—really feel that either. It's sort of like a religious theory imposed from above and usually used to beat people on the head with. Nobody takes it seriously because it doesn't mean anything, it means different things in different countries anyway. The general idea of revolution against American idiocy is good, it's still sympathetic, and I guess it's a good thing like in Cuba, and obviously Viet Nam. But what's gonna follow—the dogmatism that follows is a big drag. And everybody apologizes for the dogmatism by saying, well, it's an inevitable consequence of the struggle against American repression. And that may be true too.

But there's one thing I feel certain of, and that's that there's no human answer in communism or capitalism as it's practiced outside of the U.S. in any case. In other words, by hindsight, the interior of America is not bad, at least for me, though it might be bad for a spade, but not too bad, creepy, but it's not impossible. But traveling in countries like Cuba and Viet Nam I realize that the people that get the real evil side effects of America are there—in other words, it really is like imperialism, in that sense. People in the United States all got money, they got cars, and everybody else *starves* on account of American foreign policy. Or is being bombed out, torn apart, and bleeding on the street, they get all their teeth bashed in, tear gassed, or hot pokers up their ass, things that would be, you know, considered terrible in the United States. Except for Negroes.

So I don't know. I don't see any particular answer, and *this* month it seemed to me like actually an atomic war was inevitable on account of both sides were so dogmatic and frightened and had nowhere to go and didn't know what to do with themselves anymore except fight. Everybody too intransigent. Everybody too mean. I don't suppose it'll take place, but . . . Somebody has got to sit in the British Museum again like Marx and figure out a new system; a new blueprint. Another century has gone, technology has changed everything completely, so it's time for a new utopian system. Burroughs is almost working on it.

But one thing that's impressive is Blake's idea of Jerusalem, Jerusalemic Britain, which I think is *now* more and more valid. He, I guess, defined it. I'm still confused about Blake, I still haven't read him all through enough to understand what direction he was really pointing to. It seems to be the *naked human form divine*, seems to be Energy, it seems to be sexualization, or sexual liberation, which are the directions we all believe in. He also seems, however, to have some idea of imagination which I don't fully understand yet. That is, it's something outside of the body, with a rejection of the body, and I don't quite understand that. A life after death even. Which I still haven't comprehended. There's a letter in the Fitzwilliam Museum, written several months before he died. He says, "My body is in turmoil and stress and decaying, *but* my ideas, my power of ideas and my imagination, are stronger than ever." And I find it hard to conceive of that. I think if I were lying in bed dying, with my body pained, I would just give up. I mean, you know, because I don't think I could *exist* outside my body. But he apparently was able to. Williams didn't seem to be able to. In other words Williams's universe was tied up with his body. Blake's universe didn't seem to be tied up with his body. Real mysterious, like far other worlds and other seas, so to speak. Been puzzling over that today.

The Jerusalemic world of Blake seems to be Mercy-Pity-Peace. Which has human form. Mercy has a human face. So that's all clear.

INTERVIEWER: How about Blake's statement about the senses being the chief inlets of the soul in this age—I don't know what "this age" means; is there another one?

GINSBERG: What he says is interesting because there's the same thing in Hindu mythology, they speak of This Age as the Kali Yuga, the age of destruction, or an age so sunk in materialism. You'd find a similar formulation in Vico, like what is it, the Age of Gold running on to the Iron and then Stone, again. Well, the Hindus say that *this* is the Kali Age or Kali Yuga or Kali Cycle, and we are also so sunk in matter, the five senses are matter, sense, that they say there is absolutely no way out by intellect, by thought, by discipline, by practice, by sadhana, by jnanayoga, nor karma yoga—that is, doing good works—no way out through our own will or our own effort. The *only* way out that they generally now prescribe, generally in India at the moment, is through bhakti yoga, which is Faith-Hope-Adoration-Worship, or like probably the equivalent of the Christian Sacred Heart, which I find a very lovely doctrine—that is to say, pure delight, the only way you can be saved is to sing. In other words, the only way to drag up, from the depths of this depression, to drag up your soul to its proper bliss, and understanding, is to give yourself, completely, to your heart's desire. The image will be determined by the heart's compass, by the compass of what the heart moves toward and desires. And then you get on your knees or on your lap or on your head and you sing and chant prayers and mantras, till you reach a state of ecstasy and understanding, and the bliss overflows out of your body. They say intellect, like Saint Thomas Aquinas, will never do it, because it's just like me getting all hung up on whether I could remember what happened before I was born—I mean you could get lost there very easily, and it has no relevance *anyway*, to the existent flower. Blake says something similar, like Energy, and Excess . . . leads to the palace of wisdom. The Hindu bhakti is like excess of devotion; you just, you know, give yourself all out to devotion.

Very oddly a lady saint Shri Matakrishnaji in Brindaban, whom I consulted about my spiritual problems, told me to take Blake for my guru. There's all kinds of different gurus, there can be living and nonliving gurus—apparently whoever initiates you, and I apparently was initiated by Blake in terms of at least having an ecstatic experience from him. So that when I got here to Cambridge I had to rush over to the Fitzwilliam Museum to find his misspellings in *Songs of Innocence*.

INTERVIEWER: What was the Blake experience you speak of?

GINSBERG: About 1945 I got interested in Supreme Reality with a capital S and R, and I wrote big long poems about a last voyage looking for Supreme Reality. Which was like a Dostoevskian or Thomas Wolfeian idealization or like Rimbaud—what was Rimbaud's term, new vision, was that it? Or Kerouac was talking about a new vision, verbally, and intuitively out of longing, but also out of a funny kind of tolerance of this universe. In 1948 in East Harlem in the summer I was living—this is like the Ancient Mariner, I've said this so many times: "stoppeth one of three./ 'By thy long grey beard . . .'" Hang an albatross around your neck. . . . The one thing I felt at the time was that it would be a terrible horror, that in one or two decades I would be trying to explain to people that one day something like this happened to me! I even wrote a long poem saying, "I will grow old, a grey and groaning man,/ and with each hour the same thought, and with each thought the same denial./ Will I spend my life in praise of the *idea* of God?/ Time leaves no hope. We creep and wait. We wait and go alone." Psalm II—which I never published. So anyway—there I was in my bed in Harlem . . . jacking off. With my pants open, lying around on a bed by the window sill, looking out into the cornices of Harlem and the sky above. And I had just come. And had perhaps hardly even wiped the come off my thighs, my trousers, or whatever it was. As I often do, I had been jacking off while reading—I think it's probably a common phenomenon to be noticed among adolescents. Though I was a little older than an adolescent at the time. About twenty-two. There's a kind of interesting thing about, you know, distracting your attention while you jack off—that is, you know, reading a book or looking out of a window, or doing something else with the conscious mind which kind of makes it sexier.

So anyway, what I had been doing that week—I'd been in a very lonely solitary state, dark night of the soul sort of, reading Saint John of the Cross, maybe on account of that everybody'd gone away that I knew, Burroughs was in Mexico, Jack was out in Long Island and relatively isolated, we didn't see each other, and I had been very close with them for several years. Huncke I think was in jail, or something. Anyway, there was nobody I knew. Mainly the thing was that I'd been making it with N.C., and finally I think I got a letter from him saying it was all off, no more, we shouldn't consider ourselves lovers any more on account of it just wouldn't work out. But previously we'd had an understanding that we— Neal Cassady, I said "N.C." but I suppose you can use his name— we'd had a big tender lovers' understanding. But I guess it got too much for him, partly because he was three thousand miles away and he had six thousand girl friends on the other side of the continent, who were keeping him busy, and then here was my lone cry of despair from New York. So. I got a letter from him saying, Now, Allen, we gotta move on to *new* territory. So I felt this is like a great mortal blow to all of my tenderest hopes. And I figured I'd never find any sort of psychospiritual sexo-cock jewel fulfillment in my existence! So, I went into . . . like I felt cut off from what I'd idealized romantically. And I was also graduating from school and had nowhere to go and the difficulty of getting a job. So finally there was nothing for me to do except to eat vegetables and live in Harlem. In an apartment I'd rented from someone. Sublet.

So, in that state therefore, of hopelessness, or dead end, change of phase, you know—growing up—and in an equilibrium in any case, a psychic, a mental equilibrium of a kind, like of having no New Vision and no Supreme Reality and nothing but the world in front of me, and of not knowing what to do with *that* . . . there was a funny balance of tension, in every direction. And just after I came, on this occasion, with a Blake book on my lap—I wasn't even reading, my eye was idling over the page of "Ah, Sun-flower," and it suddenly appeared—the poem I'd read a lot of times before, overfamiliar to the point where it didn't make any particular meaning except some sweet thing about flowers—and suddenly I realized that the poem was talking about *me*. "Ah, Sun-flower! weary of time, / Who countest the steps of the sun; / Seeking after that sweet golden clime, / Where the traveller's journey is done." Now, I began understanding it, the poem while looking at it, and suddenly, simultaneously with understanding it, heard a very deep earthen grave voice in the room, which I immediately assumed, I didn't think twice, was Blake's voice; it wasn't any voice that I knew, though I had previously had a conception of a voice of rock, in a poem, some image like that—or maybe that came after this experience.

And my eye on the page, simultaneously the auditory hallucination, or whatever terminology here used, the apparitional voice, in the room, woke me further deep in my understanding of the poem, because the voice was so completely tender and beautifully . . . ancient. Like the voice of the Ancient of Days. But the peculiar quality of the voice was something unforgettable because it was like God had a human voice, with all the infinite tenderness and anciency and mortal gravity of a living Creator speaking to his son. "Where the Youth pined away with desire, / And the pale Virgin shrouded in snow,/ Arise from their graves, and aspire / Where my Sun-flower wishes to go." Meaning that there *was* a *place*, there was a sweet golden clime, and the *sweet golden*, what was that . . . and simultaneous to the voice there was also an emotion, risen in my soul in response to the voice, and a sudden *visual* realization of the same awesome phenomena. That is to say, looking out at the window, through the window at the sky, suddenly it seemed that I saw into the depths of the universe, by looking simply into the ancient sky. The sky suddenly seemed very *ancient*. And this was the very ancient place that he was talking about, the sweet golden clime, I suddenly realized that *this* existence was *it!* And, that I was born in order to experience up to this very moment that I was having this experience, to realize what this was all about—in other words that this was the moment that I was born for. This initiation. Or this vision or this consciousness, of being alive unto myself, alive myself unto the Creator. As the son of the Creator—who loved me, I realized, or who responded to my desire, say. It was the same desire both ways.

Anyway, my first thought was this was what I was born for, and second thought, never forget—never forget, never renege, never deny. Never deny the voice—no, never *forget* it, don't get lost mentally wandering in other spirit worlds or American or job worlds or advertising worlds or war worlds or earth worlds. But the spirit of the universe was what I was born to realize. What I was speaking about visually was, immediately, that the cornices in the old tenement building in Harlem across the back-yard court had been carved very finely in 1890 or 1910. And were like the solidification of a great deal of intelligence and care and love also. So that I began noticing in every corner where I looked evidences of a living hand, even in the bricks, in the arrangement of each brick. Some hand placed them there—that some hand had placed the whole universe in front of me. That some hand had placed the sky. No, that's exaggerating—not that some hand had placed the sky but that the sky was the living blue hand itself. Or that God was in front of my eyes—existence itself was God. Well, the formulations are like that—I didn't formulate it in exactly those terms; what I was seeing was a visionary thing, it was a lightness in my body . . . my body suddenly felt *light*, and a sense of cosmic consciousness, vibrations, understanding, awe, and wonder and surprise. And it was a sudden awakening into a totally deeper real universe than I'd been existing in. So, I'm trying to avoid generalizations about that sudden deeper real universe and keep it strictly to observations of phenomenal data, or a voice with a certain sound, the appearance of cornices, the appearance of the sky, say, of the great blue hand, the living hand—to keep to images.

But anyway—the same . . . *petite sensation* recurred several minutes later, with the same voice, while reading the poem "The Sick Rose." This time it was a slightly different sense-depth-mystic impression. Because "The Sick Rose"—you know I can't interpret the poem now, but it had a meaning—I mean I can interpret it on a verbal level, the sick rose is my self, or self, or the living body, sick because the mind, which is the worm "That flies in the night, In the howling storm," or Urizen, reason; Blake's character might be the one that's entered the body and is destroying it, or let us say death, the worm as being death, the natural process of death, some kind of mystical being of its own trying to come in and devour the body, the rose. Blake's drawing for it is complicated, it's a big drooping rose, drooping because it's dying, and there's a worm in it, and the worm is wrapped around a little sprite that's trying to get out of the mouth of the rose.

But anyway, I experienced "The Sick Rose," with the voice of Blake reading it, as something that applied to the whole universe, like hearing the doom of the whole universe, and at the same time the inevitable beauty of doom. I can't remember now, except it was very beautiful and very awesome. But a little of it slightly scary, having to do with the knowledge of death—my death and also the death of being itself, and that was the great pain. So, like a prophecy, not only in human terms but a prophecy as if Blake had penetrated the very secret core of the *entire* universe and had come forth with some little magic formula statement in rhyme and rhythm that, if properly heard in the inner inner ear, would deliver you beyond the universe.

So then, the other poem that brought this on in the same day was "The Little Girl Lost," where there was a repeated refrain,

> 'Do *father*, *mother*, weep?
> *Where can Lyca* sleep?
>
> '*How can Lyca* sleep
> *If her mother* weep?
>
> '*If her heart does* ache
> *Then let Lyca* wake;
> *If my mother* sleep,
> *Lyca shall not* weep.'

It's that hypnotic thing—and I suddenly realized that Lyca was me, or Lyca was the self; father, mother seeking Lyca, was God seeking, Father, the Creator; and " 'If her heart does ache / Then let Lyca wake' "—wake to what? *Wake* meaning wake to the same awakeness I was just talking about—of existence in the entire universe. The total consciousness then, of the complete universe.

Which is what Blake was talking about. In other words a break-through from ordinary habitual quotidian consciousness into consciousness that was really seeing all of heaven in a flower. Or what was it—eternity in a flower . . . heaven in a grain of sand? As I was seeing heaven in the cornice of the building. By heaven here I mean this imprint or concretization or living form, of an intelligent hand—the work of an intelligent hand, which still had the intelligence molded into it. The gargoyles on the Harlem cornices. What was interesting about the cornice was that there's cornices like that on every building, but I never noticed them before. And I never realized that they meant spiritual labor, to anyone—that somebody had labored to make a curve in a piece of tin—to make a cornucopia out of a piece of industrial tin. Not only that man, the workman, the artisan, but the architect had thought of it, the builder had paid for it, the smelter had *smelt* it, the miner had dug it up out of the earth, the earth had gone through aeons preparing it. So the little molecules had slumbered for . . . for Kalpas. So out of *all* of these Kalpas it all got together in a great succession of impulses, to be frozen finally in that one form of a cornucopia cornice on the building front. And God knows how many people made the moon. Or what spirits labored . . . to set fire to the sun. As Blake says, "When I look in the sun I don't see the rising sun, I see a band of angels singing holy, holy, holy." Well, his perception of the field of the sun is different from that of a man who just sees the sun sun, without any emotional relationship to it.

But then, there was a point later in the week when the intermittent flashes of the same . . . bliss—because the experience was quite blissful—came back. In a sense all this is described in "The Lion for Real" by anecdotes of different experiences—actually it was a very difficult time, which I won't go into here. Because suddenly I thought, also simultaneously, Ooh, I'm going *mad*! That's described in the line in "Howl," "who thought they were *only* mad when Baltimore gleamed in supernatural ecstasy"—"who thought they were *only* mad. . . ." If it were only that easy! In other words it'd be a lot easier if you just were crazy, instead of—

then you could chalk it up, "Well, I'm nutty"—but on the other hand what if it's all true and you're *born* into this great cosmic universe in which you're a spirit angel—terrible fucking situation to be confronted with. It's like being woken up one morning by Joseph K's captors. Actually what I think I did was there was a couple of girls living next door and I crawled out on the fire escape and tapped on their window and said, "I've seen God!" and they *banged* the window shut. Oh, what tales I could have told them if they'd let me in! Because I was in a very exalted state of mind and the consciousness was still with me—I remember I immediately rushed to Plato and read some great image in the *Phaedrus* about horses flying through the sky, and rushed over to Saint John and started reading fragments of *con un no saber sabiendo . . . que me quede balbuciendo*, and rushed to the other part of the book-shelf and picked up Plotinus about The Alone—the Plotinus I found more difficult to interpret.

But I *immediately* doubled my thinking process, quadrupled, and I was able to read almost any text and see all sorts of divine significance in it. And I think that week or that month I had to take an examination in John Stuart Mill. And instead of writing about his ideas I got completely hung up on his experience of read-ing—was it Wordsworth? Apparently the thing that got him back was an experience of nature that he received keyed off by reading Wordsworth, on "sense sublime" or something. That's a very good description, that sense sublime of something far more deeply inter-fused, whose dwelling is the light of setting suns, and the round ocean, and the . . . the *living* air, did he say? The living air—see just that hand again—*and* in the heart of man. So I think this ex-perience is characteristic of all high poetry. I mean that's the way I began seeing poetry as the communication of the particular ex-perience—not just any experience but *this* experience.

INTERVIEWER: Have you had anything like this experience again?

GINSBERG: Yeah. I'm not finished with this period. Then, in my room, I didn't know what to do. But I wanted to bring it up, so I began experimenting with it, without Blake. And I think it was one day in my kitchen—I had an old-fashioned kitchen with a sink with a tub in it with a board over the top—I started moving around and sort of shaking with my body and dancing up and down on the floor and saying, "Dance! dance! dance! dance! spirit! spirit! spirit! dance!" and suddenly I felt like Faust, calling up the devil. And then it started coming over me, this big . . . creepy feeling, cryptozoid or monozoidal, so I got all scared and quit.

Then, I was walking around Columbia and I went in the Columbia bookstore and was reading Blake again, leafing over a book of Blake, I think it was "The Human Abstract": "Pity would be no more. . . ." And suddenly it came over me in the bookstore again, and I was in the eternal place *once more*, and I looked around at everybody's faces, and I saw all these wild animals! Because there was a bookstore clerk there who I hadn't paid much attention to, he was just a familiar fixture in the bookstore scene and everybody went in the bookstore every day like me, because downstairs there was a café and upstairs there were all these clerks that we were all familiar with—this guy had a very *long* face, you know some people look like giraffes. So he looked kind of giraffish. He had a kind of a long face with a long nose. I don't know what kind of sex life he had, but he must have had something. But anyway, I looked in his face and I suddenly saw like a great tormented soul—and he had just been somebody whom I'd regarded as perhaps a not particularly beautiful or sexy character, or lovely face, but you know someone familiar, and perhaps a pleading cousin in the universe. But all of a sudden I realized that *he* knew also, just like I knew. And that everybody in the bookstore knew, and that they were all hiding it! They all had the consciousness, it was like a great *un*conscious that was running between all of us that everybody *was* completely conscious, but that the fixed expressions that people have, the habitual expressions, the manners, the mode of talk, are all masks hiding this consciousness. Because almost at that moment it seemed that it would be too terrible if we communicated to each other on a level of total consciousness and awareness each of the other—like it would be too terrible, it would be the end of the bookstore, it would be the end of civ— . . . not civilization, but in other words the position that everybody was in was *ridiculous*, everybody running around peddling books to each other. Here in the universe! Passing money over the counter, wrapping books in bags and guarding the door, you know, stealing books, and the people sitting up making accountings on the upper floor there, and people worrying about their exams walking through the bookstore, and all the millions of thoughts the people had—you know, that I'm worrying about—whether they're going to get laid or whether anybody loves them, about their mothers dying of cancer or, you know, the complete death awareness that everybody has continuously with them all the time—all of a sudden revealed to me at once in the faces of the people, and they all looked like horrible grotesque masks, grotesque because *hiding* the knowledge from each other. Having a habitual conduct and forms to prescribe, forms to fulfill. Roles to play. But the main insight I had at that time was that everybody knew. Everybody knew completely everything. Knew completely everything in the terms which I was talking about.

INTERVIEWER: Do you still think they know?

GINSBERG: I'm more sure of it now. Sure. All you have to do is try and make somebody. You realize that they knew all along you were trying to make them. But until that moment you never break through to communication on the subject.

INTERVIEWER: Why not?

GINSBERG: Well, fear of rejection. The twisted faces of all those people, the faces were twisted by rejection. And hatred of self, finally. The internalization of that rejection. And finally disbelief in that shining self. Disbelief in that infinite self. Partly because the particular . . . partly because the *awareness* that we all carry is too often painful, because the experience of rejection and lack-love and cold war—I mean the whole cold war is the imposition of a vast mental barrier on everybody, a vast antinatural psyche. A hardening, a shutting off of the perception of desire and tenderness which everybody *knows* and which is the very structure of . . . the atom! Structure of the human body and organism. That desire built in. Blocked. "Where the Youth pined away with desire, / And the pale Virgin shrouded in snow." Or as Blake says, "On every face I see, I meet / Marks of weakness, marks of woe." So what I was thinking in the bookstore was the marks of weakness, marks of woe. Which you can just look around and look at anybody's face right next to you now always—you can see it in the way the mouth is pursed, you can see it in the way the eyes blink, you can see it in the way the gaze is fixed down at the matches. It's the self-consciousness which is a substitute for communication with the outside. This consciousness pushed back into the self and thinking of how it will hold its face and eyes and hands in order to make a mask to hide the flow that is going on. Which it's aware of, which everybody is aware of really! So let's say, shyness. Fear. Fear of like total feeling, really, total being is what it is.

So the problem then was, having attained realization, how to safely manifest it and communicate it. Of course there was the old Zen thing, when the sixth patriarch handed down the little symbolic oddments and ornaments and books and bowls, stained bowls too . . . when the *fifth* patriarch handed them down to the sixth patriarch he told him to hide them and don't tell anybody you're patriarch because it's dangerous, they'll kill you. So there was that immediate danger. It's taken me all these years to manifest it and work it out in a way that's materially communicable to people. Without scaring them or me. Also movements of history and breaking down the civilization. To break down everybody's masks and roles sufficiently so that everybody has to face the universe *and* the possibility of the sick rose coming true and the atom bomb. So it was an immediate messianic thing. Which seems to be becoming more and more justified. And more and more reasonable in terms of the existence that we're living.

So. Next time it happened was about a week later walking along in the evening on a circular path around what's now I guess the garden or field in the middle of Columbia University, by the library. I started invoking the spirit, consciously trying to get another depth perception of cosmos. And suddenly it began occurring

again, like a sort of break-through again, but this time—this was
the last time in that period—it was the same depth of consciousness or the same cosmical awareness but suddenly it was not blissful at all but it was *frightening*. Some like real serpent-fear enter-
ing the sky. The sky was not a blue hand anymore but like a hand
of death coming down on me—some really scary presence, it was
almost as if I saw God again except God was the devil. The consciousness itself was *so* vast, much more vast than any idea of it I'd
had or any experience I'd had, that it was not even human any
more—and was in a sense a threat, because I was going to die into
that inhuman ultimately. I don't know *what* the score was there—
I was too cowardly to pursue it. To attend and experience completely the Gates of Wrath—there's a poem of Blake's that deals
with that, "To find a Western Path / Right through the Gates of
Wrath." But I didn't urge my way there, I shut it all off. And got
scared, and thought, I've gone too far.

INTERVIEWER: Was your use of drugs an extension of this experience?

GINSBERG: Well, since I took a vow that this was the area of,
that this was my existence that I was placed into, drugs were obviously a technique for experimenting with consciousness, to get
different areas and different levels and different similarities and
different reverberations of the same vision. Marijuana has some of
it in it, that awe, the cosmic awe that you get sometimes on pot.
There are certain moments under laughing gas and ether that the
consciousness does intersect with something similar—for me—to
my Blake visions. The gas drugs were apparently interesting too to
the Lake Poets, because there were a lot of experiments done with
Sir Humphry Davy in his Pneumatic Institute. I think Coleridge
and Southey and other people used to go, and De Quincy. But
serious people. I think there hasn't been very much written about
that period. *What went on* in the Humphry Davy household on
Saturday midnight when Coleridge arrived by foot, through the
forest, by the lakes? Then, there are certain states you get into with
opium, and heroin, of almost disembodied awareness, looking down

back at the earth from a place after you're dead. Well, it's not the same, but it's an interesting state, and a useful one. It's a normal state also, I mean it's a holy state of some sort. At times. Then, mainly, of course, with the hallucinogens, you get some states of consciousness which subjectively seem to be cosmic-ecstatic, or cosmic-demonic. Our version of expanded consciousness is as much as *un*conscious information—awareness comes up to the surface. Lysergic acid, peyote, mescaline, sylocidin, Ayahuasca. But I can't stand them any more, because something happened to me with them very similar to the Blake visions. After about thirty times, thirty-five times, I began getting monster vibrations again. So I couldn't go any further. I may later on again, if I feel more reassurance.*

However, I did get a lot out of them, mainly like emotional understanding, understanding the female principle in a way— women, more sense of the softness and more desire for women. Desire for children also.

INTERVIEWER: Anything interesting about the actual experience, say with hallucinogens?

---

* Between occasion of interview with Thomas Clark June '65 and publication May '66 more reassurance came. I tried small doses of LSD twice in secluded tree and ocean cliff haven at Big Sur. No monster vibration, no snake universe hallucinations. Many tiny jeweled violet flowers along the path of a living brook that looked like Blake's illustration for a canal in grassy Eden: huge Pacific watery shore, Orlovsky dancing naked like Shiva long-haired before giant green waves, titanic cliffs that Wordsworth mentioned in his own Sublime, great yellow sun veiled with mist hanging over the plant's oceanic horizon. No harm. President Johnson that day went into the Valley of Shadow operating room because of his gall bladder & Berkeley's Vietnam Day Committee was preparing anxious manifestoes for our march toward Oakland police and Hell's Angels. Realizing that more vile words from me would send out physical vibrations into the atmosphere that might curse poor Johnson's flesh and further unbalance his soul, I knelt on the sand surrounded by masses of green bulb-headed Kelp vegetable-snake undersea beings washed up by last night's tempest, and prayed for the President's tranquil health. Since there has been so much legislative miscomprehension of the LSD boon I regret that my unedited ambivalence in Thomas Clark's tape transcript interview was published wanting this footnote.

Your obedient servant
Allen Ginsberg, *aetat* 40
June 2, 1966

GINSBERG: What I do get is, say if I was in an apartment high on mescaline, I felt as if the apartment and myself were not merely on East Fifth Street but were in the middle of all space time. If I close my eyes on hallucinogens, I get a vision of great scaly dragons in outer space, they're winding slowly and eating their own tails. Sometimes my skin and all the room seem sparkling with scales, and it's all made out of serpent stuff. And as if the whole illusion of life were made of reptile dream.

Mandala also. I use the mandala in an LSD poem. The associations I've had during times that I was high are usually referred to or built in some image or other to one of the other poems written on drugs. Or after drugs—like in "Magic Psalm" on lysergic acid. Or mescaline. There's a long passage about a mandala in the LSD poem. There is a good situation since I was high and I was looking at a mandala—before I got high I asked the doctor that was giving it to me at Stanford to prepare me a set of mandalas to look at, to borrow some from Professor Spiegelberg who was an expert. So we had some Sikkimese elephant mandalas there. I simply describe those in the poem—what they look like while I was high.

So—summing up then—drugs were useful for exploring perception, sense perception, and exploring different possibilities and modes of consciousness, and exploring the different versions of *petites sensations*, and useful then for composing, sometimes, while under the influence. Part II of "Howl" was written under the influence of peyote, composed during peyote vision. In San Francisco—"Moloch." "Kaddish" was written wth amphetamine injections. An injection of amphetamine plus a little bit of morphine, plus some Dexedrine later on to keep me going, because it was all in one long sitting. From a Saturday morn to a Sunday night. The amphetamine gives a peculiar metaphysical tinge to things, also. Space-outs. It doesn't interfere too much there because I wasn't habituated to it, I was just taking it that one weekend. It didn't interfere too much with the emotional charge that comes through.

INTERVIEWER: Was there any relation to this in your trip to Asia?

GINSBERG: Well, the Asian experience kind of got me out of the corner. I painted myself in with drugs. That corner being an inhuman corner in the sense that I figured I was expanding my consciousness and I had to go through with it but at the same time I was confronting this serpent monster, so I was getting in a real terrible situation. It finally would get so if I'd take the drugs I'd start vomiting. But I felt that I was duly bound and obliged for the sake of consciousness expansion, and this insight, and breaking down my identity, and seeking more direct contact with primate sensation, nature, to continue. So when I went to India, all the way through India, I was babbling about that to all the holy men I could find. I wanted to find out if they had any suggestions. And they all did, and they were all good ones. First one I saw was Martin Buber, who was interested. In Jerusalem, Peter and I went in to see him—we called him up and made a date and had a long conversation. He had a beautiful white beard and was friendly; his nature was slightly austere but benevolent. Peter asked him what kind of visions he'd had and he described some he'd had in bed when he was younger. But he said he was *not* any longer interested in visions like that. The kind of visions he came up with were more like spiritualistic table rappings. Ghosts coming into the room through his window, rather than big beautiful seraphic Blake angels hitting him on the head. I was thinking like loss of identity and confrontation with nonhuman universe as the main problem, and in a sense whether or not man had to evolve and change, and perhaps become nonhuman too. Melt into the universe, let us say —to put it awkwardly and inaccurately. Buber said that he was interested in man-to-man relationships, human-to-human—that he thought it was a human universe that we were destined to inhabit. And so therefore human relationships rather than relations between the human and the nonhuman. Which was what I was thinking that I had to go into. And he said, "Mark my word, young man, in two years you will realize that I was right." He was right—in two years I marked his words. Two years is sixty-three— I saw him in sixty-one. I don't know if he said two years—but he said "in years to come." This was like a real terrific classical wise man's "Mark my words, young man, in several years you will realize that what I said was true!" Exclamation point.

Then there was Swami Shivananda, in Rishikish in India. He said, "Your own heart is your guru." Which I thought was very sweet, and very reassuring. That is the sweetness of it I felt—in my heart. And suddenly realized it was the heart that I was seeking. In other words it wasn't consciousness, it wasn't *petites sensations*, sensation defined as expansion of mental consciousness to include more data—as I was pursuing that line of thought, pursuing Burroughs's cutup thing—the area that I was seeking was heart rather than mind. In other words, in mind, through mind or imagination —this is where I get confused with Blake now—in mind one can construct all sorts of universes, one can construct model universes in dream and imagination, and with lysergic acid you can enter into alternative universes and with the speed of light; and with nitrous oxide you can experience several million universes in rapid succession. You can experience a whole gamut of possibilities of universes, including the final possibility that there is none. And then you go unconscious—which is exactly what happens with gas when you go unconscious. You see that the universe is going to disappear with your consciousness, that it was all dependent on your consciousness.

Anyway, a whole series of India holy men pointed back to the body—getting *in* the body rather than getting out of the human form. But living in and inhabiting the human form. Which then goes back to Blake again, the human form divine. Is this clear? In other words, the psychic problem that I had found myself in was that for various reasons it had seemed to me at one time or another that the best thing to do was to drop dead. Or not be afraid of death but go into death. Go into the nonhuman, go into the cosmic, so to speak; that God was death, and if I wanted to attain God I had to die. Which *may* still be true. So I thought that what I was put up to was to therefore break out of my body, if I wanted to attain complete consciousness.

So now the next step was that the gurus one after another said, Live in the body: this is the form that you're born for. That's too

long a narration to go into. Too many holy men and too many different conversations and they all have a little *key* thing going. But
it all winds up in the train in Japan, then a year later, the poem
"The Change," where all of a sudden I renounce drugs, I don't
renounce drugs but I suddenly didn't want to be *dominated* by
that nonhuman any more, or even be dominated by the moral
obligation to enlarge my consciousness any more. Or do anything
any more except *be* my heart—which just desired to be and be
alive now. I had a very strange ecstatic experience then and there,
once I had sort of gotten that burden off my back, because I was
suddenly free to love myself again, and therefore love the people
around me, in the form that they already were. And love myself in
my own form as I am. And look around at the other people and so
it was *again* the same thing like in the bookstore. Except this time
I was completely in my body and had no more mysterious obligations. And nothing more to fulfill, except to be willing to die when
I am dying, whenever that be. And be willing to live as a human
in this form now. So I started weeping, it was such a happy moment. Fortunately I was able to write then, too, "So that I do live
I will die"—rather than be cosmic consciousness, immortality, Ancient of Days, perpetual consciousness existing forever.

Then when I got to Vancouver, Olson was saying "I am one
with my skin." It *seemed* to me at the time when I got back to
Vancouver that everybody had been precipitated back into their
bodies at the same time. It seemed that's what Creeley had *been*
talking about all along. The *place*—the terminology he used, the
place we are. Meaning this place, here. And trying to like be real
in the real place . . . to be aware of the place where he is. Because I'd always thought that that meant that he was cutting off
from divine imagination. But what that meant for him was that
this place would be everything that one would refer to as divine,
if one were really here. So that Vancouver seems a very odd moment, at least for me—because I came back in a sense completely
bankrupt. My energies of the last . . . oh, 1948 to 1963, all completely washed up. On the train in Kyoto having renounced Blake,
renounced visions—renounced *Blake*!—too. There was a cycle that

began with the Blake vision which ended on the train in Kyoto when I realized that to attain the depth of consciousness that I was seeking when I was talking about the Blake vision, that in order to attain it I had to cut myself off from the Blake vision and renounce it. Otherwise I'd be hung up on a memory of an experience. Which is not the actual awareness of now, now. In order to get back to now, in order to get back to the total awareness of now and contact, sense perception contact with what was going on around me, or direct vision of the moment, now I'd have to give up this continual churning thought process of yearning back to a visionary state. It's all very complicated. And idiotic.

INTERVIEWER: I think you said earlier that "Howl" being a lyric poem, and "Kaddish" basically a narrative, that you now have a sense of wanting to do an epic. Do you have a plan like this?

GINSBERG: Yeah, but it's just . . . ideas, that I've been carrying around for a long time. One thing which I'd like to do sooner or later is write a long poem which is a narrative and description of all the visions I've ever had, sort of like the *Vita Nuova*. And travels, now. And another idea I had was to write a big long poem about everybody I ever fucked or slept with. Like sex . . . a love poem. A long love poem, involving all the innumerable lays of a lifetime. The epic is not that, though. The epic would be a poem including history, as it's defined. So that would be one about present-day politics, using the methods of the Blake *French Revolution*. I got a lot written. Narrative was "Kaddish." Epic—there has to be totally different organization, it might be simple free association on political themes—in fact I think an epic poem including history, at this stage. I've got a lot of it written, but it would have to be Burroughs' sort of epic—in other words, it would have to be *dis*-sociated thought stream which includes politics and history. I don't think you could do it in narrative form, I mean what would you be narrating, the history of the Korean War or something?

INTERVIEWER: Something like Pound's epic?

GINSBERG: No, because Pound seems to me to be over a course of years fabricating out of his reading and out of the museum of literature; whereas the thing would be to take all of contemporary history, newspaper headlines and all the pop art of Stalinism and Hitler and Johnson and Kennedy and Viet Nam and Congo and Lumumba and the South and Sacco and Vanzetti—whatever floated into one's personal field of consciousness and contact. And then to compose like a basket—like weave a basket, basketweaving out of those materials. Since obviously nobody has any idea where it's all going or how it's going to end unless you have some vision to deal with. It would have to be done by a process of association, I guess.

INTERVIEWER: What's happening in poetry now?

GINSBERG: I don't know yet. Despite all confusion to the contrary, now that time's passed, I think the best poet in the United States is Kerouac still. Given twenty years to settle through. The main reason is that he's the most free and the most spontaneous. Has the greatest range of association and imagery in his poetry. Also in "Mexico City Blues" the sublime as subject matter. And, in other words the greatest facility at what might be called projective verse, if you want to give it a name. I think that he's stupidly underrated by almost everybody except for a few people who are aware how beautiful his composition is—like Snyder or Creeley or people who have a taste for his tongue, for his line. But it takes one to know one.

INTERVIEWER: You don't mean Kerouac's prose?

GINSBERG: No, I'm talking about just a pure poet. The verse poetry, the "Mexico City Blues" and a lot of other manuscripts I've seen. In addition he has the one sign of being a great poet, which is he's the only one in the United States who knows how to write haikus. The only one who's written any good haikus. And everybody's been writing haikus. There are all these *dreary* haikus written by people who think for weeks trying to write a haiku, and finally come up with some dull little thing or something. Whereas Kerouac thinks in haikus, every time he writes anything—talks that way and thinks that way. So it's just natural for him. It's something Snyder noticed. Snyder has to labor for years in a Zen monastery to produce one haiku about shitting off a log! And actually does get one or two good ones. Snyder was always astounded by

Kerouac's facility . . . at noticing winter flies dying of old age in his medicine chest. Medicine cabinet. "In my medicine cabinet / the winter flies / died of old age." He's never published them actually—he's published them on a record, with Zoot Sims and Al Cohn, it's a very beautiful collection of them. Those are, as far as I can see, the only real American haikus.

So the haiku is the most difficult test. He's the only *master* of the haiku. Aside from a longer style. Of course, the distinctions between prose and poetry are broken down anyway. So much that I was saying like a long page of oceanic Kerouac is sometimes as sublime as epic line. It's there that also I think he went further into the existential thing of writing conceived of as an irreversible action or statement, that's unrevisable and unchangeable once it's made. I remember I was thinking, yesterday in fact, there was a time that I was absolutely astounded because Kerouac told me that in the future literature would consist of what people actually wrote rather than what they tried to deceive other people into thinking they wrote, when they revised it later on. And I saw opening up this whole universe where people wouldn't be able to lie any more! They wouldn't be able to *correct* themselves any longer. They wouldn't be able to hide what they said. And he was willing to go all the way into that, the first pilgrim into that new-found land.

INTERVIEWER: What about other poets?

GINSBERG: I think Corso has a great inventive genius. And also amongst the greatest *shrewdness*—like Keats or something. I like Lamantia's nervous wildness. Almost anything he writes I find interesting—for one thing he's always registering the forward march of the soul, in exploration; spiritual exploration is always there. And also chronologically following his work is always exciting. Whalen and Snyder are both very wise and very reliable. Whalen I don't *understand* so well. I did, though, earlier—but I have to sit down and study his work, again. Sometimes he seems sloppy—but then later on it always seems right.

McClure has tremendous energy, and seems like some sort of a . . . seraph is not the word . . . not herald either but a . . . not demon either. Seraph I guess it is. He's always moving—see when

I came around to, say, getting in my skin, there I found McClure sitting around talking about being a mammal! So I suddenly realized he was way ahead of me. And Wieners . . . I always *weep* with him. Luminous, luminous. They're all old poets, everybody knows about those poets. Burroughs is a poet too, really. In the sense that a page of his prose is as *dense* with imagery as anything in St.-John Perse or Rimbaud, now. And it has also great repeated rhythms. Recurrent, recurrent rhythms, even rhyme occasionally! What else . . . Creeley's very stable, solid. I get more and more to like certain poems of his that I didn't understand at first. Like "The Door," which completely baffled me because I didn't understand that he was talking about the same heterosexual problem that I was worried about. Olson, since he said, "I feel one with my skin." First thing of Olson's that I liked was "The Death of Europe" and then some of his later Maximus material is nice. And Dorn has a kind of long, *real* spare, manly, political thing—but his great quality inside also is tenderness—"Oh the graves not yet cut." I also like that whole line of what's happening with Ashbery and O'Hara and Koch, the area that they're going for, too. Ashbery—I was listening to him read "The Skaters," and it sounded as inventive and exquisite, in all its parts, as "The Rape of the Lock."

INTERVIEWER: Do you feel you're in command when you're writing?

GINSBERG: Sometimes I feel in command when I'm writing. When I'm in the heat of some truthful tears, yes. Then, complete command. Other times—most of the time not. Just diddling away, woodcarving, getting a pretty shape; like most of my poetry. There's only a few times when I reach a state of complete command. Probably a piece of "Howl," a piece of "Kaddish," and a piece of "The Change." And one or two moments of other poems.

INTERVIEWER: By "command" do you mean a sense of the whole poem as it's going, rather than parts?

GINSBERG: No—a sense of being self-prophetic master of the universe.

THOMAS CLARK

13. Edward Albee

Edward Albee was born on March 12, 1928, in Washington, D.C. He was adopted by Reed and Frances Albee, members of a family prominent in the vaudeville theater business. After graduating from Choate School in 1946, he attended Trinity College for a year. Albee then went to New York City, where he supported himself with various jobs while he wrote fiction and poetry.

In 1959, when he was thirty-one, Albee's first play, *The Zoo Story*, was produced in Berlin and opened in New York the following year. *The Death of Bessie Smith* and *The American Dream*, presented as a double bill, were named the best plays of the 1960–61 season by the Foreign Press Association. By 1962, the young author's plays, all produced off-Broadway, had gained him an enthusiastic following. With his first full-length play, *Who's Afraid of Virginia Woolf?*, which opened at the Billy Rose Theater in October 1962, he achieved his greatest triumph. This play, which caused some to call him the "new Eugene O'Neill," was a unanimous critical success, winning the Annual ANTA Award and the New York Drama Critics' Circle Award in 1963. It was made into a motion picture in 1966. Albee's other plays include *The Sandbox*, which first appeared in a program of four one-act plays entitled *4 in 1* in 1960, *Tiny Alice* (1964), and *A Delicate Balance* (1966). In addition, he has a written a libretto for William Flanagan's opera *Bartleby* (1961), and two adaptations—Carson McCullers's novella *Ballad of the Sad Café* (1963) and James Purdy's novel *Malcolm* (1965).

                    Tobias:

(Recollection) The cat that I had.

                    Agnes (~~Someone~~):

Hm?

                    Tobias:

The cat that I had....when I was ̄--well, a year or so before I <u>met</u> you. She

was very old: I'd had her since I was ~~alone~~ *very young*; she must have been fifteen, or

more. An alley cat. She didn't like people very much, I think; at least she'd

....<u>absent</u> herself. She wouldn't run, or hide; she wasn't skittish, or, or

hysterical. When people came....she'd....pick up and walk away. She liked

<u>me</u>: or, rather, when I was alone with her I could see she was content: she'd

sit on my lap, or near me, or on the basin when I shaved, or sleep on my

clothes if I left them somewhere. She was....content, I guess; I don't know

if she was happy, but she was content. We'd not had other animals --my family,

and I'd taken her to college with me, and into the city, and she was....well,

as much a fixture as....my good gold watch, my favorite bathrobe. She was

<u>there</u>. We didn't play, you understand: she was getting on, and she'd never

been....frisky --like some-- and half the time I doubt I knew she was around

--consciously. It was her absence I would have noticed. *AND I LIKED HER VERY MUC*

                    Agnes (~~Someone~~):

Yes.

                    the thing
                    Tobias:

And how ~~it~~ happened I don't really know. She....one day she....well, one day

I realized she no longer liked me. No, that's not right: one day I ~~realized~~

                    MUST HAVE
realized she ~~had~~ stopped liking me some time before. I was very busy --very

social, I guess, away weekends, nights out, parties where I lived, lots of

people in....I spent less time alone; I used my place less than I just lived

in it. But one evening I <u>was</u> alone, home, and I was suddenly aware of her

                    just
absence, not⌃that she wasn't in the room with me, but that she hadn't been.

            Manuscript page from A Delicate Balance

Edward Albee

The interview happened on a scalding, soggy-aired Fourth of July in a sunny room in Albee's small, attractive country house in Montauk, Long Island. Keeping in mind his luxuriously appointed house in New York City's Greenwich Village, one finds the country place dramatically modest by comparison. With the exception of a handsome, newly built tennis court (in which the playwright takes a disarmingly childlike pleasure and pride) and an incongruously grand Henry Moore sculpture situated high on a landscaped terrace that commands a startling view of the sea, the simplicity of the place leaves one with the curious impression that the news of the personal wealth his work has brought him has not quite reached the playwright-in-residence at Montauk. Still, it is in his country house that he generally seems most at ease, natural, at home.

Albee was dressed with a mildly ungroomed informality. He was

*as yet unshaven for the day and his neo-Edwardian haircut was
damply askew. He appeared, as the climate of the afternoon de-
manded, somewhat uncomfortable.*

*The interviewer and subject have been both friends and com-
poser-writer collaborators for about eighteen years. But Albee's
barbed, poised, and elegantly guarded public press style took over
after the phrasing of the first question—though perhaps it was
intermittently penetrated during the course of the talk.*

INTERVIEWER: One of your most recent plays was an adaptation
of James Purdy's novel *Malcolm*. It had as close to one hundred
per cent bad notices as a play could get. The resultant commercial catastrophe and quick closing of the play apart, how does this
affect your own feeling about the piece itself?

ALBEE: I see you're starting with the hits. Well, I retain for all
my plays, I suppose, a certain amount of enthusiasm. I don't feel
intimidated by either the unanimously bad press that *Malcolm*
got or the unanimously good press that some of the other plays
have received. I haven't changed my feeling about *Malcolm*. I
liked doing the adaptation of Purdy's book. I had a number of
quarrels with the production, but then I usually end up with quarrels about all of my plays. With the possible exception of the little
play *The Sandbox*, which takes thirteen minutes to perform, I
don't think anything I've done has worked out to perfection.

INTERVIEWER: While it doesn't necessarily change your feeling,
does the unanimously bad critical response open questions in your
mind?

ALBEE: I imagine that if we had a college of criticism in this
country whose opinions more closely approximated the value of
the works of art inspected, it might; but as often as not, I find
relatively little relationship between the work of art and the immediate critical response it gets. Every writer's got to pay some
attention, I suppose, to what his critics say because theirs is a
reflection of what the audience feels about his work. And a playwright, especially a playwright whose work deals very directly with

an audience, perhaps he should pay some attention to the nature of the audience response—not necessarily to learn anything about his craft, but as often as not merely to find out about the temper of the time, what is being tolerated, what is being permitted.

INTERVIEWER: Regarding adaptations in general, can you think of any by American playwrights that you admire at all?

ALBEE: No, I can't think of any that I admire. I've done adaptations for two reasons; first, to examine the entire problem of adaptation—to see what it felt like; and second, because I admired those two books—*The Ballad of the Sad Café* and *Malcolm*—very much and thought they belonged on the stage; I wanted to see them on the stage, and felt more confident, perhaps incorrectly, in my own ability to put them on the stage than in most adapters'.

INTERVIEWER: One of the local reviewers, after *Malcolm* came out, referred to it as Edward Albee's "play of the year," rather as if to suggest that this is a conscious goal you've set for yourself, to have a play ready every year.

ALBEE: Do you remember the Thurber cartoon of the man looking at his police dog and saying, "If you're a police dog, where's your badge?" It's the function of a playwright to write. Some playwrights write a large number of plays, some write a small number. I don'i set out to write a play a year. Sometimes I've written two plays a year. There was a period of a year and half when I only wrote half a play. If it depresses some critics that I seem prolific, well, that's their problem as much as mine. There's always the danger that there are so damn many things that a playwright can examine in this society of ours—things that have less to do with his artistic work than have to do with the critical and aesthetic environment—that perhaps he does have to worry about whether or not he is writing too fast. But then also, perhaps he should worry about getting as many plays on as possible before the inevitable ax falls.

INTERVIEWER: What do you mean by the inevitable ax?

ALBEE: If you examine the history of any playwright of the past twenty-five or thirty years—I'm not talking about the comedy boys,

I'm talking about the more serious writers—it seems inevitable that almost every one has been encouraged until the critics feel that they have built them up beyond the point where they can control them; then it's time to knock them down again. And a rather ugly thing starts happening: the playwright finds himself knocked down for works that quite often are just as good or better than the works he's been praised for previously. And a lot of playwrights become confused by this and they start doing imitations of what they've done before, or they try to do something entirely different, in which case they get accused by the same critics of not doing what they *used* to do so well.

INTERVIEWER: So, it's a matter of not being able to win either way.

ALBEE: Actually, the final evaluation of a play has nothing to do with immediate audience or critical response. The playwright, along with any writer, composer, painter in this society, has got to have a terribly private view of his own value, of his own work. He's got to listen to his own voice primarily. He's got to watch out for fads, for what might be called the critical aesthetics.

INTERVIEWER: Why do you think the reviews were so lacerating against *Malcolm*—a play that might simply have been dismissed as not being very good.

ALBEE: It seemed to me the critics loathed something. Now whether they loathed something above and beyond the play itself, it's rather dangerous for me to say. I think it's for the critics to decide whether or not their loathing of the play is based on something other than the play's merits or demerits. They must search their own souls, or whatever.

INTERVIEWER: When you say that the play was badly produced—

ALBEE: I didn't like the way it was directed particularly. It was the one play of mine—of all of them—that got completely out of my hands. I let the director take over and dictate the way things should be done. I did it as an experiment.

INTERVIEWER: What do you mean as an experiment?

ALBEE: As a playwright, one has to make the experiment finally to see whether there's anything in this notion that a director can contribute creatively, as opposed to interpretively.

INTERVIEWER: Do you believe that a director has any creative vitality of his own?

ALBEE: Well, that's a very "iffy" question, as President Roosevelt used to say. I imagine as an axiom you could say that the better the play the less "creativity" the director need exert.

INTERVIEWER: Have you ever had the experience of finding out that the director's way was a certain enlightenment?

ALBEE: I can't answer that honestly, because something very curious happens. In rehearsals I get so completely wrapped up with the reality that's occurring on stage that by the time the play has opened I'm not usually quite as aware of the distinctions between what I'd intended and the result. There are many ways of getting the same result.

INTERVIEWER: Well, you talk about keeping complete control of your plays. Let's say that you'd envisioned in your own mind a certain scene being done a certain way.

ALBEE: I'm not terribly concerned about which characters are standing on the right-hand side of the stage.

INTERVIEWER: That's not the point I'm trying to make. In the preparation of the early Kazan-Williams successes, Williams was in constant conflict with Kazan, and yet Kazan would come up with the one thing that would finally make the play work.

ALBEE: Do we know that it was better than Williams's original idea?

INTERVIEWER: According to his own alleged view of it, yes.

ALBEE: Some writers' view of things depends upon the success of the final result. I'd rather stand or fall on my own concepts. But there is a fine line to be drawn between pointing up something or distorting it. And one has always got to be terribly careful, since the theater is made up of a whole bunch of prima donnas, not to let the distortions occur. I've seen an awful lot of plays that I'd read before they were put into production and been shocked by what's happened to them. In the attempt to make them straightforward and commercially successful, a lot of things go out the window. I'm just saying that in the theater, which is a sort of jungle, one does have to be a little bit careful. One mustn't be so rigid or egotistical to think that every comma is sacrosanct. But at the same time there is the danger of losing control and finding that somebody else has opened a play and not you.

INTERVIEWER: Why did you decide to become a playwright? You wrote poems without notable success, and then suddenly decided to write a play, *The Zoo Story*.

ALBEE: Well, when I was six years old I decided not that I was *going* to be, but with my usual modesty, that I *was* a writer. So I starting writing poetry when I was six and stopped when I was twenty-six because it was getting a little better, but not terribly much. When I was fifteen I wrote seven hundred pages of an incredibly bad novel—it's a very funny book I still like a lot. Then, when I was nineteen I wrote a couple hundred pages of another novel, which wasn't very good either. I was still determined to be a writer. And since I was a writer, and here I was twenty-nine years old and I wasn't a very good poet and I wasn't a very good novelist, I thought I would try writing a play, which seems to have worked out a little better.

INTERVIEWER: With regard to *Zoo Story*—was its skill and power and subsequent success a surprise and revelation to you?

ALBEE: A lot interests me—but nothing surprises me particularly. Not that I took it for granted that it was going to be skillful and powerful. I'm not making any judgment about the excellence or lack of it in the play. But it did not come as a *surprise* to me that I'd written it. You must remember I've been watching and listening to a great number of people for a long time. Absorbing things, I suppose. My only reaction was, "Aha! So this is the way it's going to be, is it?" That was my reaction.

INTERVIEWER: The biggest news about you at the moment, I expect, would be the success of the film *Virginia Woolf*. The Production Code approval came hard, but apparently you approved of it yourself.

ALBEE: When the play was sold to the movies I was rather apprehensive of what would happen. I assumed they would put Doris Day in it, and maybe Rock Hudson. And I was even a little apprehensive about the actual casting. Especially Elizabeth Taylor. I wasn't apprehensive about the idea of Richard Burton being in the film, but it did seem to be a little odd that Elizabeth Taylor, who is in her early thirties, would be playing a fifty-two-year-old woman.

INTERVIEWER: At one time you were apprehensive about Mike Nichols, the director.

ALBEE: I was curious as to why they chose a man who'd never made a film before and had made his reputation directing farces on Broadway, why they chose *him* as a director to turn a serious play into a movie. I think I learned the answer: being innocent to the medium he doesn't know how to make the usual mistakes. I had a number of other reasons for apprehension. One always knows what is done to a script when it goes to Hollywood. When I saw the film in Hollywood about two or three months before it was released, I was startled and enormously taken with the picture, partially through relief I imagine. But more than that, I discovered that no screenplay had been written, that the play was there almost word for word. A few cuts here and there. A few oversimplifications.

INTERVIEWER: Oversimplifications?

ALBEE: Yes, I'll go into those in a minute. Ernest Lehman, who is credited with the screenplay, did write about twenty-five words. I thought they were absolutely terrible. So really there wasn't a screenplay, and that delighted me. It was a third of the battle, as far as I was concerned. So that was my first delight—that the play was photographed word for word. I'm not saying it was photographed action for action. The camera didn't stay thirty-five feet from the actors and it wasn't done in one set, it moved around a good deal. It behaves and acts very much like a film. In fact, it *is* a film. There are some shots, close-ups, lots of things you can't do on the stage. Then my second delight, after finding that the play was intact, was to appreciate that the director, Mike Nichols, understood not only the play, my intentions (pretty much, again with a couple of oversimplifications), but also seemed to understand the use of the camera and the film medium, all this in his first time around. Third, I was happy that Elizabeth Taylor was quite capable of casting off the beautiful-young-woman image and doing something much more than she usually does in films. And the rest of the cast was more or less fine too, Dennis and Segal. I have a few quarrels with their interpretations, but they're so minor compared to what could have happened. I found that it made an awfully good picture.

INTERVIEWER: The play as a film seems to be generally better understood by film reviewers than it was by drama critics. Is it possible that these oversimplifications you're talking about, that you blame Mike Nichols for, or somebody, are responsible for the fact that the play comes over more clearly?

ALBEE: I suppose if you simplify things, it's going to make it easier to understand. But without placing blame, I'd say there *was* an oversimplification, which I regret to a certain extent. For example, whenever something occurs in the play on both an emotional and intellectual level, I find in the film that only the emotional aspect shows through. The intellectual underpinning isn't as clear. In the film I found that in the love-hate games that George and Martha play, their intellectual enjoyment of each other's prowess doesn't show through anywhere nearly as strongly as it did in the play. Quite often, and I suppose in most of my plays, people are doing things on two or three levels at the same time. From time to time in the movie of *Who's Afraid of Virginia Woolf?* I found that a level or two had vanished. At the end of the film, for example, with the revelation about the nonexistent child and its destruction, the intellectual importance of the fiction isn't made quite as clearly as it could be. In the film it's nowhere near as important as the *emotional* importance to the characters. In my view, the two of them have got to go hand in hand. But this is quibbling, you see. It's a really very good film. There are a few things that I wish hadn't happened—that enormous error in accepting somebody's stupid idea of taking the action away from the house to the roadhouse. That's the one area of the film where somebody decided to broaden it out for film terms. Yet it was the one part of the film, curiously enough, that all the film critics thought was the most stagey.

INTERVIEWER: Incidentally, when did the title *Who's Afraid of Virginia Woolf?* occur to you?

ALBEE: There was a saloon—it's changed its name now—on Tenth Street, between Greenwich Avenue and Waverly Place, that was called something at one time, now called something else, and they had a big mirror on the downstairs bar in this saloon where people used to scrawl graffiti. At one point back in about 1953 . . . 1954 I think it was—long before any of us started doing much of anything—I was in there having a beer one night, and I saw "Who's Afraid of Virginia Woolf?" scrawled in soap, I suppose, on this mirror. When I started to write the play it cropped up in my mind again. And of course, who's afraid of Virginia Woolf means who's afraid of the big *bad* wolf . . . who's afraid of living life without false illusions. And it did strike me as being a rather typical university, intellectual joke.

INTERVIEWER: With the filming of *Who's Afraid of Virginia Woolf?* the oft-repeated evaluation of it as a play about four homosexuals who are, for the sake of convention, disguised as heterosexuals recurs. I cannot recall any public statement or comment being made by you on this interpretation of the play.

ALBEE: Indeed it is true that a number of the movie critics of *Who's Afraid of Virginia Woolf?* have repeated the speculation that the play was written about four homosexuals disguised as heterosexual men and women. This comment first appeared around the time the play was produced. I was fascinated by it. I suppose what disturbed me about it was twofold: first, nobody has ever bothered to ask *me* whether it was true; second, the critics and columnists made no attempt to document the assertion from the text of the play. The facts are simple: *Who's Afraid of Virginia Woolf?*

was written about two heterosexual couples. If I had wanted to write a play about four homosexuals, I would have done so. Parenthetically, it is interesting that when the film critic of *Newsweek* stated that he understood the play to have been written about four homosexuals, I had a letter written to him suggesting he check his information before printing such speculations. He replied, saying, in effect, two things: first, that we all know that a critic is a far better judge of an author's intention than the author; second, that seeing the play as being about four homosexuals was the only way that he could live with the play, meaning that he could not accept it as a valid examination of heterosexual life. Well, I'm sure that all the actresses from Uta Hagen to Elizabeth Taylor who've played the role of Martha would be absolutely astonished to learn they've been playing men.

I think it is the responsibility of critics to rely less strenuously on, to use a Hollywood phrase, "what they can live with," and more on an examination of the works of art from an aesthetic and clinical point of view. I would be fascinated to read an intelligent paper documenting from the text that *Who's Afraid of Virginia Woolf?* is a play written about four homosexuals. It might instruct me about the deep slag pits of my subconscious.

I believe it was Leslie Fiedler, in an article in *Partisan Review*, who commented that if indeed *Who's Afraid of Virginia Woolf?* did deal with four disguised homosexuals, the "shock of recognition" on the part of the public is an enormously interesting commentary on the public. To put it most briefly, *Who's Afraid of Virginia Woolf?* was *not* written about four homosexuals. One might make one more point: had it been a play about four homosexuals disguised as heterosexuals, the only valid standard of criticism which could be employed would be whether such license of composite characterization was destructive to the validity of the work of art. Again we come to the question of the critics' responsibility to discuss the work of art not on arbitrary Freudian terms but on aesthetic ones. Only the most callow or insecure or downright stupid critic would fault Proust's work, for example, for the transposition that he made of characters' sexes. It would be rather like faulting Michelangelo's sculptures of the male figure because of that artist's reputed leanings. So, if a play should appear, next year, say, which the critics in their wisdom see as a disguised homosexual piece, let them remember that the ultimate judgment of a work of art, whether it be a masterpiece or a lesser event, must be solely in terms of its artistic success and not on Freudian guesswork.

INTERVIEWER: It's been said by certain critics that your plays generally contain no theme; others say that you've begun to wear the same theme thin; and still others say that with each play you bravely attack a new theme.

ALBEE: I go up to my room about three or four months out of the year and I write. I don't pay much attention to how the plays relate thematically to each other. I think that's very dangerous to do, because in the theater one is self-conscious enough without planning ahead or wondering about the thematic relation from one play to the next. One hopes that one is developing, and writing interestingly, and that's where it should end, I think.

INTERVIEWER: You've spoken frequently to the effect that your involvement with music has influenced your writing for the theater. Can you elaborate on that in any way?

ALBEE: I find it very difficult. I've been involved in one way or another with serious music ever since childhood. And I do think, or rather I *sense* that there is a relationship—at least in my own work—between a dramatic structure, the form and sound and shape of a play, and the equivalent structure in music. Both deal with sound, of course, and also with idea, theme. I find that when my plays are going well, they seem to resemble pieces of music. But if I had to go into specifics about it, I wouldn't be able to. It's merely something that I feel.

INTERVIEWER: Which contemporary playwrights do you particularly admire? Which do you think have influenced you especially, and in what ways?

ALBEE: The one living playwright I admire without any reservation whatsoever is Samuel Beckett. I have funny feelings about almost all the others. There are a number of contemporary playwrights whom I admire enormously, but that's not at all the same thing as being influenced. I admire Brecht's work very much. I admire a good deal of Tennessee Williams. I admire some of Genet's works. Harold Pinter's work. I admire Cordell's plays very much, even though I don't think they're very good. But on the matter of influence, that question is difficult. I've read and seen hundreds of plays, starting with Sophocles right up to the present day. As a playwright, I imagine that in one fashion or another I've been influenced by every single play I've ever experienced. Influence is a matter of selection—both acceptance and rejection.

INTERVIEWER: In a number of articles, mention is made of the influence on you—either directly or by osmosis—of the theater of cruelty. How do you feel about the theater of cruelty, or the theories of Artaud generally?

ALBEE: Let me answer it this way. About four years ago I made a list, for my own amusement, of the playwrights, the contemporary playwrights, by whom critics said I'd been influenced. I listed twenty-five. It included five playwrights whose work I didn't know, so I read these five playwrights and indeed *now* I suppose I can say I have been influenced by them. The problem is that the people who write these articles find the inevitable similarities of people writing in the same generation, in the same century, and on the same planet, and they put them together in a group.

INTERVIEWER: The point was that the influence may not have been directly through Artaud, but perhaps, as I said, by osmosis.

ALBEE: I've been influenced by Sophocles and Noel Coward.

INTERVIEWER: Do you aspire to being more than a playwright . . . to being a sort of complete man of the theater? You've involved yourself in the production of plays by other writers; you've toyed with the idea of doing a musical; you've written a libretto for opera; you've been an articulate interpreter of the American theater as an institution; and even a public critic of professional drama critics. In retrospect, do you feel that you may have over-extended yourself in any of these areas?

ALBEE: I've certainly done myself considerable damage, though not as an artist, by attacking the critics, because they can't take it. As for involving myself with the production of other people's plays, I consider that to be a responsibility. The playwrights' unit we've been running, Playwrights 66, encourages thirty or thirty-five writers. The plays we've put on in the off-Broadway theater, the Cherry Lane, and other places, are primarily plays that I wanted to see: other people weren't putting them on, so we did. It seems to me that if one finds oneself with the cash it's one's responsibility to do a thing like that. There's certainly no self-aggrandizement. I have done adaptations because I wanted to. I don't like the climate in which writers have to work in this country and I think it's my responsibility to talk about it.

INTERVIEWER: Do you feel that in your own particular case, on the basis of a single big-time commercial hit, you have been raised to too high a position? For your own creative comfort.

ALBEE: I really can't answer that. I have no idea. As a fairly objective judgment, I do think that my plays as they come out are better than most other things that are put on the same year. But that doesn't make them very good necessarily. The act of creation, as you very well know, is a lonely and private matter and has nothing to do with the public area . . . the *performance* of the work one creates. Each time I sit down and write a play I try to dismiss from my mind as much as I possibly can the implications of what I've done before, what I'm going to do, what other people think about my work, the failure or success of the previous play. I'm stuck with a new reality that I've got to create. I'm working on a new play now. I don't believe that I'm being affected by the commercial success of *Who's Afraid of Virginia Woolf?* to make this one more commercial; I don't think I'm being affected by the critical confusion over *Tiny Alice* to make this one simpler. It's a play. I'm trying to make it as good a work of art as I possibly can.

INTERVIEWER: To talk a little about *Tiny Alice*, which I guess is your most controversial play—during your widely publicized press conference on the stage of the Billy Rose Theater, you said the critical publicity had misled the audiences into thinking of the play as a new game of symbol-hunting . . . which was at least to some degree responsible for the play's limited run. Still, you have also said that if audiences desert a play, it is either the fault of the playwright or the manner in which it was presented. With a year to reflect on the matter, how do you feel about all this now as it pertains to *Tiny Alice*?

ALBEE: I feel pretty much what I said on the stage. I keep remembering that the preview audiences, before the critics went to *Tiny Alice*, didn't have anywhere near the amount of trouble understanding what the play was about; that didn't happen until the critics *told* them that it was too difficult to understand. I also feel that *Tiny Alice* would have been a great deal clearer if I hadn't had to make the cuts I did in the third act.

INTERVIEWER: In view of the experience you had with *Tiny Alice*, the critical brouhaha and the different interpretations and the rest of it, if you were to sit down and write that play again, do you think it would emerge in any terribly different way?

ALBEE: It's impossible to tell. A curious thing happens. Within a year after I write a play I forget the experience of having written it. And I couldn't revise or rewrite it if I wanted to. Up until that point, I'm so involved with the experience of having written the play, and the nature of it, that I can't see what faults it might have. The only moment of clear objectivity that I can find is at the moment of critical heat—of self-critical heat when I'm actually writing. Sometimes I think the experience of a play is finished for me when I finish writing it. If it weren't for the need to make a living, I don't know whether I'd have the plays produced. In the two or three or four months that it takes me to write a play, I find that the reality of the play is a great deal more alive for me than what passes for reality. I'm infinitely more involved in the reality of the characters and their situation than I am in everyday life.

The involvement is terribly intense. I find that in the course of the day when I'm writing, after three or four hours of intense work, I have a splitting headache, and I have to stop. Because the involvement, which is both creative and self-critical, is so intense that I've got to stop doing it.

INTERVIEWER: If one can talk at all about a general reaction to your plays, it is that, as convincing and brilliant as their beginnings and middles might be, the plays tend to let down, change course or simply puzzle at the end. To one degree or another this complaint has been registered against most of them.

ALBEE: Perhaps because my sense of reality and logic is different from most people's. The answer could be as simple as that. Some things that make sense to me don't make the same degree of sense to other people. Analytically, there might be other reasons —that the plays don't hold together intellectually; that's possible. But then it mustn't be forgotten that when people don't like the way a play ends, they're likely to blame the play. That's a possibility too. For example, I don't feel that catharsis in a play necessarily takes place during the course of a play. Often it should take place afterward. If I've been accused a number of times of writing plays where the endings are ambivalent, indeed, that's the way I find life.

INTERVIEWER: Do *The Zoo Story* and *Virginia Woolf* both begin and continue through the longest part of their length on an essentially naturalistic course, and then somewhere toward the end of the play veer away from the precisely naturalistic tone?

ALBEE: I think that if people were a little more aware of what actually is beneath the naturalistic overlay they would be surprised to find how early the unnaturalistic base had been set. When you're dealing with a symbol in a realistic play, it is also a realistic fact. You must expect the audience's mind to work on both levels, symbolically and realistically. But we're trained so much in pure, realistic theater that it's difficult for us to handle things on two levels at the same time.

INTERVIEWER: Why did you pick the names George and Martha?

As in Washington? What did you make of Arthur Schlesinger's discovery that with those names you'd obviously written a parallel of the American sociopolitical dilemma?

ALBEE: There are little local and private jokes. Indeed, I did name the two lead characters of *Virginia Woolf* George and Martha because there is contained in the play—not its most important point, but certainly contained within the play—an attempt to examine the success or failure of American revolutionary principles. Some people who are historically and politically and sociologically inclined find them. Now in one play—*Virginia Woolf* again—I named a very old Western Union man "Little Billy"—"Crazy Billy" rather. And I did that because as *you* might recall, Mr. Flanagan, you used to deliver telegrams for Western Union, and you are very old and your name is Billy. Things like that—lots of them going on in the plays. In *Zoo Story*, I named two characters Peter and Jerry. I know two people named Peter and Jerry. But then the learned papers started coming in, and of course Jerry is supposed to be Jesus . . . which is much more interesting, I suppose, to the public than the truth.

INTERVIEWER: Going back to those "levels of understanding," in *Virginia Woolf* the audience questioned the credibility of George and Martha having invented for themselves an imaginary son.

ALBEE: Indeed. And it always struck me as very odd that an audience would be unwilling to believe that a highly educated, sensitive, and intelligent couple, who were terribly good at playing reality and fantasy games, *wouldn't* have the education, the sensitivity, and the intelligence to create a realistic symbol for themselves. To use as they saw fit.

INTERVIEWER: Recognizing the fact that it was a symbol?

ALBEE: *Indeed* recognizing the fact that it was a symbol. And only occasionally being confused, when the awful loss and lack that made the creation of the symbol essential becomes overwhelming—like when they're drunk, for example. Or when they're terribly tired.

INTERVIEWER: What you're saying is something which I guess is not really too commonly understood. You're suggesting that George and Martha have at no point deluded themselves about the fact that they're playing a game.

ALBEE: Oh, never. Except that it's the most serious game in the world. And the nonexistent son is a symbol and a weapon they use in every one of their arguments.

INTERVIEWER: A symbolic weapon rather than a real weapon. In the midst of the very real weapons that they do use.

ALBEE: Indeed, yes. Though they're much too intelligent to make that confusion. For me, that's why the loss is doubly poignant. Because they are not deluded people.

INTERVIEWER: I see. Then what you're trying to suggest now is that the last act of *Virginia Woolf* is in no way less naturalistic than the first two acts.

ALBEE: I don't find that the play veers off into a less naturalistic manner at all.

INTERVIEWER: Well, if not into a less naturalistic one, certainly into a more ritualistic, stylized one. With the Requiem Masses and all that.

ALBEE: Well, going into Latin, indeed. But that's a conscious choice of George's to read the Requiem Mass which has existed in Latin for quite a number of years. I like the sound of the two languages working together. I like the counterpoint of the Latin and the English working together.

There's one point that you've brought up that annoys me. It really annoys the hell out of me. Some critics accuse me of having a failure of intellect in the third act of *Who's Afraid of Virginia Woolf?*, merely because *they* didn't have the ability to understand what was happening. And that annoys the hell out of me.

INTERVIEWER: I can see that it would. A critic recently wrote the following paragraph: "Mr. Albee complained with *Tiny Alice* that people asked questions and would not let the play merely occur to them. He complains of those critics who judge a play's matter and do not restrict themselves to its manner. Both of these statements tend to a view much in vogue—that art consists principally of style, an encounter between us and the figurative surface of a work. This view reduces ideas to decoration, character to pageant, symbol and feeling to a conveyor belt for effects. It is to shrink art to no more than a sensual response, one kind or another of happening. To some of us this modish view is nihilistic, not progressive." Now the critic in question has come fairly close to defining a theory that might be got out of, say, Susan Sontag's *Against Interpretation* or her essay on style. I wonder how closely the critic's interpretations of your remarks—of the remarks, I guess, that you made most specifically at the *Tiny Alice* press conference—are true to your own understanding of them.

ALBEE: Well, this critic is a sophist. What he's done is to misinterpret my attitudes, Miss Sontag's attitudes, and the attitudes of most respectable creative people. What I said is that I thought it was not valid for a critic to criticize a play for its matter rather than its manner—that what was constituted then was a type of censorship. To give an extreme example, I was suggesting that if a man writes a brilliant enough play in praise of something that is universally loathed, that the play, if it is good and well enough written, should not be knocked down because of its approach to its subject. If the work of art is good enough, it must not be criticized for its theme. I don't think it can be argued. In the thirties a whole school of criticism bogged down intellectually in those agit-prop, social-realistic days. A play had to be progressive. A number of plays by playwrights who were thought very highly of then— they were very bad playwrights—were highly praised because their themes were intellectually and politically proper. This intellectual morass is very dangerous, it seems to me. A form of censorship. You may dislike the intention enormously but your judgment of the artistic merit of the work must not be based on your view of what it's about. The work of art must be judged by how well it succeeds in its intention.

INTERVIEWER: In other words, what you're saying is that a critic should separate what he takes to be the thematic substance of a play from the success or lack of success that the author brings to its presentation.

ALBEE: It's that simple. And critics who do otherwise are damn fools and dangerous, even destructive people. I don't think it can be argued.

INTERVIEWER: You have said that it is through the actual process of writing that you eventually come to know the theme of your play. Sometimes you've admitted that even when you have finished a play you don't have any specific idea about its theme. What about that?

ALBEE: Naturally, no writer who's any good at all would sit down and put a sheet of paper in a typewriter and start typing a play unless he knew what he was writing about. But at the same time, writing has got to be an act of discovery. Finding out things about what one is writing about. To a certain extent I imagine a play is completely finished in my mind—in my case, at any rate—without my knowing it, before I sit down to write. So in that sense, I suppose, writing a play is *finding out* what the play is. I always find that the better answer to give. It's a question I despise, and it always seems to me better to slough off the answer to a question which I consider to be a terrible invasion of privacy—the kind of privacy that a writer must keep for himself. If you intellectualize and examine the creative process too carefully it can evaporate and vanish. It's not only terribly difficult to talk about, it's also dangerous. You know the old story about the—I think it's one of Aesop's fables, or perhaps not, or a Chinese story—about the very clever animal that saw a centipede that he didn't like. He said, "My God, it's amazing and marvelous how you walk with all those hundreds and hundreds of legs. How do you do it? How do you get them all moving that way?" The centipede stopped and thought and said, "Well, I take the left front leg and then I—" and he thought about it for a while, and he couldn't walk.

INTERVIEWER: How long does the process of reflection about a play go on?

ALBEE: I usually think about a play anywhere from six months to a year and a half before I sit down to write it out.

INTERVIEWER: Think it through, or—

ALBEE:—think *about* it. Though I'm often accused of never thinking anything through, I think about it. True, I don't begin with an *idea* for a play—a thesis, in other words, to construct the play around. But I know a good deal about the nature of the characters. I know a great deal about their environment. And I more or less know what is going to happen in the play. It's only when I sit down to write it that I find out exactly what the characters are going to say, how they are going to move from one situation to another. Exactly how they are going to behave within the situation to produce the predetermined result. . . . If I didn't do it that way, I wouldn't be able to allow the characters the freedom of expression to make them three-dimensional. Otherwise, I'd write a treatise, not a play. Usually, the way I write is to sit down at a typewriter after that year or so of what passes for thinking, and I write a first draft quite rapidly. Read it over. Make a few pencil corrections, where I think I've got the rhythms wrong in the speeches, for example, and then retype the whole thing. And in the retyping I discover that maybe one or two more speeches will come in. One or two more things will happen, but not much. Usually, what I put down first is what we go into rehearsal with; the majority of the selections and decisions have gone on before I sit down at the typewriter.

INTERVIEWER: Could you describe what sort of reflection goes on? Do whole scenes evolve in your mind, or is the process so deep in your subconscious that you're hardly aware of what's going on?

ALBEE: I discover that I am thinking about a play, which is the first awareness I have that a new play is forming. When I'm aware of the play forming in my head, it's already at a certain degree in development. Somebody will ask, Well, what do you plan to write after the next play? And I'll suddenly surprise myself by finding myself saying, Oh, a play about this, a play about that—I had never even thought about it before. So, obviously, a good deal of thinking has been going on; whether subconscious or unconscious is the proper term here I don't know. But whichever it is, the majority of the work gets done there. And that period can go on for six months or—in the case of *The Substitute Speaker*, which is a play that I hope to be able to write this coming summer—it's a process that has been going on for three and a half years. Occasionally, I pop the play up to the surface—into the conscious mind to see how it's coming along, to see how it is developing. And if the characters seem to be becoming three-dimensional, all to the good. After a certain point, I make experiments to see how well I *know* the characters. I'll improvise and try them out in a situation that I'm fairly sure *won't* be in the play. And if they behave quite naturally, in this improvisatory situation, and create their own dialogue, and behave according to what I consider to be their own natures, then I suppose I have the play far enough along to sit down and write it.

INTERVIEWER: Is that when you know that a play has gone through this "subconscious" process and is ready to come out?

ALBEE: Not necessarily. It's when I find myself typing.

INTERVIEWER: That's not an answer.

ALBEE: It really is. There's a time to go to the typewriter. It's like a dog: the way a dog before it craps wanders around in circles —a piece of earth, an area of grass, circles it for a long time before it squats. It's like that—figuratively circling the typewriter getting ready to write, and then finally one sits down. I think I sit down to the typewriter when it's time to sit down to the typewriter. That isn't to suggest that when I do finally sit down at the typewriter, and write out my plays with a speed that seems to horrify all my detractors and half of my well-wishers, that there's no work involved. It *is* hard work, and one *is* doing all the work oneself. Still, I know playwrights who like to kid themselves into saying that their characters are so well formed that *they* just take over. *They* determine the structure of the play. By which is meant, I suspect, only that the unconscious mind has done its work so thoroughly that the play just has to be filtered through the conscious mind. But there's work to be done—and discovery to be made. Which is part of the pleasure of it. It's a form of pregnancy I suppose, and to carry that idea further, there are very few people who are pregnant who can recall specifically the moment of conception of the child—but they discover that they are pregnant, and it's rather that way with discovering that one is thinking about a play.

INTERVIEWER: When you start, do you move steadily from the opening curtain through to the end, or do you skip around, doing one scene, then another? What about curtain lines? Is there a conscious building toward the finale of each act?

ALBEE: For better or for worse, I write the play straight through —from what I consider the beginning to what I consider the end. As for curtain lines, well, I suppose there are playwrights who do build toward curtain lines. I don't think I do that. In a sense, it's the same choice that has to be made when you wonder when to start a play. And when to end it. The characters' lives have gone on before the moment you chose to have the action of the play begin. And their lives are going to go on after you have lowered the final curtain on the play, unless you've killed them off. A play is a parenthesis which contains all the material you think has to be contained for the action of the play. Where do you end that? Where the characters seem to come to a pause . . . where they seem to want to stop—rather like, I would think, the construction of a piece of music.

INTERVIEWER: You think of yourself then as an intuitive playwright. What you're saying in effect now is that superimposing any fixed theme on your work would somehow impose limitations on your subconscious imaginative faculties.

ALBEE: I suspect that the theme, the nature of the characters, and the method of getting from the beginning of the play to the end is already established in the unconscious.

INTERVIEWER: If one worked expressly by intuition, then, doesn't the form get out of control?

ALBEE: When one controls form, one doesn't do it with a stop watch or a graph. One does it by sensing, again intuitively.

INTERVIEWER: After writing a play in this sort of intuitive way, do you end by accepting its over-all structure (which must also be something of a revelation to you), or do you go back and rewrite and revise with the idea of giving it cogent shape?

ALBEE: I more or less trust it to come out with shape. Curiously enough, the only two plays that I've done very much revision on were the two adaptations—even though the shape of them was pretty much determined by the original work. With my own plays, the only changes, aside from taking a speech out here, putting one in there (if I thought I dwelled on a point a little too long or didn't make it explicit enough), are very minor; but even though they're very minor—having to do with the inability of actors or the unwillingness of the director to go along with me—I've always regretted them.

INTERVIEWER: Your earlier work, from *The Zoo Story* to *Virginia Woolf*, brought you very quick and major international celebrity, even though today at . . . thirty-eight—

ALBEE:—thirty-seven.

INTERVIEWER: When this is published it will be thirty-eight—you would otherwise be regarded as a relatively young growing writer. Do you feel this major renown, for all the doubtless pleasure and financial security it has given you, is any threat to the growth of the young playwright?

ALBEE: Well, there are two things that a playwright can have. Success or failure. I imagine there are dangers in both. Certainly the danger of being faced with indifference or hostility is discouraging, and it may be that success—acceptance if it's too quick, too lightning quick—can turn the heads of some people.

INTERVIEWER: I was thinking less in terms of what the personal effect on you would be. In terms of what you said before, there seems to be a certain pattern that's acted out in the American theater, if not exclusively in the American theater, of elevating new playwrights to enormous prestige, and then after a certain time lapse, arrived at arbitrarily, the need comes to cut them down to size.

ALBEE: Well, the final determination is made anywhere from

twenty-five to one hundred years after the fact anyway. And if the playwright is strong enough to hold on to reasonable objectivity in the face of either hostility or praise, he'll do his work the way he was going to anyway.

INTERVIEWER: Since I guess it's fairly imbecilic to ask a writer what he considers to be his best work or his most important work, perhaps I could ask you this question: which of all of your plays do you feel closest to?

ALBEE: Well, naturally the one I'm writing right now.

INTERVIEWER: Well, excepting that.

ALBEE: I don't know.

INTERVIEWER: There's no one that you feel any special fondness for?

ALBEE: I'm terribly fond of *The Sandbox*. I think it's an absolutely beautiful, lovely, perfect play.

INTERVIEWER: And as for the play you're writing now . . .

ALBEE: A *Delicate Balance*, which I am writing now. *The Substitute Speaker*, next, and then in some order or another, three short plays, plus a play about Attila the Hun.

INTERVIEWER: You say three short plays. Do you hold forth any prospect of going off-Broadway with anything?

ALBEE: Well, considering the way the critical reaction to my plays has been going in the past few years, I may well be there shortly.

INTERVIEWER: I was thinking out of choice rather than necessity.

ALBEE: I'm talking about that too.

WILLIAM FLANAGAN

Harold Pinter was born in London's East End on October 10, 1930. He left school at sixteen and drifted into a career as an actor in London and on the road.

While on tour in 1957, Pinter was asked by a director friend to write a play for the drama department of Bristol University. *The Room*, written in four days, triggered a six-year spurt of playwriting: *The Birthday Party* and *The Dumb Waiter* (1957); *A Slight Ache* (1958); *The Dwarfs*, *The Caretaker*, *Night School*, and *Revue Sketches* (1960); *The Collection* (1961); and *The Lover* (1963). In 1961 he wrote his first major film script, for *The Servant*; this was followed in 1963 by an original film script, *The Compartment*, and then the screenplays for *The Pumpkin Eater*, *The Quiller Memorandum*, and *Accident*. Among his works for television are *A Night Out* (1960), the first versions of *The Lover* (winner of the Italia Prize for television), *The Collection*, and *The Tea Party*.

The Homecoming, written in 1965, and successfully produced in London, was favorably received, by and large, during the 1966–67 New York theater season and won an Antoinette Perry Award. Critic Richard Gilman wrote that Pinter's world in his plays "is arbitrary, everything menaces, nothing is what it seems; he has broken into a new universe of drama, one in which language seldom coheres with gesture, terror is the obverse of humor, and habits of action conceal other kinds of action we can sense but never know." Pinter's use of language, he went on, "exemplifies what is never considered in our public chatter about the theater: that language can itself be dramatic, can *be* the play, not merely the means of advancing an anecdote, a decoration, or the emblem of something thought to be *realer* than itself."

I'll chop your spine off

F. - I'll ~~knock~~ your ~~nut off, sorry Jim.~~ My word of honour.
I'll have you for ~~catsmeat~~ / you talk to me like that, son.
Talking to your filthy louzy father like that.

3. - You know what, youre getting demented.

p.
What do you think of **S**econd Wi~~hd~~ in *for* the fourth race ?

F. - Second Wind ? What race ?

3. - The fourth.

F. - Dont stand a chance.

3. - Sure he does.

F. - Not a chance.

3. - Thats all you know.

F. - He talks to me about horses. *p*

3. - ~~I'll tell you one thing,~~ its about time you learned to cook *p.*

F. - ~~Yes~~ ?

3. - ~~This is what I'm saying.~~ *t ↳* I want to ~~ask~~ you ~~something.~~ The*t*
dinner we had before, what**s** *a* the name of it ? Wjat do you
call it ?

p.
Why dont you buy a dog ? Youre a dog cook. Homest. You
think youre cooking for a lot of dogs.

F. - If you dont like it get out.

3. - I am going out. I'm going out to buy myself a proper
dinner.

Choke.
Suffocate F. - ~~On. Go.~~ Leave me alone.

3. - ~~Yes~~, but I'm not going until I decide the exact moment I
want to go, you see. ~~You dont tell me to do anything, Dad.~~
I go when I like, I come back when I like. ~~You wouldnt be~~
~~here only because of me. Whose money keeps you here ?~~
~~If it wasnt for me and Joey xxxxxxxxxxxxxxxxxxxxxxx~~
~~you know where youd be ?~~ Who gives you the monet to do the
~~cooking ?~~ *Get it. You dont ever come into it.*

F. - Its my house.

3. - Dont make me laugh. You're dead if I say so.

F. - ~~Yes xx Joey xx youx lot xxx xx xxx wont let you ...~~

3. - ~~xxxx x You dont think xxx~~ *F. Get burnt.* ~~Burn.~~ *Burn.*
gets up.
Here, Daddy, you going to use your stick on me ? Dont use
your stick on me, Daddy. I havent done nothing wrong.
Dont clout me with that stick Dad.

F. I know what you do every night. silence. 3. wraps his paper, puts it in
I know all about stinking his pocket. ~~Door. Joey comes in, Uncle Sam.~~
filthy tykes ~~xx xxxxxxxx xx Exxxxxxxxxx xxxxxxxx~~
I know all about Eh, Dad, I forgot. One thing. Been meaning to ask you.
tykes. That night ... that night you .. got me .. with mum ...
what was it like ? When I was just a glint in your naughty
old eye. ~~you had me in mind, did you ?~~ *y it broken*

F. - ~~Out yourself to pieces.~~ Stuff your face into glass ~~xxxxx~~
~~Into broken glass.~~

F - Drown in your own *Shove it into a plate*
bastard blood *of glass.*

Is ~~that~~ it a fact that you had me in mind
or is it a fact that I was the last thing
you had in mind.

Manuscript page for The Homecoming

Harold Pinter

Harold Pinter had recently moved into a five-story 1820 Nash house facing Regent's Park in London. The view from the floor-through top floor where he has installed his office overlooks a duck pond and a long stretch of wooded parkland; his desk faces this view, and in late October 1966, when the interview took place, the changing leaves and the hazy London sun constantly distracted him as he thought over questions or began to give answers. He speaks in a deep, theater-trained voice which comes rather surprisingly from him, and indeed is the most remarkable thing about him physically. When speaking he almost always tends to excessive qualification of any statement, as if coming to a final definition of things were obviously impossible. One gets the impression—as one does with many of the characters in his plays—of a man so deeply involved with what he's thinking that roughing it into speech is a painful necessity.

He was not working at any writing projects when the interview took place, and questions about his involuntary idleness (many questions came back to it without meaning to) were particularly uncomfortable for him. His own work is alternatively a source of mystery, amusement, joy, and anger to him; in looking it over he often discovered possibilities and ambiguities which he had not noticed or forgotten. One felt that if only he would rip out his telephone and hang black curtains across the wide windows he would be much happier, though he insists that the "great boredom one has with oneself" is unrelated to his environment or his obligations.

When he wrote his first plays, in 1957, he was homeless, constantly on tour as an actor with a repertory stage company, playing all sorts of parts in obscure seaside resorts and provincial cities. His wife, the actress Vivien Merchant, toured with him, but when she became pregnant in 1958 it was necessary for them to find a home, and they took a basement room in London's shabby Notting Hill Gate section, in a building where Mr. Pinter worked as a caretaker to pay his rent. When their son was born they borrowed enough money to move to a less shabby district in Chiswick, but both had to return to full-time acting when Mr. Pinter's first full-length play, The Birthday Party, was a full-scale flop in 1958. The production of The Caretaker in 1960 produced enough money for a move to the middle-class district of Kew, and then, thinking he could live on his writings, Mr. Pinter moved his family to a bow-fronted Regency house in the south-coast seaside town of Worthing. But the two-hour drive to London became imperative too often, and so they moved once again, to a rented flat in Kensington, until Mr. Pinter's lucrative film scripts made it possible for them to buy the Regent's Park house. Though it is not yet completely renovated, the size and comfort of it are impressive, as is Mr. Pinter's office, with a separate room nearby for his secretary and a small bar equally nearby for the beer and Scotch which he drinks steadily during the day, whether working or not. Bookshelves line one-half the area, and a velvet chaise longue faces the small rear *garden. On the walls are a series of Feliks Topolski sketches of London theater scenes; a poster of the Montevideo production of* El Cuidador; *a small financial balance sheet indicating that his first West End production,* The Birthday Party, *earned two hundred sixty pounds in its disastrous week's run; a Picasso drawing; and his citation when he was named to the Order of the British Empire last spring. "The year* after *the Beatles," he emphasizes.*

INTERVIEWER: When did you start writing plays, and why?

PINTER: My first play was *The Room*, written when I was twenty-seven. A friend of mine called Henry Woolf was a student in the drama department at Bristol University at the time when it was the only drama department in the country. He had the opportunity to direct a play, and as he was my oldest friend he knew I'd been writing, and he knew I had an idea for a play, though I hadn't written any of it. I was acting in rep at the time, and he told me he had to have the play the next week to meet his schedule. I said this was ridiculous, he might get it in six months. And then I wrote it in four days.

INTERVIEWER: Has writing always been so easy for you?

PINTER: Well, I had been writing for years, hundreds of poems and short pieces of prose. About a dozen had been published in little magazines. I wrote a novel as well; it's not good enough to be published, really, and never has been. After I wrote *The Room*, which I didn't see performed for a few weeks, I started to work immediately on *The Birthday Party*.

INTERVIEWER: What led you to do that so quickly?

PINTER: It was the process of writing a play which had started me going. Then I went to see *The Room*, which was a remarkable experience. Since I'd never written a play before, I'd of course never seen one of mine performed, never had an audience sitting there. The only people who'd ever seen what I'd written had been a few friends and my wife. So to sit in the audience—well, I wanted to piss very badly throughout the whole thing, and at the end I dashed out behind the bicycle shed.

INTERVIEWER: What other effect did contact with an audience have on you?

PINTER: I was very encouraged by the response of that university audience, though no matter what the response had been I would have written *The Birthday Party*, I know that. Watching first nights, though I've seen quite a few by now, is never any better. It's a nerve-racking experience. It's not a question of whether the play goes well or badly. It's not the audience reaction, it's *my* reaction. I'm rather hostile toward audiences—I don't much care for large bodies of people collected together. Everyone knows that audiences vary enormously; it's a mistake to care too much about them. The thing one should be concerned with is whether the performance has expressed what one set out to express in writing the play. It sometimes does.

INTERVIEWER: Do you think that without the impetus provided by your friend at Bristol you would have gotten down to writing plays?

PINTER: Yes, I think I was going to write *The Room*. I just wrote it a bit quicker under the circumstances; he just triggered something off. *The Birthday Party* had also been in my mind for a long time. It was sparked off from a very distinct situation in digs when I was on tour. In fact, the other day a friend of mine gave me a letter I wrote to him in nineteen-fifty-something, Christ knows when it was. This is what it says: "I have filthy insane digs, a great bulging scrag of a woman with breasts rolling at her belly, an obscene household, cats, dogs, filth, tea strainers, mess, oh bullocks, talk, chat rubbish shit scratch dung poison, infantility, deficient order in the upper fretwork, fucking roll on." Now the thing about this is *that* was *The Birthday Party*—I was in those digs, and this woman was Meg in the play, and there was a fellow staying there in Eastbourne, on the coast. The whole thing remained with me, and three years later I wrote the play.

INTERVIEWER: Why wasn't there a character representing you in the play?

PINTER: I had—I have—nothing to say about myself, directly. I wouldn't know where to begin. Particularly since I often look at myself in the mirror and say, "Who the hell's that?"

INTERVIEWER: And you don't think being represented as a character on stage would help you find out?

PINTER: No.

INTERVIEWER: Have your plays usually been drawn from situations you've been in? *The Caretaker*, for example.

PINTER: I'd met a few, quite a few, tramps—you know, just in the normal course of events, and I think there was one particular one . . . I didn't know him very well, he did most of the talking when I saw him. I bumped into him a few times, and about a year or so afterward he sparked this thing off.

INTERVIEWER: Had it occurred to you to act in *The Room*?

PINTER: No, no—the acting was a separate activity altogether. Though I wrote *The Room, The Birthday Party*, and *The Dumb Waiter* in 1957, I was acting all the time in a repertory company, doing all kinds of jobs, traveling to Bournemouth and Torquay and Birmingham. I finished *The Birthday Party* while I was touring in some kind of farce, I don't remember the name.

INTERVIEWER: As an actor, do you find yourself with a compelling sense of how roles in your plays should be performed?

PINTER: Quite often I have a compelling sense of how a role should be played. And I'm proved—equally as often—quite wrong.

INTERVIEWER: Do you see yourself in each role as you write? And does your acting help you as a playwright?

PINTER: I read them all aloud to myself while writing. But I don't see myself in each role—I couldn't play most of them. My acting doesn't impede my playwriting because of these limitations. For example, I'd like to write a play—I've frequently thought of this—entirely about women.

INTERVIEWER: Your wife, Vivien Merchant, frequently appears in your plays. Do you write parts for her?

PINTER: No. I've never written any part for any actor, and the same applies to my wife. I just think she's a very good actress and a very interesting actress to work with, and I want her in my plays.

INTERVIEWER: Acting was your profession when you first started to write plays?

PINTER: Oh, yes, it was all I ever did. I didn't go to university. I left school at sixteen—I was fed up and restless. The only thing that interested me at school was English language and literature, but I didn't have Latin and so couldn't go on to university. So I went to a few drama schools, not studying seriously; I was mostly in love at the time and tied up with that.

INTERVIEWER: Were the drama schools of any use to you as a playwright?

PINTER: None whatsoever. It was just living.

INTERVIEWER: Did you go to a lot of plays in your youth?

PINTER: No, very few. The only person I really liked to see was Donald Wolfit, in a Shakespeare company at the time. I admired him tremendously; his Lear is still the best I've ever seen. And then I was reading, for years, a great deal of modern literature, mostly novels.

INTERVIEWER: No playwrights—Brecht, Pirandello . . . ?

PINTER: Oh, certainly not, not for years. I read Hemingway, Dostoevski, Joyce, and Henry Miller at a very early age, and Kafka. I'd read Beckett's novels, too, but I'd never heard of Ionesco until after I'd written the first few plays.

INTERVIEWER: Do you think these writers had any influence on your writing?

PINTER: I've been influenced *personally* by everyone I've ever read—and I read all the time—but none of these writers particularly influenced my writing. Beckett and Kafka stayed with me the most —I think Beckett is the best prose writer living. My world is still bound up by other writers—that's one of the best things in it.

INTERVIEWER: Has music influenced your writing, do you think?

PINTER: I don't know how music can influence writing; but it has been very important for me, both jazz and classical music. I feel a sense of music continually in writing, which is a different matter from having been influenced by it. Boulez and Webern are now composers I listen to a great deal.

INTERVIEWER: Do you get impatient with the limitations of writing for the theater?

PINTER: No. It's quite different; the theater's much the most difficult kind of writing for me, the most naked kind, you're so entirely restricted. I've done some film work, but for some reason or other I haven't found it very easy to satisfy myself on an original idea for a film. *Tea Party*, which I did for television, is actually a film, cinematic, I wrote it like that. Television and films are simpler than the theater—if you get tired of a scene you just drop it and go on to another one. (I'm exaggerating, of course.) What *is* so different about the stage is that you're just *there*, stuck—there are your characters stuck on the stage, you've got to live with them and deal with them. I'm not a very inventive writer in the sense of using the technical devices other playwrights do—look at Brecht! I can't use the stage the way he does, I just haven't got that kind of imagination, so I find myself stuck with these characters who are either sitting or standing, and they've either got to walk out of a door, or come in through a door, and that's about all they can do.

INTERVIEWER: And talk.

PINTER: Or keep silent.

INTERVIEWER: After *The Room*, what effect did the production of your next plays have on your writing?

PINTER: *The Birthday Party* was put on at the Lyric, Hammersmith in London. It went on a little tour of Oxford and Cambridge first, and was very successful. When it came to London it was completely massacred by the critics—absolutely slaughtered. I've never really known why, nor am I particularly interested. It ran a week. I've framed the statement of the box-office takings: two hundred sixty pounds, including a first night of one hundred forty pounds and the Thursday matinee of two pounds, nine shillings —there were six people there. I was completely new to writing for the professional theater, and it was rather a shock when it happened. But I went on writing—the BBC were very helpful. I wrote *A Slight Ache* on commission from them. In 1960 *The Dumb Waiter* was produced, and then *The Caretaker*. The only really bad experience I've had was *The Birthday Party*; I was so green and gauche—not that I'm rosy and confident now, but comparatively. . . . Anyway, for things like stage design I didn't know how to cope, and I didn't know how to talk to the director.

INTERVIEWER: What was the effect of this adversity on you? How was it different from unfavorable criticism of your acting, which surely you'd had before?

PINTER: It was a great shock, and I was very depressed for about forty-eight hours. It was my wife, actually, who said just that to me: "You've had bad notices before," et cetera. There's no question but that her common sense and practical help got me over that depression, and I've never felt anything like that again.

INTERVIEWER: You've directed several of your plays. Will you continue to do so?

PINTER: No. I've come to think it's a mistake. I work much as I write, just moving from one thing to another to see what's going to happen next. One tries to get the thing . . . *true*. But I rarely get it. I think I'm more useful as the author closely involved with a play: as a director I think I tend to inhibit the actors, because however objective I am about the text and try not to insist that *this is what's meant*, I think there is an obligation on the actors too heavy to bear.

INTERVIEWER: Since you are an actor, do actors in your plays ever approach you and ask you to change lines or aspects of their roles?

PINTER: Sometimes, quite rarely, lines are changed when we're working together. I don't at all believe in the anarchic theater of so-called creative actors—the actors can do that in someone else's plays. Which wouldn't, however, at all affect their ability to play in mine.

INTERVIEWER: Which of your plays did you first direct?

PINTER: I co-directed *The Collection* with Peter Hall. And then I directed *The Lover* and *The Dwarfs* on the same bill at the Arts. *The Lover* didn't stand much of a chance because it was my decision, regretted by everyone—except me—to do *The Dwarfs*, which is apparently the most intractable, impossible piece of work. Apparently ninety-nine people out of a hundred feel it's a waste of time, and the audience hated it.

INTERVIEWER: It seems the densest of your plays in the sense that there's quite a bit of talk and very little action. Did this represent an experiment for you?

PINTER: No. The fact is that *The Dwarfs* came from my unpublished novel, which was written a long time ago. I took a great deal from it, particularly the kind of state of mind that the characters were in.

INTERVIEWER: So this circumstance of composition is not likely to be repeated?

PINTER: No. I should add that even though it is, as you say, more dense, it had great value, great interest for me. From my point of view, the general delirium and states of mind and reactions and relationships in the play—although terribly sparse—are clear to me. I know all the things that aren't said, and the way the characters actually look at each other, and what they mean by looking at each other. It's a play about betrayal and distrust. It does seem very confusing and obviously it can't be successful. But it was good for me to do.

INTERVIEWER: Is there more than one way to direct your plays successfully?

PINTER: Oh, yes, but always around the same central truth of the play—if that's distorted, then it's bad. The main difference in interpretation comes from the actors. The director can certainly be responsible for a disaster, too—the first performance of *The Caretaker* in Germany was heavy and posturized. There's no blueprint for any play, and several have been done entirely successfully without me helping in the production at all.

INTERVIEWER: When you are working on one, what is the key to a good writer-director relationship?

PINTER: What is absolutely essential is avoiding all defensiveness between author and director. It's a matter of mutual trust and openness. If that isn't there, it's just a waste of time.

INTERVIEWER: Peter Hall, who has directed many of your plays, says that they rely on precise verbal form and rhythm, and when you write "pause" it means something other than "silence," and three dots are different from a full stop. Is his sensitivity to this kind of writing responsible for your working well together?

PINTER: Yes, it is, very much so. I do pay great attention to those points you just mentioned. Hall once held a dot and pause rehearsal for the actors in *The Homecoming*. Although it sounds bloody pretentious, it was apparently very valuable.

INTERVIEWER: Do you outline plays before you start to write them?

PINTER: Not at all. I don't know what kind of characters my plays will have until they . . . well, until they *are*. Until they indicate to me what they are. I don't conceptualize in any way. Once I've got the clues I follow them—that's my job, really, to follow the clues.

INTERVIEWER: What do you mean by clues? Can you remember how one of your plays developed in your mind—or was it a line-by-line progression?

PINTER: Of course I can't remember exactly how a given play developed in my mind. I think what happens is that I write in a very high state of excitement and frustration. I follow what I see on the paper in front of me—one sentence after another. That doesn't mean I don't have a dim, possible over-all idea— the image that starts off doesn't just engender what happens immediately, it engenders the possibility of an over-all happening, which carries me through. I've got an idea of what *might* happen —sometimes I'm absolutely right, but on many occasions I've been proved wrong by what does actually happen. Sometimes I'm going along and I find myself writing "C. comes in" when I didn't know that he was going to come in; he *had* to come in at that point, that's all.

INTERVIEWER: In *The Homecoming*, Sam, a character who hasn't been very active for a while, suddenly cries out and collapses several minutes from the end of the play. Is this an example of what you mean? It seems abrupt.

PINTER: It suddenly seemed to me right. It just came. I knew he'd have to say something at one time in this section and this is what happened, that's what he said.

INTERVIEWER: Might characters therefore develop beyond your control of them, changing your idea—even if it's a vague idea—of what the play's about?

PINTER: I'm ultimately holding the ropes, so they never get too far away.

INTERVIEWER: Do you sense when you should bring down the curtain, or do you work the text consciously toward a moment you've already determined?

PINTER: It's pure instinct. The curtain comes down when the rhythm seems right—when the action calls for a finish. I'm very fond of curtain lines, of doing them properly.

INTERVIEWER: Do you feel your plays are therefore structurally successful? That you're able to communicate this instinct for rhythm to the play?

PINTER: No, not really, and that's my main concern, to get the structure right. I always write three drafts, but you have to leave it eventually. There comes a point when you say, That's it, I can't do anything more. The only play which gets remotely near to a structural entity which satisfies me is *The Homecoming*. *The Birthday Party* and *The Caretaker* have too much writing. I want to iron it down, eliminate things. Too many words irritate me sometimes, but I can't help them, they just seem to come out—out of the fellow's mouth. I don't really examine my works too much, but I'm aware that quite often in what I write, some fellow at some point says an awful lot.

INTERVIEWER: Most people would agree that the strength in your plays lies in just this verbal aspect, the patterns and force of character you can get from it. Do you get these words from people you've heard talking—do you eavesdrop?

PINTER: I spend *no* time listening in that sense. Occasionally I hear something, as we all do, walking about. But the words come as I'm writing the characters, not before.

INTERVIEWER: Why do you think the conversations in your plays are so effective?

PINTER: I don't know. I think possibly it's because people fall back on anything they can lay their hands on verbally to keep away from the danger of knowing, and of being known.

INTERVIEWER: What areas in writing plays give you the most trouble?

PINTER: They're all so inextricably interrelated I couldn't possibly judge.

INTERVIEWER: Several years ago, *Encounter* had an extensive series of quotations from people in the arts about the advisability of Britain's joining the Common Market. Your statement was the shortest anyone made: "I have no interest in the matter and do not care what happens." Does this sum up your feeling about politics, or current affairs?

PINTER: Not really. Though that's exactly what I feel about the Common Market—I just don't care a damn about the Common Market. But it isn't quite true to say that I'm in any way indifferent to current affairs. I'm in the normal state of being very confused—uncertain, irritated, and indignant in turns, sometimes indifferent. Generally, I try to get on with what I can do and leave it at that. I don't think I've got any kind of social function that's of any value, and politically there's no question of my getting involved because the issues are by no means simple—to be a politician you have to be able to present a simple picture even if you don't see things that way.

INTERVIEWER: Has it ever occurred to you to express political opinions through your characters?

PINTER: No. Ultimately, politics do bore me, though I recognize they are responsible for a good deal of suffering. I distrust ideological statements of any kind.

INTERVIEWER: But do you think that the picture of personal

threat which is sometimes presented on your stage is troubling in a larger sense, a political sense, or doesn't this have any relevance?

PINTER: I don't feel myself threatened by *any* political body or activity at all. I like living in England. I don't care about political structures—they don't alarm me, but they cause a great deal of suffering to millions of people.

I'll tell you what I really think about politicians. The other night I watched some politicians on television talking about Viet Nam. I wanted very much to burst through the screen with a flame-thrower and burn their eyes out and their balls off and then inquire from them how they would assess this action from a political point of view.

INTERVIEWER: Would you ever use this anger in a politically oriented play?

PINTER: I have occasionally out of irritation thought about writing a play with a satirical point. I once did, actually, a play that no one knows about. A full-length play written after *The Caretaker*. Wrote the whole damn thing in three drafts. It was called *The Hothouse* and was about an institution in which patients were kept: all that was presented was the hierarchy, the people who ran the institution; one never knew what happened to the patients or what they were there for or who they were. It was heavily satirical, and it was quite useless. I never began to like any of the characters, they really didn't live at all. So I discarded the play at once. The characters were so purely cardboard. I was intentionally —for the only time, I think—trying to make a point, an explicit point, that these were nasty people and I disapproved of them. And therefore they didn't begin to live. Whereas in other plays of mine every single character, even a bastard like Goldberg in *The Birthday Party*, I care for.

INTERVIEWER: You often speak of your characters as living beings. Do they become so after you've written a play? While you're writing it?

PINTER: Both.

INTERVIEWER: As real as people you know?

PINTER: No, but different. I had a terrible dream, after I'd written *The Caretaker*, about the two brothers. My house burned down in the dream, and I tried to find out who was responsible. I was led through all sorts of alleys and cafés and eventually I arrived at an inner room somewhere and there were the two brothers from the play. And I said, So you burned down my house. They said, Don't be too worried about it, and I said, I've got everything in there, everything, you don't realize what you've done, and they said, It's all right, we'll compensate you for it, we'll look after you all right—the younger brother was talking—and thereupon I wrote them out a check for fifty quid . . . *I* gave *them* a check for fifty quid!

INTERVIEWER: Do you have a particular interest in psychology?

PINTER: No.

INTERVIEWER: None at all? Did you have some purpose in mind in writing the speech where the older brother describes his troubles in a mental hospital at the end of Act II in *The Caretaker*?

PINTER: Well, I had a purpose in the sense that Aston suddenly opened his mouth. My purpose was to let him go on talking until he was finished and then . . . bring the curtain down. I had no ax to grind there. And the one thing that people have missed is that it isn't necessary to conclude that everything Aston says about his experiences in the mental hospital is true.

INTERVIEWER: There's a sense of terror and a threat of violence in most of your plays. Do you see the world as an essentially violent place?

PINTER: The world *is* a pretty violent place, it's as simple as that, so any violence in the plays comes out quite naturally. It seems to me an essential and inevitable factor.

I think what you're talking about began in *The Dumb Waiter*, which from my point of view is a relatively simple piece of work. The violence is really only an expression of the question of dominance and subservience, which is possibly a repeated theme in my plays. I wrote a short story a long time ago called "The Examination," and my ideas of violence carried on from there. That short story dealt very explicitly with two people in one room having a battle of an unspecified nature, in which the question was one of who was dominant at what point and how they were going to be dominant and what tools they would use to achieve dominance and how they would try to undermine the other person's dominance. A threat is constantly there: it's got to do with this question of being in the uppermost position, or attempting to be. That's something of what attracted me to do the screenplay of *The Servant*, which was someone else's story, you know. I wouldn't call this violence so much as a battle for positions, it's a very common, everyday thing.

INTERVIEWER: Do these ideas of everyday battles, or of violence, come from any experiences you've had yourself?

PINTER: Everyone encounters violence in some way or other. It so happens I did encounter it in quite an extreme form after the war, in the East End, when the Fascists were coming back to life in England. I got into quite a few fights down there. If you looked remotely like a Jew you might be in trouble. Also, I went to a Jewish club, by an old railway arch, and there were quite a lot of people often waiting with broken milk bottles in a particular alley we used to walk through. There were one or two ways of getting out of it—one was a purely physical way, of course, but you couldn't do anything about the milk bottles—*we* didn't have any milk bottles. The best way was to talk to them, you know, sort of "Are you all right?" "Yes, I'm all right." "Well, that's all right then, isn't it?" And all the time keep walking toward the lights of the main road.

Another thing: we were often taken for Communists. If you went by, or happened to be passing, a Fascist street meeting and looked in any way antagonistic—this was in Ridley Road market, near Dalston Junction—they'd interpret your very being, especially if you had books under your arms, as evidence of your being a Communist. There was a good deal of violence there, in those days.

INTERVIEWER: Did this lead you toward some kind of pacifism?

PINTER: I was fifteen when the war ended. There was never any question of my going when I was called up for military service three years later: I couldn't see any point in it at all. I refused to go. So I was taken in a police car to the medical examination. Then I had two tribunals and two trials. I could have gone to prison—I took my toothbrush to the trials—but it so happened that the magistrate was slightly sympathetic, so I was fined instead, thirty pounds in all. Perhaps I'll be called up again in the next war, but I won't go.

INTERVIEWER: Robert Brustein has said of modern drama, "The rebel dramatist becomes an evangelist proselytizing for his faith." Do you see yourself in that role?

PINTER: I don't know what he's talking about. I don't know for what faith I could possibly be proselytizing.

INTERVIEWER: The theater is a very competitive business. Are you, as a writer, conscious of competing against other playwrights?

PINTER: Good writing excites me, and makes life worth living. I'm never conscious of any competition going on here.

INTERVIEWER: Do you read things written about you?

PINTER: Yes. Most of the time I don't know what they're talking about; I don't really read them all the way through. Or I read it and it goes—if you asked me what had been said, I would have very little idea. But there are exceptions, mainly nonprofessional critics.

INTERVIEWER: How much are you aware of an audience when you write?

PINTER: Not very much. But I'm aware that this is a public medium. I don't want to *bore* the audience, I want to keep them glued to what happens. So I try to write as *exactly* as possible. I would try to do that anyway, audience or no audience.

INTERVIEWER: There is a story—mentioned by Brustein in *The Theater of Revolt*—that Ionesco once left a performance of Genet's *The Blacks* because he felt he was being attacked, and the actors were enjoying it. Would you ever hope for a similar reaction in your audience? Would you react this way yourself?

PINTER: I've had that reaction—it's happened to me recently

here in London, when I went to see US, the Royal Shakespeare Company's anti-Viet-Nam-war production. There was a kind of attack—I don't like being subjected to propaganda, and I detest soapboxes. I want to present things clearly in my own plays, and sometimes this does make an audience very uncomfortable, but there's no question about causing offense for its own sake.

INTERVIEWER: Do you therefore feel the play failed to achieve its purpose—inspiring opposition to the war?

PINTER: Certainly. The chasm between the reality of the war in Viet Nam and the image of what US presented on the stage was so enormous as to be quite preposterous. If it was meant to lecture or shock the audience I think it was most presumptuous. It's impossible to make a major theatrical statement about such a matter when television and the press have made everything so clear.

INTERVIEWER: Do you consciously make crisis situations humorous? Often an audience at your plays finds its laughter turning against itself as it realizes what the situation in the play actually is.

PINTER: Yes, that's very true, yes. I'm rarely consciously writing humor, but sometimes I find myself laughing at some particular point which has suddenly struck me as being funny. I agree that more often than not the speech only *seems* to be funny—the man in question is actually fighting a battle for his life.

INTERVIEWER: There are sexual undertones in many of these crisis situations, aren't there? How do you see the use of sex in the theater today?

PINTER: I do object to one thing to do with sex: this scheme afoot on the part of many "liberal-minded" persons to open up obscene language to general commerce. It should be the dark secret language of the underworld. There are very few words—you shouldn't kill them by overuse. I have used such words once or twice in my plays, but I couldn't get them through the Lord Chamberlain. They're great, wonderful words, but must be used very sparingly. The pure publicity of freedom of language fatigues me, because it's a demonstration rather than something said.

INTERVIEWER: Do you think you've inspired any imitations? Have you ever seen anything in a film or theater which struck you as, well, Pinteresque?

PINTER: That word! These damn words and that word "Pinteresque" particularly—I don't know what they're bloody well talking about! I think it's a great burden for me to carry, and for other writers to carry. Oh, very occasionally I've thought listening to something, Hello, that rings a bell. But it goes no further than that. I really do think that writers write on . . . just write, and I find it difficult to believe I'm any kind of influence on other writers. I've seen very little evidence of it, anyway; other people seem to see more evidence of it than I do.

INTERVIEWER: The critics?

PINTER: It's a great mistake to pay any attention to *them*. I think, you see, that this is an age of such overblown publicity and overemphatic pinning down. I'm a very good example of a writer who can write, but I'm not as good as all that. I'm just a writer; and I think that I've been overblown tremendously because there's a dearth of really fine writing, and people tend to make too much of a meal. All you can do is try to write as well as you can.

INTERVIEWER: Do you think your plays will be performed fifty years from now? Is universality a quality you consciously strive for?

PINTER: I have no idea whether my plays will be performed in fifty years, and it's of no moment to me. I'm pleased when what I write makes sense in South America or Yugoslavia—it's gratifying. But I certainly don't strive for universality—I've got enough to strive for just writing a bloody play!

INTERVIEWER: Do you think the success you've known has changed your writing?

PINTER: No, but it did become more difficult. I think I've gone beyond something now. When I wrote the first three plays in 1957 I wrote them from the point of view of *writing* them; the whole world of putting on plays was quite remote—I knew they could never be done in the reps I was acting in, and the West End and London were somewhere on the other side of the moon. So I wrote these plays completely unself-consciously. There's no question that over the years it's become more difficult to preserve the kind of freedom that's essential to writing, but when I do write, it's there. For a while it became more difficult to avoid the searchlights and all that. And it took me five years to write a stage play, *The Homecoming*, after *The Caretaker*. I did a lot of things in the meantime, but writing a stage play, which is what I really wanted to do, I couldn't. Then I wrote *The Homecoming*, for good or bad, and I felt much better. But *now* I'm back in the same boat—I want to write a play, it buzzes all the time in me, and I can't put pen to paper. Something people don't realize is the great boredom one has with oneself, and just to see those words come down again on paper, I think: Oh Christ, everything I do seems to be predictable, unsatisfactory, and hopeless. It keeps me awake. Distractions don't matter to me—if I had something to write I would write it. Don't ask me why I want to keep on with plays at all!

INTERVIEWER: Do you think you'd ever use freer techniques as a way of starting writing again?

PINTER: I can enjoy them in other people's plays—I thought the *Marat/Sade* was a damn good evening, and other very different plays like *The Caucasian Chalk Circle* I've also enjoyed. But I'd never use such stage techniques myself.

INTERVIEWER: Does this make you feel behind the times in any way?

PINTER: I *am* a very traditional playwright—for instance I insist on having a curtain in all my plays. I write curtain lines for that reason! And even when directors like Peter Hall or Claude Régy in Paris want to do away with them, I insist they stay. For me everything has to do with shape, structure, and over-all unity. All this jamboree in happenings and eight-hour movies is great fun for the people concerned, I'm sure.

INTERVIEWER: Shouldn't they be having fun?

PINTER: If they're all having fun I'm delighted, but count me out completely, I wouldn't stay more than five minutes. The trouble is I find it all so *noisy*, and I like quiet things. There seems to be such a jazz and jaggedness in so much modern art, and a great deal of it is inferior to its models: Joyce contains so much of Burroughs, for example, in his experimental techniques, though Burroughs is a fine writer on his own. This doesn't mean I don't regard myself as a contemporary writer: I mean, I'm *here*.

LAWRENCE M. BENSKY